Community-Based Curriculum

Community-Based Curriculum

Instructional Strategies for Students with Severe Handicaps

SECOND EDITION

by Mary A. Falvey, Ph.D.
Division of Special Education
California State University, Los Angeles

Baltimore • London • Toronto • Sydney

Paul H. Brookes Publishing Co.
Post Office Box 10624
Baltimore, Maryland 21285-0624

Typeset by Brushwood Graphics, Inc., Baltimore, Maryland.
Manufactured in the United States of America by
McNaughton & Gunn, Ann Arbor, Michigan.

Library of Congress Cataloging-in-Publication Data

Falvey, Mary A., 1950–
Community-based curriculum.

Includes bibliographies and index.
1. Handicapped—United States—Life skills guides—Study and teaching. 2. Handicapped—Education—United States. 3. Mainstreaming in education—United States.
I. Title.
HV1553.F34 1989 371.91 88-35364
ISBN 1-55766-023-9

Contents

Contributors

Kathryn D. Bishop, M.S., has worked with adolescents and adults with severe handicaps to prepare them for the transition to competitive employment in Whittier Union High School District, California. She established a community-based adult program in Whittier, California, and currently is a supported employment trainer for the University of San Francisco. Her major research interests focus on the area of transition from school to work and quality of life for individuals with severe handicaps. She received her master of science degree from the University of Oregon. She is currently working on her doctor of philosophy degree from California State University, Los Angeles, and University of California, Los Angeles.

Jennifer Coots, M.A., worked as an elementary school teacher and mentor teacher integrating students with severe handicaps with their nonhandicapped peers in the Pasadena Unified School District, California. She is currently a research assistant for the California State Department of Education integration project. Her major research interests are integration, social skills acquisition, and friendships. She received her master of arts degree from California State University, Los Angeles. She is currently working on her doctor of philosophy degree from California State University, Los Angeles, and University of California, Los Angeles.

Lori Eshilian, M.A., is co-director of the Whittier Adult Community-Based Program serving adults with severe handicaps. She formerly taught for Los Angeles County schools where she was instrumental in establishing integrated and community-based educational programs for junior and senior students with severe handicaps. She received her master of arts degree from California State University, Los Angeles.

Mary A. Falvey, Ph.D., is a professor in the Division of Special Education at California State University, Los Angeles. She was a teacher and administrator in the public schools responsible for teaching and administering programs for students with severe handicaps. She received her doctor of philosophy degree in 1980 from the University of Wisconsin—Madison. She has authored numerous chapters, several articles, and the first edition of *Community-Based Curriculum: Instructional strategies for students with severe handicaps*. She currently serves on the TASH board of directors and is an honorary member of the California TASH board.

Marquita Grenot-Scheyer, M.A., has been instrumental in developing integrated school placements within the Los Angeles Unified School District and numerous other school districts for students with severe handicaps. She received her master of arts degree from California State University, Los Angeles, and University of California, Los Angeles. Her major research focus is on friendships between children with and without severe handicaps. She is currently an assistant professor of Special Education at California State University, Long Beach.

Michele Haney, Ph.D., has been responsible for designing, developing, and implementing parent support groups and conducting research to facilitate interactions between parents and their children. She received her doctor of philosophy degree from California State University, Los Angeles, and University of California, Los Angeles. She is currently an assistant professor in the Department of Special Education at California State University, Northridge.

FOREWORD

In 1975, when our daughter Dusty was born with Down syndrome and a visual impairment, we became depressed and discouraged. The professionals we met at the time told of how Dusty would be severely limited and would require "separate" services and schooling. They told us that because of her particular condition, people would discriminate against her, make fun of her, and deny her access to many of the activities other children enjoy. The picture they drew for us of a lonely adult going daily to a sheltered workshop or day activity program and living in a segregated facility with others "like her" made her future look bleak. The professionals we met were sincere. They believed that what they were telling us was true. However, they were not looking into the future!

We are pleased to have the opportunity to write a foreword for this book, because its premises run contrary to that bleak picture. Mary Falvey and her colleagues have presented an optimistic view of the education and future lives of children with severe disabilities, along with many practical strategies for implementation.

Central to this book is the notion that parents and significant others have crucial roles to play in the assessment, curriculum planning, and implementation of programs for their children. As parents deeply involved in the education and life planning for our child, we know this to be a fact. A major premise of this book is that people with severe disabilities are full-fledged human beings and therefore are entitled to all the rights, options, and community access afforded to all citizens. For this to be a reality, we must work to educate the total person to be successful in all aspects of his or her life. This book provides guidelines for that kind of comprehensive educational program.

Students and other readers will find this material to be straightforward and direct. Practical applications and implementation strategies are provided that will be helpful to both the preservice and inservice user. This second edition not only refines the state of the art surrounding the education and expectations of persons with severe disabilities, but also acknowledges that we are learning more all the time about the abilities of this population. We are pleased to see new material included on family, friends and community relationships, technology innovations, and adult living and working options.

Our family has not followed the path upon which we were set at the time of our daughter's birth. She has always attended a "regular school" and last year entered our neighborhood middle school, along with the other children her age on our block. She has always spent a significant portion of her day in the regular classroom, with the encouragement of creative classroom teachers and the support of dedicated special education teachers and administrators. She is an integral part of our community. In the years ahead, we can clearly see supported employment and supported living in her own apartment. She will know how to participate in the community, because that is what she is learning in school. The community will value her contribution, because that is what her peers are being shown in school. Her community-based curriculum, which includes functional academics, is preparing her for a life in our community. Her integration into the regular classroom and school activities ensures that she will know how to interact with other people and they with her. For the most part, she is accepted. She is a happy person. She does not "suffer" from Down syndrome!

Dusty's situation was not automatically provided, and we are aware that it does not yet exist everywhere for everyone. We feel that her life is on the right track because the professionals with whom we are now working share the philosophy of this book, and we are very fortunate to have been introduced to them. We will continue to support all efforts to provide an optimistic outlook for persons with severe disabilities in an integrated world to teachers, administrators, students, and their family members.

Donna and Dale Dutton

NATHAN, RICHARD,
MOM, AND DAD

Community-Based Curriculum

developing" children, see, e.g., Greer, Anderson, & Odle, 1982; Smith, 1968; Stephens, 1971). Recently, a return to a functional skills approach has been evident in publications (e.g., Brown et al., 1980; Gaylord-Ross & Holvoet, 1985; Goetz et al., 1987; Horner et al., 1986; Sailor & Guess, 1983; Wilcox & Bellamy, 1982). In order to determine if a curriculum activity is functional, teachers may ask themselves: If the student does not learn to perform a particular activity, will someone else have to do it for him or her (Brown et al., 1979)? If the answer is yes, the activity is more likely to be functional than if the answer is no. For example, Jennifer, an 8-year-old student with severe handicaps, was directed by her teacher to put pegs in a pegboard; when she did not comply, it was not necessary for someone else to do it for her. However, when Jennifer was not systematially instructed to shop for groceries, someone else had to do it for her. Grocery shopping is therefore a functional skill, while putting pegs in a pegboard is not.

Chronological age–appropriate curricula refer to curricula that result in teaching activities that are performed by nonhandicapped age peers, regardless of the students' mental ages. Teaching students with severe handicaps to perform chronological age–appropriate activities will facilitate interactions with nonhandicapped peers within a wide variety of environments.

Assessments and curricula must be based upon the *wants, needs, preferences, and culture of the student.* Since interviewing students with signficant communication difficulties regarding their wants, needs, preferences, and culture often does not furnish a complete picture, other strategies for obtaining this critical information must be considered. First, observing the student's reactions to a variety of environments, materials, activities, people, and other stimuli can yield information relating to the areas just mentioned. Second, interviewing parents, siblings, and significant others and facilitating their input regarding the student's wants, needs, preferences, and culture can be useful. Assessment and curriculum decisions based upon the joint recommendations of the student and these other individuals will more likely result in a functional educational program for the student.

Finally, assessments and curricula must reflect the student's needs with regard to *transition.* Transition refers to preparing the student for subsequent environments, expectations, norms, and rules. For example, a student participating in a preschool program located on a nursery school campus must be systematically taught the skills necessary to participate in that setting, as well as in subsequent settings (e.g., an elementary school campus). In addition, students graduating from school programs must be systematically taught to participate not only in high school, college, and/or university environments, but also in work and community environments. Students of all ages must be taught to participate in activities within nonschool environments (e.g., home, neighborhood, work, recreational environments), in order to facilitate their transition from school to nonschool and postschool environments.

Instructional Methods

Systematic and appropriate use of instructional techniques must be employed; that is, instructional procedures must be based upon the student's performance and upon his or her need for specific instructional techniques. These techniques must facilitate learning and must be faded systematically over time to increase the student's independence. *Instruction must occur frequently enough* to provide the student with the opportunity to learn to participate in new activities. In addition, instructional arrangements should vary and should include opportunities for individual, small- and large-group instruction. Students must be exposed to a variety of instructional arrangements involving other students, including nonhandicapped peers, other adults, and so forth.

In order to systematically verify students' acquisition of new activities, *data collection* must occur. Students' abilities to perform new behaviors, and the instructional interventions used to enhance student involvement, must be routinely documented through data collection.

In addition, students must be taught to perform activities in response to *natural cues and corrections*. Natural cues and corrections refer to "information typically available to persons in natural environments [that] is equivalent in intensity, duration, and frequency to that which is naturally occurring" (Falvey, Brown, Lyon, Baumgart, & Schroeder, 1980, pp. 111–112). Assessments and curricula must include information about the natural cues and corrections occurring in each natural environment that will be taught. The student must be instructed not only to perform skills in natural environments but also to perform those skills in response to the natural cues and corrections operative in those environments. For example, the motor skills needed to cross the street are only one set of skills necessary for street crossing; the student must be systematically instructed to cross the street in response to the natural cues (e.g., lights, "Walk/Don't Walk" signs, absence of cars).

Since students with severe handicaps have difficulty generalizing skills, *zero inferences* (i.e., no inferences) should be made in relation to a student's ability to transfer skills from one setting to another (Brown et al., 1979). Zero inferences result in directly teaching or at least verifying a student's skill acquisition and performance across a variety of environments.

WORK OPPORTUNITIES

Historically, educational and vocational programs have not resulted in high levels of employment for persons with severe handicaps. A survey on employment conducted by the U.S. Commission on Civil Rights in 1983 found that between 50% and 75% of all people with disabilities were unemployed. Several other studies have found similar high unemployment or underemployment levels among persons with disabilities. One such study, conducted by the Madison (Wisconsin) Metropolitan School District (VanDeventer et al., 1981), analyzed program graduates for the years 1971–1979 and found that all the graduates were either unemployed or underemployed.

These and other findings have influenced the federal government to develop new programs that will more adequately prepare persons with severe handicaps for nonsheltered, nonfacility-based, and therefore, integrated work environments. PL 98-199, the Education for Handicapped Children's Act amendments, provides resources to design, develop, implement, evaluate, and disseminate educational and vocational programs that will facilitate the transition of students with handicaps from school to nonschool and postschool environments.

Vocational and work training programs must have as their goal the acquisition of meaningful employment by those receiving the training. Generally, this can result only if training occurs within a variety of integrated, community-based work environments. Meaningful employment includes *independent, competitive employment and competitive employment with support* within integrated work environments. Competitive employment with support within integrated work environments, that is, *supported employment,* is the alternative to simulated, sheltered, and segregated work environments, such as sheltered workshops, work activity centers, and activity centers. The fiscal and human resources required to "warehouse" people with severe handicaps in those sheltered and segregated environments must be rechanneled to create integrated work opportunities. The specific characteristics of work and vocational programs within schools and adult services programs are outlined in detail in Chapters 8 and 9 of this volume.

LIVING ARRANGEMENTS AND OPPORTUNITIES

The concept of *normalization* originally developed in Europe. In 1969, Bank-Mikkelsen, then director of the Danish Mental Retardation Services, defined normalization as allowing people with mental retardation to obtain and maintain an existence in proximity to, and in a manner as similar as possible to, the "normal" population. Bengt Nirje (1969) elaborated on this principle and facilitated the development of Swedish laws governing normalized provisions and services for persons with mental retardation. Wolf Wolfensberger (1970) was responsible for the application of the principle of normalization to mentally retarded persons in the United States. However, the move from institutions to community-based, normalized living arrangements has occurred at a slow pace in this country. There are several reasons for this, among the most salient of which are:

1. Deinstitutionalization has often resulted in removing people from state-operated institutions to 60–300 bed privately owned and operated nursing homes, which exhibit the same deplorable and dehumanizing conditions.

These are not appropriate alternatives to segregated, institutional residential environments.

2. Attitudinal barriers have inhibited the development of community-based alternatives. Negative attitudes toward the development of community-based alternatives have been observed among professionals and community members. "Handicapism" refers to the stererotyping of persons with handicaps and to the prejudice and discrimination directed against them (Blatt, Bogdan, Biklen, & Taylor, 1981). A great deal of education, understanding, and sensitivity toward persons with handicaps remains to be encouraged and developed.
3. Tax dollars have and continue to be allocated toward maintaining segregated, state-operated institutional environments. The cost of "maintaining" a person with the most severe handicaps in publicly supported institutions averages $90,000 per year. In 1988, community-based alternatives costs averaged $50,000 per year according to Richard Rosenberg (personal communication, 1988).

Recent court decisions have mandated the removal of persons with severe handicaps from institutional environments to community-based, normalized living arrangements. For example, Judge Raymond J. Broderick, who tried the case *Halderman v. Pennhurst* (1978), stated that:

> Pennhurst as an institution for the retarded is a monumental example of unconstitutionality with respect to the habilitation of the retarded. As such it must be expeditiously replaced with appropriate community based mental retardation programs and facilities designed to meet the individual needs of each class member.

The exposé by Burton Blatt and Fred Kaplan (1966) of dehumanizing and devalued conditions in state institutions has, in addition to the work of other scholars, raised the consciousness of many professionals and community members; such research has also assisted in the development of community-based, normalized living arrangements and opportunities for persons with severe handicaps. Professionals, parents, politicians, and others must work together to develop alternatives to institutions within integrated community environments.

The movement from institutions has not necessarily resulted in persons with severe handicaps living in normalized settings. Most people live in a home, regardless of whether it is a house, apartment, tent, motor home, igloo, or other setting. Unfortunately, people with severe handicaps often live in "facilities" or "programs" rather than in "homes". Funding and regulations must be created to develop supported living opportunities for persons with severe handicaps to live in their own homes.

Recommended physical characteristics of such community-based, normalized living arrangements (i.e., homes) include the following:

1. The homes must be located within existing normalized communities.
2. The homes should be owned or rented by the resident, not the staff.
3. The number of people living in one home should reflect the same number of people living in other homes within that community (i.e., generally one to six people).
4. Specialized staff and resources should be provided when necessary and should work for the resident.
5. Homelike atmospheres should be present.
6. Access to neighborhood and community recreational facilities and activities with nonhandicapped peers must be present.
7. Access to neighborhood and community work opportunities with nonhandicapped peers must be present.
8. Socialization opportunities both within and outside the home must be provided.
9. Residents of homes must be provided the right to choose with whom they socialize, both within and outside the home.
10. Residents of homes must have opportunities to make decisions for themselves and, if necessary, must be provided the opportunity to acquire the skills necessary to make decisions.
11. Residents of homes must be treated with dignity and respect.

SUMMARY

This chapter reviews traditional and more functional definitions of mental retardation and severe handicaps. The focus of a diagnosis or label of mental retardation or severe handicaps should be on the development and delivery of needed resources and services, as opposed to stressing the person's deficits.

This chapter also briefly describes the characteristics of educational, work, and residential programs, services, and opportunities. The remaining chapters in this book provide more in-depth descriptions of strategies for developing and implementing such programs, services, and opportunities.

REFERENCES

Bank-Mikkelsen, N.E. (1969). A metropolitan area in Denmark: Copenhagen. In R. Kugel & W. Wolfensberger (Eds.), *Changing patterns in residential services for the mentally retarded* (pp. 227–254). Washington, DC: U.S. Government Printing Office.

Baumgart, D., Brown, L., Pumpian, I., Nisbet, J., Ford, A., Sweet, M., Messina, R., & Schroeder, J. (1982). Principle of partial participation and individualized adaptations in educational programs for severely handicapped students. *Journal of The Association for the Severely Handicapped, 7*(2), 17–27.

Blatt, B., Bogdan, R., Biklen, D., & Taylor, S. (1981). From institution to community:

A conversion model. In B. Blatt (Ed.), *In & out of mental retardation* (pp. 241–258). Baltimore: University Park Press.

Blatt, B., & Kaplan, F. (1966). *Christmas in purgatory.* Boston: Allyn & Bacon.

Bricker, D., & Filler, J. (Eds.). (1985). *Severe mental retardation: From theory to practice.* Reston, VA: Council for Exceptional Children, Division on Mental Retardation.

Browder, D.M. (1987). *Assessment of individuals with severe handicaps.* Baltimore: Paul H. Brookes Publishing Co.

Brown, L., Branston, M.B., Hamre-Nietupski, S., Pumpian, I., Certo, N., & Gruenewald, L. (1979). A strategy for developing chronological age appropriate and functional curricular content for severely handicapped adolescents and young adults. *Journal of Special Education, 13*(1), 81–90.

Brown, L., Falvey, M., Pumpian, I., Baumgart, D., Nesbit, J., Ford, A., Schroeder, J., & Loomis, R. (Eds.). (1980). *Curricular strategies for teaching severely handicapped students functional skills in school and nonschool environments.* Madison, WI: Madison Metropolitan School District.

Brown v. Board of Education, 347 U.S. 483 (1954).

Certo, N., Haring, N., & York, R. (1984). *Public school integration of severely handicapped students.* Baltimore: Paul H. Brookes Publishing Co.

Falvey, M., Brown, L., Lyon, S., Baumgart, D., & Schroeder, J. (1980). Strategies for using cues and correction procedures. In W. Sailor, B. Wilcox, & L. Brown (Eds.), *Methods of instruction for severely handicapped students.* Baltimore: Paul H. Brookes Publishing Co.

Falvey, M., Rosenberg, R., & Grenot-Scheyer, M. (1982). Strategies for assessing students with multiply handicapping conditions. In S. Ray, M.J. O'Neill, & N.T. Morris (Eds.), *Low incidence children: A guide to psychoeducational assessment* (pp. 245–273). Natchitoches, LA: Steven Ray Publishing.

Gaylord-Ross, R.J., & Holvoet, J. F. (1985) *Strategies for educating students with severe handicaps.* Boston: Little, Brown.

Goetz, L., Guess, D., & Stremel-Campbell, K. (Eds.). (1987). *Innovative program design for individuals with dual sensory impairments.* Baltimore: Paul H. Brookes Publishing Co.

Gold, M.W. (1980). *Try another way training manual.* Champaign, IL: Research Press.

Greer, J.G., Anderson, R.M., & Odle, S.J. (1982). *Strategies for helping severely and multiply handicapped citizens.* Baltimore: University Park Press.

Grossman, H.J. (Ed.). (1977). *Manual on terminology and classification in mental retardation.* Washington, DC: American Association on Mental Deficiency.

Halderman v. Pennhurst State School and Hospital, et al. C.A. No. 73-1345, E.D. PA, Order, March 17, 1978.

Horner, R.H., Meyer, L.H., & Fredricks, H.D. Bud (Eds.). (1986). *Education of learners with severe handicaps.* Baltimore: Paul H. Brookes Publishing Co.

Inskeep, A. (1926). *Teaching dull and retarded children.* New York: J.J. Little & Ives Co.

Lehr, D.H., & Brown, F. (1984). Perspectives on severely multiply handicapped. In E. Meyer (Ed.), *Topics of today: Issues of tomorrow* (pp. 41–56). Reston, VA: Council for Exceptional Children, Division on Mental Retardation.

Lutfiyya, S.M. (1988). Other than clients: Reflections on relationships between people with disabilities and typical people. *TASH Newsletter, 14*(9), 3–5.

New York State Association for Retarded Children v. Rockefeller, U.S. District Court (E.D., N.Y., 1972).

Nirje, B. (1969). The normalization principle and its management implications. In R. Kugel & W. Wolfensberger (Eds.), *Changing patterns in residential services for the mentally retarded* (pp. 51–57). Washington DC: U.S. Government Printing Office.

Pennsylvania Association for Retarded Citizens v. Commonwealth of Pennsylvania, 343 F. Supp. 279 (E.D. Pa. 1972).

PL 93-112, Vocational Rehabilitation Act of 1973, Section 504.

PL 94-142, The Education for All Handicapped Children Act of 1975. Washington, DC: U.S. Department of Education.

Sailor, W., & Guess, D. (1983). *Severely handicapped students: An instructional design.* Boston: Houghton Mifflin.

Smith, R.M. (1968). *Clinical teaching: Methods of instruction for the retarded.* New York: McGraw Hill.

Sontag, E., Burke, P., & York, R. (1973). Considerations for the severely handicapped in public schools. *Education & Training of the Mentally Retarded, 8,* 20–26.

Stephens, B. (Ed.). (1971). *Training the developmentally young.* New York: John Day Co.

Taylor, S.J. (1988) Caught in the continuum: A critical analysis of the principle of the least restrictive environment. *Journal of The Association for Persons with Severe Handicaps, 13*(1), 41–53.

Taylor, S.J., Biklen, D., & Knoll, J. (Eds.). (1987). *Community integration for people with severe disabilities.* New York: Teachers College Press.

VanDeventer, P., Yelnick, N., Brown, L., Schroeder, J., Loomis, R., & Gruenewald, L. (1981). A follow-up examination of severely handicapped graduates of the Madison Metropolitan School District from 1971–1978. In L. Brown, D. Baumgart, I. Pumpian, J. Nesbit, A. Ford, R. Loomis, & J. Schroeder (Eds.), *Curricular strategies that can be used to transition severely handicapped students from school to nonschool and postschool environments* (pp. 1–177). Madison, WI: Madison Metropolitan School District.

Wilcox, B., & Bellamy, G.T. (1982). *Design of high school programs for severely handicapped students.* Baltimore: Paul H. Brookes Publishing Co.

Wolfensberger, W. (1970). The principle of normalization and its implications to psychiatric services. *American Journal of Psychiatry, 127,* 291–296.

Wuerch, B., & Voeltz, L. (1982). *Longitudinal leisure skills for severely handicapped learners: The Ho'onanea curriculum component.* Baltimore: Paul H. Brookes Publishing Co.

TWO

PARTNERSHIPS WITH PARENTS AND SIGNIFICANT OTHERS

Mary A. Falvey and Michele Haney

PARENTS HAVE BEEN the most influential force in legislating and mandating services for their sons and daughters with severe handicaps. They have also been the most effective long-term advocates, by assisting, monitoring, and pushing the "system" to provide the services and opportunities their sons and daughters need and deserve.

In addition to parents, others who are not necessarily paid to do so have played significant roles in advocating for individuals with severe handicaps. "Significant others" have included siblings, spouses, extended family members, neighbors, friends, and other members of the community who have developed relationships and friendships with individuals with severe handicaps.

In order for people to feel connected with one another, it seems reasonable that significant others play important roles in the lives of children as they grow up. Every child should spend time with someone who is crazy about them. In other words, every child should be involved with at least one person, other than a parent, who is tremendously supportive of and involved with that child. This person should be someone who thinks that this child is more important than other people's children, and someone who is in love with this child and whom this child loves in return (Bronfenbrenner, 1975).

Parents whose sons and daughters have been labeled severely handicapped have had the responsibilities and opportunities typically associated with the challenges and joys of parenting. In addition, they have often experienced additional pressures and stresses related to parenting a child in a society that is not always committed to accepting and assisting children with disabilities.

Choice making is an assumed guarantee and right of most people. Unfortunately, however, people with severe handicaps and their families have not had such guarantees afforded them. Parents, significant others, educators, and other service providers should systematically ensure opportunities for individuals with severe handicaps to make choices about every aspect of their lives, including living, working, and playing in the community (Turnbull, Turnbull, Bronicki, Summers, & Roeder-Gordon, 1988).

This chapter is devoted to the inclusion of parents, significant others, and persons with severe handicaps in the planning, delivery, and monitoring of programs and services. The rationale for such inclusion will be articulated along with strategies for facilitating parental and significant other involvement.

FAMILY INVOLVEMENT IN SERVICES

The needs, difficulties, and unique strengths of families who have sons or daughters with severe handicaps have been documented in the professional literature (e.g., Darling, 1979; Farber, 1959; Featherstone, 1980; Hewett, 1970; Katz, 1961; Koch & Dobson, 1971; Turnbull & Turnbull, 1978). As interest in the families of children with severe handicaps has grown, the perceived role of the family in educating sons or daughters with special needs has shifted from that of being a passive recipient of services (Lyon & Preis, 1983) to that of being an active and respected part of the intervention team (Sontag, 1976; Vincent, Dodd, & Henner, 1978). The passage of Public Law 94-142 (the Education for All Handicapped Children Act of 1975) made active participation in the educational process a legal right for parents, because in the past, parents had been excluded. Government recognized the importance of parent advocacy.

Parents should be facilitated to play an active role in the development of *all* educational and support services for their sons and daughters, because parents and other family members are generally most familiar with the levels of skill proficiency of their sons or daughters. In addition, the family's preferences in terms of needs associated with existing routines, potential new skills, and future living options, should play a primary role in the establishment of priorities among skill areas to be developed. This more active role should be clearly reflected in the development and determination of the specific services and programs.

The concept of a true partnership between parents and educators is crucial to the development of an effective curriculum. Unfortunately, the evolution of this partnership has been hampered by traditional professional and parental relationships in which parents are viewed as subordinates (Darling, 1983; Schopler, 1976), and by negative professional assumptions about families whose sons or daughters are handicapped (Donnellan & Mirenda, 1984; Vincent, Laten, Salisbury, Brown, & Baumgart, 1981). According to these assumptions, parents are often viewed as ineffective, at best, and as dependent upon professionals for help in coping with their son or daughter with handicaps. Parents are rarely seen as valuable, necessary resources for the planning and possible implementation of instructional programs. Regrettably, the traditional parent-professional relationship may be largely characterized as one of distrust and avoidance (Cutler, 1981).

Creating a more effective partnership under these circumstances is not easy, but it can, and must, be accomplished. As a first step, educators and service providers must be willing to closely examine their attitudes toward parents and to attempt to understand the ways in which these attitudes have negatively influenced their interactions with them. For example, an educator may believe the parents of children with severe handicaps should be carrying out the school's instructional program at home. Such an attitude can lead to frustration with the parent who does not see himself or herself in a teaching role. "How can I be expected to toilet train that student in school if his parents won't follow through at home?" asks the educator. What this attitude fails to consider is that toilet training may not be the most important issue for the parents at this time. Perhaps they have other, far more critical concerns, or may be involved with other important activities that preclude the teaching role. Once potentially negative attitudes have been identified, examined, and modified, more constructive assumptions can be utilized for building a partnership.

The following paragraphs build upon assumptions identified by Cutler (1981), Donnellan and Mirenda (1984), and Vincent et al. (1981) to outline positive attitudes that can serve as a base for the construction of effective parent-professional relationships and interactions.

Principle 1: The emotional reactions of families of individuals with severe handicaps are normal, necessary, and protective reactions. These reactions can potentially be utilized in productive ways. It is important for educators and service providers to recognize that adjusting to the realities of raising a son or daughter with severe handicaps is an ongoing challenge. Parents may, at various times, experience grief, guilt, anger, and denial (Baum, 1962). They may also experience depression and defensiveness (Roos, 1963), as well as joy in their relationship with their son or daughter (Glidden, Valliere, & Herbert, 1988). Some of these reactions can interfere with the active involvement of the family in educating their son or daughter. However, if recognized, valued, and supported by sensitive educators and other service providers, these reactions can play an important role in the development of a working partnership between home and school and/or other services. Families need to work with professionals who understand their problems and who provide nonjudgmental emotional support and encouragement (Lyon & Preis, 1983).

Principle 2: Families are capable of solving their own problems; their solutions may not be "our" solutions, but they may be more effective for a particular family than are our solutions. Rather than the "answers," parents need information and a strong working relationship with professionals so that they can find solutions that work for them. Educators and other service providers can inform the family about programs and services that are available to them and to their son or daughter, and can help them determine strategies and interventions that are consistent with the family's needs, culture, styles, values, and coping patterns.

Principle 3: Professionals can learn to work effectively within the family system. Professionals should not try to change the family system merely to accommodate their viewpoint. A family system perspective implies an understanding of the various roles, rules, functions, and structures within a given family of the impact of a son or daughter with handicaps upon these elements, and of the changes that occur over time as the family relates both within itself and to a larger community system. Just as no two students are the same, thus necessitating an individualized approach, no two families are the same. Attitudes toward handicaps, parental expectations, family resources, parenting styles, and so on, differ from one family to another, and must be considered when developing interventions for a student.

Principle 4: The progress and/or needs of the son or daughter with handicaps may not be the most important issue for a family at a given time. Family needs will dictate family priorities. All families are involved in a variety of important activities—for example, work, play, socializing, child rearing, and homemaking. Caring for a son or daughter who is handicapped is only one part of a large group of family functions. Educators and other service providers must realize that when they devise intervention plans for a student with handicaps that involve the student's family members, they may be expecting too much of an already extremely busy family unit. The family's priorities must come first; it is the professional's responsibility to recognize and acknowledge these priorities and adapt program plans accordingly.

Principle 5: The family is the best, most committed long-term advocate for the child. Seeking the active involvement of the family in educational and other service provision decisions is a vital role for educators and other service providers. One important way that parents can serve in an advocacy role is through the individualized education program (IEP) process. Initially, parents have the right to be involved in the development of individual goals and objectives for the IEP. Educators are responsible for informing the family of the options available to them and for helping them to make knowledgeable decisions. The family's long-term commitment and knowledge of their son or daughter with severe handicaps is likely to facilitate the development of the advocacy role for family members.

Principle 6: There is no such thing as a family that cannot be actively and productively involved in the educational process of a son or daughter with handicaps. Families generally want to be involved and do what is best for their son or daughter, but they often do not know how to begin. They sometimes view the schools as alien and unreceptive environments that bear litte relationship to their "real" world of home and community. Sadly, these perceptions are often true. Educators and other service providers must find ways to bridge this gap. Direct and frequent contact with parents is necessary to foster this involvement. No family is truly uncooperative; all families can be actively and productively involved in the educational process.

Principle 7: Families have information about their son or daughter with handicaps that is critical to the development of a sound educational program. In fact, the family is the best source for information concerning the child, and it is critical to develop strategies to obtain and utilize this rich source of information. It is the role of the educator and other service providers to find ways to develop a spirit of cooperation and to facilitate this involvement.

These positive principles reflect an emphasis on serving families by helping them identify their needs and generate their own solutions to these needs. The identification of needs is often based upon skills necessary to function as a more independent member of the family unit. These needs may reflect immediate concerns (e.g., wanting the student to learn the appropriate behaviors to accompany her father, so that it is not necessary to hire a babysitter each time he wants to go grocery shopping) and long-range planning (e.g., identification of skills the student will need for transition into integrated and dignified living environments as an adult). Solutions to these and other needs can be generated with a sense of shared responsibility between school and home. In order to share such responsibility, the relationship between school staff, other service providers, and family members must be one of trust. Trust must be earned even for well intentioned teachers and service providers with good reputations and track records. Parents and significant others must see for themselves that this teacher or service provider cares about their son or daughter and has his or her best interest at heart. When a parent or significant other begins to trust a teacher or other service provider, that does not mean he or she will no longer question the service provider's actions. Parents and significant others must always be on the alert to adequately advocate for the son's or daughter's well-being.

Parents of sons and daughters with disabilities must be afforded the opportunity to feel and do what parents of nonhandicapped sons and daughters feel and do. Kay Farrell (1985) developed a "Bill of Rights" for parents that might assist professionals to allow these parents to have such "normal" feelings and reactions:

1. Right to feel angry
2. Right to seek another opinion
3. Right to privacy
4. Right to keep trying
5. Right to stop trying
6. Right to set limits
7. Right to parent
8. Right to be unenthusiastic

9. Right to be annoyed with your child
10. Right to take time off
11. Right to be expert-in-charge
12. Right to dignity (p. 73)

In addition to the varying feelings that parents have, they also have various roles. Turnbull and Turnbull (1986) identified a variety of roles parents have assumed over the years, such as: problem solvers, organization members, service developers, recipients of professionals' decisions, learners and teachers, political advocates, educational decision makers, and family members. It is critical that professionals recognize that parents have had to assume numerous responsibilities and roles in the development, delivery, and ongoing monitoring of their son's or daughter's services and opportunities. Specific strategies for involving parents and significant others are included in the following section.

Strategies for Involving Families

Families must be involved in determining the most functional and appropriate activities for their sons or daughters. In addition to participating in the planning of immediate goals and objectives, family members need to be involved over time in examining future living options and other arrangements for the son or daughter. A number of strategies can be used to develop this involvement, including frequent meetings with the family, telephone contact with them, notes home, and parent and significant other inventories and schedules. It is important for educators and other service providers to facilitate the interaction with family members, rather than direct them, so that they develop the concept of "working with" rather than "working for" the parents.

One of the most important strategies for bridging the gap between home and school and other services is to provide an atmosphere conducive to problem solving. This is best accomplished when the educator and the service provider become good listeners, encouraging family members to speak openly, to share valuable information, and to productively discuss and solve their own problems (Kroth, 1975). Techniques for effective listening have been discussed in detail by others (e.g., Bersoff & Grieger, 1971; Carkhuff, 1973; Dinkmeyer & Carlson, 1973; Gordon, 1970; Kroth, 1975, Rogers, 1961). Briefly, these techniques involve maintaining eye contact with the speaker, giving nonverbal signs of acceptance and encouragement, providing verbal feedback by paraphrasing the speaker's statements and reflecting on the feelings expressed, and avoiding judgments and moralizing. These strategies can, initially, be difficult for educators and other service providers, who are often in the role of giving out information rather than receiving information.

A good listener can assist families in defining their problems and objectives concerning sons or daughters with severe handicaps. Once identified, strategies for solving the problems or for working toward the objectives can be developed in a partnership. When working with family members in this way, the use of professional jargon and unnecessary technical terminology should be avoided. Language is critical; even seemingly harmless phrases can interfere with the developing partnership. For example, the phrase "not ready for" communicates little to the family about their son's or daughter's current educational status, much less his or her need, and at the same time places the burden of the disability back on the family. Another example is when professionals use the term or phrase that a student has reached a "plateau" and cannot learn any more about a particular subject or skill. The real issue or challenge is being avoided. The "plateau" that has been reached is probably more reflective of the lack of effective teaching techniques and strategies than it is about the student's ability or aptitude. The focus should be on what the student is able to do. Finally, educators and other service providers should use the simple phrase: "I don't know" when, in fact, they do not know "the answer."

Two useful tools for organizing an interview with parents are the parent/significant other inventory and the weekday/weekend schedule. Information obtained using these tools can be particularly helpful in the development of an appropriate, individualized curriculum. The tools also provide insights into the student's role within the family and family mechanisms for coping with the presence of a disability. Strategies for and examples of developing parent/significant other inventories and weekday/weekend schedules are contained in Chapter 3 of this volume.

It is important that family involvement be sought from the beginning of the student's educational experience and continue on a regular basis. Attempts to encourage this involvement, however, must be sensitive to the needs of the family. Meetings, for example, should be scheduled at times that are convenient for family members, rather than at times convenient solely for school personnel. Transportation to school should be provided if necessary, and educators and other service providers should be willing to hold meetings in the students' homes if requested by the family. When meetings outside the home are required, babysitting and other family needs should be identified and services and/or resources should be secured. If a family requires an interpreter in order to participate in a meeting, such services should be made available. A positive and caring attitude toward the family and their unique needs, and a belief in and commitment to family involvement in the educational process, are essential components in educating the student with severe handicaps.

The establishment of a parent-professional partnership is essential for many reasons. Heward, Dardig, and Rossett (1979) have identified the benefits to all parties involved. A productive parent-professional relationship provides professionals with:

Greater understanding of the overall needs of the child and the needs and desires of the parent

Data for more meaningful selection of specific objectives that are important to the student in his or her world outside the school
Access to a wider range of social and activity reinforcers provided by parents
Increased opportunities to reinforce appropriate behaviors in both school and home settings
Feedback from parents as to changes in behavior that can be used to improve programs being implemented by professionals and parents
The ability to comply with legislation mandating continuing parental input to the educational process

A productive parent-professional relationship provides parents with:

Greater understanding of the needs of their son or daughter and the objectives of the teacher
Information on their rights and responsibilities as parents
Specific information about their son's or daughter's school program and how they can become involved
Specific ways to extend the positive effects of school programming into the home
Increased skills in helping their son or daughter learn functional behaviors that are appropriate for the home environment
Access to additional important resources (current and future) for their son or daughter

And, of most importance, a productive parent-professional relationship provides the child with:

Greater consistency in his or her two most important environments
Increased opportunities for learning and growth
Access to expanded resources and services

Specific strategies that parents and significant others might use to become active participants in the design, delivery, and ongoing monitoring of programs, services, and opportunities for their sons and daughters are listed below:

Share your joys and your son's/daughter's hurdles—be excited and others will be, too.
Let other people know what you are striving/working toward and let them try to assist.
Create normalized settings for your son/daughter and the entire family.
Find professionals who are willing to help (job titles and degrees are not always relevant).
Feel and act as a significant member of the partnership (never say to a professional, "I am only a parent").
Do not be too patient with the "system."

Turnbull and Turnbull (1986) have developed strategies that families and significant others might use in the design and delivery of a student's IEP. Table 2.1 includes the steps of an IEP process along with suggested strategies for families and significant others.

Culturally and Linguistically Diverse Families

Involving parents in the educational planning for their sons or daughters with handicaps becomes especially challenging when working with families with culturally and linguistically diverse backgrounds. Linguistic differences are immediately recognizable obstacles to parent-teacher communication, but differences in cultural orientation and expectations can also have profound effects on parent-professional relationships. Parents of different cultural orientations may not understand their rights and responsibilities within the school system. In addition, lack of knowledge concerning available community services and limited English-speaking ability for communicating with service providers may negatively affect the parents' ability to cope with their son or daughter who has special needs (Wilson-Portuondo, 1980). Whether the family seeks information and help for their child with a severe handicap may be influenced by cultural differences as well. The parents may, for example, come from a country where services are unavailable, or where questioning those in authority is forbidden, or where asking for help is a sign of weakness.

Educators and other service providers, in general, are often ill-prepared to deal with the special issues associated with these families (Carpenter, 1983). Few service providers are multilingual. In addition, they often lack knowledge of assessment techniques, instructional methodology, and basic cultural differences pertinent to working with a culturally and linguistically diverse population (Baca, 1980). Furthermore, educators may make basic assumptions about parenting that are applicable only to traditional Anglo-American roles, norms, and rules—assumptions that are likely to severely interfere with non-Anglo parent-teacher interactions.

In order to work effectively with families who are culturally and linguistically diverse, educators and other service providers must learn not only about the students' unique characteristics, learning styles, and behavioral styles, but also about family characteristics, culture, and language that may have an educational impact. Contact with parents should be initiated in the parents' own language, through an interpreter if necessary. In addition, the following list of factors, which expands on suggestions developed by Wilson-Portuondo (1980) and Marion (1980), should be considered when working with culturally diverse populations:

1. Parents of culturally diverse backgrounds may not have access to information that will assist them in handling their son or daughter with special needs. Regularly scheduled meetings and frequent planning conferences

Table 2.1. Suggestions for involving parents in the IEP conference, developed by Turnbull and Turnbull (1986)

Preconference Preparation

1. Appoint a conference chair to coordinate all aspects of the conference. The conference chair should assume responsibility for coordinating preconference preparation, chairing the conference, and coordinating follow-up.
2. Solicit information from parents on their preferences related to their participation: persons who should attend, convenient time, convenient location, needed assistance (child care, transportation), and the type of information that they would like to receive in advance.
3. Specify the persons appropriate to attend the IEP (individualized education program) conference in light of parent and professional preferences. Be sure to consider carefully the possibility of including the student.
4. Arrange a convenient time and location for the meeting.
5. If needed, work with parents in assisting them with logistics such as child care and transportation.
6. Inform parents (in writing or verbally) of the purpose, time of conference, location, and names of participants.
7. In light of parents' preferences, share information in advance of the conference that they believe will help them prepare for participation—for example, evaluation reports, evaluation checklists to complete, list of subject areas which school personnel think should be covered by the IEP, summary of child's strengths and weaknesses in each subject area, ideas from school personnel on possible goals and objectives, information on legal rights, and information on placement options and related services.
8. If several placements are being considered for the student, encourage parents to visit each program prior to the conference.
9. Discuss the conference purpose and procedures with students and assist them in specifying their own preferences for educational programming. Encourage students to discuss their preferences with their parents.
10. Encourage parents to share any information with school personnel in advance of the conference that the parents believe will be helpful during the preparation period.
11. Gather all information from school personnel that will help prepare for the IEP conference.
12. Prepare an agenda to cover each of the remaining five components of the conference.

Initial Conference Proceedings

1. Greet and welcome parents upon arrival and welcome any persons whom the parents bring with them.
2. Introduce all conference participants and share sufficient information to identify roles and areas of responsibility. If parents are being introduced to several professionals for the first time, consider the use of name tags or make a list of the names and positions of conference participants for the parents.
3. State the purpose of the conference and review the agenda. Ask the parents and their guests if there are any issues they would like to add to the agenda.
4. Ask participants the amount of time they have available for the conference. State the intention to use time wisely but to avoid rushing through important decisions. Share the option of rescheduling another meeting if necessary.
5. Ask parents and their guests if they would like to have a clarification of legal rights. If so, fully provide the information they request.

Review of Formal Evaluation and Current Levels of Performance

1. If a formal evaluation of the student has been conducted and a separate evaluation conference to review results has not been held, ask the appropriate diagnostic personnel to identify the tests administered, the specific results of each, and the options for consideration based on the evaluation results.

(continued)

Table 2.1. *(continued)*

2. After evaluation information has been shared, summarize the major findings and encourage parents to point out areas of agreement and disagreement and their corresponding reasons.
3. Ask parents if they would like to have a written copy of evaluation results. If so, provide it to them.
4. If a formal evaluation has not been conducted (one must be conducted every 3 years), review the child's developmental progress and present levels of performance in each subject area.
5. Identify current implications of all test results for instructional programming and future implications for the next life cycle stage of the child.
6. Clarify any diagnostic jargon that is used.
7. Solicit parental input on the student's current performance levels. Identify areas of agreement and disagreement.
8. Strive to resolve disagreement through discussion or examples of student performance. If your disagreement cannot be resolved within the conference, develop a plan for collecting further evaluation information by school personnel or an independent evaluator. Solicit parental suggestions on the procedures to follow in collecting further information.
9. Proceed with the development of the IEP only when you and the parents agree on the student's type of exceptionality and current levels of performance.

Development of Goals and Objectives

1. Based on the current levels of performance, identify all subject areas requiring specially designed instruction. For each subject area, collaboratively specify appropriate goals and objectives.
2. Encourage parents and their guests to share goals and objectives they believe are important for current and future functioning in the home, school, or community environment.
3. Establish goal and objective priorities in light of relevance for the student. Discuss future educational and vocational options for the student to ensure that the goals and objectives provide sufficient preparation for future needs.
4. If the student receives instruction from two or more teachers, clarify the manner in which the responsibility for teaching the objectives will be shared.
5. Ask parents if they are willing to assume responsibility for teaching or reviewing some of the objectives with their son or daughter at home. If so, discuss their preferences for which goals and objectives they will work on.
6. Ensure that evaluation procedures and schedules are identified for goals and objectives.
7. Explain to parents that including goals and objectives in the IEP does not represent a guarantee that the student will achieve them; rather, it represents a good faith effort that school personnel will teach these goals and objectives.

Determination of Placement and Related Services

1. Based on the student's current levels of performance and the goals and objectives deemed appropriate, review the full continuum of viable placement options by identifying benefits and drawbacks of each. Solicit parent input on benefits and drawbacks from an academic and social perspective of the different placement options for their child.
2. If parents have not already visited possible placements, encourage them to do so. Agree on a "tentative placement" until the parents can visit and confirm its appropriateness.
3. Select the placement option consistent with the goals and objectives to be taught. The placement should be as close to peers who do not have exceptionalities as possible. Specify the extent of the student's participation in the regular education program.
4. Identify the related services the student needs. Discuss the benefits and drawbacks of each service and options for scheduling (i.e., frequency, the portion of class that will be missed).

(continued)

Table 2.1. *(continued)*

5. Specify the dates for initiating each related service and the anticipated duration of each.
6. If the parents have not had an opportunity to meet the teacher of the selected placement or the related service providers, share the names and qualifications of these professionals.

Concluding the Conference

1. Summarize to review major decisions and follow-up responsibility. Take notes to record this summary.
2. Assign follow-up responsibility (e.g., arranging for physical therapy) requiring attention.
3. Review with parents the responsibility (teaching objectives, increasing socialization opportunities during after-school hours, visiting adult programs) they have expressed interest in assuming.
4. Set a tentative date for reviewing the IEP document on at least an annual basis, and preferably more frequently.
5. Identify strategies for ongoing communication with parents, in light of the preferences of all involved parties.
6. Express appreciation for the shared decision making that occurred and reiterate to parents how much their participation is valued.

can provide needed information, with the educator and other service providers serving as resources.

2. Culturally diverse parents may not understand their legal rights as parents of children with handicaps. Educators and other service providers should work to help them understand these rights and responsibilities. Making sure that literature and forms (e.g., IEP forms) are available in the parents' own language is one way to facilitate this.
3. All parents need to be listened to and understood. Educators and other service providers may need to work through their own prejudices when working with culturally diverse families in order to better recognize the families' feelings and be responsive to them.
4. Parents are a tremendous source of information about themselves and their children. Discuss with parents the educational, rehabilitation, and other systems in their native country. Help them express the dissatisfactions they may have with the present system and the current educational plans for their son or daughter with handicaps. Inform them of the limits of their present program, while describing what can be provided within that program.
5. Establish contact with parents before a crisis develops. From the beginning, encourage parental support and include parents in the planning of their son's or daughter's program.
6. Cultural, linguistic, and familial priorities must be identified and addressed for each student. These priorities must be maintained within the functional skills curriculum in a multicultural class.

In all areas of the curriculum, consideration of special linguistic and cultural needs is relevant and necessary. When learning cooking skills, for example, students should be taught to purchase and prepare foods that are common in their homes. Communication skills should be developed in the student's native language to facilitate integration into the home and community. Photographs, English words, and words in the student's native language can be used simultaneously in teaching new concepts (Duran, 1985). All skills will be far more readily acquired and utilized if they have meaning and value in the student's culture and are supported in the home. It cannot be overemphasized that educators and other service providers must become familiar with the preferences, norms, and expectations that are specific to the student's culture through a program of parental involvement. Such involvement can serve as the link between the cultures of home, school, and other services, and can thus further the development of culturally diverse students with handicaps. Understanding and respecting the ways in which people are culturally different, and planning for these differences, will ensure that programs are developed that are relevant to individual student and family needs.

Siblings

A neglected aspect of family involvement in the educational planning for students with severe handicaps is the role of siblings. Although tremendous emphasis is placed on instructing students with handicaps to interact in integrated environments with nonhandicapped persons (Sailor & Guess, 1983), little attention is given to interactions within the families of these students, particularly to interactions with siblings. Educational programs must focus on the needs of the whole family, and on those skills involving interaction among members. Such programs must therefore involve all of the family's members. Siblings often have the closest, most intimate, caring, and understanding relationship with their brother or sister with a disability.

The child with handicaps is a challenge for the entire family (Chinn, Winn, & Walters, 1978; Pearlman & Scott, 1981). Siblings need to be involved in the decision-making process; they need information about what is happening to their brother or sister who is handicapped, and they can be valuable resources. Such involvement can also improve their own relationship with their siblings with handicaps.

The involvement of siblings must be sensitive to their own needs and reactions. Siblings are often expected to be responsible for their brother or sister with handicaps, and to assume parent-like roles (Myers, 1978; Seligman, 1983). These expectations can cause anger and resentment (Grossman, 1972), as well as fear and guilt (Hayden, 1974). The sibling's own work, both social and academic, may be adversely affected (Michaelis, 1980). When involving siblings in the planning process, therefore, the educator and other service provider must be careful not to place additional burdens and responsibilities on them. Siblings may come to regard any sustained interaction with their siblings with handicaps as an onerous duty (Farber, 1959). It is critical that educators and other service providers identify ways to facilitate family interactions that are beneficial not only to the student with handicaps but to all family members. Siblings may also be terrified about the future because of the responsibility they may have to assume for a brother or sister with handicaps (Featherstone, 1980). Involvement of siblings in the development of an appropriate curriculum for their brother or sister with handicaps may help to alleviate some of the siblings' immediate concerns, while providing a forum for them to express their fears and make plans for their futures.

Siblings should be invited to participate in family interviews and planning meetings. They can be asked to identify current activities within the home, neighborhood, and community in which they and their sibling with handicaps are involved. Their suggestions for goals should be solicited and incorporated into an overall plan. They may be asked to complete a weekday/weekend schedule, and their viewpoints can be compared with those of their parents. Questions about future directions should also be directed to siblings. They should be encouraged to express their feelings and concerns regarding their sibling who is handicapped, and these should be considered seriously when developing the student's educational program. Communication between family members about the child with handicaps is critical to the development of positive attitudes and adjustments on the part of the normal siblings (Grossman, 1972). By making efforts to include siblings in the planning process, educators and other service providers can do much to encourage this communication. Readers are referred to Powell and Ogle's (1985) detailed and comprehensive listing of the issues associated with siblings of children with handicaps, as well as the numerous techniques they provide for dealing with siblings' specific needs.

"Moving Out"

Most children grow up in a home with a parent or parents. Unfortunately, a large percentage of children with severe handicaps have not had such an opportunity, due to emotional, physical, social, financial, or other reasons. The government, in responding to the need to identify settings for these children, built and developed institutions, nursing homes, and group homes. Often, the result was that a child with severe handicaps was forced to live in a "program" or a "facility" rather than a home. In an effort to promote more home and family settings for children, the Center on Human Policy's Research and Training Center on Community Integration developed the policy contained in Table 2.2.

Parents, professionals, advocates, and individuals with severe handicaps have focused attention on and developed methods for facilitating more normalized living opportunities within integrated community settings. Certainly, the deinstitutionalization movement has had a very positive and significant impact on the development of more normalized opportunities (Bruininks & Lakin, 1985). Although a great deal of work has been accomplished with regard to deinstitutionalization, much remains to be done (Biklen & Knoll, 1987).

Table 2.2. A statement in support of families and their children

THESE PRINCIPLES SHOULD GUIDE PUBLIC POLICY TOWARD FAMILIES OF CHILDREN WITH DEVELOPMENTAL DISABILITIES . . . AND THE ACTIONS OF STATES AND AGENCIES WHEN THEY BECOME INVOLVED WITH FAMILIES:

All children, regardless of disability, belong with families and need enduring relationships with adults. When states or agencies become involved with families, permanency planning should be a guiding philosophy. As a philsophy, permanency planning endorses children's rights to a nurturing home and consistent relationships with adults. As a guide to state and agency practice, permanency planning requires family support, encouragement of a family's relationship with the child, family reunification for children placed out of home, and the pursuit of adoption for children when family reunification is not possible.

Families should receive the supports necessary to maintain their children at home. Family support services must be based on the principle *"whatever it takes."* In short, family support services should be flexible, individualized, and designed to meet the diverse needs of families.

Family supports should build on existing social networks and natural sources of support. As a guiding principle, natural sources of support, including neighbors, extended families, friends, and community associations, should be preferred over agency programs and professional services. When states or agencies become involved with families, they should support existing social networks, strengthen natural sources of support, and help build connections to existing community resources. When natural sources of support cannot meet the needs of families, professional or agency-operated support services should be available.

Family supports should maximize the family's control over the services and supports they receive. Family support services must be based on the assumption that families, rather than states and agencies, are in the best position to determine their needs.

Family supports should support the entire family. Family support services should be defined broadly in terms of the needs of the entire family, including children with disabilities, parents, and siblings.

Family support services should encourage the integration of children with disabilities into the community. Family support services should be designed to maximize integration and participation in community life for children with disabilities.

When children cannot remain with their families for whatever reason, out-of-home placement should be viewed initially as a temporary arrangement and efforts should be directed toward reuniting the family. Consistent with the philosophy of permanency planning, children should live with their families whenever possible. When, due to family crisis or other circumstances, children must leave the families, efforts should be directed at encouraging and enabling families to be reunited.

When families cannot be reunited and when active parental involvement is absent, adoption should be aggressively pursued. In fulfillment of each child's right to a stable family and an enduring relationship with one or more adults, adoption should be pursued for children whose ties with their families have been broken. Whenever possible, families should be involved in adoption planning and, in all cases, should be treated with sensitivity and respect. When adoption is pursued, the possibility of "open adoption," whereby families maintain involvement with a child, should be seriously considered.

While a preferred alternative to any group setting or out-of-home placement, foster care should only be pursued when children cannot live with their families or

(continued)

Table 2.2. *(continued)*

with adoptive families. After families and adoptive families, children should have the opportunity to live with foster families. Foster family care can provide children with a home atmosphere and warm relationships and is preferable to group settings and other placements. As a state or agency sponsored program, however, foster care seldom provides children the continuity and stability they need in their lives. While foster families may be called upon to assist, support, and occasionally fill in for families, foster care is not likely to be an acceptable alternative to fulfilling each child's right to a stable home and enduring relationships.

Source: *The Center on Human Policy* (1987).

An alternative to institutional settings has been to create other segregated and generally "simulated" normalized living arrangements such as: nursing homes, community intermediate care facilities (ICF), group homes, and board and care homes. These settings range in size and quality; however, no matter how well intentioned they are, they remain residential staff dominated and staff driven living "facilities" or "programs."

In order to create integrated living settings that are homes (not facilities or programs) where people have control over their own lives and have the support needed to function, a new way of funding and regulating is necessary. Government has often determined where people with disabilities can live on the basis of funding sources available and current regulatory agreements, rather than on the basis of beliefs and values or what people need and chose. "Placement decisions" have been based upon what residential facilities or programs are available. The development of new residential programs and facilities has generally been relegated to the categories of "fundable" programs and facilities (e.g., nursing homes, ICF, group homes). A discussion of what a person needs in order to be supported in integrated community settings should guide and drive the funding sources, not the preexisting facilities and programs that people must "fit" into.

There are several strategies that have been used to create integrated community living opportunities over the past several years. They include foster care, adoption, and supported living arrangements.

Foster care can offer a home-like size, choice, and setting for children with disabilities. Until recently, this opportunity was only available to children with mild and moderate disabilities. This arrangement can be temporary until the birthfamily is ready to be reunited or until an adoption is arranged either by the foster family or another family. This is generally not the first choice for integrated community living opportunities, however, it certainly is more home-like than more traditional facilities or programs (Taylor, Racino, Knoll, & Lutfiyya, 1987).

Adoption has been a very successful strategy for providing normalized home settings for children with disabilities whose birthfamilies can no longer care for them (Glidden, 1985, 1986; Glidden et al., 1988). Adoptions of children with disabilities have increased over the years. This strategy offers the child a family context while growing up. In several states, adoptive families can qualify for a financial subsidy to assist in the procurement of support services needed by their adoptive child. Glidden's research has demonstrated the positive impact that adoption has had on the family and the child with a disability (Glidden, 1985, 1986).

Finally, supported living arrangements are the most appropriate for adults, since foster care and adoption would be age inappropriate. Persons residing in supported living arrangements live in places they own or rent and have access to staff hired by the individual with severe handicaps to provide the support needed. Programs have been developed in several states that provide such supported living arrangements. One such service, Options in Community Living, in Wisconsin, has developed an extensive resource manual describing their approach (Johnson, 1985).

Living arrangements and opportunities for individuals with severe handicaps should reflect the basic values of normalization and integration in order for people with handicaps to have access to dignified living situations. In addition, financial support systems must be created and expanded in order to provide these individuals with safe and healthy living environments.

SUMMARY

The preceding chapter includes a discussion of the attitudes and values of parents and significant others that must be considered when developing good parent-professional working relationships. In addition, issues related to interacting with families of diverse cultures and languages are explored. A discussion of siblings and their relationship to the planning process is included.

Finally, the chapter closes with a discussion of living arrangements and opportunities. A supported living concept is promoted as opposed to traditional facility-based programs. The argument is made that funding and regulations must be made available, if such supported living arrangements and opportunities are to become common.

REFERENCES

Baca, L. (1980). *Policy options for insuring the delivery of an appropriate education to handicapped children who are of limited English proficiency.* Reston, VA: Council for Exceptional Children. (ERIC Document Reproduction Service No. ED 199963)

Baum, M.H. (1962). Some dynamic factors affecting family adjustment to the handicapped child. *Exceptional Children, 28*, 387–392.

Bersoff, D.N., & Grieger, R.M. (1971). An interview model for the children's behavior. *American Journal of Orthopsychiatry, 41*, 483–493.

Biklen, D., & Knoll, J. (1987). The disabled minority. In S. Taylor, D. Biklen, & J. Knoll (Eds.), *Community integration for people with severe disabilities* (pp. 3–24). New York: Teachers College Press.

Bronfenbrenner, U. (1975). Is early intervention effective? In B.Z. Friedlander, G.M. Sterritt, & G.E. Kirk (Eds.), *Exceptional Infant* (Vol. 3, pp. 449–475). New York: Brunner/Mazel.

Bruininks, R.H., & Lakin, K.C. (Eds.). (1985). *Living and learning in the least restrictive environment*. Baltimore: Paul H. Brookes Publishing Co.

Carkhuff, R.R. (1973). *The art of helping: An introduction to life skills*. Amherst, MA: Human Resource Development Press.

Carpenter, L.J. (1983). *Bilingual special education: An overview of issues*. Alamitos, CA: National Center for Bilingual Research.

Center on Human Policy. (1986). *A statement in support of families and their children*. Unpublished manuscript.

Chinn, P.C., Winn, J., & Walters, R.H. (1978). *Two-way talking with parents of special children*. St. Louis: C. V. Mosby.

Cutler, B. (1981). *Unraveling the special education maze*. Champaign, IL: Research Press.

Darling, R.B. (1979). *Families against society: A study of reactions to children with birth defects*. Beverly Hills: Sage Publications.

Darling, R.B. (1983). Parent professional interaction: The roots of misunderstanding. In M. Seligman (Ed.), *The family with a handicapped child: Understanding and treatment* (pp. 95–121). New York: Grune & Stratton.

Dinkmeyer, D., & Carlson, J. (Eds.). (1973). *Consulting: Facilitating human potential and change processes*. Columbus, OH: Charles E. Merrill.

Donnellan, A.M., & Mirenda, P.L., (1984). Issues related to professional involvement with families of individuals with autism and other severe handicaps. *Journal of The Association for Persons with Severe Handicaps, 9*, 16–25.

Duran, E. (1985). Functional skill approach: Strategies for teaching severely handicapped autistic adolescents of limited English proficiency. *Education, 105*(3), 1–9.

Farber, B. (1959). Effects of a severely mentally retarded child on family integration. *Monographs of the Society for Research in Child Development, 24*(2, Serial No. 71).

Farrell, K. (1985). *Reach out and teach: Parent handbook*. New York: American Foundation for the Blind.

Featherstone, H. (1980). *A difference in the family*. New York: Basic Books.

Glidden, L.M. (1985). Adopting mentally handicapped children: Family characteristics and outcomes. *Adoption & Fostering, 99*(3), 53–56.

Glidden, L.M. (1986). Families who adopt mentally retarded children: Who, why, and what happens. In J. Gallagher & P. Vietze (Eds.), *Families of handicapped persons: Research, programs, and policy issues* (pp. 129–142). Baltimore: Paul H. Brookes Publishing Co.

Glidden, L.M., Valliere, V.N., & Herbert, S.L. (1988). Adopted children with mental retardation: Positive family impact. *Mental Retardation, 26*(3), 119–125.

Gordon, T. (1970). *Parent effectiveness training*. New York: Peter H. Wyden.

Grossman, F. (1972). *Brothers and sisters of retarded children*. Syracuse: Syracuse University Press.

Hayden, V. (1974). The other children. *The Exceptional Parent, 4*, 26–29.

Heward, W.L., Dardig, J.C., & Rossett, A. (1979). *Working with parents of handicapped children*. Columbus, OH: Charles E. Merrill.

Hewett, S. (1970). *The family and the handicapped child: A study of cerebral palsied children in their homes*. Chicago: Aldine.

Johnson, T. (1985). *Belonging to the community*. Madison, WI: Options in Community Living.

Katz, A.H. (1961). *Parents of the handicapped*. Springfield, IL: Charles C Thomas.

Koch, R., & Dobson, J.C. (Eds.). (1971). *The mentally retarded child and his family*. New York: Brunner/Mazel.

Kroth, R.L. (1975). *Communicating with parents of exceptional children: Improving parent-teacher relationships*. Denver: Love Publishing Co.

Lyon, S., & Preis, A. (1983). Working with families of severely handicapped persons. In M. Seligman (Ed.), *The family with a handicapped child: Understanding and treatment*. (pp. 203–232). New York: Grune & Stratton.

Marion, R.L. (1980), Communicating with parents of culturally diverse exceptional children. *Exceptional Children, 46*(8), 616–623.

Michaelis, C.T. (1980). *Home and school partnership in exceptional children*. Rockville, MD: Aspen Publishers.

Myers, R. (1978). *Like normal people*. New York: McGraw-Hill.

Pearlman, L., & Scott, K.A. (1981). *Raising the handicapped child*. Englewood Cliffs, NJ: Prentice-Hall.

PL 94-142, The Education for All Handicapped Children Act of 1975.

Powell, T.H., & Ogle, P.A. (1985). *Brothers & sisters—A special part of exceptional families*. Baltimore: Paul H. Brookes Publishing Co.

Rogers, C.R. (1961). *On becoming a person*. Boston: Houghton Mifflin.

Roos, P. (1963). Psychological counseling with parents of retarded children. *Mental Retardation, 1*, 345–350.

Sailor, W., & Guess, D. (1983). *Severely handicapped students: An instructional design*. Boston: Houghton Mifflin.

Schopler, E. (1976). Towards reducing behavior problems in autistic children. In L. Wing (Ed.), *Early childhood autism*. (2d ed., pp. 221–246). New York: Pergamon Press.

Seligman, M. (1983). Siblings of handicapped persons. In M. Seligman (Ed.), *The family with a handicapped child: Understanding and treatment*. New York: Grune & Stratton.

Sontag, E. (1976). Federal leadership. In M.A. Thomas (Ed.), *Hey, don't forget about me! Education's investment in the severely, profoundly, and multiply handicapped*. Reston, VA: Council for Exceptional Children.

Taylor, S.J., Racino, J., Knoll, J., & Lutfiyya, S. (1987). Down home: Community integration for people with the most severe disabilities. In S.J. Taylor, D. Biklen, & J. Knoll (Eds.), *Community integration for people with severe disabilities* (pp. 36–56). New York: Teachers College Press.

Turnbull, A.P., & Turnbull, H.R. (Eds.). (1978). *Parents speak out: Views from the other side of the two way mirror*. Columbus, OH: Charles E. Merrill.

Turnbull, A.P., & Turnbull, H.R. (1986). *Families, professionals and exceptionality: A special partnership*. Columbus, OH: Charles E. Merrill.

Turnbull, H.R., Turnbull, A.P., Bronicki, G.J., Summers, J.A., & Roeder-Gordon, C. (1988) *Disability and the family: A guide to decisions for adulthood*. Baltimore: Paul H. Brookes Publishing Co.

Vincent, L.J., Dodd, N., & Henner, P.J. (1978). Planning and implementing a program of parent involvement. In N. Haring & D.D. Bricker (Eds.), *Teaching the severely handicapped* (Vol. 3). Seattle, WA: American Association for the Education of Severely and Profoundly Handicapped.

Vincent, L., Laten, S., Salisbury, C., Brown, P., & Baumgart, D. (1981). Family involvement in the educational process of severely handicapped students: State of the art and directions for the future. In B. Wilcox & R. York (Eds.), *Quality educational services for the severely handicapped: The federal investment* (pp. 164–179). Washington DC: United States Department of Education, Office of Special Education.

Wilson-Portuondo, M. (1980). Parent school communication: A two way approach. In M.E. Pynn & others (Eds.), *Issues in bilingual/bicultural special education personnel preparation: Workshop report*. Washington DC: Association for Cross-Cultural Education and Social Studies (ERIC Document Reproduction Service No. ED 189 795).

THREE

ASSESSMENT STRATEGIES

IN THE FOLLOWING CHAPTER, strategies for assessing the skill repertoire and needs of students with severe handicaps are delineated. The assessment strategies emphasized are those that will assist educators and parents to develop chronological age–appropriate and functional educational programs. Due to the complex and unique needs of students with severe handicaps, "formula" or "recipe" approaches to assessment are not stressed here. Instead, general parameters and strategies that must be considered when assessing students are emphasized.

Information gathered through the assessment process leads to development of an individualized eduational program (IEP). An IEP should include goals and objectives that reflect functional and chronological age–appropriate activities across a variety of integrated environments. Once an appropriate IEP is in place, teachers must develop individualized instructional programs and lesson plans. Each of these are discussed in detail in this chapter.

Traditionally, the term assessment has been used to refer to the initial evaluation of a student's performance and the end-of-term/year evaluation. However, as presented and described in this chapter, assessment has been expanded to include ongoing and continuous evaluation of a student's performance throughout his or her educational career. Assessment should initially include an identification of the student's most critical educational needs and of the student's level of participation in various activities and environments.

There are several reasons why it is crucial that assessment as a concept, set of strategies, and results should be considered in the design and development of appropriate educational programs. First, assessment allows the teacher to determine a student's ability and level of participation across a variety of activities and environments. Second, assessment provides the teacher with information about the effectiveness of ongoing instruction. Third, assessment can assist the teacher to determine the specific stimulus conditions (e.g., environments, cues, materials) that are present when the student engages in a specified behavior. Fourth, assessment provides an objective and concrete tool for communicating a student's progress with parents, other school personnel, and others. Fifth, assessment is mandated by Public Law 94-142 (PL 94-142). Specifically, PL 94-142 requires that IEP goals and objectives be based upon a student's present level of performance; this level is determined by assessing a student's skill repertoire. In addition, IEP goals and objectives must include criteria statements and timelines for reviewing the student's ability to meet those criteria statements. The student's ability level is determined through the use of assessment.

An important consideration in the assessment process is the protection of students' rights. Protections are covered by laws and ethical considerations. Following is a list of legal and ethical considerations that teachers should respect and practice (Browder, 1987):

1. Parental consent must be obtained before initial assessment or evaluation is conducted.
2. Parents must have access to review all educational records, including assessment results and evaluations.
3. Only relevant and needed assessment information should be collected; information that has no educational relevance should not be collected or reported.
4. All assessment information must be kept confidential. Such information can only be shared by other agencies and/or individuals with written parental permission. Even posting assessment data on classroom bulletin boards, if not done with student's and/or parents permission, can be in violation of the student's rights.
5. When sharing assessment data and results with parents and students, do so with sensitivity and tact. Always include a discussion of the student's strengths when discussing assessment results. Never deny parents their right to have dreams and hopes for their son or daughter.
6. Parents have the right to obtain an independent assessment or evaluation of their son's or daughter's skills and needs.
7. Placement decisions must be based upon assessment results/evaluations and shared with parents.
8. Parents have the right to participation in the development of the IEP, and teachers should encourage such participation.

DEVELOPMENT OF INITIAL DATA

The initial step or component in implementing appropriate assessment procedures for a student is to gather all of the pertinent data. This step should include at least the following:

1. Interviews with pertinent people (i.e., parents, staff, and significant others)
2. Review of pertinent data (e.g., confidential files, cumulative folders, formal and informal test results, data sheets and graphs, medical histories)
3. Collection of data (e.g., anecdotal recordings, informal observations)

Interviews with Pertinent People

A critical component in the development of educational programs is that of interviewing and interacting with parents and significant others. These interviews and interactions should be conducted in a variety of settings and at a number of different times. Ongoing and consistent communication channels should exist between school and home. It is preferred that at least some of these interviews be conducted in the home of the student, for several reasons. First, educators can inventory the student's home and neighborhood in order to determine the actual skills that are necessary for the student. Second, educators can benefit from being "on parental territory" when interviewing parents in the student's home. Parents often feel more comfortable in their own environments and are therefore likely to share more information. Parents, too, have expressed the need for educators to observe their child in his or her natural environments, particularly in the home (Turnbull, 1983). Specific strategies for collecting this critical information are: development of weekday and weekend schedules and parent/significant other inventories, and establishment of priorities among skill areas.

Development of Weekday Schedule A *weekday schedule* strategy refers to the development of a schedule that reflects the typical routine of a student during nonschool hours Monday through Friday. Such a schedule should include the time an activity typically occurs, a description of the activity (e.g., eating breakfast), the environment in which the activity takes place (e.g., eating breakfast occurs in the kitchen), and the level of assistance necessary for the student to participate in the activity (e.g., the student needs assistance when pouring). It is critical that this information—particularly the level of assistance necessary—be provided from the parents' perspective. For example, if a parent reports that Brian requires some assistance to brush his teeth, to turn on the television, and to purchase an item at the grocery store, these activities should be considered for specific assessment because they have been identified as activities within the family's typical routine, and the student is currently unable to perform all the skills for the activities independently. Parents are more likely to support and assist in developing educational programs that directly prepare their son or daughter to be the most contributing participant possible within his or her family. An example of an abbreviated weekday schedule is presented in Figure 3.1.

Development of a Weekend Schedule A *weekend schedule* strategy refers to the development of a schedule that reflects the typical routine of a student while in nonschool settings over the weekend. It is important to gain information about the student's weekend activities, especially those activities that occur on a regular basis, since they are likely to differ from activities identified by the weekday schedules. Weekend activities may include shopping, going to restaurants, visiting relatives, doing household chores, and so forth. The family, for instance, may enjoy going to restaurants, but they may be embarrassed to take their son or daughter to these establishments because of his or her inappropriate table manners. This kind of information is vital for developing and determining assessment methods and areas, as well as for developing goal areas for the student's IEP. Figure 3.2 provides an example of a student's abbreviated weekend schedule.

Development of Parent/Significant Other Inventory In addition to using weekday and weekend schedules, a *parent/significant other inventory* strategy of more general questions might be used. Such a strategy would provide an opportunity for parents and significant others to provide additional input into the development of functional educational programs for students. This information should include, at the least: the student's likes and dislikes; definition and degree of unacceptable behaviors in the home; management techniques and procedures used in the home for unacceptable behaviors; self-help skill repertoire (e.g., toileting, mobility, eating); sibling relationships, communication abilities, and preferred modalities (e.g., verbal, signs, pictures, symbols).

The weekday and weekend schedules, as well as parent/significant other inventories used to secure information from parents and significant others, should reflect at least the following eight issues and cautions:

State directions and questions in the most simple and straightforward manner possible.
Provide ample space for comments.
Include only relevant questions.
Be able to explain how the information from each question will be used.
Use the language that is most comfortable to the family.
Avoid comments, statements, or questions that are culturally unfamiliar and possibly disconcerting to the family.
Use a questionnaire as an outline for an interview.
If an interview is not a possibility, send the questionnaire with a cover letter explaining the purpose of the form and include directions for its completion.

Student: Sally Smith *Age:* 12 *Date:* January 30, 1985

Time	Environment	Subenvironment	Activity	Present level of performance/ assistance necessary	Possible skills for subsequent objections
6:45 A.M.	Home	Bedroom	Gets up	Mother wakes Sally; she complies with request to get up	Using alarm clock
7:00 A.M.	"	"	Dresses self	Dresses self independently; Requests assistance with difficult buttons	
7:10 A.M.	"	Bathroom	Washes face	Needs verbal reminders to wash face completely	Washing face
7:15 A.M.	"	"	Brushes teeth	Needs verbal reminders to brush teeth thoroughly	Brushing teeth
7:20 A.M.	"	Kitchen	Eats breakfast	Eats all foods (except breads) independently	Eating sandwiches
7:35 A.M.	"	Kitchen or livingroom	Waits for bus	Sits & waits; will not engage in recreation activities (e.g., looking through a magazine)	Looking at magazines; playing calculator and other games
7:40 A.M.	Neighborhood	Front street	Boards bus	Opens door and boards bus independently	
3:00 P.M.	Home	Entryway	Arrives home	Opens door independently; needs verbal and sometimes gestural reminders of where to put bookbag and sweater jacket	
3:10 P.M.	"	Kitchen	Eats snack	Will not initiate request for snack; cannot get snack; will eat snack independently	Getting food, untensils and other items necessary for snack

Figure 3.1. Sample abbreviated weekday schedule. (A complete weekday schedule would continue until the student goes to bed.)

Student: Sally Smith   *Age:* 12   *Date:* January 30, 1985

Time	Environment	Subenvironment	Activity	Present level of performance/ assistance necessary	Possible skills for subsequent objections
8:00 A.M.	Home	Bedroom	Gets up	Independently	
8:15 A.M.	"		Dresses self	Independently	
8:20 A.M.	"	Bathroom	Washes face	Needs verbal reminders to wash face completely	Washing face
			Brushes teeth	Needs verbal reminders to brush teeth thoroughly	Brushing teeth
8:30 A.M.	"	Kitchen	Eats breakfast	Eats all foods (except breads) independently	Eating sandwiches
8:50 A.M.	"	"	Cleans up kitchen	Will clear the table with verbal reminders; cannot wash, dry, or put dishes away	Washing dishes and general clearing up
9:10 A.M.	Community	Grocery store	Shops	Needs verbal assistance to locate items; can read grocery items on list with some assistance	Grocery shopping using picture grocery list
12:00 noon	"	Restaurant	Ordering and eating	Can use child's menu with pictures and will point to pictures when verbally prompted by mother; eats independently	Ordering and eating at a restaurant

Figure 3.2. Sample abbreviated weekend schedule. (A complete weekend schedule would include all the possible activities for weekends and holidays.)

Without this information, determining functionality for a student becomes extremely challenging. Figure 3.3 provides an example of a parent/significant other inventory.

Establishment of Priorities among Skill Areas The strategy of establishing priorities among skill areas refers to the process of considering critical dimensions relevant to the individual student's skill development. The process enables parents and educators to effectively and individually set priorities and determine the areas that need to be assessed. Establishment of priorities among skill areas is typically a long, complex process, due to the considerable number of aspects that must be considered. Brown et al. (1980) identified a number of dimensions that should be considered when establishing a student's priority skill areas. These dimensions, revised and expanded by Falvey and Anderson (1983), are listed in the form of questions, as follows:

I. What activities need to be taught?
   A. Are the activities **FUNCTIONAL** for the student?
      1. Are the activities being considered **CHRONOLOGICALLY AGE APPROPRIATE?**
      2. Are these activities required across a variety of environments?
      3. Can these activities be used often?
      4. Does someone have to do it (perform the activity) for the student?
      5. How do nonhandicapped peers participate in the activity?
      6. What activities would the student desire?
      7. What is the student's present level of performance of these activities?
      8. What family needs have been considered when determining activities?
   B. Will the activities result in NORMALIZATION for the student?
      1. What activities does the society value (particularly nonhandicapped peers)?
      2. What are nonhandicapped peers being taught?
      3. What are nonhandicapped peers doing?
      4. What activities would reduce normal/handicapped discrepancy (i.e., social significance of the activity)?
      5. What activities would result in increased opportunities for interaction with nonhandicapped peers?
      6. What activities would lead to less restrictive alternatives?
      7. What activities would promote independence?
   C. What are the **ACTIVITY** characteristics?
      1. What are the skills involved in this activity?
      2. What are the skills needed for and enhanced by this activity?
      3. What skills can be integrated across activities?

Parent/significant other ______________
Date ______________
Interviewer ______________

Date of birth ______________
Date of interview ______________
Address ______________
Phone number ______________

GENERAL QUESTIONS

1. Does your child take any medication? For what?
2. Is your child allergic to anything? If so, what?
3. How does your child learn to do new things?

COMMUNICATION/LANGUAGE

1. What languages are spoken in your home?
2. What language is spoken most often in your home?
3. How does your child communicate his/her needs to you?
4. How does your child communicate displeasure, pain or dislike to you?
5. How does your child communicate with family members and friends?
6. Does your child follow simple instructions (e.g., "Come here," "Sit down.")?
7. Do you think your child would learn skills more easily if taught in English or another language?

BEHAVIOR

1. Does your child exhibit any behaviors that you feel are inappropriate or that bother you or members of the family?
2. What do you or others do when this behavior occurs?
3. What do you do to comfort or calm your child?
4. What do you do to discipline your child or show disapproval?
5. Does your child adapt easily to changes in routine?

DOMESTIC/SELF-HELP SKILLS

1. Is your child able to feed her- or himself? If so, how did she learn to do this?
2. What are your child's favorite and least favorite foods?
3. Is your child able to dress her- or himself?
4. What personal hygiene skills would you like your child to learn?
5. Which self-help skill is most important to you for your child to learn?

COMMUNITY

1. What places in the community do you take your child to (e.g., shopping mall, restaurants, relatives' homes, others)?
2. How does your child behave when you take him/her to these places?

RECREATION/LEISURE

1. What are your child's favorite activities and toys at home?
2. What does your child do after school?
3. Does your child play with siblings and neighborhood friends?
4. Does your child enjoy playing by him/herself?
5. In what way does your child move about the house?

VOCATIONAL

1. What jobs does your child help with at home (e.g., putting away toys, cleaning up spills and messes)?
2. Do you have any suggestions as to the type of work your child might be able to do when he or she is older?
3. Have you thought of any skills that your child might enjoy that would lead to work preparation (e.g., clerical work, gardening, janitorial)?

FUTURE

1. What places do you think your child might go to when he is older?
2. In the future, where do you see your child living (e.g., supervised apartment, group home, home)?

Figure 3.3. Significant other inventory.

4. What activities can be recombined into other more complex skills processes?
5. What activities will meet the largest variety of the student's needs?
6. What activities will make maximal use of the student's learning strength and style?
7. What activities will provide opportunities for practice?
8. What families' needs have been considered when determining activities?

II. How will the activities be taught?
   A. What are the student's learning styles and strengths?
   B. What is the student's learning rate?
   C. How well is this student able to tolerate change, confusion, chaos, etc.?
   D. How well is this student able to generalize?
   E. How well is this student able to respond to natural and instructional cues and consequences?
   F. Where does the student have difficulty in a given sequence or activity?
   G. What patterns emerge across environments, materials, cues, persons, etc., when the student has difficulty?
   H. Is the student's communication understood across persons and environments?

III. Where should the activities be taught?
   A. Are the environments chronologically age appropriate?
   B. Are the environments accessible for teaching during school hours?
   C. Are the environments preferred by the student?
   D. Are the environments frequently used by the student, nonhandicapped peers, and the student's family?
   E. Are there opportunities to teach many activities in these environments?
   F. Is there a high probability that the student will acquire the activities needed to function in these environments?
   G. Are the environments appropriate for the student now (current) and in the future (subsequent)?
   H. Are the environments safe for the student, and/or will the student likely acquire the safety skills necessary to participate in the activities within the environment?

Throughout meetings with parents and students, discussion must be devoted to the areas of priority that should be assessed and eventually taught. Each of the foregoing questions should be addressed and considered when determining specific skill areas of priority for each student.

REVIEW OF PERTINENT DATA

Included in the development of the initial data should be a review of pertinent data. It is essential that current as well as former records and information regarding the student be reviewed. Pertinent data include: cumulative/confidential folders, formal and informal test results, current and past goals and objectives, progress demonstrated on past goals and objectives, medical histories, educational histories and changes in the family unit. These data should be considered in conjunction with other information (e.g., actual observations, interviews with parents and significant others) when determining appropriate assessment strategies and areas. Caution should be exercised with regard to negative descriptions of students that might result in limiting their options and possibilities.

Collection of Informal Data

The final component in the development of the initial data is the actual collection of informal data. Since this is the initial data collection step, informal observation and anecdotal recording would generally be the most appropriate data collection strategies to use. The term *anecdotal recording* refers to a written description of behaviors and of the environmental conditions under which these behaviors occur. Following is a list of sample behaviors and analyses of behaviors that might be informally observed and recorded during the collection of data:

1. Speed or rate at which the student performs a task
2. Attention span of the student
3. Initiative of the student
4. Rate of acquisition of new skills
5. Flexibility displayed by the student when adapting to new tasks, materials, environments, or persons
6. Student's learning modalities (e.g., auditory, visual)
7. Student's preferences concerning activities, materials, or friends
8. Student's overall strengths
9. Student's overall weaknesses

These anecdotal recordings and informal observations should be performed in the student's natural environments. Examples of such environments include: home, school, playground, classroom, cafeteria, grocery store, laundromat, or job training site. If possible, these observations should be performed by persons familiar with the student. If the person is unfamiliar with the student, or if new staff are making the observations, the observations should be recorded in each environment more than once. The data that is collected and analyzed should be reviewed by persons who are knowledgeable about the student, for example, the parent.

Several issues and cautions have been delineated by Vanderheiden (1984) that should be considered when using observational techniques:

1. Select target behaviors.
2. Define target behaviors in observable terms.
3. Define the criteria to be used in judging occurrence or nonoccurrence.
4. Select no more than two targets to observe at one time.
5. Keep coding on data sheet simple and efficient.
6. Gather reliability data.
7. Run pilot observations when possible.
8. Know, specifically, what the observation is to reveal.

DEVELOPMENT OF ASSESSMENT PLAN

The types of assessment tools, instruments, and/or strategies must be individually identified for each student; a variety of these are available to educators and can be categorized into one or more of the following types of assessment strategies or methods:

1. *Norm-referenced assessment*, which is a standardized measurement of a person's performance relative to the performance of others (Salvia & Ysseldyke, 1978). There are two categories of norm-referenced measures:
   a. *Development scales*, which are a summary of behaviors observed at various ages (e.g., Uzgiris and Hunt's Ordinal Scales of Psychological Development [1975])
   b. *Intelligence scales*, which are samples of behaviors observed, calculated, and compared against the norm in order to determine an intelligence quotient (e.g., Stanford-Binet Intelligence Scale [Terman & Merrill, 1973])
2. *Normal developmental models*, which are sequences of behaviors exhibited by "normal" children as they progress through the maturational stages; these sequences of behaviors have not been standardized (e.g., Brigance Diagnostic Inventory of Early Development [Brigance, 1978])
3. *Criterion-referenced measures*, which are sequences of behaviors defined in terms of some prearranged or predetermined standard of scores, without comparison to previous performance of any group of persons (e.g., task analysis of shoe tying)
4. *Ecological and student repertoire inventory strategies,* which are sequences of behaviors that reflect the actual skills necessary to participate within community environments (Brown et al., 1979). Items are identified from an extensive inventory of the skills performed by nonhandicapped age peers in a variety of community environments. Specifically, the steps for conducting ecological inventories are:
   a. Divide the curriculum into the following curricular domains: domestic, vocational, recreation, and community.
   b. Delineate the environments within each domain that are available to nonhandicapped age peers.

   c. Delineate the subenvironments within each environment.
   d. Delineate the activities that occur within each subenvironment.
   e. Delineate the specific skills required or expected in order to participate in each activity.
5. Once the skills have been identified through the process of conducting ecological inventories, student repertoire inventories are necessary. These inventories are a method of measuring a student's existing performance repertoire against the skills identified in the ecological inventory, that is, against skills performed by nonhandicapped age peers (Falvey, Brown, Lyon, Baumgart, & Schroeder, 1980). The steps for conducting student repertoire inventories are:
   a. Delineate the skills performed by nonhandicapped age peers for a given activity (i.e., the previously listed step *e* of the ecological inventory).
   b. Observe and record whether the student is able to perform the skills performed by nonhandicapped age peers for a given activity.
   c. Conduct a discrepancy analysis of the student's performance against his or her nonhandicapped peers' performance. Specifically, if a student is unable to perform a skill, educators should observe and analyze the characteristics of that skill (e.g., natural cues and correction procedures, materials, performance criteria). A determination is then made of the specific aspect(s) of the skill with which the student has difficulty. For example, a student may be able to perform the motor components of crossing a street, but is unable to determine when it is safe to cross the street. That student presumably is unable to respond to the natural cues provided in that environment. Specific knowledge of this inability provides educators with critical information concerning what and how the student will be taught.
   d. Utilize one of the following three options (if the student is unable to perform any of the skills): 1) teach the student to perform the skill, or 2) develop an adaptation that the student can use to assist in the performance of the skill. Then, teach the student to perform the skill utilizing the adaptation, or 3) teach the student to perform a different but related skill.

Figure 3.4 provides an example of an ecological inventory completed within a hospital coffee shop (see Item 4 on the list). Additional examples of ecological inventories can be found in subsequent chapters.

Figure 3.5 provides an example of a student repertoire inventory. Like Figure 3.4, this was conducted for a student in a coffee shop at a hospital.

The use of norm-referenced assessments and normal developmental model assessments presents substantial problems if the student being assessed is functioning significantly below his or her chronological age peers. These as-

Domain: Community
Environment: Torrance Hospital
Subenvironment: Coffee Shop

Activity:	Locating a seat
Skills:	Enter doorway
	Scan area for empty table/chair
	Go to empty table/chair
	Sit down in empty chair
Activity:	Looking at menu
Skills:	Scan selections
	Determine desired food and beverage
	Replace menu in menu holder
Activity:	Ordering desired food and beverage
Skills:	State or point to choice
	Answer waitress/waiter's questions
	Wait for order

Figure 3.4. Sample abbreviated ecological inventory.

sessments often yield a developmental age or intelligence score. For students in whom there is a significant discrepancy between their chronological and mental ages, developmental ages and/or intelligence scores will not provide specific information regarding their needs and preferred learning methods. Because the majority of students with severe handicaps are functioning substantially below their chronological age peers, the use of norm-referenced assessments should be minimized. If used, extreme caution should be exercised when interpreting the results. For example, when assessing the skill repertoire of a 10-year-old student who had severe handicaps, a psychologist utilized a normal developmental test and determined that the student's developmental age was approximately 2 years. The psychologist and teacher developed curricula for that student utilizing materials and activities most often used and performed by $2\frac{1}{2}$- and 3-year-old children, without regard for that student's chronological age, which was that of a 10-year-old child. Instead, this student should have been assessed in terms of the skills necessary to participate in as many activities as possible that were appropriate to the student's chronological age. Activities should include community, domestic, recreational, and vocational environments that 10-year-old nonhandicapped peers utilize (e.g., playing in the neighborhood park, crossing streets, shopping in stores, performing chores at home).

This is not to suggest that developmental skills are not critical to teach. Developmental skills such as object permanence, classification, and one-to-one correspondence are inherent in and required across a variety of materials, ac-

Student: Kraig Rosenberg
Date: 8/23

Domain: Community
Environment: Torrance Hospital

Subenvironment: Coffee Shop
Teacher: Shellie Coots

Nonhandicapped person inventory	Student inventory	Discrepancy analysis	What-to-do options
Activity: Locating a seat Skills: Enter doorway	+		
Scan area for empty table/chair	–	No strategy for scanning	Teach scanning skills
Go to empty table/chair	–	Result of no scanning strategy	Teach scanning skills
Sit down in empty chair	+		
Activity: Looking at menu Skills: Scan selections	–	No strategy for scanning	Teach scanning skills
Determine desired food and beverage	–	Not able to read	Develop pictorial menu
Replace menu in menu holder	+		and teach
Activity: Ordering desired food and beverage Skills: State or point to choice	–	Unable to communicate	Develop and teach an alternative communicative system
Answer waitress/waiter's questions	–	Unable to communicate	Develop and teach an alternative communicative system
Wait for order	+		

Code: + = correct response; – = incorrect response.

Figure 3.5. Sample student repertoire inventory.

tivities, and environments. For instance, understanding of the concept of object permanence is required when locating straws hidden from view in a fast food restaurant, or when searching for cleaning materials that are located in a closed cabinet. Classification skills are required when locating an item in the grocery store according to the aisle markers, or when identifying a soda pop vending machine among several vending machines. One-to-one correspondence skills are required when setting a table for several people or when stuffing envelopes. It is insufficient to assess and measure these skills only through the use of existing developmental tests. The materials, activities, cues, and environments for these tests are generally artificial and are presented out of context. Additionally, they generally are not chronological age appropriate. It would be imprudent to assume that the student could demonstrate these skills in a functional and appropriate way, having only been assessed with artificial materials, activities, and/or in artificial environments.

Caution should also be exercised when using criterion-referenced measures. These measures can result in the teaching of splinter skills, that is, skills that are taught separately from other related skills and apart from the contexts and environments where those skills would naturally be performed. Since there is no set basis for determining the skills identified by criterion-referenced measures, teachers might teach skills that they personally feel are important, or that the test regards as important, without considering the community in which the student resides, or the student's or family's needs.

The ecological and student repertoire inventory strategies are especially useful and appropriate when assessing students' skills. Since the purpose of education is to prepare students to participate in a variety of community environments to the maximal extent possible, the ecological and student repertoire inventory strategies are important tools. These tools can provide educators with information on actual skills necessary for functioning in community environments, as well as on the skill repertoire of a student in such environments (Falvey et al., 1980). This process involves assessing basic and developmental skills, such as cognitive, academic, motor, communication, and social skills in the context where they naturally occur. This is referred to as *infusion of basic or developmental skills*. By infusing these skills in the assessment process, the teacher is more likely to develop a functional and age-appropriate curriculum for the students.

In summary, assessment strategies and tools must provide relevant information about a student's skill repertoire in order for educators to develop appropriate educational goals and objectives for that student. Caution must be used when relying on the traditional methods of securing such information, such as norm-referenced, normal developmental models, and criterion-referenced measures. Developmental tests or measures, if used appropriately, can provide information regarding a student's learning strengths, styles, and concept development. The ecological and student repertoire inventory strategies will yield information about a student's skill repertoire in relevant, functional, community-based environments. The development of an assessment plan involves determining the most appropriate and relevant assessment instruments and procedures for evaluating the student's skill repertoire, learning strengths and styles, and concept development.

IMPLEMENTATION OF ASSESSMENT PLAN

Once the specific procedures for the assessment plan have been determined, the next step is to implement that plan (i.e., conduct the assessments). A number of major issues must be considered when implementing the assessment plan.

First, the materials and tasks used to assess a student's performance should be chronological age appropriate. For example, when assessing a 13-year-old student's sequencing and memory skills, the electronic game, Simon, would be more appropriate than blocks or "preschool" pictures. Second, the materials and tasks used to assess a student's performance should be functional for that student. For example, when assessing a 5-year-old student's object permanence skills, the student's own toys or other belongings should be used, rather than "test kit" materials that might have little or no meaning to the student. Third, the environment and context in which a skill is assessed should be natural. For example, when evaluating a student's eating skills, assessments should be performed at naturally occurring mealtimes. In addition, assessment of a student's grocery shopping skills should be conducted in a grocery store familiar to the student, if possible. Fourth, adaptations should be used when necessary. For example, students requiring glasses, large printed material, or directions given in sign language, should be provided such materials during the assessment process. Finally, a student's culture and native language must be considered when determining assessment materials, directions, and environments.

Implementation of the assessment plan consists of at least the following activities:

1. Select the skill(s) to be assessed.
2. Select the materials to be used.
3. Determine the environment(s) in which the assessment(s) will occur.
4. Develop data collection procedures.
5. Collect and record data.
6. Assess at different times.
7. Assess in different environments.
8. Assess in the presence of different persons (e.g., nonhandicapped peers, staff, community members).
9. Assess in the presence of various natural cues.

Formal tests and test instruments provide methods of recording students' behaviors. Informal methods (e.g., the ecological and student repertoire inventory strategies) provide opportunities to use a variety of methods or approaches to record student behaviors. This allows the educator to develop data collection procedures that will record the behaviors and conditions of concern. A data collection procedure must be developed after determining the specific behaviors and conditions that are to be measured. Once the behaviors and conditions have been identified, data collection procedures are generally obvious, provided that the educator is aware of various options. Following is a description of data collection procedures frequently used when measuring student behaviors:

1. Baseline data: a recording of the behaviors exhibited by a student prior to intervention. The purpose of this procedure is to determine objective and precise information about a behavior before developing an objective or instructional procedure to change that behavior. All behaviors, skills, and activities that make up a student's educational plan should reflect the baseline data previously collected.
2. Event recording: a recording of how often a behavior occurs (i.e., its frequency). Frequency can be determined by documenting the number of occurrences, then dividing this number by the number of minutes that the behavior was observed. This will allow for comparing the frequencies of behaviors observed at various time intervals. Also used in this context are *interval recording* and *time sampling* (Alberto & Troutman, 1982) procedures. Interval recording and time sampling are particularly useful when determining the percentage of times students engage in specific behaviors.
3. Duration recording: a recording of the length of time a student engages in a specific behavior (Snell, 1978). This data collection procedure is especially applicable when measuring, for example, the amount of time a student spends interacting with nonhandicapped peers in recreational activities.
4. Latency recording: a recording of the time between the presentation of the cue to perform a task and the student's actual initiation of the task (Alberto & Troutman, 1982). This procedure is particularly relevant when measuring, for example, the amount of time it takes a student to begin washing the floor at a fast food restaurant once the employer has given the directive to begin.
5. Scoring by levels: a recording of the levels of assistance or intervention necessary to facilitate the student's performance of a task. The level is determined by using ecological and student repertoire inventories. This procedure is also useful when measuring a student's performance once teaching begins in natural environments. The levels of assistance a person might use to facilitate the student's performance of a skill are listed from the most

intense to the least intense and assigned a value or number. The student is evaluated in terms of his or her ability to perform given skills. In addition, the level of intervention necessary for a given student is repeatedly recorded until the student is able to perform the skill independently. Finally, this measurement procedure is useful when recording the level of intervention at designated intervals to ensure a student's progress toward, or maintenance of, the independent performance of the skill.

For examples of event recording using intervals and samples of time (Item 2), see Figure 3.6. For an example of duration recording (Item 3), see Figure 3.7. An example of latency recording (Item 4) may be found in Figure 3.8. Figure 3.9 provides an example of the scoring by levels data collection procedure (see Item 5).

DEVELOPMENT OF ASSESSMENT SUMMARIES

Once the assessment plan has been implemented, the next component is to interpret and summarize the findings. There are at least three categories of information that should be included in such a summary.

First, the actual results of the assessments conducted should be organized and included in the assessment summary. A listing of the actual skills and activities assessed, and the student's skill repertoire of those skills and activities, should be made available.

Second, determination of the student's learning strengths and weaknesses should be made. Throughout the assessment process, student's learning strengths and weaknesses should be observed and recorded. For example, a student who consistently performs more correct responses when provided with pictorial versus verbal directions would be considered a visual learner rather than an auditory learner, at least in the situations observed.

Third, the student's entry level skill repertoire should be noted. For each skill area assessed, a statement specific to the student's abilities and inabilities should be made. For example, when measuring a student's skill repertoire of ambulating her wheelchair in the community, it was concluded that the student was able to ambulate at an acceptable pace, stop at all curbs, and point to various safety signs. However, this student was unable to make the correct decision of when to cross the street safely. The summary would suggest that this student be provided with opportunities to respond correctly to the natural cues for crossing a street.

ORGANIZATIONAL TECHNIQUES

The major focus of this chapter thus far has been on developing an understanding of assessment techniques and strategies. Assessment out of the context of

Event recording: Number of times student is out of her seat

Date	Frequency	Total #
8/23	✓ ✓ ✓ ✓ ✓ ✓ ✓ ✓	8
8/24	✓ ✓ ✓ ✓ ✓ ✓	6
8/25	✓ ✓ ✓	3

Code: ✓ = Number of times student is out of her seat inappropriately during the school day

---

Interval recording: Number of times student initiates a communicative behavior and number of times student responds to others' communicative efforts

Time: 9:15 A.M.– 9:30 A.M.

Environment: Free/play area Activity: Playing with nonhandicapped peers

	Frequency	Total #
Initiations	✓ ✓ ✓ ✓ ✓ ✓	6
Responses	✓ ✓ ✓ ✓ ✓ ✓ ✓ ✓ ✓ ✓	10

Time: 12:00–12:15 P.M.

Environment: Cafeteria Activity: Eating lunch with nonhandicapped peers

	Frequency	Total #
Initiations	✓ ✓ ✓ ✓ ✓ ✓ ✓ ✓	8
Responses	✓ ✓ ✓ ✓ ✓ ✓ ✓ ✓ ✓ ✓ ✓ ✓	12

Time sampling: Number of times student is able to maintain head control across environments and samples of time

Environment	Homeroom	Street and sidewalks	Grocery store	Cafeteria	Theater (job site)	Home (laundry)	Total #
Intervals	9:00 A.M.– 9:30 A.M.	10:00 A.M.– 10:30 A.M.	11:00 A.M.– 11:30 A.M.	12:00– 12:30 P.M.	1:00 P.M.– 1:30 P.M.–	2:00 P.M.– 2:30 P.M.	—
Frequencies	✓ ✓ ✓ ✓ ✓ ✓ ✓ ✓	✓ ✓ ✓ ✓ ✓ ✓ ✓	✓ ✓ ✓ ✓	✓ ✓ ✓ ✓	✓ ✓ ✓ ✓	✓ ✓	29

Code: ✓ = Number of times student positions head in upright position

Figure 3.6. Sample event recording data sheets.

developing and implementing educational plans has little meaning or purpose. The assessment results of a student's current functioning obtained through the use of the techniques and strategies previously delineated must be the basis for the development of a student's educational plan. This section includes strategies for organizing and sequencing an overall individualized program plan.

Duration recording: Amount of time student is "on task" when stacking boxes in bookstore (job-training site)

Begins stacking	9:30 A.M.	9:46 A.M.	9:59 A.M.	10:15 A.M.	10:20 A.M.	10:27 A.M.	Total time (min.) "on task"	Percentage of time "on task"
Ends stacking	9:37 A.M.	9:52 A.M.	10:13 A.M.	10:17 A.M.	10:25 A.M.	10:30 A.M.		
# of min. "on task"	7	6	14	2	5	3	37	61

Figure 3.7. Sample duration recording data sheet.

Two organizational tools that will be given specific attention are the individualized education program (IEP) and the daily program plan.

IEP

The education of all children with special needs is guided and monitored by an IEP. In the language of PL 94-142, this term means a written statement developed individually for each student with handicaps, to include:

1. A statement of the student's present levels of educational performance
2. A statement of annual goals for the student, including short-term instructional objectives
3. A statement of the specific special education and related services to be provided to the student
4. A statement of the extent to which the student will be able to participate in regular educational programs
5. The projected dates for initiation of services and the anticipated duration of services

Latency Recording: Amount of time between when the "Walk" sign appears on the corner and the student begins walking across the street

	Time		
Date	Cue issued	Student walked	Total latency
1/17	8:55 A.M.	8:57 A.M.	2 min.
	9:05 A.M.	9:06 A.M.	1 min.
	9:10 A.M.	9:10 A.M.	0 min.
	11:15 A.M.	11:17 A.M.	2 min.
	11:23 A.M.	11:23 A.M.	0 min.
	11:28 A.M.	11:29 A.M.	1 min.

Figure 3.8. Sample latency recording data sheet.

Scoring by levels: Using a walker to move from classroom to office

Skills	Dates 9/2	9/3	9/4	9/5	9/6	9/9	9/10
1. Grasp handles	3	3	2	2	2	4	5
2. Raises self from wheelchair	6	6	6	6	6	6	6
3. Turn walker clear of wheelchair	1	2	2	2	4	2	4
4. Look up	1	2	4	4	4	5	5
5. Step with alternating feet	6	6	6	6	6	6	6
6. Walk straight	2	2	2	2	2	2	4
7. Make left turns	2	2	2	2	2	2	2
8. Make right turns	2	2	2	2	2	2	2
Student's Total	23	25	26	26	28	29	34
Independence level = 8 skills performed in response to natural cues (i.e., 6 × 8)	48	48	48	48	48	48	48
Percentage of independence (independence level ÷ student's level)	48%	52%	54%	54%	58%	60%	70%

Code: Physical guidance = 1; model = 2; direct verbal = 3; indirect verbal = 4; gestural = 5; natural cue = 6.

Figure 3.9. Sample scoring-by-levels data sheet.

6. Appropriate objective criteria and evaluation procedures for determining, on at least an annual basis, whether instructional objectives are being achieved

The IEP is developed annually with input from various school representatives, including: the student's teacher and parents; the student, when appropriate; and other professionals as needed (e.g., related service providers). The requirements of the IEP provide a starting point for educational planning for students with handicaps. Additional requirements must be added to this basic outline to guarantee that the design, implementation, and evaluation of these individualized plans result in comprehensive, longitudinal, and chronological age-appropriate curricula for each student. For example, while PL 94-142 requires that a statement delineating the amount of time a student will spend in the regular school environment be included in an IEP, it does not mandate that such time be provided. A statement indicating that a student will spend no time in a regular educational program meets the letter, but not the intent, of the law and is otherwise unacceptable. Brown et al. (1980) added the following requirements to the IEP:

> IEPs will ensure that all severely handicapped students have opportunities to interact with nonhandicapped students.
>
> IEPS will contain goals and objectives directed toward teaching severely handicapped students to perform chronological age–appropriate functional skills in natural environments.

> IEPs will contain systematic strategies for including parents/guardians in the educational programs of their children.
> IEPs will contain functionally relevant methods and procedures for determining existing and needed student skill repertoires.
> IEPs will contain strategies that can be used to put in priority order the skills that might be selected for instruction, using the collective input of a variety of persons, disciplines, and perspectives.
> IEPs will contain descriptions of how severely handicapped students might be taught chronological age–appropriate skills.
> IEPs will contain clearly articulated statements pertaining to performance criteria. (p. 202)

For students with severe handicaps, the organization of the instructional program must include the following considerations.

Strategies for Developing the IEP The IEP provides the basic system for organizing the essential and relevant curricular content for a student. To assist educators in implementing the IEP, Williams, Brown, and Certo (1975) identified a number of critical dimensions that must be taken into account when developing educational plans for students with severe handicaps. These have been further expanded upon by Brown et al. (1980) and Falvey, Grenot-Scheyer, and Luddy (1984). Briefly, these dimensions include consideration of what skills need to be taught and why, how the skills will be taught and how their acquisition will be verified empirically, where these skills should be taught, the student's potential for learning to perform the skill at an acceptable rate and standard of performance, and what instructional materials and procedures will be used to assist the student in acquiring and performing the skills. Once an educator has implemented the various strategies for determining what skills might be needed by a particular student, these components can be considered in relation to the IEP format and the resulting information can be organized into a comprehensive educational plan. Suggested expansions to the IEP format are provided below.

Component 1: A statement of the student's current level of educational performance must be provided. This component should include the present chronological age of the student, the student's level of independent functioning within and across domains, the student's present level of performance of the individual functional skills to be included in the instructional program, the student's current level of social and interactional skills, specific performance-related information about the student (e.g., learning style, learning rate, ability to generalize, areas of difficulty), and an individual skill analysis for each proposed instructional objective. The information obtained from individual student assessments should be included as attachments to the IEP itself.

Component 2: A statement of annual goals for the student must be provided, including short-term instructional objectives. This component should include a description of the specific skill sequences needed by the student; a rationale for the teaching of these sequences at this time; a delineation of the curricular domain, the environments, the subenvironments, and the activities for teaching these skills; a description of the instructional arrangements for teaching these skills (e.g., natural environments, cues and corrections, reinforcement procedures, instructional strategies); specific performance criteria for each skill sequence; and a description of strategies to be used to determine the meeting of performance criteria. Again, much of this information can be included in attachments to the IEP.

Component 3: A statement of the specific special education and related services to be provided to the student must be included. This component should include a description of strategies for incorporating related service activities into the student's overall educational program in addition to the coordination of time and scheduling factors.

Component 4: A statement of the extent to which the student will be able to participate in regular educational programs must be provided. This component should include descriptions of the naturally occurring environments in which specific skills will be taught (i.e., community and school environments), a statement of the percentage of time the student will spend in interactions with nonhandicapped age peers and provisions for developing this interaction, and a description of strategies for developing positive interactions between the student and nonhandicapped peers.

Component 5: A statement of the projected dates for the initiating and anticipated duration of services must be included. This statement should include provisions for school days to be at least comparable in length and frequency to those of nonhandicapped students, a statement of expected school arrival and departure times, and provisions for extending the school year through summer school.

Component 6: Appropriate objective criteria and evaluation procedures for determining, on at least an annual basis, whether instructional objectives are being achieved must be provided. This component should include measurement strategies (e.g., graphs, data sheets, anecdotal record formats) that will be used to monitor and communicate student progress toward individualized objectives. Actual examples of measurement formats should be attached to the IEP.

Daily Program Plan

The daily program plan provides a format for organizing individualized lessons that are developed to assist the student in achieving IEP objectives. Daily plans should include the objective for the specific lesson, the IEP goal and objective being reinforced, the teaching procedures to be used, the specific materials needed, a description of the natural environment in which the skill is to be used, and methods for evaluating both the specific lesson and progress toward the IEP objective.

Individualized daily plans must be developed for each student, emphasizing age-appropriate and functional skills. The plans should develop in a sequence leading from the student's entry-level abilities in a particular skill toward the acquisition of that skill as written in the student's IEP.

ONGOING ASSESSMENT

Once an IEP and daily program plan have been developed and implemented, it is necessary to, on an ongoing basis, record and monitor a student's progress. The more frequently a teacher records and monitors a student's progress, the more quickly and accurately an identification of that student's progress or lack of progress can be noted. This will avoid using teaching techniques, settings, and materials that inhibit a student's progress.

When a teacher is recording ongoing data reflecting a student's behavior(s), a lack of progress is sometimes noted. This lack of progress may be a reflection of an ineffective data collection procedure rather than a student's lack of progress. A list of skills containing "yes" or "no" checkmarks might reflect for an extended period of time that the student was unable to correctly perform the skill. After further analysis, however, it might be noted that the student has made progress in terms of performing the skill with less assistance now than in the past. This would indicate that a simple "yes" or "no" checklist is an ineffective ongoing data collection tool for this student for the behavior(s) in question. An alternative to this approach might be to use a scoring by levels data collection procedure described previously in this chapter.

When it has been determined that the data collection instrument is sensitive enough to reflect the student's behavior(s) and no changes in the student's behavior(s) are observed, there are several other considerations. First, a student's basic/developmental skill repertoire (e.g., motoric or communication skill) might be inhibiting the student's progress to perform a particular skill. For example, if an elementary age student who is nonverbal is not participating in the recess activities, teaching more recess/game skills may not be enough. This student's lack of participation might be due to an inability to communicate or interact. Providing that student with an augmentative communication aide and teaching him or her and the peers to respond appropriately would more likely facilitate participation.

Second, the activity itself might not be motivating to the student. In such an instance, the teacher might build into the activity some motivating characteristics or determine a different, although related, activity to teach.

Third, sometimes when a student's skill repertoire becomes more proficient and independent, he or she receives less teacher attention. For a student who enjoys and needs a teacher's attention, his or her inability to perform skills more independently might be directly related to less teacher attention. Teachers should be sure to interact with students in such a way that the students continue to receive the attention desired and needed while at the same time gain their independence (Falvey et al., 1980).

Finally, in order for students to acquire skills, particularly challenging ones, teachers must convey to those individuals their confidence in them. If teachers are not convinced and convey a message of limited ability, students are likely to accept and emulate such an attitude. Therefore, when a student is not progressing at a reasonable rate, teachers might evaluate their own attitudes and expectations toward that student and his or her potential.

Ongoing assessment involves making instructional decisions based upon objective, concrete, and specific information about the student; the behavior(s) expected; the setting; and several other factors. Ruling out the possible misinterpretation of the progress or lack of progress demonstrated by a student, teachers must have some decision rules for what or when the student makes good progress, marginal progress, no progress, or regress. Browder (1987) and Haring, Liberty, & White (1980), while conducting research, produced sets of rules that can be used to assist the teacher in making data-based instructional decisions. Listed below is a summary of these instructional decisions by Browder (1987).

1. When the student has met his or her objective, extend the performance to more and/or different activities.
2. When the student is demonstrating progress at an acceptable rate (to be individually established for each student for each activity), but has not met the objective, make no changes in the program.
3. When the student demonstrates initial progress, but such progress tapers off, consider changing or improving the consequences for continued progress. In addition, provide intensive training on difficult steps of the activity.
4. When the student is making no progress or regresses from baseline, one of three suggestions should be considered. First, increase the type and/or intensity of the initial prompts (i.e., the antecedents). Second, simplify the program or task analysis into smaller components. Third, improve the motivational factors associated with the activity itself. Be sure to consider this from the student's perspective.

In summary, ongoing data collection and analysis is essential to the development and maintenance of appropriate educational programs for students with severe handicaps. Teachers must regularly review such data and make decisions to discontinue, continue, or make modifications to a program based on those data.

SUMMARY

Assessment procedures must be individualized for each student. However, the actions in which teachers engage inorder to gather their assessment data should at least include conducting parent or significant other weekday and weekend inventories, ecological and student repertoire inventories, and informal data collection. These steps are most likely to result in the development of an individualized program for a student that reflects chronologically age-appropriate and functional activities across a variety of integrated natural environments.

Assessment data must be the basis for IEP goals and objectives. Such goals and objectives should reflect the baseline data gathered during the assessment process. The mechanism used to ensure the teaching of the goals and objectives specified in the IEP is the development of the daily program.

Finally, ongoing data collection is a crucial step in ensuring accountability and relevance of a student's program over time. Decisions about eliminating, changing, or maintaining an instructional program should be made based upon ongoing assessment information.

REFERENCES

Alberto, P., & Troutman, A. (1982). *Applied behavior analysis for teachers*. Columbus, OH: Charles E. Merrill.

Brigance, A.L. (1978). *Brigance Diagnostic Inventory of Early Development*. Woburn, MA: Curriculum Associates.

Browder, D. (1987). *Assessment of individuals with severe handicaps: An applied behavior approach to life skills assessment*. Baltimore: Paul H. Brookes Publishing Co.

Brown, L., Branston, M.B., Hamre-Nietupski, S., Pumpian, I., Certo, N., & Gruenewald, L. (1979). A strategy for developing chronological age appropriate and functional curricular content for severely handicapped adolescents and young adults. *Journal of Special Education, 13*(1), 81–90.

Brown, L., Falvey, M., Vincent, L., Kaye, N., Johnson, F., Ferrara-Parrish, P., & Gruenewald, L. (1980). Strategies for generating comprehensive, longitudinal, and chronological-age-appropriate individualized education programs for adolescent and young-adult severely handicapped students. *Journal of Special Education, 14*(2), 199–215.

Falvey, M., & Anderson, J. (1983). Prioritizing curricular content. In A. Donnellan, J. Anderson, L. Brown, M. Falvey, G. LaVigna, L. Marcus, R. Mesaros, P. Mirenda, G. Olley, & L. Schuler (Eds.), *National society for children & adults with autism: National personnel training. Module 111*. Unpublished curriculum materials.

Falvey, M., Brown, L., Lyon, S., Baumgart, D., & Schroeder, J. (1980). Strategies for using cues and correction procedures. In W. Sailor, B. Wilcox, & L. Brown (Eds.), *Methods of instruction for severely handicapped students* (pp. 109–133). Baltimore: Paul H. Brookes Publishing Co.

Falvey, M., Grenot-Scheyer, M., & Luddy, E. (1984). Developing and implementing integrated community referenced curricula. In D.J. Cohen & A.N. Donnellan (Eds.)., *Handbook of autism and pervasive developmental disorders* (pp. 238–250). New York: John Wiley & Sons.

Haring, N., Liberty, K., & White, O. (1980). Rules for data-based strategy decisions in instructional programs: Current research and instructional implications. In W. Sailor, B. Wilcox, & L. Brown (Eds.), *Methods of instruction for severely handicapped learners* (pp. 159–192). Baltimore: Paul H. Brookes Publishing Co.

PL 94-142, *The Education For All Handicapped Children Act of 1975*.

Salvia, J., & Ysseldyke, J. (1978). *Assessment in special and remedial education*. Boston: Houghton Mifflin.

Snell, M.E. (1978). *Systematic instruction of the moderately and severely handicapped.* Columbus, OH: Charles E. Merrill.
Terman, L., & Merrill, M. (1973). Stanford-Binet Intelligence Scale. Chicago: The Riverside Publishing Co.
Turnbull, A.P. (1983). Parent professional interactions. In M. Snell (Ed.), *Systematic instruction of the moderately and severely handicapped* (pp. 18–44). Columbus, OH: Charles E. Merrill.
Uzgiris, I.C., & Hunt, J. McV. (1975). *Assessment in infancy: Ordinal Scales of Psychological Development.* Urbana: University of Illinois Press.
Vanderheiden, C. (1984). Workshop material. Nonverbal Communication Workshop.
Williams, W., Brown, L., & Certo, N. (1975). Basic components of instructional program. *Theory into Practice, 14*(2), 123–136.

FOUR

INSTRUCTIONAL STRATEGIES

Michele Haney and Mary A. Falvey

AN EFFECTIVE EDUCATOR is able to utilize a variety of strategies to determine what skills to teach an individual student and how to teach those skills. The "how" of teaching includes finding ways to motivate individual students and reinforce developing behaviors, as well as organizing and implementating instructional plans. This chapter describes teaching methods that have been used successfully with students with severe handicaps, and the issues associated with their use. The methods outlined here have been extensively researched and described by a number of authors, and are based primarily on applied behavior analysis. Although this chapter provides a basic introduction to these powerful teaching strategies, the references supplied throughout provide supplementary sources of information.

MOTIVATION

The learning process for all individuals begins with motivation. Motivation may be defined as the strength of desire to engage and persist in achievement-related behaviors (Ruble & Boggiano, 1980). The correlation between motivation, on the one hand, and learning and achievement, on the other, has been explored by many researchers (Atkinson & Raynor, 1974; Ball, 1977; Hull, 1943; McClelland, Atkinson, Clark, & Lowell, 1953; Skinner, 1974; Tolman, 1959; Weiner, 1972). There are a variety of theories about how motivation affects people. Motivation has been shown to be influenced by individual differences, by expectations about the likelihood of success or failure at a particular task, and by task incentives, both intrinsic and extrinsic. High levels of motivation, whatever the basis, generally result in high levels of performance. However, even the best teaching strategies may fail to result in the desired achievement if the proper motivation is not considered and incorporated. Ensuring appropriate motivation for each student is an essential component of any instructional plan.

Motivation provides the incentive to perform the skills or behaviors being taught. In behavioral terms, motivation can be viewed as the specific consequences that follow or accompany a skill or an activity. The consequence or motivation may be within the activity, that is, it may be an intrinsic consequence or motivation. For example, a student learning to draw with colored markers may find the activity pleasurable and thus be highly motivated to develop skills necessary to participate in this activity. Alternatively, consequence or motivation may be extrinsic, such as a reward for the correct performance of a desired behavior. For instance, the student who likes to draw might be given a set of colored markers as a reward for learning a difficult or disagreeable task.

It is hard to identify situations in which motivation does not assume an important role. School performance, for example, is affected by a wide variety of motivational variables. The reward of a good grade, of praise from a teacher or parent, or of the opportunity for advancement are typically sufficient incentives for most students. Some students enjoy learning for its own sake. Students with severe handicaps, however, often show little motivation to learn skills typically acquired by their nonhandicapped peers in school (Sailor & Guess, 1983).

Students with severe handicaps are often outer-directed. In other words, they are more dependent on external, and often artificial, cues and rewards in their task orientation (Falvey, Brown, Lyon, Baumgart, & Schroeder, 1980; Yando & Zigler, 1971). Because of a forced dependence on others in meeting even a few basic needs, they often have significantly fewer experiences with initiating activities and with personal success. As a result, a major challenge for teachers is to develop, foster, and facilitate self-motivation. Carefully chosen and implemented motivational procedures can aid in teaching new behaviors, in strengthening existing behaviors, and in decreasing undesirable behaviors. Motivation is thus an important first step in the development of instructional strategies.

The term reinforcement is often used to refer to motivation in the discussion of intervention strategies. The choice of effective reinforcement is a major element in an instructional program for students with severe handicaps. This could imply that motivation is often external in cause, that it is developed and determined by someone other than the student himself or herself, and is extrinsic in nature. However, extrinsic reward is the least desirable option in attempting to develop motivation. Careless use of extrinsic reward can undermine students' intrinsic motivation (Green & Lepper, 1974). Educators must first determine specific skills and activities to be taught that are themselves interesting, relevant, and meaningful to the student. Ideally, the instructional activities should be highly motivating. Successful completion of these activities should result in natural consequences that provide natural reinforcement to the student. The traditional use of mindless repetition of meaningless and nonfunctional educational tasks does not provide intrinsic reward and should be eliminated. When activities and skills themselves are functional and relevant but the student is unable to obtain or maintain sufficient motivation, carefully developed external reinforcements may then be necessary. The development of appropriate external reinforcement and of a reinforcement schedule must be accompanied by a plan for phasing out the use of the external reinforcement as soon as possible. The section following discusses different types of external reinforcement choices.

CLASSIFYING REINFORCEMENT CHOICES

Reinforcement may be defined as a specific stimulus that is awarded contingent upon the initiation of a particular behavior. There are two basic types of reinforcement: primary and secondary. Primary reinforcers are unlearned; that is, they are naturally rewarding to an individual. If one is hungry, for example, food can be a primary reinforcer. Secondary reinforcers are those stimuli that become valuable to an individual through association with an existing reinforcer. Generally, reinforcement affects the action or response in some way, increasing it when the reinforcement is undesirable or negative. Sailor and Guess (1983) have provided a useful model for classifying reinforcement choices (they refer to choices as "motivational effects") into three categories: objects, events, and actions.

Objects include food or other tangible items (toys, tokens, etc.) that may be used as primary reinforcement under carefully controlled circumstances. Objects provide a direct and immediate external consequence for a specific response. The use of object reinforcement is illustrated by the following example:

Tom, a 4-year-old student with autism, is learning to use signs for communication purposes. At snacktime in the classroom, he is first given small amounts of his favorite foods (i.e., those foods previously observed by his teacher and parents to be his favorite). When he finishes eating, his teacher verbally asks him if he wants more, and uses the sign for "more." His response, initially an imitation of the sign "more," is promptly rewarded with "seconds" of his favorite foods. Gradually, Tom begins to use the sign at snacktime, lunchtime, and mealtime at home without the model provided by the teacher, thus connecting the action (the sign for "more") with the object consequence (an additional serving of a favorite food).

Events can also provide reinforcement in learning situations. Some are social in form, such as a hug, or words, or praise. Pleasant sounds, vibratory stimulation, and other forms of sensory input may also be considered in this category. Events may be used as primary reinforcers that provide direct consequences for desired responses. For example, a student learning to turn on a tape recorder may be immediately rewarded by the sounds of his or her favorite music when the switch is in the "on" position. Events may also be secondary reinforcers when, paired with a tangible consequence such as food, they eventually become motivating in themselves. In this case, the reinforcing event is called a *conditioned reinforcer*.

A conditioned reinforcer is one that assumes its reinforcing properties through frequent pairings with strong unconditioned or previously conditioned reinforcers (Sulzer-Azaroff & Mayer, 1977). Praise, for example, may not be initially motivating to a student who is unaccustomed to it, but it may take on motivational properties when paired, over time, with something already meaningful to that student (e.g., listening to the "Walkman"). Initially, each time that student completes a desired activity, she can be rewarded with the Walkman paired with the words of praise, as in: "What a great job, Sue!" Gradually, as praise becomes conditioned as reinforcing to her, the use of the Walkman can be phased out.

The *action* category of reinforcement choices refers to the use of behaviors to reinforce other behaviors. In other words, actions engaged in by the student at a high frequency can often be considered motivating, and may therefore be used as a reward for low frequency behaviors. This reinforcement category is based on the Premack Principle: "Any response A will reinforce any other response B if and only if the independent rate of A is greater than that of B" (Premack, 1959, p. 220). This can be stated more simply as: "First, I must work on this skill that is not easy and pleasant; however, I can then do something I really like to do." For example, a student who enjoys listening to music may choose to spend 10 minutes engaging in that activity upon completing the chore of sweeping the room. The action of listening to music reinforces the acquisition of the skill of sweeping the room.

REINFORCEMENT PROCEDURES

Reinforcement may be positive or negative, and may be used to increase a desired behavior or to decrease an undesired behavior. Positive reinforcers strengthen the action they follow by providing a reward for those actions. When a stimulus—an object, event, or action—is made contingent upon a behavior and leads to an increase in that behavior, positive reinforcement occurs (Snell & Smith, 1978). The careful use of positive reinforcement techniques provides the most effective and durable strategy for the shaping of student behaviors. Reinforcers that are individually determined, that are closely related to the desired behavior, and that are immediately and systematically administered, are the most powerful reinforcers.

Negative reinforcers may also increase behaviors by making the removal of a negative stimulus contingent upon that behavior. For example, a student who has a difficult time making eye contact in a social situation may make eye contact when the teacher takes hold of his chin and forces him to face her. The student may quickly learn to make eye contact to avoid the unpleasant stimulus of the teacher's rough physical prompt to do so. Although initially effective, and thus dangerously appealing, there are two major problems with the use of aversive stimuli, and its effects tend not to last. Concerns about the use of aversive procedures have recently been debated (Horner, 1988), and their use have been proscribed on both moral and legal grounds. Further, students quickly develop escape or avoidance behaviors in response to negative reinforcers, behaviors that are often difficult to control. For these reasons, negative reinforcement techniques should be avoided in instructional settings.

In cases where negative reinforcement has been used to develop a behavior, careful substitution of positive reinforcement must be planned to maintain that behavior. In the example of the student who learned to make eye contact when the teacher held his chin forcibly, that behavior might initially diminish upon the removal of the negative reinforcer. The systematic substitution of positive reinforcement (e.g., praise from the teacher when eye contact is made in response to her request, or the reward of a sticker when the behavior is exhibited without prompting) will be necessary. The negative reinforcer may have initially inhibited the undesired behavior, but the positive reinforcer will strengthen the desired behavior and thus ensure that it will become a part of the student's behavioral repertoire. It is generally unnecessary to use negative reinforcement, since positive reinforcement is usually necessary to sustain a behavior.

The subsection that follows discusses the identification and use of reinforcers to increase behaviors. The examples featured emphasize positive reinforcement, as this is the preferred method of reinforcement.

CHOOSING REINFORCERS TO INCREASE BEHAVIORS

Several important principles can be applied to the effective use of reinforcement procedures to increase behaviors. The first concerns the *immediacy of the reinforcement*. To be effective, reinforcement procedures must be individually and systematically developed and delivered as close as possible to the actual performance of the desired behavior. The more immediately a reinforcer is presented following a desired behavior, the more likely that the reinforcer will be associated with the desired behavior. For example, a student who is learning to use a communication board may initially not understand that pointing to a pictorial representation of an object will result in obtaining that object. However, if the behavior of pointing to the picture is immediately reinforced by the presentation of the object, the association will be reinforced.

The *frequency with which the reinforcement is delivered* is a second important consideration. A schedule for the delivery of a reinforcement may be continuous or intermittent; that is, a reinforcer may be administered each time the desired behavior occurs, or it may be administered after a specified number of instances of the occurrence of the desired behavior. The schedule of reinforcement frequency should be based upon the student's previous success with continuous or intermittent reinforcement schedules. If intermittent schedules are determined to be the most effective, specific schedules must be based upon those that previously resulted in the student's acquisition of skills. When a new behavior is being introduced to a student, the frequency of reinforcement should be high enough to result in acquisition. As the behavior becomes more familiar, the frequency of reinforcement must be faded. It is also important to remember that constant and frequent reinforcement does not naturally occur in typical community settings, particularly in work settings. The frequency of reinforcement must be faded as quickly as possible to the type and frequency generally provided to nonhandicapped persons in those settings, while still maintaining the skill performance.

A final important consideration in the choice and use of reinforcers is the *age appropriateness* of the object, event, or action chosen. For instance, an opportunity to play with a preferred stuffed toy when a classroom task has been completed may be an appropriate reward for a young child, but it is not appropriate for a teenager. Likewise, a hug is a common consequence for work well done in a primary level classroom. For an older student, it can be inappropriate and stigmatizing, particularly in school and community settings such as in a grocery store or in a high school cafeteria. More appropriate choices must be made to reinforce work done well under those circumstances, especially in light of the natural consequences provided in integrated school and community environments. Money, for example, is a common reward for vocational efforts.

No reinforcer is effective in every situation; neither can something that is reinforcing for one student be assumed to be reinforcing for another student. Further, even the best reinforcer wears out quickly when made contingent upon multiple behaviors. Reinforcers must, therefore, be carefully selected for a specific individual and a specific target behavior. The most effective reinforcers are those that arise as a natural consequence to a given task, or that have a logical relationship to that task (Wilcox & Bellamy, 1982). For example, a student being trained to use vending machines may be naturally reinforced by what he or she is able to purchase from a vending machine. In this case, it would be important to select machines for training that carry items of interest to that student.

Occasionally, reinforcers natural to a given situation are either not motivating in themselves or fail initially to motivate a given student. Only when this happens should a gradual move toward more artificial reinforcement begin (Sulzer-Azaroff & Mayer, 1977). This principle serves a threefold purpose. First, natural reinforcers are less intrusive and thus are less likely to set the student apart from others in the "real world." Second, natural consequences have been shown to result in more efficient learning than arbitrary or generalized reinforcers (Wilcox & Bellamy, 1982). Natural consequences reinforce a more immediate connection between the task and the reinforcer. Finally, it is often difficult to develop a logical fading sequence of artificial reinforcers to natural reinforcers.

If the desired behavior itself lacks positive natural consequences, reinforcers natural and appropriate to the community setting in which the desired behavior is being taught should be used to the maximum extent possible. For example, sweeping floors in a community center may not be rewarding, but being able to use the recreation facilities once the floors are swept may be rewarding and can be appropriate to the setting. Highly artificial reinforcers such as tokens, lavish praise, and physical displays of affection should be used only as last resorts. If they are used, they must be dispensed in nonstigmatizing and dignified ways and faded quickly (Ford & Miranda, 1984).

To determine effective reinforcers for students, the following guidelines should be considered:

1. Identify consequences that are natural to the behavior itself and/or to the environment in which the behavior will take place.
2. Survey others familiar with the student's likes and dislikes and record those that are reinforcing to the student, and that may be relevant to the behavior/environment of interest.
3. Observe the student both on and off task in the natural setting and record those naturally occurring consequences that appear to have particular salience for that student.
4. Offer the student paired choices from those potential reinforcers identified in Items 1, 2, and 3, and establish priority choices based on the student's responses.

Identify Natural Consequences

Many activities and skills involve consequences that may themselves provide sufficient reinforcement to promote the acquisition of those activities and skills. A strategy that can be used to identify consequences natural to an activity or skill is to conduct a skill analysis of that activity. Each step of the skill analysis can be examined for potential naturally occurring consequences. Figure 4.1 provides an example of a condensed skill analysis of the activity of washing dishes, conducted in order to determine the natural consequences of the behavior.

Not all behaviors have easily identified natural consequences to serve as reinforcers of student performance. When a reinforcing consequence natural to the behavior cannot be identified, a survey of the environment may identify other potential reinforcements. For example, Fred, a student with severe handicaps, is learning to perform activities within an integrated community-based

Environment: Home (domestic)
Subenvironment: Food preparation area
Activity: Washing the dishes

Skills	Naturally occurring consequence
1. Place drain in sink.	1. No immediate consequence, but if done correctly, will provide additional reinforcement in Step 2 (sink will fill).
2. Turn on water.	2. Water will begin to flow and fill sink.
3. Adjust water flow temperature.	3. Correct water temperature provides pleasing sensation.
4. Put soap in water.	4. Soap bubbles appear.
5. Turn off water when sink is full.	5. Water flow stops; sink does not overflow (potentially a negative consequence).
6. Place dishes in sink.	6. Student can begin to wash dishes. As it has been determined that student enjoys water-play activities, this should provide natural reinforcement for the remaining steps in the sequence.
7. Use sponge to wash each dish.	7. Same as number 6.
8. Rinse each dish.	8. Same as number 6.
9. Place dish in rack to dry.	9. Activity completed (potentially a negative consequence).

Figure 4.1. A brief analysis of the skills used in washing dishes, conducted to determine the (possible) naturally occurring consequences of performing those skills.

vocational setting. Upon conducting an analysis of the activity of dusting the tapes in a video store, the teacher is initially unable to identify potential naturally occurring reinforcers. A survey of the environment in which the job takes place, however, reveals a video game and vending machines in the laundromat next to the video store. These had been previously determined to be reinforcing events and activities for this student. The teacher arranges short breaks (contingent upon appropriate on-task behavior) for the student at regular intervals during his work time. While on break, Fred is able to go to the laundromat and purchase something from one of the vending machines or to play a video game. The money for the purchases is earned on the job. Gradually, the time between breaks can be increased until Fred is working and taking breaks that were typically available to nonhandicapped employees in that work environment.

Survey Student Likes and Dislikes

What is motivating to one student may not be motivating to another. A teacher must, therefore, be thoroughly familiar with a student's likes and dislikes when attempting to determine reinforcers for that student relevant to a given situation. The student can be requested to assist in the identification of desirabled reinforcers. Parents and others familiar with the student can also be surveyed in order to determine their suggestions for desirable reinforcers. The teacher may wish to develop a series of questions to aid in gathering this information. The following areas should, at a minimum, be considered:

The student's favorite foods
The student's favorite activities at home
The student's favorite activities away from home
Rewards and punishments used at home to manage student behaviors

This information can be matched with activities and skills relevant to the environment of interest. For example, a home survey may identify that a preschool-age student's favorite activity is to listen to music. By introducing a record player into the classroom environment, the teacher may build in a natural reinforcement for a desired classroom behavior for that student.

Observe the Student

One of the most effective ways to determine what is motivating for a given student in a given situation is to observe the student in that situation. While an initial survey of the environment may produce a list of potential reinforcers, the teacher may overlook less obvious ones or those that have relevance only to the student in question. The following example illustrates this point.

John, a student with multiple handicaps, is placed in a bookstore for vocational training. His task is to dust. First, he empties a shelf of books. Then, using a cloth sprayed with water, he dusts the shelf, dusts each book, and then returns the books to the shelf. John is easily distracted and has a difficult time staying on task. He is not initially motivated by praise or by the prospect of a break when the task is completed. His teacher, observing him on the job, notes that John really enjoys spraying his dusting cloth with the cleaning fluid. She restructures the activity so that John can respray the cloth each time he completes a small shelf of books. Getting to respray the cloth is an effective reinforcement for John, and on-task behavior increases significantly. Gradually, he is instructed to spray less often until he is spraying the dusting cloth only at appropriate intervals.

Offer Paired Choices

Occasionally, a situation will offer a number of potential reinforcers, and careful analysis by the teacher of the student's likes and dislikes may reveal many more. When this is the case, the student may be offered paired choices from the list of potential reinforcers. These can be ordered according to priority, based on the student's responses. The necessity of involving the student in the choice of reinforcement cannot be overstressed. To be effective, the reinforcement must be highly desirable to the student in the situation to which it is applied.

In summary, naturally occurring consequences are the least obtrusive and often the most effective reinforcement choices. If systematic efforts to identify naturally occurring consequences fail, knowledge of student likes and dislikes across a variety of environments may provide the teacher with many potentially strong reinforcers with which to begin shaping the desired behavior. Gradually, natural consequences can be substituted for the more artificial ones. Information from parents and others who know the student well, in addition to systematic observation of the student, will assist in the determination of potential reinforcers or motivators. Figure 4.2 illustrates a format for the systematic recording of an individual student's food preferences. This format may be adapted for use in recording preferences for games and any other potentially reinforcing activities, events, or objects.

INSTRUCTIONAL PROCEDURES

Once appropriate reinforcement has been determined for a given student in a given teaching situation, a variety of teaching strategies may be employed to facilitate the acquisition of the desired behavior(s). One set of instructional procedures involves using selective reinforcement of behaviors that are already, in some way, part of the student's repertoire. This will strengthen the existing behaviors and will encourage their appearance under appropriate circumstances. Bringing existing behaviors under the control of the circumstances in which they should occur is known as *stimulus control. Differential reinforcement, prompting,* and *fading* are techniques used to develop stimulus control. More complex strategies, such as *shaping* and *chaining*, may need to be employed to develop new behaviors. Finally, a number of positive alternatives to punishment have been developed to aid in decreasing undesirable behaviors. These techniques, which encourage the development of new behaviors to replace those targeted for reduction, include *differential reinforcement of other behaviors (DRO), differential reinforcement of low rates of responding (DRL),* and *differential reinforcement of competing behaviors (DRC).* The sections that follow define and illustrate the use of these strategies.

BRINGING EXISTING BEHAVIORS UNDER STIMULUS CONTROL

Stimulus control is said to exist when there is a high probability that a particular response will occur in the presence of a particular antecedent stimulus (Sulzer-Azaroff & Mayer, 1977). In other words, the response is under the control of that stimulus. This technique can be used effectively to ensure that behaviors or skills that are part of an individual student's existing repertoire will be exhibited by that student under the appropriate conditions. The antecedent stimulus acts to cue or prompt the desired behavior at the specified time. For example, many student's skill repertoires include the ability to sit, but not all students will sit when told to do so. Sitting at one's desk is a desirable class-

Survey of Weekly Lunch Preferences

Week of: ____________________

Key:
+ Likes
− Dislikes
0 Unsure

Day	Menu	Students												Comments
	Main course													
	Vegetable													
	Fruit													
	Starch													
	Dessert													
	Beverage													
	Other													
	Main course													
	Vegetable													
	Fruit													
	Starch													
	Dessert													
	Beverage													
	Other													
	Main course													
	Vegetable													
	Fruit													
	Starch													
	Dessert													
	Beverage													
	Other													
	Main course													
	Vegetable													
	Fruit													
	Starch													
	Dessert													
	Beverage													
	Other													
	Main course													
	Vegetable													
	Fruit													
	Starch													
	Dessert													
	Beverage													
	Other													

Figure 4.2. Format for the systematic recording of an individual student's food preferences.

room behavior during academic instruction times, yet some students have a difficult time settling down or staying seated. The action, sitting down, needs to be brought under the control of the antecedent stimulus, the teacher's instruction to "Sit down." Stimulus control is generally accomplished by careful reinforcement of the desired behavior or skill when it is exhibited under the specified circumstances.

Before using stimulus control procedures, the educator must first determine that the desired behavior or skill is part of the student's repertoire of behaviors or skills. If it is not, more complex teaching procedures must first be applied to develop the behavior or skill (these teaching procedures are discussed in detail in a later section of this chapter). Once it has been determined that the behavior or skill is present, the antecedent stimulus that will control the behavior under specified circumstances must be identified. Three types of stimuli can be used to control behaviors: *instructional control, materials control*, and *setting control* (Donnellan, Gossage, LaVigna, Schuler, & Traphagen, 1977). Instructional control involves instructions, verbal or nonverbal, given by the educator to prompt a desired student behavior. Materials control exists when the specific materials to be used in performing the desired behavior serve to prompt the student to engage in that behavior. Setting control exists when the aspects of the environment in which the behavior is to take place trigger the behavior.

Stimulus control is most effective when the antecedent stimulus used to cue a desired behavior is a natural part of the environment in which that behavior is to take place. For example, it is appropriate for a student to learn to sit down at a typing table for instruction when told to do so. The command from the teacher is a natural part of the educational environment. To use that same command in the community to signal to the student that he or she has reached the place to sit and wait for the bus would be inappropriate. In the latter instance, the command to sit causes the student to be dependent upon an artificial cue that is not likely to exist each time the student needs to sit and wait for a bus. A natural antecedent stimulus, or cue, in this instance, might be the bus stop sign or bench.

When determining antecedent stimuli, educators must also be careful to identify all the relevant characteristics of potential antecedent stimuli, that is, all the natural cues. Failure to identify all the natural cues might result in the student attending to the irrevelant aspects of antecedents and, therefore, engaging in the behavior at the wrong time or under inappropriate circumstances. For instance, the relevant characteristics of a bus stop sign include its shape, its color, the words that are written on it, and, perhaps, the presence of a bench to sit on while waiting. All of these aspects may be important when trying to bring the student behavior of waiting for the bus under the control of the antecedent stimulus, the bus sign. If, for example, the student learns to attend to the shape only, he or she may incorrectly wait at a "yield" sign because it is the same shape. On the other hand, if the student has learned to attend primarily to the presence of a bench, he or she may fail to wait for the bus at a stop where a bench is not present. Careful advance consideration of relevant characteristics and the use of numerous instructional trials under a variety of circumstances will facilitate bringing the behavior under the control of only the most relevant aspects of the antecedent stimuli.

A final step in the development of stimulus control for a particular behavior or skill is to determine reinforcement strategies. This includes determining the rewards or consequences for the student when the desired behavior is exhibited under the specified circumstances and developing a reinforcement on the use of naturally occurring consequences. For instance, when the student waits for a bus at the bus stop sign, the natural consequence is that the bus comes. Initially, however, other forms of reinforcement may need to be paired with the natural consequence to develop the desired behavior. The three steps: identifying the antecedent stimuli, determining the relevant characteristics of the stimuli, and establishing reinforcement strategies, are critical in the development of stimulus control procedures. Figure 4.3 illustrates the use of these steps in bringing behavior under stimulus control.

Differential Reinforcement

Once a behavior has been specified, the antecedent stimuli described, and the reinforcement determined, stimulus control procedures can be used to teach the student to exhibit the behavior when the antecedent stimuli are presented. Differential reinforcement is one technique for developing this stimulus control. It involves the deliberate reinforcement of the specified behavior when, and only when, it occurs under the specified stimulus conditions. As students are con-

Environment: Community
Subenvironment: Street corner bus stop
Activity: Waiting for the bus

Antecedent stimuli	Relevant characteristics	Reinforcement
Bus stop sign and waiting bench at northwest corner of Fifth and Main Street.	Sign is triangular. Sign is yellow. Black lettering on sign: "Bus Line 54" "Main Street North." Green wooden bench. Advertisement on bench: "Joe's Cafe" "Fine Foods at Reasonable Prices" Picture of hamburger. People waiting for bus.	Natural: Bus arrives. Other: Verbal praise if student stops near bench. Give student bus money when seated at waiting bench.

Figure 4.3. Illustration of the use of three steps for assessing the environment in order to plan for bringing behavior under stimulus control.

tinually reinforced for the behavior in the presence of a specified antecedent, they will come to associate the reinforcement with the antecedent. Gradually, the antecedent itself will trigger the desired behavior.

Toilet training provides a good example of the use of differential reinforcement to bring an existing behavior under stimulus control. In this case, the specified behavior is having the student empty her bladder, the antecedent stimulus is the condition of being seated on the toilet, and the reinforcement should be something previously determined as highly motivating to the student. When the behavior is exhibited under the specified conditions, it is reinforced. When the behavior is exhibited at other times (for example, the student wets her pants in the classroom), it is not reinforced. Gradually, the student learns to empty her bladder only when seated upon the toilet.

Prompting

For many students with severe handicaps, more specific guidance and instructional assistance may initially be necessary to acquire new skills. A range of instructional stimuli may need to be provided in order to direct the student toward the performance of a desired response. This technique is known as *prompting*. Prompts may take the form of *cues*, which are used to provide instructional information to a student before a skill is performed. Prompts may also be provided as *corrections*, which communicate to a student that a skill already performed is inappropriate or needs to be reattempted in a different way (Falvey et al., 1980).

Suppose, for example, that a teacher wanted to teach a student to wash her hands after using the toilet. The natural cue, which would indicate that the behavior was under stimulus control, is the setting. In other words, when the student had finished toileting, the presence of the sink would remind her to wash her hands. If this did not occur, the teacher might first gesture to the sink, providing a correction. The next level of prompt would be to ask: "Have you forgotten something?" At the most extreme level, the teacher would actually motor the student through all or part of the whole cycle of hand washing.

The presentation of prompts must be carefully controlled to minimize student dependence, to provide maximum clarity, and to facilitate the student's learning of the desired behavior(s). A *discrete trial format (DTF)* is an effective teaching procedure that enables the educator to control the presentation of stimulus, prompts, and consequences. In *DTF*, prompts are used after the natural stimulus fails to control the desired behavior and prior to the end of the student's response. *DTF* is added to the stimulus to bring about a correct response and to thus provide frequent and immediate reinforcement to the student for correct performance of the behavior. The components of the *DTF* include: the discriminative stimulus, the prompt (only if necessary), the desired response, and the reinforcement, or consequence, for a correct response. A trial is measured as a student's attempt to perform the desired behavior. One trial ends when the behavior is correctly performed and subsequently reinforced, or when the student performs incorrectly. In the case of incorrect performance, the student is returned to the stimulus point and a new trial is begun, perhaps using a more intensive level of prompt.

There are eight levels in the hierarchy of prompt usage. As indicated earlier, the highest level, level eight, is the natural cue or stimulus, indicative of stimulus control. Level seven is the gestural prompt. This may include: pointing, shaking one's head to indicate approval or disapproval, or a facial cue, such as a smile or a frown. Level six is the indirect verbal prompt: the use of words to imply that some behavior needs to occur. At level five, a direct verbal prompt explicitly states the behavior that needs to happen. In the previous example, the teacher might have said directly: "Wash your hands." To prompt at level four is to actually model the desired behavior for the student, to encourage the student's imitation of that behavior. A minimal physical prompt is used at level three, that is, slight physical contact to guide a student toward a behavior. At level two, a partial physical prompt is applied; at this level, the teacher physically starts the student in the desired behavior, but then releases the student to complete the behavior independently. Finally, at level one, a full physical prompt may be used, in which the student is motored through the entire activity. Figure 4.4 illustrates a format for consideration of a prompting hierarchy for a particular behavior.

Just as the most effective reinforcers are those that are natural consequences of the skill to be developed, the most effective cues to use are those that are natural to the situation in which the desired behavior is to occur. Students must learn to perform in response to natural cues as quickly as possible, because artificial prompts will generally not be available to them in integrated community environments. A major consideration when using prompts is that they must eventually be removed on the basis of the data collected on the student's performance (Koegel & Schreibman, 1982). Students can quickly become dependent on artificial or intense levels of prompts. Thus, part of the use of prompts must involve a systematic plan to reduce the student's dependency on prompts until he or she is able to perform the behavior solely in response to the natural cues. The technique for reducing prompting levels is known as *fading*.

Fading

Fading procedures are necessary when artificial or intense levels of prompts have been used to develop a skill. When fading procedures are properly executed, the student maintains existing high levels of performance. This means that fading procedures must be gradually applied, moving down the levels of prompts and also reducing the numbers of prompts provided. The following example illustrates this process.

Carol, a 6-year old student with severe handicaps, is learning to use a

Environment: Home (recreational leisure)
Subenvironment: Living room
Activity: Listening to the radio

Stimuli	Level of prompt	Behavior	Consequence
Radio is available in the home for student use; music has been determined to be a favorite activity for the student; student has free time.	8—Natural	Without prompting, and given leisure time and the presence of the radio, student turns on radio.	Student listens to music.
	7—Gestural	Adult points toward radio; student turns on radio.	Student listens to music; adult may nod approval.
	6—Indirect verbal	Adults says, "Why don't you listen to music?" Student turns on radio.	Student listens to music; adult says, "Good idea!"
	5—Direct verbal	Adult says, "Turn on the radio"; student complies.	Student listens to music; adult may verbally reinforce for turning on radio.
	4—Model	Adult models turning on radio for student, then gives student a turn to do so.	Student is reinforced for attending to model, and gets to listen to music when he turns radio on himself.
	3—Minimal physical	Adult points student in direction of radio and pushes student's hand toward radio if necessary; student turns on radio.	Student listens to music; adult may need to provide additional verbal praise.
	2—Partial physical	Adult positions student's hand on radio knob, but releases hand so student can turn it.	Music may be enough, but student may require additional verbal or object reinforcement.
	1—Full physical	Adult motors student through the turning on of the radio.	Again, music may be sufficient, but additional reinforcement may be necessary.

Figure 4.4. Format for consideration of a prompting hierarchy.

spoon for eating. At first, physical prompts are needed for several steps of the eating process. A full physical prompt is necessary to assist her in scooping her food from the dish. A partial physical prompt is needed to cue her to bring the food to her mouth. A verbal prompt reminds her to steady the spoon when it reaches her mouth. As these behaviors become established, the teacher begins to fade the levels of prompts provided. Rather than full physical guidance in scooping, a light touch prompts Carol to complete the movement. A gesture, the teacher motioning upward with her hand from the table toward Carol's mouth, encourages Carol to bring the food to her mouth. The verbal prompt is eliminated completely. This gradual fading process continues systematically until Carol has reached independence in eating with a spoon.

Fading should be done slowly so that the student maintains the desired behavior. If, as prompts are being faded, the student begins to perform the behavior incorrectly, the fading sequence has been too rapid. At this point, it may be necessary for the instructor to return to the last level of prompting at which the behavior was performed correctly, and to begin the fading sequence again.

DEVELOPING NEW BEHAVIORS

The previous discussion focused on developing behaviors that were already a part of a student's repertoire of skills. Many important behaviors, however, are not likely to occur spontaneously, and therefore cannot be increased by reinforcement and prompting. The development of new behaviors requires the more sophisticated use of the procedures described previously, paired with two major teaching strategies: shaping and chaining. The use of these procedures requires a specific delineation of the new behavior as well as of the circumstances under which that behavior should be exhibited.

Shaping

Shaping involves the reinforcement of successive approximations of better and better attempts at a complex response (Snell & Smith, 1978). Shaping begins with reinforcement of the closest approximation of the target behavior that exists in the student's repertoire, and systematically builds on slight changes in that behavior, leading toward the target behavior itself. Before beginning shaping procedures, the target behavior must be operationally defined, that is, the exact characteristics of acceptable performance must be specified. From this point, all possible steps in the direction of that target behavior must be outlined, and careful observations of the students must take place to determine the student's starting point toward that behavior. At first, the closest approximation that the student is able to make toward the target behavior is reinforced. The required level of performance is then gradually increased, and only responses that move in the direction of the target behavior are reinforced. In this way, the student's behavior is shaped toward the target behavior.

Many different behaviors can be developed using shaping procedures. To illustrate one use of shaping, let us consider how to teach Mario, a 10-year-old student with autism, to interact with nonhandicapped peers on the school playground. At first, any movement by Mario toward a group of peers would be reinforced. The next step would be to make reinforcement contingent upon Mario playing next to a group of peers. Next, Mario's use of the same playground equipment, side by side with his peers, would be reinforced. As this behavior became well established, the next step would be to make reinforcement contingent upon Mario sharing a piece of equipment with a peer, and so on.

Shaping can be used with various levels of prompts to further encourage the development of behaviors when close approximations fail to progress using shaping alone. For example, if Mario fails to independently move closer to his peers at play, his teacher might prompt him to do so by using the least intensive level of prompt needed. Reinforcement would then be given to this guided response. As in any use of prompts, this prompt should be faded as quickly as possible to encourage independence. When the guided behavior has been well established and the use of the guide eliminated, the next step toward the target behavior should be developed.

Chaining

Another procedure that can be used to develop new behaviors and skills is chaining. Chaining involves breaking a target behavior down into its smallest component parts in order to teach the parts one at a time (Koegel & Schreibman, 1982). The first behavior in the chain is the first response taught. A chain should begin at the level at which the student is able to successfully learn the first behavior, and should move in successive steps toward the target behavior.

A distinction can be made between forward chaining and backward chaining, depending on which step in the chain is taught first (Sulzer-Azaroff & Mayer, 1977). Teaching steps using forward chaining begins with teaching the first step in the chaining procedure until all the steps have been learned. Backward chaining progresses in the opposite direction, with the student motored through all the steps in the chain and then teaching the last step first and progressing until all the steps have been learned.

Chaining begins with a *task analysis* of the target behavior. In task analysis, each component behavior of the target behavior is identified, and the sequence of those behaviors is defined. The analysis of the task should be linked to the student's ability level (Gold, 1980). For example, one student may learn to wash his hands through a 10-step process, while another student may need that same behavior broken down into a 30-step process in order to acquire the necessary skills. Each step in a task analysis should be clearly stated in order to objectively measure the student's performance of the behavior. There should be just enough steps in the task analysis to allow efficient and systematic teaching; each step can itself be analyzed if the student has special difficulty in successfully performing that step. A task analysis should be individually developed and applied. Bellamy, Horner, and Inman (1979) suggest procedures for developing an effective and efficient task analysis. A modified version of their plan follows:

1. Perform the task yourself.
2. Break the task down into a logical number of parts based on your own performance.
3. Prompt the student through the task.
4. Reanalyze the task based on student areas of difficulty.

When an individualized task analysis has been developed, it can be used as a teaching sequence to develop a desired target behavior. If forward chaining is being used, the student is taught to perform the first unlearned step in the chain. When this step is mastered, instruction proceeds to the next step, and so on. For example, a student learning to use a record player must first learn to turn the record player on, then to place the record on the turntable, then to follow each remaining step in the chain. Reinforcement is given as each step in the chain is successfully completed.

In backward chaining, the steps are taught in reverse order. This method can be useful for linking the natural reinforcement inherent in the completion of the activity with the performance of the activity. For example, if the teaching sequence for shoe tying starts with the last step in the sequence, pulling the bow tight, the student is immediately reinforced by the successfully tied shoe. Conversely, when starting with the first step, the student may not see the end result, the tied shoe, immediately, and may require a more artificial reinforcement.

Backward chaining can also be beneficial when baseline testing of the student indicates that he or she has mastered some of the steps at the end of a teaching chain. For example, if the student is able to place a dish in the dish rack, the last step in the sequence for washing a dish, instruction should begin with the next to the last step, checking the dish for remaining soap. At the same time, the student would be expected to continue to perform previously mastered step(s). Figure 4.5 provides a task analysis for a dishwashing procedure, numbered for both forward and backward teaching order.

As with shaping, prompts can be used to encourage the development of behaviors in a chain. Each step as it is introduced may first have to be prompted. In addition, most target behaviors are composed of component behaviors that are only meaningful in the context of the target behavior. They should not, therefore, be taught in isolation. For example, students being taught an isolated dishwashing step may ask themselves: "Why learn to put the drain in the sink if you are not going to wash the dishes?" Although the instructional energy for the moment may be concentrated on putting the drain in the sink, the other component dishwashing behaviors can be completed at more intensive prompting levels, as necessary, so that the activity itself maintains its meaning.

Environment: Home (domestic)
Subenvironment: Food preparation area
Activity: Washing the dishes

Skills:

Forward teaching order	Backward teaching order	
1.	20.	Put drain in sink.
2.	19.	Turn on hot water.
3.	18.	Adjust hot water flow.
4.	17.	Turn on cold water.
5.	16.	Adjust cold water flow.
6.	15.	Put correct amount of soap in sink.
7.	14.	Determine when sink is full.
8.	13.	Turn off hot water.
9.	12.	Turn off cold water.
10.	11.	Place dirty dish in water.
11.	10.	Pick up sponge.
12.	9.	Use sponge to wash front of dish.
13.	8.	Turn dish over.
14.	7.	Use sponge to wash back of dish.
15.	6.	Check front and back of dish for dirt.
16.	5.	Place sponge in water.
17.	4.	Rinse front of dish.
18.	3.	Rinse back of dish.
19.	2.	Check dish for remaining soap.
20.	1.	Place dish in rack.

Figure 4.5. Task analysis conducted for the activity of washing dishes, numbered for forward or backward chaining instruction.

INSTRUCTIONAL APPROACHES FOR DECREASING UNDESIRABLE BEHAVIORS

The major emphasis of education should be on increasing desirable behaviors. However, methods have also been developed to assist educators in manipulating reinforcement to eliminate or decrease undesirable behaviors. Three of these methods involve use of negative reinforcement procedures and should be used, if at all, with the utmost caution. Further, their use must always be paired with a positive component that improves or builds replacement behaviors (Snell & Smith, 1978). Included are: methods involving the withholding of reinforcement (extinction), the removal of reinforcement (a form of punishment), and the presentation of aversive reinforcement (also a form of punishment). These procedures have limited applicability and effectiveness (Bandura, 1975). Also, many programs, agencies, state departments, local school districts, and so on, have policies and procedures that do not allow the use of punishment.

The remaining procedures have been developed as alternatives to negative reinforcement strategies, particularly punishment. These preferred strategies are: differential reinforcement of other behaviors (DRO), differential reinforcement of low rates of responding (DRL), and differential reinforcement of competing behaviors (DRC). A built-in component of each of these strategies is the systematic development of positive behavioral alternatives to the undesirable behavior. Each procedure is reviewed in detail in the following sections.

Extinction

Extinction is a procedure in which behavior that has been reinforced is no longer reinforced (Sulzer-Azaroff & Mayer, 1977). Extinction is often used to eliminate undesirable attention-getting behaviors. For example, extinction was appropriately applied in a classroom situation with a student who was constantly disrupting recreational activities with loud noises and aggressive actions, such as grabbing at items on the game board. The teacher and the other students were able to ignore this behavior, thus withholding the desired reinforcement of attention. At the same time, the teacher reinforced that student with positive attention whenever he exhibited more appropriate behaviors. The use of extinction, paired with the reinforcement of a positive alternative, largely eliminated the student's undesirable actions.

Extinction can be used to decrease a behavior. However, caution must be considered when using extinction procedures. First, extinction is not recommended for use with all undesirable behaviors. Some behaviors, such as those that are potentially harmful to the student or to others, are difficult, and even dangerous, to ignore. Although extinction might ultimately be effective in reducing these behaviors, the danger that someone may be hurt in the process far outweighs the usefulness of the procedures.

Second, to be most effective, extinction procedures must be continuously and consistently applied. If the behavior in question is even occasionally reinforced, it will be difficult to eliminate. If a student's undesirable behaviors have been reinforced over a long period of time, it may take an equally long period to extinguish those behaviors. Before beginning an extinction procedure, the teacher must be sure that he or she will be able to ignore the student or otherwise withhold reinforcement when the behavior is exhibited, and to apply this procedure for as long as necessary. Furthermore, even the most consistently applied extinction procedures may initially cause an increase in the targeted undesired behavior. If a student, for example, is acting out to get attention and is accustomed to that attention, he or she may act out with greater intensity when that attention is first withheld. Again, the teacher must also be able to recognize when the escalation period has continued too long.

Finally, extinction procedures can only be used when the teacher has control over the stimulus that is reinforcing the undesirable behavior. In the example of the student whose disruptive behaviors were interfering with leisure activities, extinction was effective because the teacher was able to encourage the student's peers to ignore the behavior as she did. She had full control over the reinforcement situation. At other times, the behavior is itself reinforcing (e.g., self-stimulatory behavior), and the teacher will be unable to withhold or control the reinforcement. In such instances, extinction cannot be used effectively.

Punishment

Two different operations may be considered as punishment: the removal of positive reinforcement and the delivery of a negative consequence. Punishment has been used to decrease behaviors that are inappropriate in some situations. The motivation to decrease or eliminate a behavior results from a negative stimulus associated with the behavior. As with all forms of reinforcement, punishment must be individually determined and relevant to the situation in which it is applied. Issues of immediacy, frequency, age appropriateness, and natural consequences (discussed in the previous section on positive reinforcement) also apply to the use of punishment.

The use of "time-out" is the most common example of punishment that involves removal of positive reinforcement. In time-out, the student is isolated from a situation that provides enjoyable stimuli when he or she exhibits a particular undesirable behavior. The student is allowed to return to the enjoyment stimuli when the inappropriate behavior ceases.

The removal of reinforcement works to decrease undesirable behaviors only if the reinforcement being removed is highly desirable to the student. Taking away privileges, for example, is effective only if the student desires those privileges. Although this principle may seem simple, it is frequently overlooked. Educators are often quick to send a disruptive student into time-out, without realizing that the student may not be motivated to return to classroom activities. Time-out, in these instances, merely serves to reinforce the student's disruptive behavior by removing him or her from the unpleasant stimulus of the classroom. Careful choice of motivating instructional activities and supportive positive reinforcement is often more effective than punishment procedures in isolation.

The second type of punishment involves the presentation of an aversive event or action. Punishment of this type can be verbal, such as a firm reprimand following an undesired behavior (e.g., "Stop that!"), or it can take a physical form (e.g., a slap or shock). Serious ethical issues must be considered if these methods are used for changing behavior (LaVigna & DonnellanWalsh, 1976). The degree of inappropriateness of the behavior to be punished and the rights of the individual student must be weighed seriously. In addition, all of the potentially positive procedures must first be exhausted.

Negative side effects associated with the use of punishment make its usefulness limited at best. These side effects include: negative emotional reactions, avoidance behaviors, aggression, increased anxiety, and the association of negative events with the punisher. Far too often, punishment is used as the treatment of choice when trying to decrease undesirable behaviors; it appears easier to punish a student for an undesirable behavior than to reinforce the student for a desired behavior. The authors of this volume advocate the use of punishment only as a last resort, for controlling behaviors that are immediately dangerous to the student or to others in the environment. Even in these situations, educators are obligated to use the least aversive effective procedure. Positive behavior control strategies are most effective over time and should be the first choice. For a further discussion of these issues, the reader is referred to LaVigna and Donnellan's (1984) excellent work on alternatives to punishment in the school setting.

Differential Reinforcement of Other Behaviors

Undesirable behaviors can be difficult to diminish because they are often being inadvertently rewarded. For example, students might act out because they receive attention when they do so. That brief time when the teacher is telling them to stop the behavior, or punishing them for the behavior, may be the only time they actually get to spend with the teacher on a one-to-one basis. All their desirable behaviors may go unnoticed, but the undesirable one gets the attention. That attention is reinforcing no matter what form it takes. In the DRO procedure, reinforcement is deliberately given to the student after a specified period of no undesired behavior (LaVigna & Donnellan-Walsh, 1976). In this way, the student is being reinforced, positively, for all behaviors except the one undesirable behavior. To illustrate, a student who is abusive to others might be reinforced with a previously determined effective reinforcer for each 5-minute block of time in which he is not abusive. The other behaviors occurring during these time blocks would be strengthened by the reinforcement, and the undesired behavior would be diminished by the lack of reinforcement.

Friman, Barnard, Altman, and Wolf (1986) described an intervention in which DRO procedures were effectively applied by a mother of a girl with severe handicaps who exhibited behavior problems marked by aggressive pinching. In one situation during the intervention, the mother positively reinforced the girl (with praise and gentle touch) when she did not pinch during specified time periods. If the mother was pinched during the time period, she used response prevention techniques, gently holding the girl's hand stationary for 2 minutes after the pinch. DRO was suspended during response prevention. This intervention resulted in a sharp decrease in pinching behavior, to near-zero levels at the end of the intervention and at follow-up.

DRO can be quick and effective when individually developed and systematically applied. The reinforcement period must be reasonable for the student and should be increased gradually as the behavior comes under control. Careful recording of the frequency of the undesirable behavior before instituting the DRO procedure is therefore necessary. For example, observation may indicate that a student is self-abusive at least once every 5 minutes during structured periods and once every 2 minutes during unstructured periods. DRO schedule in this case should be set up for that student at 5-minute intervals for the structured periods, and at 3-minute intervals for the unstructured periods. Gradually, the intervals should be lengthened until eventually the student is no longer engaged in the undesired behavior.

Differential Reinforcement of Low Rates of Responding

A procedure similar to DRO is DRL. In DRL, reinforcement is made contingent upon the particular behavior occurring at a specified low rate (Sulzer-Azaroff & Mayer, 1977). The student is reinforced if the desired behavior occurs only after a specified time period, or if it occurs a limited number of times during a specified time period. DRL can be used when the goal is to reduce an undesirable behavior but not to eliminate it completely. For example, a teacher might want to eliminate "yelling out" behavior in the classroom, but may consider that same behavior appropriate on the playground. Baseline data might show that the student yelled out, on average, 10 times in a 10-minute period. During specified time intervals while in the classroom, the student would receive reinforcement only for lower rates of yelling out (e.g., five times in a 10-minute period). Similarly, the student might receive reinforcement contingent upon not yelling out in the last 10-minute period in class, and then be allowed to yell out on the way to the playground. In this way, the teacher can reduce the behavior during times that it is disruptive, without eliminating it at other times.

DRL can also be used as a preliminary step to DRO, when a behavior is so frequent or well established in a student that it is unlikely that it will diminish quickly or completely. In this case, a student would be reinforced for diminishing incidences of the behavior, but would not have to eliminate the behavior entirely. For example, observation might indicate that a student engages in self-stimulating behavior 85% of the time in a given 5-minute period. The first goal might be to reduce the incidence of that behavior to 75% in a 5-minute period, and reinforcement would be provided for those periods in which the self-stimulating behavior was reduced to 75% of the time. Gradually, the expectation could be increased, and reinforcement given for fewer and fewer incidences of the behavior.

Differential Reinforcement of Competing Behaviors

Students often engage in undesirable behaviors because they do not know what else to do. Procedures to reduce undesirable behaviors that do not provide the student with reasonable alternatives may, therefore, have limited success. DRC is based on the premise that undesirable behaviors cannot occur simultaneously with competing desirable behaviors. The procedure involves the systematic reinforcement of alternatives to undesirable behaviors (LaVigna & Donnellan-Walsh, 1976). On a basic conceptual level, every new skill and desirable behavior that is developed in a student is an alternative to an undesirable behavior, but DRC involves a more systematic matching of desirable with undesirable behaviors. The educator first defines the exact parameters of the problem behavior and then searches for alternatives that will interfere with that behavior. These alternatives are then systematically reinforced.

For example, Jennifer, a 3-year old child with severe developmental delays, spends a large portion of time wringing her hands in front of her face, attending to little else in her environment. Her teacher developed a DRC program whereby Jennifer is rewarded every time her hands are holding a toy. When holding a toy, a behavior in Jennifer's repertoire, Jennifer cannot engage in the self-stimulatory hand wringing. The reinforcement of this competing behavior, toy holding, causes a significant reduction in the undesirable hand wringing and results in an increase in Jennifer's ability to attend to her environment.

As another example, Chris engages in the undesirable behavior of pulling food off shelves when he is in the supermarket. The reaction of others in this community environment is highly reinforcing to Chris, and thus his teacher is having a difficult time bringing this behavior under control. The teacher decides to teach Chris to push a shopping cart when in the supermarket. She provides systematic reinforcement to Chris whenever he pushes the cart. Because he has to use both hands to push the cart, Chris is unable to pull things off the shelves. The reinforcement of the new and desirable behavior serves to bring the undesirable behavior under control.

Maintenance and Generalization

Newly developed behaviors or reductions in undesirable behaviors are of limited benefit if they disappear when instruction ceases, or if they occur only under instructional conditions. Therefore, any instructional plan to develop or decrease behaviors must include strategies for maintaining those behavioral changes and for generalizing them to other situations.

Maintenance refers to procedures that ensure that newly developed desirable behaviors or decreases in undesirable behaviors will last (Kazdin & Esveldt-Dawson, 1981). Maintenance procedures are begun after an acceptable level of performance has been attained. They involve the gradual reduction in the frequency and immediacy of reinforcement, from previous levels that were necessary for the student to attain the desired level of performance, to the minimal levels necessary for the student to maintain that performance. This reduction can involve intermittent reinforcement, that is, reinforcement after some, but not all, occurrences of the behaviors in question. It can also involve delayed reinforcement, that is, an increase in time between the performance of the behavior and the delivery of the reinforcement. Reinforcement can be faded, or gradually withdrawn, in these two ways to the point where acceptable levels of performance are maintained under natural consequences.

If the instructional emphasis has from the beginning been on the use of natural cues and consequences, plans for maintenance of behaviors are generally minimal. Natural cues and consequences should continue to be available for the student in the environment in which the specified behavior occurs. If the behavior has been initially developed or decreased through the use of artificial reinforcement, the maintenance of the behavioral change will be assisted by a shift in emphasis from artificial to natural reinforcement. Techniques for accomplishing this shift have been discussed elsewhere in this chapter.

In addition to maintenance, the student may need to learn to perform skills across a variety of circumstances and situations. Techniques to facilitate this transfer are known as generalization techniques. Generalization is best accomplished by using natural teaching cues and reinforcement options and by teaching the desired behaviors in the actual settings in which they will need to be performed (Stokes & Baer, 1977). For example, teaching a student to read a street signal in a classroom setting may not result in that student being able to cross a street using signals in the community. At the same time, teaching the student to cross at a particular street may not mean that the student will be able to cross a different street (Horner, Sprague, & Wilcox, 1982). The best way to see that the skill is generalized is to teach it at a number of different streets, using the variety of natural aids and reinforcements that are available in the community. The generalization of the appropriate behavior can then be assessed in novel situations.

SUMMARY

This chapter reviews strategies for implementing individualized instructional programs for students with severe handicaps. Basic intervention techniques are discussed, organized around the premise that determining what is motivation or reinforcement for a given student in a given instructional situation provides the basis for any intervention plan. Various reinforcement procedures are described, with emphasis placed on positive reinforcement. Specific instructional strategies are discussed, including stimulus control, shaping, chaining, and differential reinforcement of various kinds.

REFERENCES

Atkinson, J.W., & Raynor, J.O. (Eds.). (1974). *Motivation and achievement*. Washington, DC: Winston.

Ball, S. (1977). *Motivation in education*. New York: Academic Press.

Bandura, A. (1975). The ethics and social purposes of behavior modification. In C.M. Franks & G.T. Wilson (Eds.), *The annual review of behavior therapy theory and practice* (Vol. 3, pp. 13–20). New York: Brunner/Mazel.

Bellamy, G.T., Horner, R.H., & Inman, D.P. (1979). *Vocational habilitation of severely retarded adults: A direct service technology*. Baltimore: University Park Press.

Donnellan, A., Gossage, L.D., LaVigna, G.W., Schuler, A., & Traphagen, J.D. (1977). *Teaching makes a difference*. Sacramento: California State Department of Education.

Falvey, M., Brown, L., Lyon, S., Baumgart, D., & Schroeder, J. (1980). Strategies for using cues and correction procedures. In W. Sailor, B. Wilcox, & L. Brown (Eds.), *Methods of instruction for severely handicapped students* (pp. 109–133). Baltimore: Paul H. Brookes Publishing Co.

Ford, A., & Miranda, P. (1984). Community instruction: A natural cues and corrections decision model. *Journal of The Association for Persons with Severe Handicaps, 9*(2), 79–87.

Friman, P.C., Barnard, J.D., Altman, K., & Wolf, M.M. (1986). Parent and teacher use of DRO and DRI to reduce aggressive behavior. *Analysis and Intervention in Developmental Disabilities, 6*, 319–330.

Gold, M.W. (1980). *Try another way. Training Manual.* Champaign, IL: Research Press.

Green, D., & Lepper, M.R. (1974, September). Intrinsic motivation: How to turn play into work. *Psychology Today, 8*, 49–54.

Horner, R. (1988, August). A look at recent *TASH* articles on positive programming for behavior problems. *TASH Newsletter, 14*(8), p. 11.

Horner, R.H., Sprague, J., & Wilcox, B. (1982). General case programming for community activities. In B. Wilcox & G.T. Bellamy, *Design of high school programs for severely handicapped students* (pp. 61–98). Baltimore: Paul H. Brookes Publishing Co.

Hull, C.L. (1943). *Principles of behavior. An introduction to behavior theory.* New York: Appleton-Century Crofts.

Kazdin, A., & Esveldt-Dawson, K. (1981). *How to maintain behavior.* Lawrence, KS: H & H Enterprises.

Koegel, R.L., & Schreibman, L. (1982). *How to teach autistic and other severely handicapped children.* Lawrence, KS: H & H Enterprises.

LaVigna, G.W., & Donnellan, A.M. (1984). *Alternative to punishment: Solving behavior problems with non-aversive strategies.* New York: Irvington Publishers.

LaVigna, G.W., & Donnellan-Walsh, A.M. (1976). *Alternatives to the use of punishment in the school setting.* Paper presented at the eighth annual Southern California Conference on Behavior Modification, California State University, Los Angeles.

McClelland, D.C., Atkinson, J.W., Clark, R.A., & Lowell, E.L. (1953). *The achievement motive.* New York: Appleton-Century-Crofts.

Premack, D. (1959). Toward empirical behavioral laws: I. Positive reinforcement. *Psychological Review, 66*, 219–233.

Ruble, D.N., & Boggiano, A.K. (1980). Optimizing motivation in an achievement context. In B.K. Keogh (Ed.), *Advances in special education* (Vol. 1). *Basic constructs and theoretical orientations.* Greenwich, CT: JAI Press.

Sailor, W., & Guess, D. (1983). *Severely handicapped students: An instructional design.* Boston: Houghton Mifflin.

Skinner, B.F. (1974). *About behaviorism.* New York: Random House.

Snell, M.E., & Smith, D.D. (1978). Intervention strategies. In M.E. Snell (Ed.), *Systematic instruction of the moderately and severely handicapped* (1st ed.) (pp. 74–99). Columbus, OH: Charles E. Merrill.

Stokes, T.R., & Baer, D.M. (1977). An implicit technology of generalization. *Journal of Applied Behavior Analysis, 10*, 341–367.

Sulzer-Azaroff, B., & Mayer, G.R. (1977). *Applying behavior-analysis procedures with children and youth.* New York: Holt, Rinehart & Winston.

Tolman, E.C. (1959). Principles of purposive behavior. In S. Koch (Ed.), *Psychology: A study of a science* (Vol. 2). New York: McGraw-Hill.

Weiner, B. (1972). *Theories of motivation: From mechanism to cognition.* Chicago: Rand McNally.

Wilcox, B., & Bellamy, G.T. (1982). *Design of high school programs for severely handicapped students*. Baltimore: Paul H. Brookes Publishing Co.

Yando, R., & Zigler, E. (1971). Outer directions in the problem-solving of institutionalized and non-institutional normal and retarded children. *Developmental Psychology, 4*, 277–288.

FIVE

COMMUNITY SKILLS

TEACHING STUDENTS WITH severe handicaps to perform skills necessary to function within a variety of community environments is essential. For years, the "experts" in special education, rehabilitation, medicine, and other related areas have placed unnecessary restrictions and limitations on what can be expected of persons with severe handicaps. These restrictions and limitations led to the development of isolated and segregated living, educational, vocational, and recreation/leisure environments for persons with severe handicaps. Although many restrictions still persist in the attitudes of some professionals, these are gradually declining; the result is that the remaining isolated and segregated environments are being broken up. Recent research has provided new perspectives and new expectations for the potentials of persons with severe handicaps.

Several studies have documented success in teaching students to perform the skills necessary to use public transportation (Coon, Vogelsberg, & Williams, 1981; Sowers, Rusch, & Hudson, 1979; Welch, Nietupski, & Hamre-Nietupski, 1985). Street crossing, another critical community skill, has also been successfully taught to persons with handicaps (Horner, Jones, & Williams 1985; Marchetti, McCartney, Drain, Hooper, & Dix, 1983; Matson, 1980; Page, Iwata, & Neef, 1976; Vogelsberg & Rusch, 1979). Several studies have demonstrated the success of teaching purchasing skills (Gaule, Nietupski, & Certo, 1985; McDonnell & Horner, 1985; McDonnell, Horner, & Williams, 1984; Nietupski, Clancy, & Christiansen, 1984; Nietupski, Welch, & Wacker, 1983; Smeets & Kleinloog, 1980; Storey, Bates, & Hanson, 1984; Wheeler, Ford, Nietupski, Loomis, & Brown, 1980). Finally, studies have demonstrated the successful teaching of laundromat skills to students with severe handicaps (McDonnell & McFarland, 1988; Morrow & Bates, 1987).

In order for students to acquire the skills necessary to interact with a variety of people, opportunities for interactions must be provided. Community environments offer numerous and varied opportunities for interactions. Students must learn to interact not just with family members, their peers, and school personnel, but also with the grocery store clerk, the fast food restaurant cashier, and the public transportation bus driver, among numerous other individuals. Without the chance to be taught directly within a variety of community environments, students are unlikely to acquire such interaction skills.

Although much more research is needed to assist in the determination of specific instructional procedures necessary for a given student within community environments, existing research raises the expectations for students with severe handicaps within community environments. In addition to research findings, the characteristics of community environments—that is, the stimulus dimensions present—must be used for direct instruction, since students with severe handicaps exhibit difficulty in generalizing skills across stimulus dimensions.

GENERAL CASE PROGRAMMING

When teaching takes place in the environments where the skills naturally occur, the difficulties in generalizing skills from simulated to natural environments are minimized. Community environments frequented by the student and by his or her family now and in the future should be the environments used to directly teach. Students taught in artificial environments (for instance, a simulated grocery store) to perform skills that appear to be functional have, in reality, not been taught to perform functional skills. For students who have difficulty with the generalization of skills, a skill can only be functional if it is taught in the environments where it naturally occurs. By directly teaching in community environments, educators and parents make no inferences about skill generalization across stimulus dimensions from artificial or simulated to natural environments (Brown et al., 1979). Horner, Sprague, and Wilcox (1982) presented a strategy for teaching skills that would most likely generalize across environments. This procedure is referred to as General Case Programming and consists of specific strategies for educators and parents to identify the specific community environments that will be used for direct instruction and that will most likely result in the student being able to generalize the skills (perform them in other community environments that were not directly taught). For instance, the specific steps for applying general case programming to street crossing, as presented by Willliams and Horner (1984), are as follows:

1. Defining the Instructional Universe (i.e., specifying all the streets that the student will be expected to cross after the student has been trained)

2. Selecting the streets that will be trained (include streets that contain the stimulus dimensions present in the student's instructional universe)
3. Conducting the training and collecting the data reflecting the student's performance
4. Modifying the instruction based upon an analysis of the "error patterns"
5. Training street crossing under exceptional traffic conditions (e.g., emergency vehicles with sirens, malfunctioning traffic signals)
6. Determining when to stop training based upon verification of the student's performance on nontrained streets

Specific information regarding the stimulus dimensions present in community environments must be incorporated into instructional programs. Following is a discussion of some of the stimulus dimensions that should be thoroughly identified and directly used to teach skills in community environments.

Stimulus Dimensions

The stimulus dimensions that are present and that direct us to perform skills in specific environments and at specific times have been referred to as *natural cues and corrections* (Falvey, Brown, Lyon, Baumgart, & Schroeder, 1980). In addition to learning to perform the skills in natural environments, students must be taught to perform those skills at the appropriate times and in the presence of the appropriate cues, people, and materials. Learning the motor skills to walk or move a wheelchair across a street are relatively easy skills to teach, as compared to teaching the student when it is "safe" to cross the street. The natural cues and corrections for performing a skill such as street crossing are numerous—for example, lights, walk signs, presence or absence of cars, presence or absence of emergency vehicles with sirens and/or lights, or traffic police directing cars and pedestrians. Without the opportunity to directly and frequently teach students to respond to the natural cues and corrections in their natural environments, students are likely to be denied entrance and access to those environments.

In order for students to acquire the skills necessary to function in a variety of community environments, the effects of natural consequences on a student's behavior must be taught. Although initially teaching a skill might include the use of contrived or artificial reinforcers, those reinforcers must be faded as the student becomes more proficient at performing the skill. In order for students to become active and participating members of a community, they must be systematically taught the natural consequences of acceptable and unacceptable behaviors. Those consequences are best taught where they would naturally occur, that is, within community environments.

In order to teach students the motor, visual, auditory, and other components of activities within a variety of community environments, materials natural to those environments must be used. For example, to teach students to deposit their paychecks in a bank, the specific bank deposit slips for that bank should be employed during instruction. In addition, when teaching students to perform the skills to purchase items, real money or other appropriate exchanges (e.g., credit cards, checks) must be used. Furthermore, when teaching students the motor components of using grocery carts, actual grocery carts and store aisles should be used. Finally, when teaching students to independently eat a meal at a fast food restaurant, the actual utensils, condiment containers, and other materials should be used. Without actually utilizing community environments for direct instruction, educators and parents might overlook teaching students to use natural materials.

COMMUNITY TRAINING ISSUES/LOGISTICS

In order to design and develop frequent, comprehensive, and direct instruction within a variety of community environments, several practical and logistical issues need to be resolved as educators examine and modify the services provided to students with severe handicaps. Each local school and/or school district must address these issues individually in order to establish the necessary policies and procedures that will allow for safe and responsible instruction to occur within their communities. These issues offer new challenges for school personnel, parents, and community members. This section contains a description of some of the most salient issues and challenges for community training, as well as suggested strategies for resolving those issues and challenges.

Funding

Fiscal support for community training is essential for a program to sustain itself. The information regarding the cost of community training programs from local school districts suggests that it does not cost more money to operate these programs than classroom-based programs. However, creative methods and procedures are required for allocating the money necessary to operate these programs (Hamre-Nietupski, Nietupski, Bates, & Maurer, 1982). In many instances, funds are necessary to cover the expenses for transportation, whether the transportation is provided by public transit, private cars, or school vehicles. Funds are also needed to allow participation in a variety of community activities, such as eating at a restaurant, making a purchase at a grocery store, or using the local YWCA or YMCA. In order to provide students with opportunities to learn to respond to natural cues and corrections, to use natural materials, and to respond appropriately to natural consequences, real money must be used, even during instructional periods. Numerous strategies for financing community training have been developed by educators, parents, and community members. Following are some of those strategies:

1. Develop procedures with the business/accounting departments within the school districts to redirect monies traditionally used for instructional supplies, equipment, petty cash, and other funds to be used instead for com-

munity training. Methods for securing monies before the training occurs, or for reimbursing personnel for any out-of-pocket expenditures for training, must be developed and systematized.

2. Recruit contributions from student body funds, parents, parent organizations, service organizations (e.g., Kiwanis Club or Lions Club) for community training.
3. Organize parents, school personnel, and/or community members or clubs to hold fund-raising activities to raise money for community training.
4. Organize school personnel and/or nonhandicapped students to assist in fund-raising activities in which the students with severe handicaps are actively involved and are learning vocational skills (e.g., bake sales, car washes, selling breakfast or lunch to school personnel and/or the student body).
5. Request that the student and his or her family develop shopping lists based upon items needed at home, with the family supplying the money for the purchases.
6. Recruit school personnel, members of the community who are confined to their homes, and others who are willing to have the student make needed purchases for them with monies provided by the recruited persons (Hamre-Nietupski et al., 1982).
7. Use money, if available, for individual student lunches or lunch programs to purchase necessary groceries to prepare lunches.
8. Use reduced fares or "no-charge bus passes" for public transit.
9. Offer a shopping service to staff wherein the students receive a list (pictorial if necessary) of the item(s) needed by a staff member and also the money necessary to purchase the item(s).

Staffing Needs

Implementing educational programs within a variety of community environments usually requires educators to develop student/staff ratios and schedules that vary from those typically used in traditional classroom-based programs. Each program must develop an individualized schedule reflecting the needs of the students, the community environments that need to be used for instruction, the available staff, the additional resources required, and the strategies for acquiring such additional resources. Although research is not yet available to provide guidelines for determining the student/staff ratios necessary for community instruction, many educators have reported that a ratio of one adult to two to four students allows for appropriate instruction to occur (Hamre-Nietupski et al., 1982). Since many classrooms are not staffed with such an adult/student ratio, creative strategies must be developed in order to provide community training in the appropriate manner. Infrequent trips to the community with large numbers of students with severe handicaps, that is, more than four students at a time, would result in the creation of an artificial environment, since the presence of numerous students would change the stimulus dimensions within those environments. In addition, large numbers of students, whether they have handicaps or not, are often overwhelming to business owners, commuters on public transportation, and other community members. A variety of strategies should be considered when developing individualized schedules aimed at achieving appropriate student/staff ratios for community training. Following are some of those strategies:

1. Use a cooperative or team-teaching approach with other teachers. Work with the teachers in the team arrangement to program for all the students, utilizing all the available resources across all the classrooms. In addition, if teacher certification is necessary for supervising students, sharing the supervision across teachers can allow more flexibility. For example, one teacher can be in the community with two appropriately sized groups of students and a volunteer, while the rest of the students can remain in the school with the aide under the supervision of the teacher in the team arrangement.
2. Use support personnel (e.g., speech therapists, occupational or physical therapists, psychologists, administrators, nurses, social workers, physical education teachers) to participate in the community training program. These support personnel can be directed to implement the goals and objectives established by them in their speciality areas. For example, a speech therapist might work with a group of students in the community to teach communication skills, instead of working with them in the classroom or clinical therapy room. Teaching communication skills as well as other skills within the context of where they would naturally occur would decrease the difficulties students are likely to have in generalizing communication skills from artificial to natural environments.
3. Use volunteers to assist in the implementation of a community-based program. Volunteers might be recruited from the following sources: parents, nonhandicapped students, service organizations, university and college programs, or senior citizens (e.g., Foster Grandparent Program). These volunteers must be systematically trained to provide the necessary teaching procedures and to implement those procedures in a safe and ethical manner. Volunteers must be familiar with the student and with his or her strengths and deficiencies in order to implement such a program.
4. If teacher certification is necessary for direct supervision, aides and volunteers can assume the responsibility for directly teaching a small group of students far enough away from the teacher so as to not create a large group, but close enough so that if an emergency arises the teacher can intervene. For example, a teacher teaching four students to shop at a grocery store might have an aide in the same store teaching three other students to shop for different items; the teacher would interact only with the students in his

specific group. The teacher is there in case of an emergency, but he is interacting only with the students in his group.

5. Use environments that can serve multiple purposes. For example, a grocery store can be used to teach a group to purchase a loaf of bread, while another group is working on the vocational skills of returning the grocery carts from the parking lot to the store, and still another group is learning to order lunch from the fast food counter in the grocery store.
6. Create classes of students with heterogeneous needs so that no single class is overwhelmed. This is particularly important for students in wheelchairs or for students with severe behavior problems. Establishing heterogeneous groupings of students will allow for more flexibility in staffing arrangements and assignments, and will provide the opportunity for students to learn from each other.
7. Nonhandicapped peers can be available for supervising students and/or directly participating in community training. Once these peers have been trained and their permission and their parents' permission have been secured, they can serve as tutors or peers in a community training.

Liability

Providing instruction across a variety of environments requires that educators develop specific policies and procedures that will enable them to implement their programs in a safe and resonsible manner. Often, the issue of liability—that is, who is responsible for injury or property damage when students are involved in community training—is a major challenge in the development and implementation of a community training program. Liability issues must be dealt with, and policies and procedures must be developed in order to ensure adequate insurance protection for students, staff members, school districts, local businesses, and local city governments. Negligence is the major reason that a school district would be found liable in the case of an accident or incident. Negligence is simply the absence of reasonable policies/procedures, actions, and behaviors that reflect common sense safety decisions. The determination of what constitutes adequate coverage usually entails, first of all, conducting a comprehensive analysis of existing school policies and procedures. Although community training should not be viewed as a "field trip" in the traditional sense, existing school district field trip policies and procedures frequently provide adequate insurance protection for community training activities. If such protection is not present or is not sufficient, educators, parents, board of education members, community members, and other concerned individuals must determine the revisions necessary for the protection of all groups when conducting community training. In addition, the following strategies can be employed to develop community training programs with the appropriate insurance protection:

1. Contact other school districts providing community training, particularly those of a similar size and extent of services to determine the coverage provided for community training.
2. Involve parents in every aspect of developing and implementing a community training program. Secure written parental permission for all community training experiences. Be sure parents are informed about the purpose and need for community training.
3. Develop individualized education program (IEP) goals and objectives that reflect the skills necessary to function in various community environments. Since the IEP should dictate the services provided for a given student, those goals and objectives can serve as a guarantee for community training.
4. Encourage the school board (or board of directors) to adopt community training as the curriculum/program strategy that will be used for teaching students.
5. Arrange for administrators to contact the school district liability insurance carrier to discuss community-based training and current liability coverage. Generally, the liability coverage for a school is sufficient, although if additional coverage is needed, such coverage should be obtained (Nietupski, Hamre-Nietupski, Donder, Houselog, & Anderson, 1988).
6. Ensure that staff involved in providing training in the community are provided with CPR and first aid training in case of a medical emergency (Nietupski et al., 1988).

Community Access

In order to teach students to perform the variety of skills required across community environments, direct instruction must occur in those environments. Access to those environments is a critical consideration when determining which community environment skills to teach directly. At least two types of accessibility must be considered when conducting ecological inventories of community environments: attitudinal accessibility and physical accessibility. Attitudinal accessibility refers to environments containing persons who are supportive of, or at least not opposed to, the concept of training students with severe handicaps in their businesses, on their buses, in their parks, and so forth. It has been demonstrated that peoples' attitudes will be positively influenced once they have had the opportunity to observe not only a program in operation but the students acquiring new skills in the community, and the responsibility assumed by school personnel. However, when identifying initial community training environments, those environments where attitudinal barriers do not exist or are not likely to interfere with the success of the program should be considered. Environments characterized by physical accessibility are those in which substantial physical barriers are not present or are sufficiently minor that no obstacles are posed for students with disabilities. Thus, initial consideration should be given to environments where substantial physical barriers are not present or where they can easily be eliminated. In addition to accessibility, the following issues should be considered when determining community environments for teaching:

1. Environments that are frequented by the student and by his or her family
2. Environments that would be frequented by the student and by his or her family if the student acquired the skills necessary to participate in those environments
3. Environments that are frequented by nonhandicapped peers
4. Environments preferred by the student and by his or her family
5. Environments that involve skills that would be requirements preferred by the student and by his or her family
6. Environments that involve skills that would be required in the largest number of other community environments
7. Environments that would be accessible to the student during nonschool hours

Figure 5.1 provides an example of an ecological inventory demonstrating the large assortment of activities and skills that can be taught across several environments.

Administrative, Teacher, and Parental Support

Support and understanding of the purpose and need for community training from various people is particularly important in the development and maintenance of community-based educational programs. Specifically, support from administrators (including board of education members), from other teachers, and from parents is critical. Administrators who understand and support the program can, for example, facilitate the implementation, establish the logistics, investigate and obtain liability coverage, and identify and secure fiscal support. Other teachers can, for example, assist in the implementation by team teaching, by systematically teaching, or by verifying generalization of community-based skills. They can also assist by following up and enhancing the students' community mobility and independence the year after the training. Parents can aid in the implementation by helping to determine the functional skills that should be taught, by providing other essential input regarding how and what their son or daughter can learn, or by recruiting additional assistance for community training. Some of the strategies for securing support for community-based programs from administrators, teachers, and parents are listed as follows:

1. Assume the responsibility to inform administrators, teachers, and parents about the program. Do not assume they understand the purpose or program components.

Student's name ______________________

Beginning date ______________________

DOMAIN: Community

ENVIRONMENT: Alpha Beta Grocery Store

SUBENVIRONMENT: Front of store									
Activity 1: Entering door									
1. Walks to front of store									
2. Identifies "in" door (welcome)									
3. Steps on door mat									
4. Waits for door to open									
5. Walks into store									
SUBENVIRONMENT: Inside foyer of store									
Activity 1: Entering body/main part of store									
1. Locates turn style									
2. Walks to turn style									
3. Puts hand on turn style stick									
4. Pushes turn style stick forward and takes a step									
5. Walks through turn style									
SUBENVIRONMENT: Inside store									
Activity 1: Getting a basket									
1. Locates baskets									
2. Walks over to baskets									
3. Selects a basket									
4. Holds handle of first basket with one hand and puts one hand on second basket									
5. Pulls first basket away from second basket until separated									
6. Turns basket around in direction to head in									
7. Uses two hands to push cart									
Activity 2: Pushing a basket									
1. Pushes cart with two hands									

(*continued*)

Figure 5.1. Ecological inventory.

SUBENVIRONMENT: Inside store *(continued)*									
Activity 2: Pushing a basket *(continued)*									
2. Guides cart through clear paths									
3. Looks for other paths if one is cluttered									
4. Waits for another cart to pass									
5. Pushes cart to side when looking for item									
6. Pushes cart to avoid hitting stacked items									
Activity 3: Observation of store environment									
1. Looks around the store									
2. Names various items pointed to									
3. Classifies products (vegetables, fruits, meat, etc.) in groups									
4. Identifies and names people									
5. Identifies checkstand									
Activity 4: Shopping									
1. Takes out shopping list/cue card wallet									
2. Looks at item(s) to buy									
3. Walks up and down the aisles while looking for item									
4. Stops in aisle where item is									
5. Scans the shelves for item									
6. Picks out item									
7. Puts item in basket									
8. Looks for next item									
9. Pushes cart to next aisle									
10. Pushes cart to checkstand									
Activity 5: Checkstand									
1. Locates checkstand									
2. Pushes cart over to line with less people									
3. Pushes cart behind last person									
4. Stands behind basket									
5. Moves up with the line									

(continued)

SUBENVIRONMENT: Inside store *(continued)*									
Activity 5: Checkstand *(continued)*									
6. Pushes cart into checkstand									
7. Places items on counter									
8. Leaves item with checker									
9. Moves to middle of counter									
Activity 6: At check register									
1. Greets cashier									
2. Gets money ready (take out of purse or wallet)									
3. Looks at items being checked while waiting									
4. Watches register for price verification									
5. Listens for price (total) from checker									
6. Gives money to checker									
7. Holds hand out									
8. Waits for change and/or receipt									
9. Puts money away									
10. Grabs bag									
11. Thanks, says good-bye to checker									
SUBENVIRONMENT: Foyer of store									
Activity 1: Walks out → Exit									
1. Locates exit									
2. Identifies "out" door (thanks for shopping)									
3. Steps on door mat									
4. Waits for door to open									
5. Walks out door									

2. Reinforce and show genuine enthusiasm when these individuals become involved in the program, even if only minimally.
3. Make arrangements for them to visit the program, particularly when conducting actual community training.
4. Make arrangements for them to visit other programs that provide exemplary community training and to discuss with other administrators, teachers, and parents their attitudes toward the program.
5. Make presentations, both formal and informal, to teacher groups, admin-

istrator groups, parent groups, and at professional meetings regarding the community training program.

6. Keep everyone informed of when and where community training will occur. Send notices home, post announcements on classroom doors, include the community training schedule in the school or district newsletter, and inform office staff and others of specific training schedules.
7. Be sure the students' IEP goals and objectives include the community participation and mobility skills that need to be taught.
8. Become familiar with school district policy and initially develop the specific program components and characteristics consistent with current policy. If it is necessary to include program components or characteristics that are inconsistent with district policy, be sure to actively and rapidly work toward the needed changes in policy.

In addition to securing the support of administrators, other teachers, and parents for community training, it is essential to maintain such support. Several strategies have been delineated below that can be used to maintain administrative, teacher, and parental support:

1. Be sure the administration (including the school secretary), other staff, and parents are informed about with whom, where, when, and how the community training will occur. A schedule identifying this information can be left with the school office, given to parents, and posted on the classroom door.
2. Input by administrators, by other teachers, and by parents should be solicited for community environments appropriate for training. Not only will they feel more involved, but they can suggest appropriate training environments not previously identified.
3. All reports, including IEPs, assessment findings, and memorandums to parents, administration, or other teachers must be professionally prepared and presented.

Safety

In order to develop and implement educational programs for students with severe handicaps within a variety of community environments, a number of safety issues must be considered. Safety procedures must be established in order to maximize students' participation and minimize the risks within the community training program. Procedures must be developed that minimize the risks for the students as well as the school personnel and school district. Students must be systematically taught, and their ability to function safely within community environments must be continually assessed. Educational programs should ensure that while students are participating in community training programs at least the following preparations are made:

1. Designate who will have which responsibilities.
2. Designate who should be telephoned at school in case of an emergency.
3. Carry first aid materials on all community trainings and have all staff experienced in administering first aid.
4. Have each student carry an identification card containing his or her name, the name and telephone number of the school, and the names and telephone numbers of the student's parents.
5. Have the teachers carry copies of the students' emergency cards containing the students' doctors' names and telephone numbers, current medications, and telephone numbers of local paramedics and police.
6. Have the students and staff carry enough change in case a need arises to make an emergency phone call.
7. Develop a detailed information form with a current photograph for each student so if an emergency arose, or a student became lost, a detailed description could be provided to law enforcement officials immediately. The list below represents the minimum information that should be on file in an easily accessible setting in case of an emergency:
   a. Name
   b. Date of birth
   c. Social Security number
   d. Height
   e. Weight
   f. Hair color
   g. Eye color
   h. Skin tone
   i. Nationality
   j. Communication mode(s)
   k. Student's current schedule
   l. Home address
   m. Home telephone number
   n. Home contact person
   o. Emergency telephone numbers
   p. Relevant medical information
8. Contact local law enforcement agencies to inform them of the community aspect of the program so they have some understanding of why school-age children are not at school during the day. In addition, this contact should include a description of the students and their needs.

For an example of a student's identification card (see Item 4), refer to Figure 5.2. For an example of an emergency card, see Figure 5.3. Before moving into community environments, educators should notify the school office regarding the upcoming community training. Specifically, they should inform the

I am in a community training program with the ______________________
School District. I may need assistance to dial an emergency number.
Name ____
School Number ______________________________________
Home Number _______________________________________

Figure 5.2. Student identification card.

office staff who will be participating (including students and staff), and what the exact locations will be, along with approximate times of arrival and departure. Regarding those students remaining at school, educators should inform the school office what their activities will be and who will be responsible for them.

If a student becomes ill or injured in the community, there are several steps that educators should take. Specifically:

1. Assess the student's medical situation.
2. Provide necessary first aid.
3. Send someone to call paramedics, if necessary. If possible, *do not* leave the student unattended.
4. Send someone to call the school to receive back-up assistance for other students, if necessary.
5. Document all events and activities, as well as time, people present, and setting.
6. Remain calm at all times.
7. If necessary, provide paramedics and hospital employees with the student's emergency card.
8. Be sure the student's parents have been contacted (particularly if the student is a minor).

Name ______________________ Medication ______________
Address ____________________ ______________________
__________________________ Allergic reactions
Birthdate ___________________ ______________________
Parents/guardian _____________ ______________________
Work # _____________________ Social Security #
Physician ___________________ ______________________
Phone # ____________________
In case parents/guardians are unavailable whom can we contact
Name ______________________ Phone # ________________

Figure 5.3. Emergency card.

Mobility

Providing instruction in various community environments requires that decisions be made on current as well as subsequent mobility needs of the students. School buses can be a convenient, accessible solution for immediate community training. However, the end goal of community training is maximum participation and independent community utilization; therefore, it is essential that students be afforded the opportunity to learn to use transportation that will be available once they have graduated from the school program. Following are suggested and appropriate transportation modes that are often available for students participating in community training programs:

1. Walking and/or using wheelchairs
2. Bicycling
3. Public bus lines
4. "Dial-a-Ride" or other specialized transportation
5. Taxis
6. Carpooling

If independent community mobility skills have not been identified as a priority for a given student, the following transportation modes might be considered:

1. District vehicles (e.g., career education buses, driver education vehicles, school maintenance trucks, school buses or vans)
2. Cars or vans purchased through fund raising or through donations for community training purposes
3. Arrangements with school transportation to drop off and pick up the students at community training locations instead of school
4. Private vehicles owned by teachers, parents, or volunteers (be sure to use these vehicles in accord with district policy and carry the appropriate amount and type of insurance.)
5. Other transportation resources made available by other agencies (e.g., local Association for Retarded Citizens [ARC], local Department of Rehabilitation)

Specific strategies for mobility training should be employed when teaching a student to travel around in his or her community. Once the available mode of transportation appropriate for a student has been identified, assessment of that student's current level of participation must be conducted. The skill sequences listed below can be used when determining a student's ability to walk in the community. (Note that walking can be substituted for ambulating a wheelchair in the following listing.)

1. Walks in the direction intended
2. Slows walking at driveways to check for traffic

3. Stops at driveways if traffic is present
4. Stops at intersections and responds appropriately to safe street cues (e.g., waits if there is a red light, a "Don't Walk" sign, or if cars are present; walks across the street if there is a green light, a "Walk" sign, or if no moving cars are present). Specifically, determine whether the student responds appropriately to:
   a. Red/yellow/green lights
   b. "Walk"/"Don't Walk" signs
   c. Presence or absence of moving cars
   d. Traffic director (police, school guard, etc.)
   e. Presence of an emergency vehicle (i.e., ambulance, fire engine, police car)
5. Continues to check for cars while crossing the street and responds appropriately when one appears
6. Stops at desired destination

In addition, the use of public transportation (e.g., buses, taxis, trains) would be an appropriate mobility skill to teach students in those communities where such transportation is available. The skill sequence listed below can be used when determining a student's bus transportation skills:

1. Determines which bus to take and which bus stop location to use in order to get to desired location
2. Goes to desired bus stop at appropriate time
3. Waits appropriately at bus stop (e.g., sitting/standing appropriately)
4. Takes out bus pass/money as bus approaches
5. Boards correct bus
6. Shows bus pass to driver or puts bus money in correct slot
7. Requests transfer if needed
8. Sits in an empty seat; sits appropriately in bus
9. Looks for landmarks to identify destination
10. Locates landmarks and rings buzzer
11. Once bus has stopped moving, disembarks bus

In order to learn the skills to independently move around one's community, students need to be given opportunities to be independent. The opportunity should only be given once the student has been observed exercising the safety skills required in the community.

STRATEGIES FOR COMMUNITY TRAINING

In order to design, develop, and implement a chronological age–appropriate community training program, educators and parents must consider a number of factors, particularly, the student's chronological age. Figure 5.4 provides exam-

Environments	Activities			
	Preschool	Elementary	Adolescent	Adult
Bob's Big Boy Restaurant	Look at pictures in "children's" menu	Read "children's" menu	Read "regular" menu	Read "regular" menu
Sears, Roebuck and Company store	Go to Children's Department with Dad Observe Dad purchasing "E.T." tee shirt for self	Go to Children's Department with Dad Purchase toy with Dad	Go to Juniors' Department alone or with friend Purchase blue jeans	Go to Woman's department alone or with a friend Purchase blouse
Grocery store	Ride in pushcart	Purchase gum ball from gum ball machine	Purchase milk, bread, and orange juice	Purchase weekly groceries

Figure 5.4. Inventory of community environments and activities appropriate for training across ages.

ples of environments and activities appropriate for training across a variety of environments and ages.

Each school and/or school district must develop a community training program that consists of environments and activities that reflect the community the students reside in, the current and subsequent needs of the students and of their families, and the most efficient and effective use of available resources.

How to Get Started

This chapter includes a great deal of information on developing and implementing a community-based program for students with severe handicaps. The following sequence represents the basic steps to initiate such a program:

1. Develop a proposal for administrators addressing all logistics previously identified.
2. Secure administrative support.
3. Host a meeting for parents to discuss community-based programs and secure input and support.
4. Conduct ecological inventories.
5. Conduct specific student, parent/significant other inventories (see Chapter 3, this volume, for an example of a parent/significant other inventory).
6. Conduct student repertoire inventories of those specific activities identified by the parent/significant other and/or student.
7. Revise or develop an IEP that reflects functional and chronological age-appropriate goals to be taught in integrated community settings.
8. Develop an emergency procedure for the specific community that considers available staff, the specific behavioral/medical needs of students, and the characteristics of the community.
9. Identify environments, times, students, and staff for community training.
10. Secure permission from parents for specific community instruction.
11. Develop specific lesson plans for each community training.
12. GO FOR IT!!!!

Adaptations

If a student is unable to acquire and perform skills to participate in activities within community environments, that student should *not* be excluded from those environments. Adaptations can be developed to assist a student to participate in or perform activities that occur within community environments. Adaptations might be developed to assist a student in the performance of activities that involve motor skills, mathematics, reading, verbal communication, or other skills.

Since some students might not be able to acquire the complex mathematics, reading, verbal communication, or motor skills necessary to participate in a variety of community environments, individualized adaptations can be developed. Table 5.1 provides examples of adaptations that might be used to assist a student in the performance of skills required in various community environments.

Ongoing Monitoring of Community Programs

In order to effectively create and develop community-based training programs and to monitor the success of these programs and the resulting student progress, systematic data collection must be designed and instituted. Data collection procedures must allow for the collection of data reflecting specific behaviors targeted for a given student. For example, when collecting data regarding a student's ability to cross various streets in response to the natural cues, the data collected must include a delineation of the skills necessary to perform the street

Table 5.1. Examples of adaptations that might be used in teaching skills required in various community environments

Domain: Community	
Environment: Grocery store	
Activities	Possible adaptation(s)
1. Using grocery shopping list	Picture shopping lists
2. Determining if there is enough money for groceries.	Calculators
3. Pushing grocery cart	Adapted carts provided by some grocery stores for accessibility with wheelchair
4. Obtaining items out of reach	Asking for assistance; using a broomstick handle with clamp attached
5. Requesting assistance	Communication books/boards with pictures or words representing vocabulary needed in grocery stores
Environment: Video arcade	
Activities	Possible adaptation(s)
1. Determining correct change or token(s) needed to activate video machines	Cards containing pictures of actual money or token(s) needed (student matches amount needed by placing money or token[s] on top of picture indicating correct amount)
2. Following written sequence for playing video game	Cards containing pictures of sequence needed to activate video game
3. Verbally interacting with peers	Communication books/boards with pictures or words representing vocabulary needed in video arcades
Environment: Fast food restaurants	
Activities	Possible adaptation(s)
1. Ordering food	Picture and/or word cards indicating desired order based upon food items available
2. Paying for food	Using $5, which should cover the cost of a "typical meal"
3. Locating correct restroom	Picture and/or word card indicating sign for correct restroom door

crossing, and of the natural cues available at the various types of streets the student is learning to cross. Figure 5.5 provides an example of such a data collection procedure.

When designing data collection procedures within community environments, several issues should be considered. First, the data collection procedures should be acceptable to the general community. For example, when collecting data regarding students' abilities to function within a shopping center, a teacher was stopped by security guards and questioned. The shopping center had outlawed the use of political petitions on the premises, and the security guards thought that the clipboards the teachers were carrying to record the data were politically related petitions. Once the purpose of the program was explained to the security guards and the teachers modified their data collection procedures, there were no problems with teaching in that shopping center. The modifications adopted by the teachers included: omitting the use of clipboards, since most people do not walk around shopping centers with clipboards; splitting up the groups of students so that their numbers were not overwhelming to the shoppers and business owners; developing data collection procedures that involved recording the most essential information on 3″ × 5″ cards that were carried in the teachers' pockets.

A second issue to keep in mind when designing data collection procedures is that data should be collected across environments and analyzed in terms of the various demands and stimulus dimensions that exist in these environments. In order to develop a comprehensive program, skills should be targeted and reinforced across the array of environments in which the student functions.

Third, since community training is likely to involve the use of volunteers, other teachers, teachers' aides, and support staff, the data collection procedure must be understood by all persons collecting data. The objectives for each student, the coding system to be used to record the students' responses, and the time when the data should be collected must be clearly stated and understood by all those who will collect the data.

Another consideration when attempting to maintain a community training program over time is to develop a task force of teachers, parents, administrators, and others as appropriate, who can assist in the development, maintenance, expansion, and modification of the community training program. Such a task force would meet regularly or when issues or challenges are raised. They would create or modify policies and procedures, share strategies and information, and alleviate fear on the part of those persons who are apprehensive of a community program.

SUMMARY

This chapter includes a rationale for developing and implementing community-based educational programs. Strategies for developing and maintaining such

Scoring: 1 = Physical
2 = Modeling
3 = Direct verbal
4 = Indirect verbal
5 = Gesture
6 = Independently

Name: ____________________
Date: ____________________

Ordering								
1. Locate entrance door.								
2. Read "pull" sign and open door.								
3. Locate end of line.								
4. Get in line.								
5. Move up in line.								
6. Wait for clerk to look/ask for order.								
7. Tell clerk your order.								
8. Ask for ketchup, salt, and so on.								
9. Use communication cards (if necessary).								
10. Listen for clerk to give price/total.								
11. Get wallet from pocket/purse.								
12. Take money from wallet/purse.								
13. Give money to clerk.								
14. Wait for your change.								
15. Put money left back in wallet/purse.								
16. Step to side (letting others order).								
17. Put wallet in pocket/purse.								
18. Wait for food ordered.								
19. Go to door and push open.								
20. Watch for cars coming.								
21. Walk to patio.								
22. Find an empty seat.								
23. Sit down and eat quietly.								
24. After eating, remove all trash.								
25. Pick up papers and put in trash (if wind blows them away).								

Comments:

Figure 5.5. Sample data sheet for evaluating a student's skills at McDonald's Restaurant.

programs are included. Since providing instruction in the community can be viewed as risky, emergency procedures and other safeguards are addressed, and examples are provided. Sample data collection instruments and activity lists are also included.

REFERENCES

Brown, L., Branston, M. B., Hamre-Nietupski, S., Pumpian, I., Certo, N., & Gruenewald, L. (1979). A strategy for developing chronological age appropriate and functional curricular content for severely handicapped adolescents and young adults. *Journal of Special Education*, *13*(1), 81–90.

Coon, M. E., Vogelsberg, T., & Williams, W. (1981). Effects of classroom public transportation instruction on generalization to the natural environment. *Journal of The Association for the Severely Handicapped*, *6*(2), 46–53.

Falvey, M., Brown, L., Lyon, S., Baumgart, D., & Schroeder, J. (1980). Strategies for using cues and correction procedures. In W. Sailor, B. Wilcox, & L. Brown (Eds.), *Methods of instruction for severely handicapped students* (pp. 109–133). Baltimore: Paul H. Brookes Publishing Co.

Gaule, K., Nietupski, J., & Certo, N. (1985). Teaching supermarket shopping skills using an adaptive shopping list. *Education & Training of the Mentally Retarded*, *20*(1), 53–59.

Hamre-Nietupski, S., Nietupski, J., Bates, P., & Maurer, S. (1982). Implementing a community based educational model for moderately/severely handicapped students: Common problems and suggested solutions. *Journal of The Association for the Severely Handicapped*, *7*(4), 38–43.

Horner, R. H., Jones, D. N., & Williams, J. A. (1985). A functional approach to teaching generalized street crossing. *Education and Training of the Mentally Retarded*, *10*(2), 71–78.

Horner, R.H., Sprague, J., & Wilcox, B. (1982). General case programming for community activities. In B. Wilcox & G. T. Bellamy, *Design of high school programs for severely handicapped students*. Baltimore: Paul H. Brookes Publishing Co.

Marchetti, A. G., McCartney, J. R., Drain, S., Hooper, M., & Dix, J. (1983). Pedestrian skills training for mentally retarded adults: Comparison of training in two settings. *Mental Retardation*, *21*, 107–110.

Matson, J. L. (1980). A controlled group study of pedestrian-skill training for the mentally retarded. *Behavior Research and Therapy*, *18*, 99–106.

McDonnell, J. J., & Horner, R. H. (1985). Effects of in vivo simulation vs. in vivo training on the acquisition and generalization of grocery item selection by high school students with severe handicaps. *Analysis and Intervention in Developmental Disabilities*, *5*(4), 323–344.

McDonnell, J. J., Horner, R. H., & Williams, J. A. (1984). Comparison of three strategies for teaching generalized grocery purchasing to high school students with severe handicaps. *Journal of The Association for Persons with Severe Handicaps*, *9*(2), 123–133.

McDonnell, J.J., & McFarland, S. (1988). A comparison of forward and concurrent chaining strategies in teaching laundromat skills to students with severe handicaps. *Research in Developmental Disabilities*, *9*, 177–194.

Morrow, S.A., & Bates, P.E. (1987). The effectiveness of three sets of school-based instructional materials and community training on the acquisition and generalization of community laundry skills with students with severe handicaps. *Research in Developmental Disabilities*, *8*, 113–136.

Nietupski, J., Clancy, P., & Christiansen, C. (1984). Acquisition, maintenance and generalization of vending machine purchasing skills by moderately handicapped students. *Education and Training of the Mentally Retarded*, *19*(2), 91–96.

Nietupski, J., Hamre-Nietupski, S., Donder, D.J., Houselog, M., & Anderson, R.J. (1988). Proactive administrative strategies for implementing community-based programs for students with moderate/severe handicaps. *Education and Training in Mental Retardation*, *23*, 138–146.

Nietupski, J., Welch, J., & Wacker, D. (1983). Acquisition, maintenance, and transfer of grocery item purchasing skills by moderately and severely handicapped students. Education and Training of the Mentally Retarded, *18*(4) 279-286.

Page, T.J., Iwata, B.H., & Neef, N.A. (1976) Teaching pedestrian skills to retarded persons: Generalization from the classroom to the natural environment. *Journal of Applied Behavior Analysis*, *9*, 433–444.

Smeets, P.M., & Kleinloog, D. (1980). Teaching retarded women to use an experimental pocket calculator for making financial transactions. *Behavior Research of Severe Developmental Disabilities*, *1*, 1–20.

Sowers, J., Rusch, F.R., & Hudson, C. (1979). Training a severely retarded young adult to ride the city bus to and from work. *AAESPH Review*, *4*(1), 15–23.

Storey, K., Bates, P., & Hanson, H.B. (1984). Acquisition and generalization of coffee purchase skills by adults with severe disabilities. *Journal of The Association for Persons with Severe Handicaps*, *9*(3), 178–185.

Vogelsburg, R.T., & Rusch, F.R. (1979). Training severely handicapped students to cross partially controlled intersections. *AAESPH Review*, *4*(3), 264–273.

Welch, J., Nietupski, J., & Hamre-Nietupski, S. (1985). Teaching public transportation problem solving skills to young adults with moderate handicaps. *Education and Training of the Mentally Retarded*, *20*(4), 287–295.

Wheeler, J., Ford, A., Nietupski, J., Loomis, R., & Brown, L. (1980). Teaching moderately and severely handicapped adolescents to shop in supermarkets using pocket calculators. *Education and Training of the Mentally Retarded*, *15*, 105–111.

Williams, J.A., & Horner, R.H. (1984). *General case street crossing instructional package*. Unpublished manuscript, University of Oregon, Eugene.

SIX

DOMESTIC SKILLS

Lori Eshilian, Michele Haney, and Mary A. Falvey

SPECIAL EDUCATION PROGRAMS for students with severe handicaps have often included self-help skills training as a major focus of the overall curricula. The mechanical skills of dressing, grooming, toileting, self-feeding, and simple household chores have been the major emphasis of most self-help curricula. Although these self-help skills are most essential to developing independence for persons with severe handicaps, curricula in this area have traditionally been used to teach only a small portion of the skills needed to function within a variety of integrated domestic environments.

The "domestic domain" is the area of the curriculum that includes self-help and social-sexual skills, and encompasses home and neighborhood skills that are necessary for individuals to participate fully in all aspects of life. All students need to learn to care for their personal needs as independently as possible. All students also need to learn to function as part of a larger familial and societal unit. They have the right to live in a home of their liking, and to be a part of their home and neighborhood activities to the highest level possible. Those students who may always require a certain level of assistance have the right to establish the necessary level of interdependence with others of their choice. Education's basic goal should be to prepare students to handle the rights and responsibilties of adult life and to help individuals develop the interdependence that is necessary to maintain a high quality of life. For students with severe handicaps, this preparation is accomplished through direct instruction of skills within the domestic domain.

Teaching students to perform skills within their home and neighborhood environments—that is, skills within the domestic domain—is critical for several reasons. First, students' self-esteem is likely to increase the more independent they become in those environments. Their self-esteem also increases as they realize the rights and power they have for making decisions that affect their lives. Second, the development of age-appropriate social-sexual skills increases the likelihood for interactions with others in their personal lives, at work, and in their neighborhoods. Third, as the student's level of independence increases in the domestic domain, or as "interdependent support networks" are established, parent and family responsibilities are likely to be reduced (Meyer, McQuarter, & Kishi, 1985). When parental responsibilities are reduced, a more normalized process of "growing up" can occur for persons with severe handicaps. Fourth, since independence is valued in our society, students' abilities to perform independent living skills will likely result in more acceptance and interaction with the community. Finally, domestic skill acquisition, maintenance, and generalization can be developed into vocational or career opportunities (e.g., becoming a chambermaid at a hotel, a janitor, a dishwasher, or a receptionist).

The goal of a comprehensive domestic skills curriculum is to facilitate for students the acquisition of skills necessary to function within domestic environments and to become contributing members of their households and communities. Objectives identified within the domestic domain maximize the students' overall progress toward independence based upon the skills required to function in natural living environments familiar to the student. Objectives must reflect parental preferences and needs. The role played by parents, families, and care providers in developing and implementing the curriculum, for cultural and familial relevance, is a critical component of teaching domestic skills. Objectives must also look toward the future by anticipating the adult living arrangement that provides the level of independence and support needed by the individual. Most importantly, objectives must reflect the individual's choice for his or her priority areas of skill development and must reflect their plans for the future. This chapter provides strategies for developing, implementing, and evaluating an appropriate domestic skills curriculum. Both traditional and nontraditional aspects of a domestic skills curriculum are addressed; emphasis is placed on methods of establishing priorities and strategies for teaching in natural environments. Strategies for facilitating the involvement of the family are discussed, and ways for including the student in decision making and self-advocacy are outlined.

FAMILY INVOLVEMENT

Parents, families, and supported living staff should be encouraged to play an active role in the development of all areas of the curriculum, especially the area of domestic skills. Parents, family members, and significant others are generally the most familiar with the domestic skill proficiency of their sons or daughters. They are also aware of existing routines, potential new skills, and future living options, all of which are primary considerations when establishing priorities among the domestic skill areas to be taught. For this reason, issues and strategies related to facilitating active family and significant other involvement are delineated in this chapter. Chapter 2 of this volume provides a more comprehensive discussion of these and additional issues and strategies for parent and family involvement. (The term family will be used here to include parents, siblings, other family members, supported living staff and/or other significant others.) Following are several points that need to be considered:

1. It is important for educators to facilitate interaction with the family rather than to direct it, so that they develop the concept of "working with" rather than "working for" families. A number of strategies can be used to develop this involvement, including frequent meetings with the family both at school and in their home, telephone contact with them, and regular notes home that reflect positive feedback about their son or daughter, as well as occasional suggestions or areas of concern. When families identify concerns and problems, solutions should be generated with a sense of shared responsibility between school and home.
2. It is important to use a "Parent/Significant Other Inventory" as an assessment tool in determing the current level of functioning and in developing an appropriate individualized domestic skills curriculum. Chapter 3 of this volume delineates strategies and provides examples for developing a parent questionnaire and weekday/weekend schedules. Both the questionnaire and the weekday/weekend schedule are useful tools for obtaining valuable information and providing an opportunity for the family to actively establish priority domestic goals and objectives.
3. In the domestic domain, the identification of needs is often based upon skills necessary to function as a more independent member of the family unit. These needs may reflect both immediate and anticipated concerns (e.g., identification of skills the student will need for transition into adult environments). It is important to encourage families to look toward the future with optimism and realistic expectations.
4. In the domestic domain, it cannot be overemphasized that the educator must become familiar, through a program of family involvement, with the preferences, norms, and expectations that are specific to the student's culture. For example, consideration of special linguistic and cultural needs is relevant and necessary. When learning domestic skills, students should be taught the skills that are common in their homes. For example, a student from a Hispanic home might be taught to prepare quesadillas rather than grilled cheese sandwiches, while a student from a Chinese family might be taught to prepare rice rather than baked potatoes (if these are, in fact, fam-

ily preferences). Cultural practices must also be taken into consideration when instruction is being provided in the performance of household chores. For instance, some cultures do not view all household chores as being appropriately performed by both genders. Communication and social skills should also be developed in the student's native language and with culturally appropriate skills in mind so as to facilitate integration into the home and community. Domestic skills will be far more readily acquired and utilized if they have meaning and value in the student's culture and are supported in the home.

It is important that family involvement be sought from the beginning of the student's educational experience. (Figure 6.1 provides a sample parent/significant other questionnaire in the domestic domain.) Attempts to encourage this involvement, however, must be sensitive to the needs of the family. Meetings, for example, should be scheduled at times that are convenient for family members, rather than at times convenient to school personnel only. If necessary, transportation to school should be provided, and educators should be willing to hold meetings in the students' homes, particularly when seeking input for a domestic skills curriculum. When meetings outside the home are required, babysitting and other family needs should be identified and services and/or resources secured. A positive and caring attitude toward the family and their unique needs, and a belief in, and commitment to, family involvement in the educational process, are essential components in educating the student with severe handicaps.

NEIGHBORHOOD INTEGRATION AND LIVING ARRANGEMENT OPTIONS

Neighborhood integration refers to where and how persons with disabilities live, and the relationships they have with other people in their neighborhood. The strategy for achieving integrated neighborhoods is relatively simple: providing the student with severe handicaps the same options that are available to others in that neighborhood and community. The type of housing options available for persons with disabilities should reflect the types of options available in the community to anyone (e.g., owned or rented houses, apartments, duplexes, condos, townhouses).

Options for living arrangements are more varied: living with one's own family, relatives, or foster family, living alone, or living with a friend or compatible person of one's choice. In order to successfully participate in a safe, dignified, and active manner in any of the living arrangements identified above, hiring full- or part-time support may be necessary (Taylor, Biklen, & Knoll, 1987). Each of these represents a choice, not a continuum, of living arrangements. Variables that often affect the choice of one of these options are: age of the individual, family support system, domestic skill level, physical needs and/

Parent Questionnaire

1. What types of jobs does your son or daughter perform at home?
   For example: Making his or her bed
   Setting the table
   Watering the lawn
   Preparing a meal
   Raking leaves

2. Does your son or daughter have any jobs outside the home?

3. What jobs do the nonhandicapped siblings perform at home?

4. Does your son or daughter have any special hobbies or interests?

5. What types of responsibilities at home would you like your son or daughter to be able to perform?

6. In terms of feeding himself or herself, are there any skills you would like your son or daughter to learn?
   For example: Using a knife
   Cooking

7. What dressing skills would you like your son or daughter to learn?
   For example: Buttoning
   Caring for clothing

8. In terms of personal hygiene, what are the skills your son or daughter has now and what would you like him or her to learn?

9. What types of home recreational and leisure activities would you like your son or daughter to learn?

10. How does your son or daughter get along with other family members?

11. What skills would enable him or her to participate more in family activities?

12. What places do you think your son or daughter might go when he or she is older?

13. In the future, where do you see your son or daughter living?
    For example: Supervised apartment
    Group home

(continued)

Figure 6.1. Sample parent questionnaire for developing a domestic skills curriculum.

Parent Questionnaire
(continued)

14. What type of work do you think your son or daughter might do when he or she is older?

15. What activities does your son or daughter now enjoy that might lead to vocational preparation?

16. What skills and/or activities not already mentioned would you like your son or daughter to learn so that you don't always have to do them for him or her?

or personal preferences, and/or a local, state, and federal funding support system.

Relationships with other persons in one's neighborhood are based on longitudinal positive interactions. People develop friendships and aquaintances within their neighborhoods over months or years after seeing one another engage in functional daily routines (e.g., getting the mail or paper, watering the yard, taking walks, purchasing items from a neighborhood store). In order to establish these relationships, a person with disabilities must be visible in his or her community and must be competently involved in functional domestic activities.

For persons with severe handicaps, segregation out of neighborhoods, segregation within neighborhoods, and educational and adult programs and services that inadequately prepare individuals to participate fully in their homes and neighborhoods have served in the past as barriers to successful neighborhood integration. When neighborhood segregation occurs, persons with severe handicaps are not provided the opportunity to develop basic living or social skills that are relevant to their neighborhoods. In addition, other members of the neighborhood do not have an opportunity to recognize the positive qualities of each individual who has been segregated. The segregated group of persons with handicaps in a neighborhood soon becomes recognized for their disabilities and differences, rather than for their abilities and similarities. When persons with handicaps are placed together in large homogeneous groups within the community, neighborhood integration is extremely difficult to achieve.

Two critical goals of the domestic skills curriculum is to increase an individual's options for current or future living arrangements and to increase positive interaction within that individual's neighborhood. Such goals imply that it is important for educational programs to address the current and future domestic skill needs of each individual within his or her home and neighborhood. It is also critical for families and other support services and agencies to establish goals for ensuring individuals that their rights will be respected for living in homes of their choice, for living with persons and support systems of their choice, and for living within neighborhoods that allow them access to work, community resources, and social contact with friends and family.

DECISIONS, CHOICE MAKING, AND SELF-ADVOCACY

Lipsky and Gartner (1987) remind us that "choice-making is a characteristic of persons who society respects. . . . Failure to teach and provide for this in our educational programs is a function of our professional attitudes rather than of our student's disabilities" (p.70). Educational programs at all age levels and across all domains need to incorporate decision-making and self-advocacy skills into the curriculum, particularly within the domestic domain. Individuals may not always have control over the variables and options in the community or at work, but within their home they should have more power to direct and control their lives with the support of advocates of their choice. Table 6.1 provides a questionnaire that gives individuals with disabilities an opportunity to think about options and make choices that affect their domestic lives.

Freedom of choice is a basic human right. Such freedom, especially in the areas of living arrangements and social-sexual relationships, has been limited, or most often, nonexistent, for persons with severe handicaps. Obtaining the services and training needed to be more independent and productive members of the community increases one's freedom. It is also important to choose where to live, with whom to spend time, whom to love, with whom to live, whom to marry, and so on. Good choices do not happen by chance. It is imperative that persons with severe handicaps have the opportunity to acquire the skills necessary to make informed choices in this important area (WACSEP, 1984).

Allen (1988) points out that while systems need to provide advocates for persons with disabilities, the best "method of advocacy is self-advocacy" (p. 94). Educational programs can encourage students to develop decision-making strategies, to understand their options, and to gain a sense of control over their lives by incorporating the philosophy of self-advocacy into their curriculum. Allen (1988) outlines the following objectives for developing self-advocacy skills and increased independence:

1. *Control over the timing of events.* For example, choosing when to get up on the weekend, when to get a hair cut, or when to watch TV
2. *Making personal choices.* For example, choosing what clothes to buy, which cereal to eat, what friends to play with, or where to live.
3. *Choosing environments and methods of training.* For example, choosing to learn to make one's own bed, or learning to cook on an electric stove, and choosing who will provide that instruction.
4. *Opportunity to evaluate services and programs.* For example, being asked

Table 6.1. Sample questionnaire for developing self-advocacy for persons with disabilities (modified from Allen, 1988)

Home

Where do you live now: parent's home, own home/apartment, community care residence, other?
Where do you want to live now or in the future?
Whom do you live with?
Do you have your own room or share your room?
Do you like your roommate?
How do you get along with others in your home?
Whom do you want to live with now or in the future?
What domestic tasks do you need help with?
What domestic tasks would you like to learn?

Recreation/Leisure

What do you do for fun in your home or neighborhood?
What kinds of things would you like to do for fun?
Do you need more recreation and leisure skill training?
Where do your friends live?
How do you get to see your friends and how often?
Do you have relatives who live near you?
How do you get to see your relatives and how often?
Do you know your neighbors?
Do you have someone you can turn to in the neighborhood?

Financial

Are you currently receiving SSI, SSDI, other?
Who is the payee?
Do you have a guardian or conservator?
Do you work and receive a paycheck?
Do you participate in banking, budgeting, and spending of your money?
Do you currently have enough money for all your needs?
Do you have any financial concerns?

Advocacy

Do you need someone to be an advocate for you in your current home?
Do you need an advocate for future planning?
Do you need more information about life options?
Do you need more training: self-advocacy, sex education, independent mobility?
Do you get to make decisions for yourself in your current home?
Do you have any concerns currently or for the future?

if they like the staff where they live, or being listened to when they have a concern and seeing positive results derived from their evaluation.

5. *Involvement in the hiring of staff.* For example, if an individual needs an attendant for personal care during the school day, he/she should be given the opportunity to select that person.
6. *Attendance in all planning meetings.* For example, individuals with disabilities, at all ages, should attend all program planning meetings to assist in the development of appropriate goals and objectives.
7. *Opportunity for self-charting and self-monitoring.* For example, having a picture symbol calendar for scheduling self-care, chores, and planned activities.

8. *Receive assertiveness and self-advocacy training*. For example, joining a local chapter of People First, and/or being reinforced for speaking up for oneself.

TEACHING DOMESTIC SKILLS

Preparing students with severe handicaps to become participating and contributing members of their home environments requires that the family and educators work together to develop appropriate and systematic educational programs. Skill concepts to be addressed when developing plans in the domestic domain include: personal health care, home care and management, family relationships, human sexuality, and home leisure activities. The teaching of these critical skills must begin early in the life of the student with severe handicaps, and the sequencing of these skills must be developed systematically in response to the changing needs of the student and the home environment. In addition, domestic skills must be taught in natural domestic environments, that is, in the students' own homes and neighborhoods, to ensure that the students can utilize the skills being taught in the environments for which they are required. A number of issues and standards must be considered in the development and implementation of an appropriate domestic curriculum. The section following addresses these issues and standards, and provides strategies for generating a domestic skills curriculum.

Establishing Priorities among Curricular Content

Brown et al. (1979) have identified a list of 16 dimensions to be considered when developing and establishing priorities for curricular content. Of these, eight are considered particularly relevant to the development of domestic skills curricula (Pumpian, Livi, Falvey, Brown, & Loomis, 1980). First, *information and input from the student and his or her family* must be considered. This dimension was discussed earlier in this chapter, as well as in Chapter 2 of this volume, however, its importance bears reemphasizing. Input from a student and his or her family regarding the student's preferences, current skill repertoires within the home and neighborhood, current social skills, current levels of participation in domestic activities, plans for future domestic environments, and specific family cultural/linguistic considerations, provides important direction for choosing relevant curricular content.

The *functional nature of the skills* chosen must also be considered. This means that the skill must be relevant in the student's present and future domestic environments. The skill must be one that the student will need, and one that would otherwise have to be performed by someone else. For example, if the student does not acquire the skills necessary to dress him- or herself, someone else will have to do it. Choosing domestic skills that are functional in nature reduces some of the care responsibilities for the family and allows time for more positive interactions between family members and the student with severe handicaps.

The *number of current and subsequent environments* in which the skills are required must also be a consideration. The skills should have utility in other environments in addition to the present home environment. For example, vacuuming is a skill that is useful both at home and in vocational environments. Students can use leisure activities both within the home and in community or vocational environments (e.g., playing cards, sewing, baking).

Fourth, *skills that will be used a number of times* during a given day or week should be chosen over those that are used infrequently. Doing the laundry, for example, a skill that is used at least weekly, should be considered for teaching before learning to put up wallpaper, an activity that occurs more infrequently (unless, of course, putting up wallpaper is the student's career or job).

The *social significance of the skills* chosen is a particularly important consideration in the domestic skill domain. Good personal hygiene, appropriate social interaction skills, and cleanliness in home care can enhance the social acceptance of the student with severe handicaps. Being clean and well-groomed, making clothing choices appropriate to a given situation, maintaining basic standards in housecleaning, using appropriate social greetings, and expressing one's needs in a relationship, are but a few examples of domestic skills that enhance one's social status. In addition, students with severe handicaps need training to deal with interpersonal relationships and issues related to sexuality. The independence that results from learning functional and socially relevant domestic and interpersonal skills will enhance the overall quality of the interactions between the student with severe handicaps and others.

Consideration should be given to choosing skills that *minimize the potential for physical harm* to the student with severe handicaps. Students need to learn the proper use of appliances and materials with which they come in contact in their natural environments. Potential sources of danger within the natural domestic environments should be inventoried, and safety skills should be taught. Students also need to be taught awareness of danger within their work and community environments, and they should learn routine emergency procedures.

Another consideration is the *logistical and practical realities and complexities of a skill*. Skills that can be taught in other environments and generalized to the home should take precedence over those that can be taught (or used) in only one environment. Skills chosen to be taught in the domestic domain should be skills that can be practiced in other environments. In addition, skills should be chosen that provide maximum opportunities for independent performance, or maximum participation in domestic and community environments (e.g., showering skills can be taught in the school gym, at a YMCA/YWCA, or other recreation facility, as well as in the home). The complexity of a skill should also be considered. For example, learning to bake a cake from scratch may not be feasible due to the length of time it would take to teach such a complex set of skills. It may be more useful to teach an individual how to make a cake from a boxed cake mix, or how to locate and select a cake from a bakery. For most families, the practical reality is that they find ways to simplify their lives. Cleaners, bakeries, prepared food or fast food restaurants, and house cleaners if present in the family/neighborhood culture and community, should also be available to the student.

Finally, the *chronological age–appropriate nature of a skill* must be considered. Skills that are performed routinely by nonhandicapped age peers should be given priority to reduce the distance between the person with handicaps and his or her peers. Within the domestic domain, this can mean training the elementary-age student with severe disabilities to perform household chores, such as clearing the dining room table of dishes or making the bed, because such chores are expected of his or her siblings and peers. For a junior high school–age female, it could involve teaching the skill of applying make-up, because it is a skill used by her peers in the locker room at school and thus has social significance. It may also result in selecting certain leisure activities for skill training, such as the selection and "enjoyment" of popular tapes or videos, for a high school–age student, because that skill is valued by other teenagers in the school or neighborhood.

The eight dimensions just discussed must be considered in total when developing curricular content in the domestic domain. Each dimension has an equally strong impact on the choices to be made. The first skill to be taught should be the skill that satisfies all dimensions. Figure 6.2 provides a domestic skills checklist that may be used to establish priorities among curricula across the eight dimensions. Once potential domestic skills have been identified through ecological inventories and other means of assessment, the educator can rank each skill on the eight dimensions. Skills can then be placed in order of priority according to the number of dimensions they satisfy.

Where to Teach

The domestic skills curriculum must be designed to provide direct training in a variety of domestic environments (Freagon et al., 1983). Skills and behaviors are best taught in the settings and at the same times in which students will naturally be required to perform them. This approach makes the activities more relevant for the student, and minimizes problems of generalization. For example, it would be a more natural sequence to make one's own bed after getting up in the morning than to make a bed that no one sleeps in, that is located in a classroom, or that has just been deliberately "messed up" in the presence of the student. This means that in implementing a domestic skills curriculum, educators must utilize natural home environments as much as possible. Logistics and

Domestic Skills Priority Checklist

Student name: ____________________ Date: ____________________

Activity: ____

	No	Somewhat	Average	Very much
1. Family input:				
Is this a skill the student routinely needs at home?	1	2	3	4
Is this a skill the family considers critical?	1	2	3	4
Will this skill increase the student's participation in family routines?	1	2	3	4
Is this skill relevant to the student's home culture?	1	2	3	4
Average score for this item: ________				
2. Functional nature:				
Is this a skill that someone else must now perform for the student?	1	2	3	4
Is this a skill the student must use often?	1	2	3	4
Is this a skill that will continue to be useful in later domestic environments?	1	2	3	4
Average score for this item: ________				
3. Current and subsequent environments:				
Is this a skill that can be used in a number of environments other than the present home environment?				
For example: Vocational	1	2	3	4
Community	1	2	3	4
Other domestic environments	1	2	3	4
Later domestic environments	1	2	3	4
Average score for this item: ________				
4. Number of uses:				
Is this a frequently occurring activity?	1	2	3	4
Average score for this item: ________				
5. Social significance:				
Will performing this skill increase the student's social acceptance?	1	2	3	4
Will this skill enhance the student's interpersonal skills?	1	2	3	4
Average score for this item: ________				
6. Physical harm:				
Will learning this skill increase the student's personal safety?	1	2	3	4
Is the skill itself safe to perform, even when done inappropriately?	1	2	3	4
Can the skill be performed without adult supervision?	1	2	3	4
Average score for this item: ________				

(continued)

Figure 6.2. Domestic skills priority checklist.

Domestic Skills Priority Checklist
(continued)

7. Logistics:
   Can this skill be taught or practiced in other environments? 1 2 3 4
   Is this a skill that will increase the student's independent participation in domestic and other environments? 1 2 3 4
   Average score for this item: ________
8. Age appropriateness:
   Is this a domestic skill a nonhandicapped peer is likely to perform? 1 2 3 4
   Is this a skill preferred by nonhandicapped peers? 1 2 3 4
   Is this a skill expected of siblings in the home? 1 2 3 4
   Average score for this item: ________

Total skill score (add average scores): ________________

cost most often interfere with the utilization of natural domestic environments, but these are concerns that must be overcome if domestic skill training is to be effective. A number of strategies may be used to develop natural training sites.

The first and most logical choice is to utilize the student's own home environment. Using this environment ensures that the training a student receives is relevant to the environment in which he or she will use the skills. The method of turning on a washing machine, for example, differs from one washing machine to another. For students who have a difficult time learning a sequence, problems can be kept to a minimum if there is only one sequence to learn, in this case, that of operating the home washing machine. Parents are often willing to allow their home to be used as a site for domestic skill training on a regular and frequent basis, or, at the least, they will allow their home to be used for generalization training to compensate for differences between the home and other natural training sites.

Unfortunately, students are often bused to school sites that are far away from their homes, making the regular utilization of the home for training logistically difficult. The easiest solution to this would be to provide appropriate educational programs for all students in their neighborhood schools. However, since this is not yet the case, educational program staff may want to arrange heterogeneous classroom groupings according to geographical locations in order to provide easier access to students' homes and communities (WACSEP, 1984). Small groups of students from the class can spend portions of their days or weeks within their own homes, in the homes of classmates, or within their general neighborhood, working on similar domestic skills.

Another solution is to develop natural training sites close to the school. The homes of other students, of staff members, or of community volunteers who live close to the school, can be utilized. A variety of options should be selected so as to provide the variety of settings that represent features of the student's home environment (e.g., electric and gas home appliances; carpeted, wood, or tiled floors). Regular visits to the student's home, and family support in providing additional skill training and practice time, are essential for ensuring generalization of domestic skills from the training site(s) to the home.

The school district could also maintain its own domestic skills training site. One such program is described by Freagon et al. (1983). The school maintained a three-bedroom home in a residential neighborhood. All students had access to the home during regular school days for domestic skill training. Small groups of students were involved in an intensive, live-in training period to prepare them for postschool living arrangements. A domestic trainer lived at the house when students were present and coordinated home and school domestic skill training.

The provision of an itinerant domestic skills trainer provides an additional solution to the problem of conducting domestic skill training in natural environments. This professional can provide training in the students' homes during nonschool hours, at the times when domestic skill performance is most likely to occur. In addition, he or she can provide assistance to parents so that they may implement their own domestic training program.

The school administration must be committed to community-based programs if natural domestic training environments are to be developed and utilized. Support personnel (e.g., speech therapists, occupational therapists, physical therapists) can be utilized effectively in the home as well. The selection and utilization of natural environments makes transportation an additional issue to consider. When natural environments are within walking distance of the school site, traffic, safety, time, and scheduling problems are kept to a minimum. However, when distance requires mobility training for students, and the utilization of public transportation for students and teaching personnel, logistical issues such as insurance, liability, and funding must be addressed, and appropriate strategies must be developed. Creative solutions can and must be found for the problem of natural environment utilization. (Chapter 5, this volume, provides a detailed discussion of strategies for teaching community mobility skills.)

Self-Care and Basic Living Skills

Curriculum in the domestic domain focuses on the development of skills that will enable students with severe handicaps to function as independently as possible within their home environments. Basic self-care skills, including feeding, dressing, toileting, and grooming, represent traditional beginnings for the development of this independence (Snell, 1983). However, these personal-care skills have tended to be defined in simple listings of skill components that assume a level of independence upon mastery. It is inappropriate to assume that mastery of skill mechanics is equivalent to independence. Personal care, within the context of independent living, involves the total physical well-being of the individual; it involves not only independence, but also a positive self-concept and acceptance by others. Curriculum in this domain, then, must go beyond the mechanics of physical appearance and hygiene to include an understanding of the need for task performance, as well as an awareness of the choices and options involved. Some examples serve to illustrate this point.

Mastery of the mechanical skills necessary for dressing oneself (e.g., putting on clothing items, using fasteners) does not imply that the student has achieved independence in dressing. In addition to the specific mechanical skills of dressing, the student must also develop an awareness of what clothes should be worn together, which clothing choices are appropriate for different environments and current fashion, which clothing choices are appropriate for various weather conditions, and how and when to care for one's clothing. Similarly, learning to feed oneself must include not only the specific mechanical skills of eating, but also the ability to make choices about what and when to eat, to develop good nutritional habits, and to understand social norms associated with eating. It is important to note that obtaining the mechanical skills in the areas of dressing and feeding are not prerequisites for being provided the opportunity to learn the other important related skills. In fact, the mechanical skills maybe the least important skills to focus on for individuals who are severely physically challenged, or whose other skill needs are more important at the time. All persons, however, should be provided continual opportunities to practice their skills in decision and choice making concerning the selection of the clothing they wear, the foods that they eat, and so on.

As another example, the skills related to self and home care, which include meal preparation, laundry, and housekeeping skills, are often taught in isolation or as individual, unrelated sequences. Home care skills include all of the activities that contribute to the daily routine of the family and home, and they reflect the participation of each family member in the care of the home. When to do the laundry is as important as how to do the laundry. Learning to share chore responsibilities with others is also important. For example, one person can separate, wash, and dry the clothes, another person can fold and put the clothes away, and another person can be responsible for ironing. Domestic skills curriculum must therefore include developing an awareness of the family as a functioning unit and of the integral role of each person in that unit. Meal preparation for some families is also a time for getting together and sharing the day's experiences. Each family member may have a role in the preparation of the meal, but the role of participating in the family interaction at mealtime is equally important. In this case, teaching the student to cook without teaching him or her to participate in interactions with others would be unfortunate and would result in incomplete training.

This more comprehensive approach necessitates the inclusion of specific skills for home management in the domestic curriculum to facilitate a sense of personal and family organization. The term *home management* is used here to refer to teaching the mechanics of performing money, time, and mobility skills. It includes the development of responsibility and of decision-making skills. Incorporating home management domestic skills into the curriculum provides the student experiences that lead to making personal choices regarding schedules and routines. The curriculum thus includes the large number of skills that will enable the student to become an active member of a household.

In summary, domestic skills should not be taught in isolated, discrete activity units. Instead, these skills must be placed in the larger context in which they occur, including the social context. Skill sequences should be developed that allow the person to more fully participate in the total living environment, rather than to merely perform separate tasks within that environment.

The ecological inventory strategy discussed in Chapter 3 of this volume is a useful tool for looking at the total living environment and for generating appropriate and responsive domestic skill curricula. Pumpian et al. (1980) identified the following steps for conducting domestic ecological inventories:

1. *Delineate the current and subsequent least restrictive functional domestic environments.* This refers to identifying those environments that are currently or potentially available for the performance of domestic activities. They may include the person's place of residence, homes of relatives or friends, and homes or apartments where the person may choose to live in the future.
2. *Delineate the subenvironments that architecturally divide each domestic environment.* For most domestic environments this will include bedrooms, bathrooms, kitchen, dining area, living room, and closets. In addition, some domestic environments may include garages, basements, yards, stairways, shared living space (e.g., laundry room of an apartment house, pool area), immediate neighborhood, and so on. These are the specific environments in which skill sequences may be performed.
3. *Delineate the most relevant and functional domestic activities that occur, or might occur, within each domestic subenvironment.* Activities that should receive priority are those that occur most frequently and those that are currently being performed by someone else for the student. Areas to consider include grooming, personal care, dressing, eating, cleaning, food preparation, social interaction, and management activities.
4. *Delineate skill clusters and functional objects used and required to complete functional and relevant delineated activities.* This should include consideration of various adaptations that may be available, and of family styles, preferences, and habits. This step should incorporate relevant information about the way a given family performs an activity and the unique skills that are associated with their performance.

For a listing of sample personal, home care, home management, and social interaction skills for consideration within the domestic domain, see Table 6.2.

Incorporating Social-Sexual Skills into the Domestic Domain

An area frequently overlooked in the development of a domestic skills curriculum is that of social-sexual skills. Although it is generally accepted that human relationships significantly increase the quality of life for all persons, this is an area where persons with disabilities have often been excluded (Bullard & Knight, 1981; Haavik & Menninger, 1981). When social behaviors, social skills, and human sexuality have been addressed in relation to persons with severe handicaps, the emphasis has generally been on providing rudimentary knowledge based on myths, prejudices, and limited expectations. Some educational programs have used these prejudices and limited expectations as justifications to excuse persons with disabilities from social opportunities (Lipsky & Gartner, 1987).

Educators and families have long recognized that the success of a person with a handicap, in any integrated environment, is dependent upon that person's social abilities (Chadsey-Rusch, 1986; Greenspan & Schoultz, 1981; Storey & Gaylord-Ross, 1987; Wehman, Kregel, Shafer, & Hill, 1987). It cannot be assumed that by merely placing persons with and without disabilities together that modeling, imitation, social interaction, and social acceptance will take place (Gresham, 1982). Systematic instruction in a variety of age-appropriate activities and integrated environments must take place in order to facilitate social-sexual development of individuals with severe handicaps.

There are two approaches to teaching social skills: affective education and social skills training. Affective education emphasizes an individual's feelings and explores appropriate behavior through problem-solving activities and role-playing, with the teacher as a facilitator. Social skills training is a systematic approach, often using models, prompts, and instructional adaptations, with the teacher providing reinforcement and feedback to influence and maintain appropriate behavior (Wood, 1982). The affective and social skills training approaches should be used as complementary teaching strategies when providing social-sexual skill education for individuals with severe handicaps. Due to the disabilities in communication, language, and behavior that may exist, individuals with severe handicaps often benefit from the use of age-appropriate models, prompts, adaptive instructional devices, and consistent reinforcement when learning appropriate social skills. However, problem-solving activities, role-playing, and opportunities that encourage decision making and positive self-concepts should also be an integral part of the curriculum.

A comprehensive social-sexual skills training program must include the teaching of the following concepts:

Table 6.2. Sample personal health care, home care, home management, and social interaction skills for consideration within the domestic curriculum

Personal health care	Home care	Home management	Social interaction
Physical appearance Dressing oneself Grooming Hair styling Dental care Use of cosmetics Social norms	Laundry Using washing machines Sorting clothes Ironing	Schedules/routine Cleaning sequence Total home vs. personal space	Family Sharing space and appliances (e.g., using the bathroom or TV) Sharing responsibilities (e.g., chores, bills) Communication skills Respect of others' belongings Respect of privacy
Hygiene Toileting Routine cleanliness Use of deodorants Care of menstrual needs	Clothing Regular care Choosing Purchasing Repair of Sewing	Time Concept of Use of Management of	Neighbors Appropriate greetings Borrowing and lending skills "Neighborly kindness" (e.g., watching pets or watering while away, picking up newspapers, sharing vegetables or flowers from the garden)
Safety Awareness of dangers First aid What to do in emergencies	House cleaning Basic standards Materials needed How to (e.g., dust, vacuum, mop, make beds)	Money Concepts of Value Budgeting	
		Materials Purchase of Storage of Maintaining and replacing supplies	

- Wellness
  - Exercise
  - Use of medications
  - Diet/weight control
  - Effects of smoking
- Nutrition
  - Eating a balanced diet
  - Use of food supplements
  - Caloric and nutritional content of foods
- Emotional/mental health
  - Self-concept
  - Recognizing and dealing with emotions
  - Community resources
  - Relationships with others

- Meals
  - Choice: what to eat and when
  - Preparation
  - Food purchase
  - Clean up
- Eating skills
  - Basic skills
  - Adaptations
  - Table manners
- Home maintenance
  - Basic repairs
  - Upkeep
  - Decorating
- Yard maintenance
  - Trash removal
  - Basic care (e.g., raking, mowing)
- Appliances
  - Use of
  - Safety

- Use of space
  - Design
  - Safety
  - Accessibility
- Organization
  - Location of items
  - Sharing responsibilities
  - Establishing routines
- Choices

  - Respect of neighbors' property and privacy
  - Communication skills
- Friends
  - Calling friends on the phone
  - Inviting friends over
  - Communication skills
  - Planning foods and/or activities
  - Social skills/manners

Appropriate/inappropriate dress, grooming, touching of self and others, social behaviors, and language
Private/public clothing, body parts, places, conversation, voice level, touching, and thoughts
Assertive/passive/aggressive behavior, language, and voice tone
Respect for self, by developing independence, being private,taking ownership of one's body, making positive choices, and demonstrating a good self-concept
Respect for others/making friends by allowing for others' privacy, discriminating between strangers, acquaintances, and friends, initiating appropriate social interactions, and sharing places/interests/activities/thoughts/feelings

Social-sexual skill training of the concepts stated above can be accomplished by utilizing both the affective and social skills training teaching strategies. For example, students can learn the appropriate social distance to maintain in role-play situations in the classroom using tape on the floor, as well as through the use of prompts and an "arms length" measurement strategy when in a grocery store check out line (McClennen, 1988). Students can learn to whisper when talking about private matters. Whispering can be practiced in public restrooms, when having discussions about sex education, or when purchasing private clothing (e.g., underwear, bras), and can be prompted and reinforced by having educators whisper (Edwards, 1986). Students can also learn assertive and aggressive behaviors for self-protection through modeling and role-playing of different situations that encourage the student to decide the appropriate protective behavior response. Students can also learn respect for themselves and for others by being treated with respect by persons who work with them. When people with severe handicaps are treated with dignity and respect, are allowed to make choices, and are provided privacy, they will most often model that behavior in their interactions with others.

Another important consideration for teaching social-sexual skills is the number of opportunities to practice in natural environments. Social skills practiced across a variety of relevant environments and age-appropriate activities are more likely to be learned and generalized to a broad range of situations and environments where the social behavior is useful (Breen, Haring, Pitts-Conway, & Gaylord-Ross, 1985; Horner, Sprague, & Wilcox, 1982; Stainback & Stainback, 1983; Storey & Gaylord-Ross, 1987). For example, teaching persons with disabilities to make positive statements to others can be taught in a recreation and leisure activity (Storey & Gaylord-Ross, 1987). This same skill, however, should also be taught and practiced at home, in a work setting, in a grocery store, and in any other relevant environment, to facilitate the generalization of that skill.

Another factor that has been found to influence generalization of social skills is the nature of the skill itself. If a social skill is naturally reinforcing, then it is more likely to be generalized from one situation to the next (Stainback & Stainback, 1983). The simple skill of smiling to others is naturally reinforcing because it usually elicits a smile in return. Most social skills are naturally reinforcing; the educational challenge is to assist students in recognizing the naturally reinforcing qualities.

Besides social skill training, practical sexual knowledge must also be incorporated into the domestic skill curriculum on a regular and systematic basis. Such information includes: terminology for body parts, understanding of male and female anatomy, knowledge of body functions, and ways to deal with genital sexual feelings, intercourse, and contraception. Developing and implementing such curriculum requires the close participation and involvement of parents, teachers, and school district personnel. Parental support and consent is required when providing sex education to students who are minors. A variety of appropriate sex education programs have been outlined in current literature (Haavik & Menninger, 1981; Hamre-Nietupski, Ford, Williams, & Gruenewald, 1978; Hingsburger, 1987; Kempton, 1977; L.A.C.O.E., 1987; Monat, 1982). Table 6.3 provides an outline of sample skill areas related to appropriate social-sexual curriculum. Social-sexual skills, like self-care and basic living skills, should not be taught in isolated, discrete activity units, but incorporated throughout the curriculum so that they have relavance to the student's total life.

In providing an appropriate social-sexual education, the issue of exploitation and abuse of people with disabilities cannot be overlooked. A large percentage of people with disabilities are victims of sexual abuse; this suggests there is a critical need to provide appropriate sex education, especially when it encourages a sense of control and choice over one's own life (Baladerian, 1985). Educators must also be aware of the nonverbal indicators of sexual abuse so that they will be able to recognize and assist students in reporting abuse, in obtaining protection, and in gaining the skills to protect themselves (Aguilar, 1984). Table 6.4 is a list of nonverbal signs that may indicate the existence of sexual abuse.

Hingsburger (1987) has outlined other challenges to be faced when providing appropriate social-sexual education or counseling for persons with severe handicaps. The challenges arise from the social-sexual problems often present for students with severe handicaps. The problems are: confused self concepts, isolation from heterogenous groups of peers, lack of sexual knowledge, learned patterns of inappropriate sexual behavior, inconsistent social-sexual environments, and lack of personal power. Many of these problems can be addressed by providing, at an early age, appropriate and ongoing social-sexual education, and training in decision making and self-advocacy skills to students with severe handicaps. This also strongly implies the need for more appropriate training for those who live and work with persons with severe handicaps, including: teachers, parents, social workers, care providers, and the community at large (Adam, Tallon, & Alcorn, 1982; May, 1980). It also demonstrates the impor-

Table 6.3. Sample social-sexual educational curriculum

- Self-awareness/self-esteem
  - Identifying information
    - Knowledge of gender
    - Knowledge of public/private body parts
    - Knowledge of likes/dislikes
    - Knowledge of personal qualities
  - Feelings of self in relationship to others
    - Recognition of personal feelings
    - Sensitivity to feelings of others
    - Knowledge of interaction skills
  - Values and decision making
    - Knowledge of individual values
    - Decision-making strategies
    - Knowledge of appropriate/inappropriate social behaviors
    - Knowledge of private/public places, vocabulary, and actions
    - Knowledge of social rules for self and others
- Health and hygiene
  - Body parts
    - Knowledge of body parts and their functions
    - Knowledge of male/female differences
    - Knowledge of appropriate hygiene and grooming
  - Puberty
    - Recognizing signs of male/female changes
    - Knowledge of hygiene and grooming changes
    - Understanding the function of physiological changes
  - Physical stimulation
    - Identifying touching/hugging/kissing
    - Identifying masturbation
    - Identifying sexual intercourse or sex acts with others
    - Identifying choice making in relationships
    - Identifying appropriate/inappropriate places, situations, vocabulary
  - Reproductive process
    - Understanding conception
    - Knowledge of fetal development and birth
    - Knowledge of birth control
    - Understanding the responsibility of parenthood
    - Knowledge of sexually transmitted diseases
  - Nutrition
    - Knowledge of food groups
    - Knowledge of meal planning
    - Understanding the importance of good nutrition
  - Drugs, alcohol, cigarettes
    - Knowledge of the effects of drugs
    - Understanding peer pressure
    - Understanding drug abuse
- Self-protection
  - Recognizing relationships and situations
    - Identifying strangers/acquaintances/community workers/family/friends
    - Recognizing appropriate/inappropriate interactions and relationships with strangers/acquaintances/family/friends/careproviders/community workers

(continued)

Table 6.3. *(continued)*

- Recognizing safe/unsafe situations
- Participating safely in the community

Assertiveness training
- Assertiveness through body language
- Assertiveness through verbal expression
- Identifying where to get help in the community
- Physical self-protection techniques

Reporting abuse
- Identifying persons to tell
- Identifying agencies to go to

Relationships
- Identifying different kinds of relationships
    - Family
    - Friends
    - Community
- Family
    - Identifying roles and responsibilities within a family
    - Understanding family transitions: growing up, independence, separation, death
    - Dealing with conflict, decision making, and finding solutions
- Friends
    - Knowledge of social interaction skills
    - Developing friendships
    - Sharing interest
    - Understanding liking and loving relationships
- Community
    - Understanding social rules and etiquette
    - Knowledge of appropriate/inappropriate social behaviors
    - Understanding consequences of behavior
- Making informed choices
    - Understanding different life-styles
    - Understanding different living arrangements
    - Understanding responsibilities of marriage and family

tance of integrated school and community settings, and of providing more heterogeneous age-appropriate and normalized activities within those settings. Social-sexual educational programs must utilize appropriate teaching strategies, and provide for the practice of learned skills in a variety of environments for generalization to occur.

SUMMARY

A number of issues associated with the development of an appropriate curriculum within the domestic domain are presented in this chapter. The focus of a domestic skill curriculum is to prepare students to function with maximum independence within their present and future home environments. Starting early in life, students with severe handicaps must begin to acquire skills that will allow them some level of participation in domestic activities and that will lead to fuller participation and interaction with others in domestic environments.

Table 6.4. Nonverbal indicators of sexual abuse

Physical	Behavioral	Emotional
Difficulty in walking or sitting	Bizarre or unusual behavior	Difficulty in sleep
Torn, stained, or bloody clothing	Sophisticated or unusual sexual behavior or knowledge	Avoidance of a trusted person
Pain, itching in the genital area	Sudden infantile behavior	Bed-wetting
Bruises or bleeding in the genital area	Refusal to undress or bathe	Fear of being alone or unusual desire to be alone
Veneral disease	Change of eating habits	Hypochondria
Pregnancy		Unexplained stomach aches

Skills chosen for development must reflect parental preferences in terms of existing routines, priorities, and future living options. Student's needs and preferences must also be considered, by providing a curriculum that allows for individual choice and decision making.

The traditional self-help curriculum generally subsumed under the rubric of the domestic domain has been expanded in this chapter to include the often neglected aspects of family interactions, neighborhood integration, future living options, self-advocacy, and social-sexual development. A wide spectrum of community-based living options is now available for students with severe handicaps, and students must be fully prepared to function within these options. All students need to learn skills that will allow them to live fully as individuals, as family members, and as members of a larger society. All students also have the right to total participation and maximum independence based on individual potential. A comprehensive and systematic domestic skill program that begins early in life will lead to independence and participation by these individuals in the full range of natural living environments.

REFERENCES

Adam, G.L., Tallon, R.J., & Alcorn, D.A. (1982). Attitudes toward sexuality of mentally retarded and nonretarded persons. *Education and Training of the Mentally Retarded, 17*(4), 307–312.

Aguilar, S. (1984). Prosecuting cases of physical and sexual assault of the mentally retarded. Unpublished manuscript, Sacramento County Prosecutor's Office, Sacramento, CA.

Allen, W.T. (1988). *The right to be heard: Ways to increase consumer participation in the service system: A guide for case managers.* Sacramento, CA: A.R.C.A.

Baladerian, N. (1985). *Prevention of sexual exploitation of developmentally disabled adults.* Paper presented at the California Association of Post-secondary Educators of the Disabled.

Breen, C., Haring, T., Pitts-Conway, V., & Gaylord-Ross, R. (1985). The training and generalization of social interaction during breaktime at two job sites in the natural environment. *Journal of The Association for Persons with Severe Handicaps, 10,* 41–50.

Brown, L., Branston, M.B., Hamre-Nietupski, S., Pumpian, I., Certo, N., & Gruenewald, L. (1979). A strategy for developing chronological age appropriate and functional curricular content for severely handicapped adolescents and young adults. *Journal of Special Education, 13*(1), 81–90.

Bullard, D.G., & Knight, S.E. (Eds.). (1981). *Sexuality and physical disability.* St. Louis: C.V. Mosby.

Chadsey-Rusch, J. (1986), Identifying and teaching valued social behaviors. In F.R. Rusch (Ed.), *Competitive employment issues and strategies* (pp. 273–287). Baltimore: Paul H. Brookes Publishing Co.

Edwards, J. (1986, November) *Social sexual considerations for the developmentally disabled.* Paper presented at the National TASH conference, San Francisco.

Freagon, S., Wheeler, J., Hill, L., Brankin, G., Costello, D., & Peters, W. (1983). A domestic training environment for students who are severely handicapped. *Journal of The Association for Persons with Severe Handicaps, 8,* 49–61.

Greenspan, S., & Shoultz, B. (1981). Why mentally retarded adults lose their jobs: Social competence as a factor in work adjustment. *Applied Research in Mental Retardation, 2,* 23–28.

Gresham, F.M. (1982). Misguided mainstreaming: The case for social skills training with handicapped children. *Exceptional Children, 48*(5), 422–433.

Haavik, S.F., & Menninger, K.A. (1981). *Sexuality, law, and the developmentally disabled person. Legal and clinical aspects of marriage, parenthood, and sterilization.* Baltimore: Paul H. Brookes Publishing Co.

Hamre-Nietupski, S., Ford, A., Williams, W., & Gruenewald, L. (1978). *Sex education and related home and community functioning skill programs for severely handicapped students: Toward appropriate functioning in less restrictive environments* (Vol. 8, Part 2). Madison, WI: Madison Metropolitan School District.

Hingsburger, D. (1987). Sex counseling with the developmentally handicapped: The assessment and management of seven critical problems. *Psychiatric Aspects of Mental Retardation Reviews, 6*(9), 41–45.

Horner, R.H., Sprague, J., & Wilcox, B. (1982). General case programming for community activities. In B. Wilcox & G.T. Bellamy (Eds.), Design of high school programs for severely handicapped students (pp. 61–98). Baltimore: Paul H. Brookes Publishing Co.

Kempton, W. (1977). The sexual adolescent who is mentally retarded. *Journal of Pediatric Psychology, 2,* 104–107.

L.A.C.O.E. (1987). *Family Life Curriculum.* Downey, CA: Los Angeles County Office of Education.

Lipsky, D.K., & Gartner, A. (1987). Capable of achievement and worthy of respect: Education for handicapped students as if they are full fledged human beings. *Exceptional Children, 9,* 69–73.

May, D.C. (1980). Survey of sex education coursework in special education programs. *The Journal of Special Education, 14*(1), 107–112.

McClennen, S. (1988). Sexuality and students with mental retardation. *Teaching Exceptional Children, 20*(4), 59–63.

Meyer, L.H., McQuarter, R., & Kishi, G.S. (1985). Assessing and teaching social interaction skills. In S. Stainback & W. Stainback (Eds.), *Integration of students with severe handicaps* (pp. 66–86). Reston, VA: The Council for Exceptional Children.

Monat, R.K. (1982). *Sexuality and the mentally retarded.* San Diego: College Hill Press.

Perske, R. (1974). Sexual development. *Exceptional Parent, 4,* 36–39.

Pumpian, I., Livi, J., Falvey, M., Brown, L., & Loomis, R. (1980). Strategies for generating curricular content to teach adolescent and young adult severely handicapped students domestic living skills. In L. Brown, M. Falvey, D. Baumgart, I. Pumpian, J. Schroeder, & L. Gruenewald (Eds.), *Strategies for teaching chronological age appropriate functional skills to adolescent and young adult severely handicapped students* (Vol. 9, pp. 61–101). Madison, WI: Madison Metropolitan School District.

Snell, M.E. (1983). Self-care skills. In M.E. Snell (Ed.), *Systematic instruction of the moderately and severely handicapped* (2d ed., pp. 358–409). Columbus, OH: Charles E. Merrill.

Stainback, W., & Stainback, S. (1983). Generalization of positive social behavior by severely handicapped students: A review and analysis of research. *Education and Training of the Mentally Retarded, 12,* 293–297.

Storey, K., & Gaylord-Ross, R. (1987). Increasing positive social interaction by handicapped individuals during a recreational activity using a multicomponent treatment package. *Research in Developmental Disabilities, 8*(4), 627–624.

Taylor, S.J., Biklen, D., & Knoll, J. (1987). *Community integration for people with severe disabilities,* New York: Teachers College Press.

WACSEP. (1984). *A curriculum for individuals with severe handicaps.* Whittier, CA: Whittier Area Cooperative Special Education Programs.

Wehman, P., Kregel, J., Shafer, M., & Hill, M. (1987). *Competitive employment for persons with mental retardation: From research to practice* (Vol. II). Richmond: Rehabilitation Research and Training Center, Virginia Commonwealth University.

Wood, F.H. (1982). Affective education and social skills training : A consumer's guide. *Teaching Exceptional Children, 14*(6), 212–216.

SEVEN

RECREATION SKILLS

Mary A. Falvey and Jennifer Coots

TRADITIONAL CURRICULA FOR students with severe handicaps have often included recreation/leisure activities. Unfortunately, many of the activities contained in these curricula have been patronizing, demoralizing, and generally not valued by nonhandicapped persons. This chapter provides a rationale, a description, and strategies for developing and implementing chronological age–appropriate and valued recreation/leisure activities for persons with severe handicaps.

The term *leisure* refers to: "a. freedom or spare time provided by the cessation of activities: as 1) free time as a result of temporary exemption from work or duties; 2) time at one's command that is free of engagements or responsibilities; b. a period of unemployed time" (Guralnick, 1970, p. 807). The term *recreation* refers to: "1. refreshment in body and mind, as after work, by some form of play, amusement, or relaxation; 2. any form of play, amusement, or relaxation used for this purpose, as games, sports, hobbies, etc." (Guralnick, 1970, p. 1188).

The recreation/leisure curricular domain involves activities reflective of Guralnick's definitions, as well as activities that are chronological age appropriate and that occur within a variety of natural integrated environments. The recreation/leisure domain must be included in students' curricula, and learning opportunities must be systematically provided in this domain in order to ensure that students' education prepares them to recreate and/or perform leisure skills in and across a wide variety of natural and integrated environments. More specifically, the following is a list of reasons for developing curriculum in the recreation/leisure domain:

1. Recreation/leisure is a set of activities in which most nonhandicapped people engage; therefore, providing opportunities to acquire skills to enable persons with severe handicaps to engage in recreation/leisure activities is normalizing.
2. Recreation/leisure activities provide opportunities to avoid "dead time"; in other words, recreation/leisure activities provide for constructive use of free time in one's life.
3. Recreation/leisure activities occur and/or exist across a variety of environments. They facilitate an individual's participation in diverse community, neighborhood, and home environments.
4. Recreation/leisure activities are considered physically and emotionally beneficial for people of all ages.
5. Recreation/leisure activities often facilitate creative thinking and behavior.
6. Many recreation/leisure activities provide opportunities to teach interaction, social, communication, and other related behaviors between persons with severe handicaps and nonhandicapped peers.
7. Constructive use of leisure time often reduces inappropriate social behaviors (Schleien & Ray, 1988).
8. Persons with severe handicaps rarely acquire skills, such as recreation/leisure skills, unless systematic instruction is provided (Schleien & Ray, 1988).
9. Recreation/leisure activities can be developed into vocational and career opportunities.
10. Recreation/leisure skill development can and should facilitate parent, teacher, and community involvement and cooperation.
11. Recreation/leisure activities, once acquired, can provide parents, siblings, and others with support for the care, supervision, and entertainment of their sons or daughters, siblings, or other relatives with severe handicaps.
12. Recreation/leisure activities can provide opportunities for friendships to develop for persons with severe handicaps.

Recent research has demonstrated that students with severe handicaps can acquire and perform functional, chronological age–appropriate recreation/leisure skills (Adkins & Matson, 1980; Hamre-Nietupski, Nietupski, Sandvig, Sandvig, & Ayers, 1984; Hill, Wehman, & Horst, 1982; Nietupski, Hamre-Nietupski, & Ayers, 1984; Nietupski & Svoboda, 1980; Schleien, Certo, & Muccino, 1984; Schloss, Smith, & Kiehl, 1986; Sedlak, Doyle, & Schloss, 1982; Voeltz, Wuerch, & Bockhart, 1982; Wehman, Renzaglia, Berry, Schultz, & Karan, 1978). In addition, several researchers have demonstrated the value of substituting inappropriate and/or unacceptable behaviors with appropriate recreation or leisure activities and/or social interaction opportunities (Flavell, 1973; Horner, 1980; Kissel & Whitman, 1977; Wahler & Fox, 1980).

Providing opportunities for students with severe handicaps to receive their education in the same school as their neighbors (generally their neighborhood school), has become increasingly prevalent (Stainback, Stainback, & Forest, 1989). In addition, employment opportunities with support have increased for adults with severe handicaps, for example, in supported employment programs (see Chapter 8, this volume). Establishing such school and employment opportunities only increases the need for, and access to, neighborhood community recreation/leisure opportunities. The remainder of this chapter provides a detailed discussion of strategies for developing and implementing chronological age–appropriate recreation/leisure opportunities in integrated neighborhood environments.

DEVELOPMENT OF A RECREATION/LEISURE CURRICULUM

Programs for persons with severe handicaps have often included leisure skill development components. Unfortunately, most of the traditional leisure skill development programs have not produced increased student participation in a wide variety of integrated community and home recreation/leisure activities. Such programs and opportunities have generally taught all persons with severe handicaps the same leisure activities without regard for individual preferences. In addition, recreation activities that occur in the community have often taken the form of large group "field trips" (e.g., bowling with 30 adolescents with severe handicaps every Thursday morning at the same bowling alley).

Recently, a number of papers and curricula have been published that attempt to identify the critical characteristics of appropriate recreation/leisure curricula for individuals with severe handicaps (Bambara, Siegel-Causey, Shores, & Fox, 1984; Banks & Aveno, 1986; Coleman & Whitman, 1984; Dattilo & Rusch, 1985; Ford et al., 1981; Guess, Benson, & Siegel-Causey, 1985; Hamre-Nietupski et al., 1984; Nietupski et al., 1986; Voeltz, Wuerch, & Wilcox, 1982; Wacker, Berg, & Moore, 1984; Wehman, Schleien, & Kiernan, 1980; Wuerch & Voeltz, 1982). An analysis of these excellent resources reveals several characteristics that should be considered when designing, developing, implementing, and monitoring recreation/leisure programs. These characteristics are discussed in the following paragraphs.

Chronological Age–Appropriate Activities

Chronological age–appropriate activities, materials, environments, expectations, and other relevant stimuli must be determined and taught. If persons with severe handicaps are to be accepted and integrated into their communities, then providing them with the skills and experiences of their nonhandicapped peers is likely to increase their interactions and ultimately result in friendships. The person's current age and his or her subsequent needs must be identified. For example, it would be chronological age–appropriate to teach a 3-year-old to play with a "Busy Box," but it would not be chronological age appropriate to teach a 10-year-old to play with that toy. To determine chronological age–appropriate materials or toys, it would be appropriate to inventory or interview a nonhandicapped 10-year-old child. Figure 7.1 provides a questionnaire that can be given to 10-year-old children to determine some of the toys and materials they use. Parents, educators, recreators, and others can use the information obtained from the questionnaire to develop activities to teach 10-year-old students with severe handicaps. Such a process should be used and modified for different ages of students.

Peer Recreation/Leisure Activities Survey

Age ____________ Name ______________________________

Date ______________________________

1. List at least 3 things that you do in your free time.

____

____

____

2. List 5 of your favorite toys or games.

______________________ ______________________

______________________ ______________________

____

3. List 3 activities that you and your family do together in your free time.

____

____

____

4. List 3 of your most favorite outdoor activities.

____

____

____

5. List any clubs or groups you belong to.

____

____

____

6. List 5 of your favorite records or singers.

______________________ ______________________

______________________ ______________________

____

Figure 7.1. Questionnaire for nonhandicapped students for use in determining chronological age–appropriate recreation/leisure activities.

Interaction with Nonhandicapped Peers

Activities that involve interactions between persons with severe handicaps and their nonhandicapped peers must be identified and taught. Interactions with nonhandicapped peers provide opportunities for persons with severe handicaps to acquire social and communication skills, and to develop friendships and build more caring communities. More specifically, creating opportunities for students to participate in recreation/leisure activities that involve heterogeneous groups of people must be developed (i.e., students with handicaps should avoid the use of "handicapped times" or "handicapped only" recreation/leisure activities). Cooperative recreation/leisure activities should be facilitated between students with and without handicaps (Wacker et al., 1984).

Activities that Can Be Adapted

Since some individuals with severe handicaps do not possess all the skills necessary to participate in all chronological age–appropriate recreation/leisure activities, adaptations can be used to enhance their participation. Recreation/leisure activities that can be adapted that facilitate increased participation should be considered (Banks & Aveno, 1986; Baumgart et al., 1982).

Several types of recreation/leisure adaptations specifically for students who are deaf and/or blind have been identified by Hamre-Nietupski et al. (1984). They include: attaching a permanent tactile prompt to a toy or game, such as placing a raised and brightly colored tab on the "on" switch of a tape recorder; stabilizing materials, such as putting rubber suctions on the bottom of a game or toy; enhancing the visual or auditory response of the material, such as using enlarged print or headphones; simplifying the task for more participation, such as modifying the rules of a card game.

In addition to modifying individual tasks or activities for more participation, Schleien and Ray (1988) recommend that community programs can also be modified to facilitate more participation for individuals with severe handicaps and their nonhandicapped peers. Specifically, Schleien and Ray present several examples of how community recreation programs can be adapted for more accessibility to members of the community. Those examples include:

1. A designated runner can be used for the baseball batter who is a double amputee.
2. Cumulative team scores are the only basis for winning a recreation league bowling tournament. A person in a wheelchair can be a member of the bowling team and can compete by using a tubular steel bowling ramp.
3. Participants in the photography class are told to work in two-person teams to complete their class project. One person in the class happens to be mentally retarded.
4. Participants in a woodworking class work in groups of four to complete a shelving unit. Three of the participants are not disabled and do the cutting and joining of the parts. The fourth member, who happens to be severely disabled with cerebral palsy, does the varnishing.

5. Children are gathered in groups of three to explore the "Haunted House" at the recreation center. One child holds the flashlight, while another hides effectively behind the third friend's wheelchair, which she helps to push.
6. Players at a frisbee "golf" tournment in a park are awarded individual stroke handicaps similiar to those awarded in a regular golf game. The person who earns second place is severely mentally retarded. (p. 76)

Opportunities For Self-Initiation and Choice

Recreation/leisure activities must be those activities that are systematically and intentionally chosen by the individual. The concept of "learned helplessness" has been used to characterize the results of programming and intervention that inhibit individual choice making (Guess et al., 1985). In order to learn to express oneself, one needs systematic instruction in self-initiation as well as opportunities to initiate interactions.

The concept of self-initiation is particularly critical in the development of recreation/leisure opportunities. The definitions of recreation and leisure imply activities that are desired, preferred, and chosen by the individual. A program to enhance and increase the recreation/leisure skills for persons with severe handicaps must therefore include instruction in self-initiation and choice making (Dattilo & Rusch, 1985). In addition, teachers and recreators must systematically identify all opportunities available for students to express themselves and make choices, and must capitalize on the teaching opportunities for each of those situations (Guess et al., 1985). For a more detailed discussion of teaching self-initiation and choice making, the reader is referred to Chapter 11 of this volume.

A Variety of Activities

The characteristics of recreation/leisure activities vary greatly, not only in terms of number of typical participants but in type of activity. For instance, activities may involve a single person, small groups, or large groups. In addition, some activities primarily consist of observing (e.g., watching a football game), while other activities involve active participation (e.g., playing football). Persons with severe handicaps must have opportunities to acquire the skills necessary to participate in activities that involve a single person, a small group, and a large group. Moreover, they must be given the chance to acquire the skills necessary both for actively observing and for participating directly in activities. The array of recreation/leisure activities available to nonhandicapped persons should be similarly available to their peers with severe handicaps.

Accessible Recreation/Leisure Activities

Activities must be considered that are accessible in a number of ways to students with severe handicaps. First, activities should be affordable or have no financial cost. Second, activities should have reasonable, minimal, or no transportation requirements. Third, activities should be considered that do not require the presence of specialized staff, such as a special education teacher. Finally, activities should pose minimal safety hazards for the individual.

Activities Preferred by the Individual

Since, by definition, recreation/leisure activities involve activities that are preferred by the individual, determining an individual's favorite activities is essential. Once preferences are determined, those activities must be taught. Observing across activities and environments, as well as interviewing the individual and his or her family, can assist staff in identifying his or her likes and dislikes with regard to recreation/leisure activities.

Activities Preferred by the Individual's Family

Recreation/leisure activities that reflect the cultural norms, values, expectations, and preferences of the family and community in which the individual resides must be taken into account when determining what recreation/leisure activities to teach. In order for a recreation/leisure activity to be functional for an individual, the activity must be available in his or her home or home community during nonschool hours. Facilitating activities that are preferred and valued by the individual and his or her family increases the likelihood that the student will participate in that activity.

Activities Relevant to Other Environments

Recreation/leisure activities that involve skills that need to be performed in other recreation/leisure environments, as well as in environments within other domains—that is, domestic, vocational, and community domains—should be taught. For example, some of the skills involved in playing computer-assisted games in a video arcade are the same or similar to the skills necessary to use a computer in many work settings. Teaching the use of the computer in a recreation/leisure setting can reinforce and provide practice of the skills required to use a computer within an employment setting.

Activities with Reasonable Time Requirements

Recreation/leisure activities should be considered that have time requirements (i.e., duration and frequency) that match the individual's abilities to endure and perform that activity at acceptable intervals. For example, a student who has demonstrated the ability to "sit and observe" for no more than 10 minutes should not be expected to "sit and observe" a movie for 90 minutes. Initially, the student can engage in activities that require "sitting and observing" for no more than 10 minutes. Gradually, the student can be provided opportunities to increase his or her ability to participate in activities of longer duration.

Activities that Include Active Participation

Individuals with multiple handicaps, particularly those with significant physical challenges, are unfortunately often expected to be passive observers of events and activities, rather than active participants. Learning is more effective when people are actively involved in activities they are learning. Recreation/leisure activities that actively involve individuals are more appropriate than those that involve exclusively passive behaviors. In addition, Bambara et al. (1984) have found that reactive toys contain more reinforcing value than non-reactive toys. Therefore, educators and recreators must systematically identify materials, activities, and events that facilitate the active involvement of individuals with severe handicaps.

All of the foregoing characteristics need to be individually applied to each individual in order to determine the most appropriate recreation/leisure curriculum for him or her. Figure 7.2 provides a data sheet that can be used to analyze and evaluate specific recreation/leisure activities based upon the dimensions described in this chapter. In order to assist the reader in the use of this data sheet, examples of recreation/leisure activities that were analyzed and evaluated by the author for several individuals are presented below.

The first individual, Shannon, is 4 years old. She is nonambulatory and has a visual impairment. Her parents have stated that she responds well to toys and other materials that have auditory stimuli. She does not like playing with "baby toys." Figure 7.3 provides a data sheet analyzing and evaluating the appropriateness of several activities for Shannon, based upon the dimensions already delineated.

The second individual, Sean, who is 10 years old, has no intelligible speech. He uses a picture communication board and likes cars and trucks. His family speaks only Spanish, although he is able to understand some basic English phrases and words. Figure 7.4 provides a data sheet analyzing and evaluating several activities for Sean, based upon the dimensions already described.

The third individual, Tara, a 22-year-old, works at a movie theater that is located next door to a video arcade and within walking distance of her home. She is ambulatory and uses some pictures to augment her speech. She dislikes activities that involve detailed eye-hand coordination and fine motor skills, and prefers activities that involve gross motor skills. Figure 7.5 provides a data sheet analyzing and evaluating several activities for her.

IMPLEMENTING A RECREATION/LEISURE CURRICULUM

In order to implement an educational program for individuals with severe handicaps, detailed instructional programs must be developed. Williams, Brown, and Certo proposed that prior to engaging in instructional interactions with a student, educators should identify the components of instructional pro-

Code: + yes – no o unknown	Student:											Age:							Date:		
	Activity characteristics												Student characteristics								Comments
								Accessibility											Time requirements		
Recreation/ leisure activities	Chronological age appropriate	Interactions with nonhandicapped peers	Individual	Small group	Large group	Observing	Participating	Cost	Transportation	Specialized staff needs	Safety	Adaptability	Student preference	Family preference	Reflects culture	Skills needed in other environments	Activities that can be taught	Activities that can be adapted	Duration	Frequency	
1.																					
2.																					
3.																					
4.																					
5.																					

Figure 7.2. Sample data sheet for individualized recreation/leisure activity analysis.

Code:
+ yes
− no
o unknown

Student: *Shannon* Age: *4* Date: *11/1*

Recreation/ leisure activities	Activity characteristics												Student characteristics								Comments
								Accessibility											Time requirements		
	Chronological age appropriate	Interactions with nonhandicapped peers	Individual	Small group	Large group	Observing	Participating	Cost	Transportation	Specialized staff needs	Safety	Adaptability	Student preference	Family preference	Reflects culture	Skills needed in other environments	Activities that can be taught	Activities that can be adapted	Duration	Frequency	
1. *Climbing on neighborhood park equipment*	+	+	+	+	+	+	+	+	−	+	+	+	+	+	+	+	+	+	+	+	*Meets most criteria. Develop objective and teach.*
2. *Playing with rattles*	−	−	+	−	−	−	+	+	+	+	+	+	−	−	−	+	+	+	−	−	*Does not meet several critical criteria. Do not develop objective.*
3. *Playing "Ring Around the Rosie"*	+	+	−	+	+	−	+	+	+	+	+	+	+	+	+	+	+	+	+	+	*Meets several critical criteria. Develop objective and teach.*
4. *Playing with wooden puzzles*	+	*o*	+	−	−	−	+	+	+	+	+	+	−	−	−	+	+	+	+	+	*Does not meet several critical criteria. Do not develop objective.*
5. *Playing with toy radio*	+	−	+	−	−	+	+	−	+	+	+	+	+	−	−	+	+	+	+	+	*Meets several critical criteria. Develop objective and teach.*

Figure 7.3. Sample recreation/leisure activity analysis for Shannon, a 4-year-old nonambulatory student with a visual impairment.

Code:
+ yes
− no
o unknown

Student: *Sean* Age: *10* Date: *11/1*

Recreation/leisure activities	Activity characteristics												Student characteristics								Comments
	Chronological age appropriate	Interactions with nonhandicapped peers	Individual	Small group	Large group	Observing	Participating	Accessibility					Student preference	Family preference	Reflects culture	Skills needed in other environments	Activities that can be taught	Activities that can be adapted	Time requirements		
								Cost	Transportation	Specialized staff needs	Safety	Adaptability							Duration	Frequency	
1. *Playing with "Busy Box" (preschool toy)*	−	−	+	−	−	−	+	−	+	+	+	+	−	−	−	−	−	−	−	−	*Does not meet several critical criteria. Do not develop objective.*
2. *Putting a model car together*	+	+	+	+	−	+	+	−	+	+	+	+	+	+	+	+	+	+	+	+	*Meets most critical criteria. Develop objective and teach.*
3. *Looking at automotive magazines in Spanish*	+	+	+	+	−	−	+	+	+	+	+	+	+	+	+	+	+	+	+	+	*Meets most critical criteria. Develop objective and teach.*
4. *Listening to early childhood records (e.g., "Rock A Bye Baby")*	−	−	+	+	−	+	−	−	+	+	+	+	−	−	−	−	−	−	−	−	*Does not meet several critical criteria. Do not develop objective.*
5. *Making churros (Mexican pastry)*	+	+	+	+	−	−	+	+	+	+	+	+	+	+	+	+	+	+	+	+	*Meets most critical criteria. Develop objective and teach.*

Figure 7.4. Sample recreation/leisure activity analysis for a 10-year-old who has no intelligible speech and whose family is monolingual in Spanish.

Code:
\+ yes
− no
o unknown

Student: *Tara* Age: *22* Date: *11/1*

Recreation/ leisure activities	Activity characteristics												Student characteristics								Comments
	Chronological age appropriate	Interactions with nonhandicapped peers	Individual	Small group	Large group	Observing	Participating	Accessibility: Cost	Accessibility: Transportation	Accessibility: Specialized staff needs	Accessibility: Safety	Accessibility: Adaptability	Student preference	Family preference	Reflects culture	Skills needed in other environments	Activities that can be taught	Activities that can be adapted	Time requirements: Duration	Time requirements: Frequency	
1. *Enrolling in aerobics class*	+	+	+	+	+	+	+	−	−	+	+	+	+	+	+	+	+	+	+	+	*Meets most critical criteria. Develop objective and teach.*
2. *Doing embroidery*	+	−	+	−	−	−	+	+	+	+	+	+	−	−	−	+	+	+	−	−	*Does not meet several critical criteria. Do not develop objective.*
3. *Playing with video games at video arcade*	+	+	+	+	+	−	+	+	+	+	+	+	+	+	+	+	+	+	+	+	*Meets most criteria. Develop objective and teach.*
4. *Playing with "Simon" (battery-operated toy)*	+	+	+	+	−	+	+	−	+	+	+	+	+	+	+	+	+	+	+	+	*Meets most critical criteria. Develop objective and teach.*
5. *Playing "hop scotch" at park*	−	−	−	+	−	+	+	+	+	+	+	+	−	−	−	−	−	−	−	−	*Does not meet several critical criteria. Do not develop objective.*

Figure 7.5. Sample recreation/leisure activity analysis for 22-year-old Tara, who uses some pictures to augment her speech, works at a movie theater, and prefers activities involving gross motor skills to activities requiring fine motor skills.

grams (1975). The components have been extensively used and revised several times (Brown et al., 1980; Falvey et al., 1979; Ford et al., 1981). Following is a list of these components:

1. *What* activity should be taught?
2. *Why* should an activity be taught?
3. *Where* should an activity be taught?
4. *How* should an activity be taught?
5. What *performance criteria* should be sought?
6. What *materials* should be used?
7. What *measurement strategies* should be used?

Each component is discussed in this chapter as it applies to developing curriculum within the recreation/leisure domain.

What Activities Should Be Taught?

This component emphasizes the need to obtain and take into account the information secured from the ecological and student repertoire inventories. The ecological inventory is a strategy for systematically identifying the activities performed by nonhandicapped persons. In order to determine chronological age–appropriate recreation/leisure activities, a delineation of the activities that nonhandicapped peers are performing is necessary. A more detailed discussion of strategies for conducting ecological inventories is presented in Chapter 3 of this volume. Figure 7.6 provides an example of an ecological inventory of recreation/leisure environments and activities that was conducted across age groups by the author.

The student repertoire inventory is a strategy for determining the specific skill repertoire of an individual. This involves assessing the individual's current skill repertoire of recreation/leisure activities. In addition, comparing and analyzing his or her repertoire in relation to the repertoire of nonhandicapped peers is essential for determining what recreation/leisure activities need to be learned. For example, in order to determine which chronological age–appropriate recreation/leisure activities to teach at a neighborhood park, an ecological inventory (i.e., nonhandicapped peer repertoire) of the specific park an individual will use is crucial, since parks vary in terms of available activities, resources, materials, behavior norms and expectations, and so forth. The individual's performance of the skills necessary to engage in the identified activity at the specific park is observed and recorded. Finally, a discrepancy analysis of the individual's performance is conducted to determine what skills the individual needs in order to perform the activity, or if appropriate, what adaptations might be developed to enhance his or her participation. A more detailed discussion of strategies for conducting student repertoire inventories is outlined in Chapter 3 of this volume.

	Sample activities across ages			
Environment	Preschool	Elementary	Adolescent	Adult
Culver City Movie Theatre	Accompany older sibling to matinée Accompany older sibling to purchase popcorn Eat popcorn	Accompany friend to matinée Purchase popcorn Eat popcorn	Accompany friend to movie theater at night Purchase popcorn Eat popcorn	Go alone to movie theatre Purchase popcorn Eat popcorn
Venice Beach	Play with toys in the sand	Play in the waves	Go surfing	Sunbathe
Griffith Park	Play in sandbox and on "tots" equipment	Play on regular equipment	Play "organized" softball	Have a picnic

Figure 7.6. Example of ecological inventory or recreation/leisure activities and environments, conducted across ages.

Why Should an Activity Be Taught?

It is important to determine what to teach, based on the "criterion of ultimate functioning" (Brown, Nietupski, & Hamre-Nietupski, 1976). Similarly, it is important to identify the reasons for teaching an activity and the potential consequences of not teaching the activity. For example, an adult with severe handicaps who is not taught to engage in appropriate leisure activities during breaktime at his or her place of employment may be denied access to the break room, and ultimately, the job itself. In deciding whether or not to teach an activity, educators and recreators should address whether the activity will help to prepare the individual to function as independently as possible, in as many environments as possible. A major factor in determining why to teach a particular activity is to consider the individual's and family's preferences. As stated earlier, to determine an individual's preferences, systematic and frequent observations of the individual engaging in a variety of recreation/leisure activities must be conducted. Interviews with the individual, with his or her parents, and with significant others to determine his or her family preferences are also appropriate. Figure 7.7 provides an example of a parent questionnaire regarding recreation/leisure activities that was developed by Wuerch and Voeltz (1982).

How Should an Activity Be Taught?

It is important to systematically identify the appropriate instructional arrangements for each student, that is, the cues and corrections, the hierarchy of reinforcement contingencies, and the fading procedures. When conducting a student repertoire inventory, educators can evaluate how an individual is currently performing an activity and can observe the natural cues and corrections that exist. This information should be used to determine the cues, corrections, materials, reinforcement, and other stimuli that will be used when teaching the individual the recreation/leisure activity. Adaptations, as well as instructional cues, corrections, reinforcement, and materials, should be faded as quickly and effectively as possible. This is done to enhance his or her opportunity to function as independently as possible in as many recreation/leisure environments as possible.

What Performance Criteria Should Be Sought?

There is a need for systematically determining how well an individual performs an activity. When judging how well a student performs an activity, educators and recreators should compare his or her performance to that of nonhandicapped peers. Performance criteria are usually based upon latency, rate, and/or duration. *Latency* refers to the amount of time it takes an individual to begin performing a skill from the time the cue to begin is given. For example, when inventorying the skills necessary to play a video game, it is essential that the amount of response time between when the coin or token is inserted, and when

Home Leisure Activities Survey

Student: ____________ Date: ____________ Completed by: ____________

1. Please list any leisure activities available in your home, including other children's toys and games, in which your child has shown some interest.

2. What are your child's favorite leisure activities?

3. What does your child typically do during his or her free time?

4. Can you list some indoor or outdoor activities your family enjoys doing together? (Please list these beginning with those you *most prefer*).

5. Are there any special *space* or *transportation* needs that we should consider in planning leisure or recreation activities for your child?

6. People resources: Are there other people in the home who spend leisure time with your child? What would you like your child to be able to do with these persons?

7. Which of these activities are available in the home?

____ Lego	____ TV Video Games	____ Portable Bowling	____ Marble Rollway	____ Target Games
____ Pinball Games	____ Lite-Brite	____ Simon	____ Remote Control Toys	____ Musical Toys

8. Please assign a rating to each activity to indicate how interesting you think your child would find the activity.
   1 = not very interesting; 2 = somewhat interesting; 3 = very interesting

____ Lego	____ TV Video Games	____ Portable Bowling	____ Marble Rollway	____ Target Games
____ Pinball Games	____ Lite-Brite	____ Simon	____ Remote Control Toys	____ Musical Toys

9. Which of these activities is your child permitted to play with?

____ Lego	____ TV Video Games	____ Portable Bowling	____ Marble Rollway	____ Target Games
____ Pinball Games	____ Lite-Brite	____ Simon	____ Remote Control Toys	____ Musical Toys

10. Which of these activities do you feel are appropriate leisure time activities for your child?

____ Lego	____ TV Video Games	____ Portable Bowling	____ Marble Rollway	____ Target Games
____ Pinball Games	____ Lite-Brite	____ Simon	____ Remote Control Toys	____ Musical Toys

Figure 7.7. Example of parent questionnaire regarding recreation/leisure activities, developed by Wuerch and Voeltz (1982; reprinted by permission).

the individual should begin playing (so as not to lose his or her "turn"), should be specified as the performance criterion that must be demonstrated. *Rate* refers to the number of times an individual performs an activity divided by the number of minutes. For example, when teaching someone to play the card game, "Uno," it is necessary to determine the speed typically demonstrated and acceptable when dealing cards to all the players. To determine this, educators and recreators can observe nonhandicapped peers dealing cards and can specify the rate based on their performance. *Duration* refers to the total amount of time an individual requires to perform an activity. For example, after observing 10 nonhandicapped persons purchasing sodas from a vending machine, a teacher concludes that each purchase took 15–30 seconds. The performance criterion expected of an individual with severe handicaps when purchasing a soda in the same environment should then be 15–30 seconds.

What Materials Should Be Used?

It is necessary to use natural materials rather than artificial materials when teaching persons with severe handicaps to function in integrated recreation/leisure environments. For instance, if an individual is being taught to give a street vendor 35¢ for an ice cream bar, it would be absurd to use "play" money to teach this specific activity. When artificial material adaptations—such as picture communication books—are necessary, they should be habilitative in nature. Additionally, it should be dignifying, and should ensure the individual's participation in as many activities as possible.

What Measurement Strategies Should Be Used?

It is important to empirically verify an individual's performance. Because of the variety of stimulus dimensions present in recreation/leisure environments, it is particularly critical that strategies for evaluating a student's performance be developed and implemented. These strategies should be designed so that the maximum amount of evaluative information is secured with the least amount of disruption in teaching and in interactions with the individual being taught. Evaluative information provides not only an individual's progress data, but also information that assists educators and recreators in justifying teaching recreation/leisure activities within a variety of natural environments. Figure 7.8 provides a sample data sheet that can be used to evaluate a 5-year-old student's progress in recreation/leisure activities.

AFTER-SCHOOL AND WORK RECREATION OPPORTUNITIES

Historically, when persons with severe handicaps have been afforded the opportunity to engage in recreation/leisure activities after school, or after other programmed hours (e.g., after sheltered workshop hours), these activities were generally designated as "handicapped only." That is, they were conducted as

Leisure Materials	Materials chosen? (✔ = yes)	Amount of time played	Appropriately played with material?	Comments
Doll	✔ ✔ ✔ ✔ ✔	*10 min.* *5 min.* *8 min.* *2 min.* *1 min.*	*Yes* *Yes* *Hit another student* *Banged doll on floor* *Yes*	*Seems to choose this toy most often*
Toy truck				*Never chose this toy*
Dollhouse	✔	*3 min.*	*Did not seem to know what to do*	*Chose toy once, but if instructed, might choose more often*
Record player				*Never chose to play with this toy, but enjoys music if someone else turns on record player*

Figure 7.8. Sample data sheet for evaluating students' progress in recreation/leisure activities.

segregated activities, such as in the Special Olympics, or in special camps (Schleien & Larson, 1986). As the goal to provide full integration for all individuals with severe handicaps is realized, it is necessary to work with local services, organizations, and programs that provide recreation to the general community to increase the skill and confidence of such groups in actively involving individuals with severe handicaps in their programs.

To facilitate the inclusion by local school districts and recreation centers of students with severe handicaps in after-school programs, Schleien and Ray (1988) have developed a task analysis that is presented in Table 7.1. In addition to the actions suggested by Schleien and Ray, developing a task force of parents, educators, recreators, and other interested persons might be helpful. This task force should assist in the creation, modification, and expansion of after-school and community programs for all students. School-based as well as community-based recreation programs should be represented on this task force and explored in terms of access.

In working with recreation centers and other organizations that offer community recreational activities for the general community, educators, recreators, and parents can conduct awareness inservice training sessions on the abilities, disabilities, and needs of people with disabilities. In addition, it would be use-

Table 7.1. A process for including persons with disabilities in after-school recreation programs

Step 1. School Personnel:
- a. Contact recreation personnel for class and registration information.
- b. Inform recreation personnel of the general abilities and interests of their students with disabilities who may be potential participants.

Step 2. Recreation Personnel:
- a. Highlight programs that would provide the most appropriate, successful, and enjoyable integrated experiences.
- b. Send class and registration materials.

Step 3. School Personnel:
- a. Send registration materials home with students, along with highlighted recommended programs.

Step 4. School Personnel:
- a. Once received from students and/or parents, send registration information to the appropriate staff person for processing.

Step 5. School Personnel or Recreation Personnel:
- a. Call recreation personnel or school personnel to arrange meeting to discuss participant characteristics with program instructor(s) and/or complete Environmental Analysis Inventory.

Step 6. Recreation Personnel:
- a. Contact program instructors for meeting established in Step 5.

Step 7. The meeting agenda should address, but not be limited to:

	Content	*Provided by*
a.	Description of participant's abilities	School personnel
b.	Need for volunteer advocate	School personnel
c.	Expectations and basic skills needed in class	Instructor
d.	Anticipated modifications or adaptations	All
e.	Date and time of follow-up meeting (either during or at conclusion of program) to address following questions: 1. Could process be improved? How? 2. Is there a resource to solicit and train volunteer advocates? 3. Is there a need for more staff training? 4. Other:	All

ful to assess the specific settings used for recreation and to recommend adaptations that would facilitate an individual's involvement. Finally, reinforcing inclusion efforts by the various centers and simultaneously pushing for more integration is likely to facilitate full integration.

Finally, it would be helpful to develop a "resource bank" of available recreation/leisure opportunities within the community. The bank could include information from the following agencies:

Parks and recreation
Recreation centers
YMCA and YWCA
Boys' and girls' clubs
Scouting organizations
Community colleges

Adult education
Churches and synagogues
Hobby groups and clubs
Neighborhood gyms and sports clubs

Each agency listed in the bank should include an address, phone number, director's name, and brochure listing programs and available services. This information should be updated regularly to ensure accuracy.

SUMMARY

Neighborhood schools and community jobs are environments that enable students to meet playmates and co-workers with whom to engage in recreation. Such environments must be available to individuals with severe handicaps. There are several critical steps that should be employed that will assist educators and recreators to develop, establish, implement, and monitor appropriate recreation/leisure programs. The components and steps presented in this chapter are summarized below:

Insist on participation in "regular" programs and discourage maintainance of "special" programs.
Instruct individuals to engage in chronological age–appropriate preferred activities alone, with peers, friends, siblings, and family.
Encourage and facilitate self-initiation and choice making.
Develop after-school and after-program recreation opportunities that offer interactions with nonhandicapped peers.

This chapter provides a rationale for including systematic and frequent instruction in a wide variety of chronological age–appropriate recreation/leisure activities and environments. In addition, strategies for developing and implementing instructional programs are included. The importance of identifying individuals' preferences as the basis for determining the specific recreation/leisure skills to be taught is articulated. In addition, strategies for establishing community recreation opportunities for individuals with severe handicaps are identified.

REFERENCES

Adkins, J., & Matson, J. (1980). Teaching institutionalized mentally retarded adults social appropriate leisure skills. *Mental Retardation, 18,* 249–252.

Bambara, L., Siegel-Causey, P., Shores, R.E., & Fox, J.J. (1984). A comparison of reactive and nonreactive toys on severely handicapped children's manipulative play. *Journal of The Association for Persons with Severe Handicaps, 9*(2), 142–149.

Banks, R., & Aveno, A. (1986). Adapted miniature golf: A community leisure program for students with severe physical disabilities. *Journal of The Association for Persons with Severe Handicaps, 11*(3), 209–215.

Baumgart, D., Brown, L., Pumpian, I., Nisbet, J., Ford, A., Sweet, M., Messina, R., & Schroeder, J. (1982). Principle of partial participation and individualized adaptations in educational programs for severely handicapped students. *Journal of The Association for the Severely Handicapped, 7*(2), 17–27.

Brown, L., Falvey, M., Vincent, L., Kaye, N., Johnson, F., Ferrara-Parrish, P., & Gruenewald, L. (1980). Strategies for generating comprehensive, longitudinal and chronological age appropriate individual educational plans for adolescent and young adult severely handicapped students. *Journal of Special Education, 14*(2), 199–215.

Brown, L., Neitupski, J., & Hamre-Nietupski, S. (1976). The criterion of ultimate functioning and public school services for severely handicapped students. In M. A. Thomas (Ed.), *Hey, don't forget about me! Education's investment in the severely, profoundly and multiply handicapped* (pp. 2–15). Reston, VA: Council for Exceptional Children.

Coleman, R.S., & Whitman, T.L. (1984). Developing, generalizing, and maintaining physical fitness in mentally retarded adults: Toward a self-directed program. *Analysis and Intervention in Developmental Disabilities, 4*(2), 109–128.

Dattilo, J., & Rusch, F.R. (1985). Effects of choice on behavior: Leisure participation for persons with severe handicaps. *Journal of The Association for Persons with Severe Handicaps, 10*(4), 194–199.

Falvey, M., Ferrara-Parrish, P., Johnson, F., Pumpian, I., Schroeder, J., & Brown, L. (1979). Curricular strategies for generating comprehensive, longitudinal and chronological age appropriate functional individual vocational plans for severely handicapped adolescents and young adults. In L. Brown, M. Falvey, D. Baumgart, I. Pumpian, J. Schroeder, & L. Gruenewald (Eds.), *Strategies for teaching chronological age appropriate functional skills to adolescents and young adult severely handicapped students* (Vol. 9, pp. 102–161). Madison, WI: Madison Metropolitan School District.

Flavell, J. (1973). Reduction of stereotypes by reinforcement of toy play. *Mental Retardation, 11,* 21–23.

Ford, A., Brown, L., Pumpian, I., Baumgart, D., Nesbit, J., Schroeder, J., & Loomis, R. (1981). Strategies for developing individualized recreation/leisure plans for adolescent and young adult severely handicapped students. In L. Brown, M. Falvey, D. Baumgart, I. Pumpian, D. Baumgart, J. Nesbit, A. Ford, J. Schroeder, & R. Loomis (Eds.), *Curricular strategies for teaching severely handicapped students functional skills in school and nonschool environments* (Vol. 10, pp. 14–151). Madison, WI: Madison Metropolitan School District.

Guess, D., Benson, H., & Siegel-Causey, E. (1985). Concepts and issues related to choice-making and autonomy among persons with severe handicaps. *Journal of The Association for Persons with Severe Handicaps, 10*(2), 79–86.

Guralnick, D.B. (Ed.). (1970). *Webster's New World Dictionary.* New York: World Publishing Company.

Hamre-Nietupski, S., Nietupski, J., Sandvig, R., Sandvig, M. B., & Ayers, B. (1984). Leisure skills instruction in a community residential setting with young adults who are deaf/blind severely handicapped. *Journal of The Association for Persons with Severe Handicaps, 9,* 49–54.

Hill, J.W., Wehman, P., & Horst, G. (1982). Toward generalization of appropriate leisure and social behavior in severely handicapped youth: Pinball machine use. *Journal of The Association for the Severely Handicapped, 6,* 38–44.

Horner, R.D. (1980). The effects of an environmental enrichment program on the behavior of institutionalized profoundly retarded children. *Journal of Applied Behavior Analysis, 13,* 473–491.

Kissel, R.C., & Whitman, T.L. (1977). An examination of the direct and generalized effects of a play-training and over correction procedure upon the self-stimulatory behavior of a profoundly retarded boy. *AAESPH Review, 2,* 131–146.

Nietupski, J., Hamre-Nietupski, S., & Ayres, B. (1984). Review of task analytic leisure skill training efforts: Practitioner implications and future research needs. *Journal of The Association for Persons with Severe Handicaps, 9*(2), 88–97.

Nietupski, J., Hamre-Nietupski, S., Green, K., Varnum-Teeter, K., Twedt, B., LaPera, D., Scebold, K., & Hanarahan, M. (1986). Self-initiated and sustained leisure activity participation by students with moderate/severe handicaps. *Education and Training of the Mentally Retarded, 21*(4), 259–264.

Nietupski, J., & Svoboda, R. (1980). Teaching a cooperative leisure skill to severely handicapped adults. *Education and Training of the Mentally Retarded, 17,* 38–43.

Schleien, S.J., Certo, N., & Muccino, A. (1984). Acquisition of leisure skills by a severely handicapped adolescent: A data based instructional program. *Education and Training of the Mentally Retarded. 19*(4), 297–305.

Schleien, S.J., & Larson, A. (1986). Adult leisure education for the independent use of a community recreation center. *Journal of The Association for Persons with Severe Handicaps, 11*(1), 39–44.

Schleien, S.J., & Ray, M.T. (1988). *Community recreation and persons with disabilities: Strategies for integration.* Baltimore: Paul H. Brookes Publishing Co.

Schloss, P.J., Smith, M.A., & Kiehl, W. (1986). Rec club: A community centered approach to recreational development for adults with mild to moderate retardation. *Education and Training of the Mentally Retarded, 21*(4),282–288.

Sedlak, R.A., Doyle, M., & Schloss, P. (1982). Video games: A training and generalization demonstration with severely retarded adolescents. *Education and Training of the Mentally Retarded, 17,* 332–336.

Stainback, W., Stainback, S., & Forest, M. (Eds.). (1989). *Educating all students in the mainstream of regular education.* Baltimore: Paul H. Brookes Publishing Co.

Voeltz, L.M., Wuerch, B.B., & Bockhaut, C.H. (1982). Social validation of leisure activities training with severely handicapped youth. *Journal of The Association for the Severely Handicapped, 7,* 3–13.

Voeltz, L.M., Wuerch, B.B., & Wilcox, B. (1982). Leisure and recreation: Preparation for independence, integration, and self-fulfillment. In B. Wilcox & G.T. Bellamy, *Design of high school programs for severely handicapped students* (pp. 175–209). Baltimore: Paul H. Brookes Publishing Co.

Wacker, D.P., Berg, W.K., & Moore, S.J. (1984). Increasing on task performance of students with severe handicaps on cooperative games. *Education and Training of the Mentally Retarded, 19*(3), 183–190.

Wahler, R.G., & Fox, J.J. (1980). Solitary toy play and time out: A family treatment package for children with aggressive and oppositional behavior. *Journal of Applied Behavior Analysis, 13,* 23–29.

Wehman, P., Renzaglia, A., Berry G., Schultz, R., & Karan, O. (1978). Developing a leisure skill repertoire in severely and profoundly handicapped persons. *AAESPH Review, 3,* 162–172.

Wehman, P., Schleien, S.J., & Kiernan, J. (1980). Age appropriate recreation programs for severely handicapped youth and adults. *Journal of The Association for the Severely Handicapped, 5*(4), 395–408.

Williams, W., Brown, L., & Certo, N. (1975). Basic components of instructional programs. In L. Brown, T. Crowner, W. Williams, & R. York (Eds.), *Madison's alternative for zero exclusion: A book of readings* (Vol. 5). Madison, WI: Madison Public Schools.

Wuerch, B.B., & Voeltz, L.M. (1982). *Longitudinal leisure skills for severely handicapped learners: The Ho'onanea curriculum component.* Baltimore: Paul H. Brookes Publishing Co.

EIGHT

EMPLOYMENT SKILLS

Kathryn D. Bishop and Mary A. Falvey

We do not exist in order to work,
but we work in order to be.
—R. Ruether (1977)

EMPLOYMENT IS OFTEN the prerequisite for acceptance of adults in contemporary societies. If individuals are excluded from participation in the work of a society and from completion of contributory tasks, they cannot be free from economic dependence on family or governmental subsistence. Consequently, if individuals with severe handicaps are unskilled and inexperienced in meaningful work, they cannot escape their readily sanctioned segregated existence. Work that is carefully chosen and creatively structured to match an individual is essential to personal growth that will result in less compulsive institutional needs and dependencies.

Employment means work for pay. Volunteer work or nonpaid prevocational tasks, which many adults with severe handicaps are "allowed" to do, can truly be regarded as acts of complaisance and not as chosen options. Volunteer work or work activities are often viewed subjectively as therapeutic options. Such options can actually be work that is reduced to a level of diversional pursuits similar to the self-expressive productivity of basket weaving. There is a difference, however, between volunteerism that serves to maintain an individual's dependent status and volunteerism that leads to change. Appropriate volunteerism consists of activities in which active participation allows greater autonomy, increased opportunity, and enhanced decision making. Meaningful volunteerism and meaningful employment need not preclude each other, and both should be engaged in for the purpose of increasing one's quality of life.

The opportunities for individuals with severe handicaps to become employed in the community and to be paid for the work they produce alongside nonhandicapped co-workers have increased significantly in the last few years. The criterion of ultimate functioning as defined and described by Brown, Nietupski, and Hamre-Nietupski (1976) challenges educators, adult service providers, parents, vocational counselors, employers, and members of the community to develop services that will result in the student or adult acquiring skills in natural environments. These skills should allow him or her greater opportunities for integrated interactions in a variety of community settings, one of which is a place of employment.

Employment training must begin as soon as possible in the course of a student's education, and the training must be coordinated from training site to training site, so that students' experiences build upon each other (Lynch, 1984; Wehman, 1983). Employment training for preschool students and primary elementary–age students might consist of learning to perform jobs in the classroom, school yard, and at home. Junior and senior high school–age students might learn jobs such as busing tables, delivering newspapers, or cleaning hotel rooms. Table 8.1 lists several of the employment training activities that would be appropriate across ages.

The purpose of this chapter is to provide an overview of integrated, paid, meaningful work opportunities that possess the necessary support for individuals with severe handicaps (i.e., supported employment), and its components. Specifically, the chapter includes a brief historical perspective of the conception of supported employment, and discussions of marketing, job development, job match, work site analyses, job coaching, and follow-along services.

Adults with severe handicaps have historically been provided with a variety of day program options. However, those options were generally available in restrictive sheltered or segregated settings (Falvey, Bishop, Grenot-Scheyer, & Coots, 1988). These settings (adult development centers, work activity centers, and sheltered workshops) were developed as a continuum of sheltered training programs which individuals would "flow through" before moving into competitive employment (Bellamy, Rhodes, Bourbeau, & Mank, 1986). This continuum usually begins at age 21 after graduation from public schools; such schools traditionally lacked transition programs (see Chapter 9, this volume, for more information on transition). According to Bellamy (1983), the average length of stay per individual is 37 years for development centers, 10 years for work activity centers, and 9 years for sheltered workshops. If a student/client started in the adult development center and matriculated through the continuum, he or she would be 77 years old before being eligible for work in competitive employment. In other words, the continuum does not allow thousands of individuals to take advantage of integrated employment opportunities.

Table 8.1. Vocational environments and activities across ages

	Activities			
Environment	Preschool	Elementary	Adolescent	Adult
Elementary school playground	Pick up papers and garbage	Wash tables	Bus tables	Do all custodial chores
Home	Pick up toys	Set table	Prepare sandwich	Prepare lunch to take to work
Neighborhood paper route	Assist older sibling fold papers and put them into canvas bag	Deliver paper and assist older sibling in collecting fees	Walk around neighbor-hood delivering papers and collecting fees	Drive pick up truck around community delivering papers and collecting fees

In addition to the fact that individuals are not moving through the continuum, it is apparent that time served in the sheltered or segregated options may actually be antihabilitative. Following are some of the antihabilitative and restrictive characteristics of these training environments:

1. Work performed often requires minimal learning on the part of the workers (Brown et al., 1983).
2. The best workers are often retained for the more demanding work, instead of being placed in and trained for a nonsheltered vocational environment.
3. Adequate time is not available for training workers in nonsheltered environment.
4. Personnel often lack training in critical areas, such as effective teaching methods, production, and providing "real" job training (Brown et al., 1983).
5. "Down time" or "dead time" is frequent.
6. Formal vocational evaluation is often based upon inferences, not upon actual observation of that student/client in actual community jobs (Wehman, 1981).
7. All the students/clients receiving training are handicapped and are therefore afforded no contact with nonhandicapped workers (Brown et al., 1983).
8. Inappropriate assumptions are made that persons in sheltered workshops and activity centers "enjoy" or are more competent at tasks that involve sitting or standing at tables using predominantly fine motor and coordination skills.
9. Tasks vary according to the contracts secured (Brown et al., 1983) rather than according to the student's/client's training needs.
10. Equipment is often out of date and in poor condition, resulting in worthless training.
11. Frequently, normal workdays or workweeks are not followed. As a consequence, persons in workshops or at centers do not have sufficient opportunity to build endurance. Historically, workshops and centers have interrupted work periods, particularly at holiday times, with events such as dances that featured age-inappropriate music (Brown et al., 1983).
12. Systematic strategies are not developed to assist the student/client to make the transition to less restrictive settings (Brown et al., 1983).
13. Irrelevant exit requirements or prerequisite skill requirements are often higher than requirements in "real" community jobs (Bellamy, 1983).

Early research (Bellamy, Horner, & Inman, 1979; Gold, 1972) demonstrated that individuals with severe handicaps could complete vocational products when given appropriate instruction. At the same time, other leaders in the field began to demonstrate the value and benefit of enabling individuals with severe disabilities to receive services in integrated settings (Brown et al., 1977; Kenowitz, Zweibel, & Edgar, 1978; Strain, 1983). Combining the fact that these individuals are able to be productive along with the fact that integrated services are more appropriate resulted in the concept of supported employment.

SUPPORTED EMPLOYMENT

In 1985, the Office of Special Education and Rehabilitation Services issued a supported employment initiative indicating that supported employment should be the primary service option for adults with mental retardation. Supported employment is a concept that focuses on outcomes and does not function as a "program" (McDaniel & Flippo, 1986). The outcomes for supported employment make up its definition:

Involves paid meaningful work (i.e., work that others would be paid to do)
Features work performed in integrated settings (i.e., settings that approximate natural proportions of employees with and without handicaps)
Includes a place and train approach (i.e., elimination of ineffective prevocational training programs)
Is appropriate for individuals who need ongoing support, not in a time limited manner (i.e., a zero reject service)

Current studies are now being published that demonstrate the success and further potential of people receiving supported employment services. Wehman, Hill, Wood, and Parent (1987) completed a study of 21 persons labeled severely mentally retarded which demonstrated that "positive, paid, vocational outcomes can accrue for people with severe intellectual impairments" (p.15). Hill, Wehman, Kregel, Banks, and Metzler (1987) provided a longitudinal cost/benefit analysis of supported employment that showed "a substantial savings to taxpayers . . . along with significant financial benefits to all consumers" (p. 182).

Beyond demonstrating that individuals with severe handicaps can be successful in paid integrated employment, and that providing them support to do so is fiscally beneficial, there are other benefits of supported employment. The following list represents the way in which supported employment has affected various constituency groups:

1. Local Secondary Programs and Adult Service Providers
   - more motivated staff
   - harder working staff
   - integrated into the community
   - adjusting to new regulations and expectations
   - exploring creative and fiscally responsible building usages
   - reexamination of mission and the purpose of service provision
   - need for new and increased inservice training

2. Statewide Agencies
    consortium of agencies facilitating collaboration
    creating supported life options
    regulating community-based integrated school programs
    provide lobbying efforts and feedback to federal agencies
3. Employers
    high quality, reliable employment service
    cost effective services
    prestige and good publicity
    meeting hiring quotas
    raising awareness of the capabilities of people who are handicapped
4. Employeees/Co-workers
    new friends
    high quality, reliable co-workers
    increase in job satisfaction
    raising awareness of disability issues
5. Students/Clients
    higher quality of life
    more disposable income
    greater dignity
    new friends, social interactions
    challenging work
    productive life-style
    greater community access and awareness
6. Families/significant others
    more dignified individual
    self-supporting, contributing individual
    sharing common experiences with other family members
    greater community awareness and support
    less dependence by the individual

Belief that supported employment is a viable option is the first step toward delivery of successful services. Service providers must place a strong value on integration and meaningful work, or the logistical challenges of involving people with the most severe handicaps will be looked upon as insurmountable barriers. Without the philosophical value base, most efforts will be rendered futile. If one values the concept, however, accepting and creatively working through the logistical challenges becomes the motivation, excitement, and reward for service providers.

Supported employment may be offered through a number of modes, depending on the needs of an individual. Individual placement allows the greatest individualization, integration, and independence, and it is achieved by placing and supporting a single individual with severe handicaps into an employment site. Small group placements (preferably no more than four individuals) and mobile crews are viable options that allow more on-the-job supervision but may inhibit maximal interaction opportunities with nonhandicapped co-workers. Affirmative industry is an option that may prove successful in rural areas or in areas of high unemployment. This model introduces a needed business to the community which happens to employ a small number of people with handicaps and a greater number of people without handicaps who had previously been unemployed. Following are some specific examples of supported employment placements:

> Steve is a young man who is labeled as deaf and severely mentally retarded. He shares a job with George, who is legally blind, is severely mentally retarded, and uses a wheelchair due to paraplegic cerebral palsy. Betsy and Stephanie are also a part of this group. They both have Down syndrome resulting in moderate mental retardation. This group of individuals, along with 75 nonhandicapped co-workers, are employed by a beer distributor which is a major employer in their community. Steve's job is to unload the trucks returning expired beer and carry the cases to George. George opens each can and pours the expired beer into a disposal system. Betsy and Stephanie take the empty cans from the bin near George to another section of the plant where both women treat and recycle the cans.
>
> Each employee is paid according to his or her productivity. A Department of Labor subminimum wage certificate was obtained because of George's low productivity rate. A job coach supports the crew by facilitating interactions with co-workers, assisting George with physical needs, and teaching strategies for self-monitoring and increased productivity. The agency provides transportation for the group.
>
> Mario is a young man who is labeled with autism and who exhibits aggressive/assaultive behaviors. He reacts very strongly to changes in his routine and to unfamiliar people. Mario is employed at a 40-acre wholesale nursery where he is assigned his own area; he waters trees and plants and removes dead leaves. Mario, like his co-workers, works alone, but he eats lunch and takes breaks with five co-workers who do similar work in other areas of the nursery. Mario receives support related to his behavior when new staff are added or if his job changes that day due to employer needs. Mario is also learning to use a picture communication system in his interactions at work, at home, and in the community.
>
> Although Bonnie is nonambulatory and requires assistance with catheterization and gavage feeding, she is in an individual placement. Bonnie is employed by a computer access corporation where she and two nonhandicapped women work as part of a sales team. While the nonhandicapped women discuss payment options, programming capabilities, and peripheral equipment, Bonnie demonstrates sample software while operating a variety of adaptations and accommodations that promote adaptive hardware. A job coach initially supported and trained Bonnie full time but he has gradually phased out his support. Now the job coach comes 1 hour a day to assist with Bonnie's physical needs and teach her to use any new equipment. Bonnie receives a commensurate wage and is paid directly by the employer.

Supported employment provides individualized training at the job site, as well as training related to other areas that may be needed to maintain employment. For example, Ronda needed direct instruction on sorting the mail at Adam's Office Machines, while Kenni, who can already sort the mail, needed direct instruction on riding the bus to work. Areas such as transportation, social skills, and banking may need to be addressed in order for some individuals to successfully maintain their employment.

Regardless of the specific type of supported employment model that is being implemented, there are several key components of supported employment. Each component is a necessary mechanism for providing supported employment services. It is important to note, however, that the components do not occur in a linear sequence, and frequently overlap in implementation. The reader should also note that the term "service provider" is used throughout the text to refer to school districts and/or adult agencies.

MARKETING AND JOB DEVELOPMENT

Promoting supported employment in the community and developing jobs with specific employers requires a new perspective on the part of service providers. Service provision agencies are typically staffed by people who have backgrounds in human service fields (e.g., rehabilitation, special education, social work). However, marketing and job development in supported employment require staff to take a business-like approach, since one customer of the service is the private sector employer. Marketing requires creating, promoting, funding, and distributing services that accommodate the needs of the employment community, as well as the needs of the consumers who have disabilities. Marketing revolves around a system that provides services that are valued by employers and consumers, and does not necessarily mean marketing an individual client.

The following list from Robinson, Andrew, Bishop, Dutton, and LaMar (1988) delineates some of the services and benefits featured in marketing to employers:

Individual Placement Options:
- pre-screening based on client abilities
- job analysis based on employer needs
- no cost on-the-job training
- guarantee that job gets done to employer satisfaction
- systematic evaluation of job performance
- open-ended, not time limited support to employer/employee through duration of employment

Contracted Service Options
- management services providing full range of personnel support for one or more positions
- hiring, training services provided
- reliability guaranteed, absenteeism and turn-over eliminated

- quality control assured through supervised option
- no-risk, probationary trial period leading to potential hire
- job redesign, if required (p. 3)

In addition to marketing supported employment services to employers, job development may also be new to service providers. While marketing introduces and promotes the concept, job development means actually securing specific jobs that can then be matched with an individual seeking employment. Most development techniques are techniques commonly used in acquiring jobs. One can become familiar with local employment opportunities by determining the needs of community employers. This can be achieved by:

Making telephone calls—contacting businesses listed in the local phone book and setting up an appointment to meet with them
Reading local newspapers (particularly want ads) and publications
Attending Chamber of Commerce or other service club meetings
Working with other employment placement services (e.g., university employment office, temporary help agencies)
Developing a business or employer advisory committee
Utilizing the Employment Development Department resources (e.g., job banks)
Utilizing personal contacts—student/consumer, parents, friends, colleagues, relatives, neighbors

Once access to an employer has been gained, it is important for the service provider to sell the employer on the benefits of the service. To do this, the service provider must have a good understanding of the service being offered and of the potential needs of the employer. Supported employment relies on the services provided by the agency rather than on the particular strengths of any specific student or client. Therefore, the mission statement of the organization should emphasize those services and should have a business focus. This point is illustrated in the following two mission statements:

> The purpose of the Heavenly Hearts Mission is to help handicapped people receive the love and attention they deserve. By allowing us to work in your business, you will be serving the less fortunate in your community.
>
> versus
>
> Employment Plus provides employers with access to a labor pool and offers training, evaluation, and supervision of the employees at no extra cost. Employment Plus also guarantees production that meets the standards of the employer.

The second mission statement is more dignified, and reflects appropriate services, and because it has a "business tone," it is more likely to result in greater employer participation.

The aspect of job development that differs from regular placement agencies is that of "development." Typically, job developers seek positions that are being advertised or have existing standard job descriptions. For persons with severe handicaps, job development requires studying existing jobs and businesses and potentially creating or developing jobs that are not currently in existence or are not currently an intact position. This is not to say that unnecessary or artificial jobs are created. By actually studying the business, a good job developer may see more efficient and effective ways of personnel utilization.

For example, by observing the daily routine at Jaana's Scandinavian Bakery, a job developer noted that the highly paid pastry chef was spending half his time designing and baking intricate pastries. The other half of his time was spent placing spoonfuls of cookie dough onto cookie sheets and putting the sheets in the oven. Jaana, who owned the bakery, spent her time bagging the freshly baked cookies and balancing the finances of the business, often taking the books home. A third employee alternated between waiting on customers and washing dishes. Although the bakery was not advertising an opening, the job developer was able to point out that her agency could provide someone to scoop the cookie dough and bag the cookies every morning for 4 hours at a reasonable wage. This would allow the pastry chef to concentrate on the fancy baked goods and the owner could work on the accounting during that time. This type of job development takes a developer who can see potential, envision change, and deliver efficient options. The well-developed job is one that matches the potential abilities of the student/client and helps the business as well.

Job Match

The process of pairing an individual with a specific job is called "job match." Creating a successful job match consists of careful client assessment and analysis of job site requirements. The information gathered for the job match focuses not on task specific skills but on job-related factors that can truly "make or break" job success.

Traditional vocational assessments have focused on evaluating an individual's ability or inability to perform simulated work tasks in isolated evaluation units. Although there are precise procedures for conducting evaluations, and a great deal of time and money are spent in this process, traditional assessments virtually reveal no more than the fact that an individual is severely handicapped. Other concerns about the use of traditional assessments include the questionable validity of studies comparing assessments of severely handicapped persons with those of nonhandicapped persons (Gaylord-Ross, 1987).

Assessment relies on the intuitiveness of the professional and his or her ability to gather functional information from as many sources as possible. The goals of assessment as delineated by Gaylord-Ross (1987) are to:

1. Describe overt skills
2. Infer underlying abilities
3. Predict future performance

4. Suggest instructional strategies
5. Determine individual preferences

These goals would best be met through historical and situational assessments as opposed to traditional assessment procedures. Historical assessment consists of gathering information from the individual and from parents and/or significant others, siblings, or former teachers or service providers, as well as from medical records, school records, and previous work histories (see Chapter 3, this volume, for more specific information on how to gather this data). Situational assessments consist of collecting information about an individual while he or she is actually performing tasks in a natural work environment. Situational assessments provide actual information based upon the individual's participation in a potential work site.

For example, after completing a simulated work evaluation (traditional assessment), it was determined that Adam could be successfully employed with support as a mechanic's aide in an auto repair garage, although no situational assessment was completed. This placement lasted for 10 minutes, because Adam hates to get dirty and displays significant behavior problems when asked to do something that will result in getting his hands dirty. This placement was not successful, because it relied only on traditional assessments and not on any functional information. Had the evaluator interviewed Adam's parents or taken Adam to visit a garage, more valuable information would have been gathered and a better job match completed.

The above example helps to illustrate why assessment should not focus on task specific information and should attempt to ascertain information related more to job-related demands. The reason for not focusing on task specific behaviors is twofold. First, the fields of special education and rehabilitation have developed sophisticated instructional and training strategies that enable individuals with severe disabilities to complete even complex tasks (see Chapter 4, this volume). Second, research by Gaston (1988) and Greenspan and Schoultz (1981) demonstrated that individuals with severe handicaps do not lose their jobs due to poor task performance, but more often due to factors related to social skills or external forces. In other words, it is possible to teach someone to change oil, but it is not possible to teach that person to like dirty environments.

Job match is proving to be a critical component of supported employment. Service providers are beginning to report that individuals maintain their jobs for a period of 2–3 months and then begin to develop problems at the workplace. In following up evaluations with these providers, it was found that virtually no job match process was being completed. The most common practice was to find a job and place the first available student/client in the job regardless of any matching. The placements enjoyed a "honeymoon" period, but as soon as the new job became a day-to-day routine, person-job incompatibilities became apparent and were not overcome.

Another factor in the job match process that supports job retention is the assessment and provision of additional resources. Regardless of the individual's interests and the compatiblility of a specific job, other factors must be in place as well. Parent and significant other support must be elicited, transportation issues resolved, and other program options considered. Involving an individual in supported employment addresses only one domain of the individual's life. Assessment includes determining, arranging, and supporting the individual in nonwork related activities, such as recreation and social functions, which enhance the individual's success at work.

Workplace Analyses

Once a potential job match has been made, the service provider gathers more in-depth information about the job itself. At this point, the individual's tasks are to learn the job, know the employment site as a business, and become familiar with personnel. From this process the training plan is developed. The major components of workplace analysis are work site orientation and job site analysis (Mcloughlin, Garner, & Callahan, 1987).

Work site orientation focuses on becoming familiar with the formal and informal policies, practices, and personnel of the business as a whole. This should be viewed as being similar to an orientation for a typical new employee, and should consider the following as delineated by Robinson et al. (1988):

The application form
The interview process
Hiring and firing procedures
Personnel paperwork required (time cards, emergency information)
Layout of plant and location of time clock, restrooms, break areas, and offices
Safety requirements and procedures
Detailed understanding of benefits and work schedules
Channels of communication
Job description

After the service provider has gained a sense of the employment site as a whole, the perspective narrows, and the focus is on the specific job that has been developed. Through job analysis, the service provider should have a good understanding of what the job is, how it is typically done, why it is done, who is involved in doing it, and what skills and equipment it takes to do it. The following list from Robinson et al. (1988) identifies the information that should be obtained in a job analysis:

Set up of work area
Location of tools and supplies
Required production forms and other paperwork
All components of the job
Difficult or tiring parts of the job

Variations within the task sequence or with the job tasks
Procedure for obtaining parts and materials
Procedure for handling finished goods
Expected work behavior (e.g., talking, eating)
The names of all things involved with the job
The person to ask for answers to work questions
Clean up, repair, or maintenance responsibilities
Personalities in the work area
Proper clothing and safety equipment
Procedures for what to do if there is "down time"
Production standards (norms and agreed upon) (p. 8)

A job analysis should be arranged for by scheduling a visit to observe the specific job at a time that is similar to that which the student/client will be performing the job (working at a restaurant during peak hours looks very different from working at the same restaurant during early or late shifts). Note the name of the person being observed and accept all statements from this person in a nonjudgmental fashion. View the employee as an expert and avoid topics of conflict such as union battles or shop gossip. It is also important to verify the information that has been gathered with the supervisor who will be checking the work of the student/client. Figure 8.1 provides an example of a job analysis form.

Once a complete understanding of the job itself has been ascertained, a task analysis can be done. Since a specific client has probably been targeted at this time, the task analysis can be completed with this individual in mind. The task analysis is most useful when used in conjunction with a Student/Client Repertoire Inventory (see Chapter 3 of this volume). The discrepancy analysis and the proposed strategies are the basis from which the job coach (the person providing on-site training to the employee) will begin training.

At this time, strategies for job accommodation should be considered. Accommodation may include restructuring the job or job carving. This consists of taking pieces of jobs or changing the existing job to create a position more suited to a specific individual. Modifications to the work equipment may also aid an individual in being more successful with certain tasks. The time and place the tasks are performed may also be arranged to enhance success. Rehabilitation Engineering, a service offered by the Department of Rehabilitation, is an excellent source of creative accomodation and adaptation strategies, especially for individuals with severe physical disabilities.

Falvey et al. (1979) have described types of adaptations that might be provided within the vocational domain. They are as follows:

1. Adaptations that involve altering student/client characteristics, for example:
   a. Providing physical prompts and assistance by other persons (e.g., guiding a person's hand, gesturing)

Job Site Analysis

Job site: ______________________________

Address: ______________________________

Telephone number: ______________________________

Supervisor(s): ______________________________

Significant co-workers: ______________________________

____

Teacher/vocational specialists: ______________________________

____

Job placement staff: ______________________________

Student(s): ______________________________

____

Work days/hours: ______________________________

Relevant Information (obtain prior to student training)

1. Location of time clock, lounge, lockers, restrooms, pay telephone, etc.:
____
____
____

2. Location of work area and specific set up instructions: ______________
____
____
____

3. Location of materials and supplies: ______________________________
____
____

4. Required paperwork, production forms, documents, etc.: ______________
____
____

5. Procedure for obtaining required job task assignments, materials, and task priorities/sequence: ______________________________
____
____

6. Variations within the task sequence or within the job task: ______________
____
____

7. Procedure for handling finished goods and completing tasks: ______________
____
____

8. Expected work/break behavior (e.g., you can sit, eat, leave business):
____
____
____

(continued)

Job Site Analysis *(continued)*

9. Person(s) to ask for answers to work questions: ______
10. Clean up, maintenance, or repair responsibilities: ______
11. The names of all things involved with the job: ______
12. Procedure for what to do when you run out of work or the equipment breaks down: ______
13. Proper clothing and safety equipment: ______
14. Production and quality expectations: ______
15. Schedule for pay days: ______
16. Initial pay rate: ______
17. Details of benefits, work schedule, and procedures for notification of vacation/sick days: ______
18. Channels of communication: ______
19. Job description: ______
20. Procedure to ensure employer communication of problems: ______

Job Tasks (in prioritized order): ______

Figure 8.1. A sample job site analysis form.

   b. Providing prosthetic devices (e.g. wheelchairs, walkers, arm extensions, picture cards depicting job activities, natural cues, sequences)
   c. Altering dress or cosmetic appearance (e.g., overalls worn in a factory, appropriate haircut, use of deodorant)
2. Activity adaptations that involve alterations in the process of the activity but that do not affect outcomes of the activity, for example:
   a. Altering the sequence of the skills needed to perform the job activity (e.g. obtaining all the necessary materials before cleaning a hotel room, instead of obtaining materials as needed)
   b. Altering the method of performing the activity (e.g., standing when sorting towels instead of sitting)
   c. Providing aids (e.g., cue cards, sequence charts, communication booklets)
   d. Increasing the number of directions for an activity in order to provide more precise information (e.g., changing the directions, "Wash the floor" to, "Get the mop and bucket, fill the bucket with water, place the mop in the bucket, squeeze the mop, and wash the floor")
   e. Changing the materials used to complete the activity (e.g., using a short handled scrubber instead of a dishrag; using Windex and a rag instead of ammonia water and squeegee)
   f. Changing the length of time needed to perform the activity (e.g., allowance for piecework rather than only salary per hour)
   g. Adapting and/or modifying job descriptions so that the student/client might perform a portion of a job (e.g., instead of having all the secretaries at a given job answering phones, composing letters, filing, stuffing envelopes, and performing other job tasks that would not necessarily involve complex verbal and written communication skills)
3. Environmental adaptations that involve changes made within the specific vocational environments, for example:
   a. Providing changes in physical characteristics (e.g., providing ramps, elevators, partitions, changes in noise levels and in lighting)
   b. Effecting attitude changes (e.g., providing information to co-workers about seizures, wheelchair use, valuing people, deemphasizing labels)

Job Coaching

Job coaching is the actual process of providing training to the new employee at the job site. The role of the job coach is perhaps the most critical aspect of successful supported employment. In addition to providing intensive task-related training at job sites, the job coach is the most logical liaison between the employer, the student/client, the parent and/or significant other, and the agency. The high visibility status of the job coach means that her or his attitudes and actions have an impact not only on the individual receiving the training, but also on co-workers, supervisors, and community members in general. The job coach is seen as representing not only him- or herself, but also the individual, the employer, and the school or agency. In a sense, the job coach also reflects the global movement toward supported employment for all persons with severe handicaps.

The training/instructional strategies that a job coach may utilize are similar to strategies that would be used for teaching any task. These strategies will not be discussed at length in this section, but in Chapter 4 of this volume, information is provided on techniques and strategies. The job coach must realize, however, that regardless of the strategies used in training, there are certain characteristics that must always be maintained. These characteristics have been specified by Leitner and Bishop (1988):

> 1. Dignity—the job coach should provide training in such a manner that allows the trainee to maintain his/her dignity. Trainees should not be requested to engage in any training activities that would offend and/or embarrass her/him.
> 2. Appropriateness—the appropriateness of a training activity should be considered in regard to the trainee's chronological age, cultural background, preference for meaningful work, and integration with non-disabled individuals. In addition, any training strategies should be appropriate to the worksite in regard to both formal and informal rules.
> 3. Instructional content—when delivering cues and corrections, the content should be specific and task related.
> 4. Instructional affect—the attitudes and behaviors of the job coach should be appropriate to the particular work site.
> 5. Timing—the job coach should demonstrate the ability to deliver training cues in a timely fashion. That is, training cues should be paired with natural cues whenever possible. In the initial stages of learning, corrections should be provided immediately after the undesired response. Timing should change gradually, as the job coach attempts to fade her/his presence and allow the trainee the opportunity to problem solve, self-correct and receive natural reinforcement.
> 6. Flexibility—job coaches should expect fluctuations and incongruencies in the day-to-day behavior of the trainee, as well as the work place. The job coach should adjust her/his attitudes and/or strategies to meet these changing needs. (p. iv)

Because supported employment services are offered in the community in integrated settings, it is important for job coaches to realize that they are now working in the business world. Therefore, job coaches should realize and act appropriately, according to the norms of that particular business. For example, many businesses expect employees to arrive 10 minutes early for work, dress in a certain way, and follow formal or informal protocols. Therefore, the job coach and the student/client must also display these behaviors.

For the job coach, the student/client and the employer are both customers. A relationship with both must be developed and maintained over time. This relationship is necessary for the initial acceptance and the long-term success of the individual in the workplace. A job coach is also a salesperson and may develop more employment opportunities within a particular business. A good job coach will assess each situation and spend an appropriate percentage of time interacting with employers and/or co-workers. He or she will also spend time on direct instruction or interaction with the student/client, and communication with other support services and the parent/significant other. An important responsibility of the job coach is to instill confidence in those involved with supported employment. The job coach maintains close contact with the client, the co-workers, the employer, and the parent/significant other, and coordinates ongoing communication regarding the student's/client's progress. This can be accomplished by demonstrating commitment to the philosophy of normalization and integration, and by being available when problems or doubts arise, as well as by responding quickly to concerns, and understanding and acknowledging the individual as more than a student/client in a special day program. In other words, for the job coach, technical knowledge is not enough.

Job Coach Support

The concept of job match for individuals in supported employment is important for the job coach as well. Selection of job coaches for a specific site should consider personalities of the job coach and the student/client, the work site culture (e.g., all men or all women, certain language or dialect is predominant), and the skills and interests of the job coach. If a job coach is not well matched to a certain employment site, the placement may be lost through no fault of the student/client, but because of conflicts with the job coach.

Providing management and supervision of job coaches is an issue to which service providers should attend before implementing supported employment services. Scheduling and time management become critical factors due to the number of students/clients being served in different employment locations. A paging or beeper system is helpful here, as in any community-based program, so that staff may be reached easily at any time during their shift. Also, as with other community programs, preservice and inservice training and ongoing supervision are necessary for a successful program. Both formal and informal methods for providing and receiving communication and feedback should be established.

Concerns that may arise are that the job coach may be using inappropriate techniques or may have difficulty with decision-making responsibilities related to fading or changes in strategies. Frequent discussions with supervisors and consistent data collections are appropriate for supporting the job coach in these decisions. Another common problem job coaches face is that they are often expected to do the employer's work and are seen as an extra employee, instead of a specialist providing training to the individual in supported employment. The job coach will need to make his or her function clear from the beginning. He or she must carefully balance the task of viewing the employer as a customer, being friendly and supportive, yet ensuring that the individual being served is receiving appropriate support. Finally, the job coach may get to the point of being so familiar with the student/client that the coach is no longer able to see the student's/client's potential social inappropriateness. When this occurs, the job coach is not providing social skills training that facilitates more appropriate behavior by the student/client, and is not encouraging more interaction by the student/client with nondisabled peers. It is the responsibility of the supervisor to actually observe the job coach in various situations to help the coach to take advantage of every training opportunity.

It is important to provide support to the job coach in other ways as well. Often, job coaches are not given any space of their own in the office, because they are out in the community most of the day. Having a desk, file drawer, or telephone to use can be extremely helpful to a job coach. Also, job coaches should be included in meetings and social events sponsored by the agency. Their work in the community may prohibit them from developing work relationships and can make them feel isolated. Therefore, any social support and inclusion is helpful. Some communities have begun "T.G.I.F." gatherings for job coaches in the community from various agencies, and have started to encourage relationships in that way.

Although the job coach's responsibilities vary from agency to agency (some are responsible for job development as well as training), there are some minimum competencies for which all job coaches should be held responsible prior to being independent in the community. The following competencies are adapted from Leitner and Bishop (1988):

1. Understand the principles of normalization.
2. Discuss the role of the job coach as an advocate.
3. Determine a composite picture of each client's/student's life in relation to his or her job.
4. Complete a work site analysis, job site analysis, task analysis, and Student/Client Repertoire Inventory.
5. Identify natural cues and consequences.
6. Determine data collection procedures.
7. Identify and develop adaptations.
8. Apply training strategies to assist in skill acquisition.
9. Revise training plans based on data.
10. Implement fading techniques.
11. Teach responses to natural cues and consequence.
12. Facilitate advocacy relationships between the trainee, co-workers, parents, and community members.
13. Facilitate the trainee's maintenance and/or increase in production.
14. Identify the need, then develop and implement plans for behavioral challenges.
15. Develop and implement plans for trainee evaluation, supervision, support, promotion, change, or maintenance.

With all of the responsibilities of the job coach, data collection is often overlooked. Data collection, as in all areas of training, is important in supported employment. Data collection becomes the basis for making training decisions, for knowing how the client is progressing, and knowing when specific parts of the task are learned. Data collection provides motivation for the student/client and the job coach as well (see Chapter 3 of this volume for more information on data collection).

In supported employment, data collection is important for other reasons as well. Production rates must be acccounted for to determine wages for Department of Labor regulations, and to monitor Social Security information. Department of Labor regulations mandate that wages be based upon the type, quality, and quantity of work produced by each individual. The wage must be proportionate to wages received by nonhandicapped employees for similar work (Wehman, Wood, Everson, Goodwyn, & Conley, 1988). Supplemental Security Income (SSI) recipients are now able to receive cash and medical benefits when they continue to work and earn additional income. Section 1619 of the Social Security Disability Amendments of 1980 authorizes special SSI payments and continued Medicaid coverage for persons with handicaps. Individuals with severe handicaps are allowed to have earnings in excess of the "substantial gainful activity" (SGA) and are still entitled to receive special SSI cash benefits. Also, even if an individual has lost his or her entitlement to cash benefits due to excess earnings, he or she can continue to receive Medicaid coverage as long as he or she has a handicapping condition or needs Medicaid coverage in order to work.

Data collection also provides accountability to supporting agencies providing other services, and to funding agencies such as the Department of Rehabilitation. Data collection is essential in documenting training and decisions related to liability (see Chapter 9 of this volume).

Another training issue for job coaches is behavior management. Many techniques that were utilized and presumed to be successful in segregated settings may not be acceptable in a workplace environment. All behavior management techniques must be nonaversive in nature and must coincide with the ethics of the work site culture. For example, in the sheltered workshop, it was common for Chip to be placed in the supervisor's office for "time out" when he would begin throwing tantrums. However, in his new supported employment job at Matt's Produce Market, it is not appropriate to ask the manager to leave his office so that Chip can be shut in there for "time out."

Behavior management plans must be determined prior to placement, and the logistics of management implementation must be worked out with regard to the specific employment site. This is not to say that individuals with severe behavior disorders should not be involved in supported employment. To the contrary, such individuals should be placed in work sites that have been very carefully matched to meet their needs. Included in the match for persons with severe behavior challenges should be a functional analysis of the behaviors, so that the best possible placement can be made while intervention continues appropriately. Chapter 4 of this volume discusses behavior managment in more detail.

FOLLOW-ALONG SERVICES

Follow-along services are implemented after placement is made, after training has been successfully implemented, and after the job coach's services are being faded from support as the individual stabilizes in his or her work performance. Follow-along services ensure that routine follow-up with the employer, the student/client, the parent/significant other, and other support services will take place. This routine formal and informal process allows problems or concerns to be discovered at an early stage when intervention can be implemented. Otherwise, small problems that arise may, with time, escalate to the point that a placement, or necessary support, is lost. Ongoing follow-along allows a relationship of mutual trust to develop between the parties involved, and ensures ongoing communication and advocacy for the student/client.

Frequent review of the student's/client's progress is part of the follow-along process. Data collection and production records may indicate that it is time for the employee to receive a raise, take on more responsibility, or receive more training in certain tasks. It is also a time to re-assess the individual's interests and the overall picture of his or her life and determine if changes are necessary in other areas. A student or client may develop different interests and wish to work at another type of business. Social interactions may be more easily facilitated in a different type of work. However, relationships may have been developed at the existing workplace. In this case, it may be best to determine a different type of job within the existing business so that relationships remain intact.

Follow-along services include the transition of students from school-age providers to adult service providers (see Chapter 9, this volume). These services also include: 1) an examination of the individual's residential options, 2) recreation/leisure activities, 3) transportation access and mobility skills, and 4) other necessary support such as medical attention and community/consumer skills. Supported employment is an important facet of an individual's life, but all facets of life must be working together to be successful.

SUMMARY

This chapter discusses the definition, history, and components of supported employment. Supported employment is a viable employment option that allows individuals with severe handicaps to be employed in jobs that are integrated into the normal work force of the community. The extensive use of sheltered workshops and activity centers is challenged in the chapter. An individual's success in employment does not depend on the four walls of a sheltered environment, but on the support of the professionals who are involved with him or her and on the opportunity for interaction with nonhandicapped peers.

The necessary components of supported employment include: marketing and job development, job match (assessment and analysis), job coaching (training and on-site or off-site support), and follow-along services. Each of these components should be carefully planned and developed before any individual is placed in a supported employment position. Supported employment services also require ongoing communication and cooperation with school transition programs, other service providers (e.g., integrated recreation/leisure services, residential providers, transportation services), funding agencies, and parents or significant others. The success of the individual relies on all relevant parties working together toward the goal of the individual's full participation in all aspects of adult life in the community.

REFERENCES

Bellamy, G.T. (1983). *Competitive employment training.* Paper presented at a conference by the California Chapter of the Association for the Severely Handicapped, San Diego, CA.

Bellamy, G.T., Horner, H., & Inman, D. (1979). *Vocational habilitation of severely retarded adults: A direct service technology.* Baltimore: University Park Press.

Bellamy, G.T., Rhodes, L.E., Bourbeau, P.E., & Mank, D.M. (1986). Mental retardation services in sheltered workshops and day activity programs: Consumer benefits and policy alternatives. In F.R. Rusch (Ed.), *Competitive employment issues and strategies* (pp. 257–271). Baltimore: Paul H. Brookes Publishing Co.

Brown, L., Nieptupski, J., & Hamre-Nietupski, S. (1976). The criterion of ultimate functioning and public school services for severely handicapped students. In M.A. Thomas (Ed.), *Hey, don't forget about me! Education's investment in the severely, profoundly and multiply handicapped* (pp. 2–15). Reston, VA: Council for Exceptional Children.

Brown, L., Shiraga, B., Ford, A., VanDeventer, P., Nesbit, J., Loomis, R., & Sweet, M. (1983). Teaching severely handicapped students to perform meaningful work in nonsheltered vocational environments. In L. Brown, J. Nesbit, A. Ford, M. Sweet, R. Loomis, & P. VanDeventer (Eds.), *Educational programs for severely handicapped students* (Vol. 13, pp. 1–100). Madison, WI: Madison Metropolitan School District.

Brown, L., Wilcox, B., Sontag, E., Vincent, B., Dodd, N., & Gruenwald, L. (1977). Toward the realization of the least restrictive educational environments for severely handicapped students. In L. Brown, J. Nietupski, S. Lyon, S. Hamre-Nietupski, T. Crowner, & L. Gruenwald (Eds.), *Curricular strategies for teaching functional object use, nonverbal communication, problem solving, and mealtime skills to severely handicapped students* (Vol. 7, pp. 106–173). Madison, WI: Madison Metropolitan School District.

Falvey, M., Bishop, K., Grenot-Scheyer, M., & Coots, J. (1988). Issues and trends in mental retardation. In S. Calculator & J. Bedrosian (Eds.), *Communication assessment and intervention for adults with mental retardation* (pp. 45–65). Boston, MA: College Hill Press.

Falvey, M., Ferrara-Parrish, P., Johnson, F., Pumpian, I., Schroeder, J., & Brown, L.

(1979). Curricular strategies for generating comprehensive, longitudinal and chronological age appropriate functional individual vocational plans for severely handicapped adolescents and young adults. In L. Brown, M. Falvey, D. Baumgart, I. Pumpian, J. Schroeder, & L. Gruenwald (Eds.), *Strategies for teaching chronological age appropriate functional skills to adolescents and young adult severely handicapped students* (Vol. 9, pp. 102–161). Madison, WI: Madison Metropolitan School District.

Gaston, D. (1988). What are the reasons for job terminations of people with mental retardation who are severely handicapped? Unpublished master's thesis, California State University, Los Angeles.

Gaylord-Ross, R. (1987). The role of assessment in transitional, supported employment. *Career Development for Exceptional Individuals, 9*(2), 129–134.

Gold, M. (1972). Stimulus factors in skill training of the retarded on a complex assembly task: Acquisition, transfer, and retention. *American Journal of Mental Deficiency, 76,* 516–526.

Greenspan, S., & Shoultz, B. (1981). Why mentally retarded adults lose their jobs: Social competence as a factor in work adjustment. *Applied Research in Mental Retardation, 2,* 23–28.

Hill, M., Wehman, P., Kregel, J., Banks, D., & Metzler, H. (1987). Employment outcomes for people with moderate and severe disabilities: An eight year longitudinal analysis of supported-competitive employment. *Journal of The Association for Persons with Severe Handicaps, 12*(3), 182–189.

Kenowitz, L., Zweibel, S., & Edgar, E. (1978). Determining the least restrictive educational opportunity for the severely and profoundly handicapped. In N. Haring & D. Bricker (Eds.), *Teaching the Severely Handicapped* (Vol. 3, pp. 49–61). Seattle, WA: AAESPH.

Leitner, R., & Bishop, K. (1988). *Competency-based training for job coaches: A self guided study course for trainers in supported employment.* San Francisco, CA: University of San Francisco-Rehabilitation Administration.

Lynch, B. (1984). Acquisition and performance by mentally retarded children and young adults on a complex benchwork task. *Exceptional Children, 50*(5), 444–448.

McDaniel, R.H., & Flippo, K. (1986). *Telesis: Supported employment resource manuals.* San Francisco, CA: University of San Francisco-Rehabilitation Administration.

McLoughlin, C., Garner, J., & Callahan, M. (1987). *Getting employed, staying employed.* Baltimore: Paul H. Brookes Publishing Co.

Robinson, R., Andrew, P., Bishop, K., Dutton, D., & LaMar, K. (1988). *A supported employment overview.* San Francisco, CA: University of San Francisco-Rehabilitation Administration.

Ruether, R. (1977). *Mary—The feminine face of the Church.* Philadelphia, PA: Westminster Press.

Strain, P. (1983). Generalization of autistic children's social behavior change: Effects of developmentally integrated and segregated settings. *Analysis and intervention in developmental disabilities, 3,* 23–34.

Wehman, P. (1981). *Competitive employment: New horizons for severely disabled individuals.* Baltimore: Paul H. Brookes Publishing Co.

Wehman, P. (1983). Toward employability for severely handicapped children and youth. *Teaching Exceptional Children, 15*(4), 220–225.

Wehman, P., Hill, M., Wood, W., & Parent, W. (1987). A report on competitive employment histories of persons labeled severely mentally retarded. *Journal of The Association for Persons with Severe Handicaps, 12*(1), 11–18.

Wehman, P., Wood, W., Everson, J.M., Goodwyn, R., & Conley, S. (1988). *Vocational education for multihandicapped youth with cerebral palsy.* Baltimore: Paul H. Brookes Publishing Co.

NINE

TRANSITION ISSUES AND STRATEGIES

Kathryn D. Bishop and Mary A. Falvey

TRANSITION HAS BEEN defined as the passage from one state, place, stage, or subject to another (Merriam-Webster, 1974). The concept of facilitating the transition from school-age community life to adult community life for persons with severe handicaps has become highly significant in recent years. With the passage and implementation of Public Law 94-142, the existence and quality of education for students with severe handicaps has improved dramatically. However, as thousands of students each year face graduation or "aging out" of school programs into adult life, the question becomes, "What now?" Van Deventer et al. (1981) state that, "it cannot be assumed that when a student with severe handicaps graduates to new environments the skills previously taught will be applied, adapted, or generalized to the extent they were performed in old environments" (p. 188). This statement is supported by the research of Colvin and Horner (1983); Horner and McDonald (1982); Stokes and Baer (1977); Zeaman and House (1963).

DEVELOPMENT AND IMPLEMENTATION OF TRANSITION PROGRAMS

Early data provided from the Madison Metropolitan School District (Van Deventer et al., 1981) indicated that although the quality of school-age programs may have increased, its actual effect on postgraduation life-styles has been negligible. The study reviewed the life-styles of 53 program graduates with severe handicaps. Of these graduates, only one worked in a nonsheltered vocational environment. Forty-nine graduates participated in segregated sheltered workshops or day activity centers, and 3 persons had no employment or day program involvement at all. Of those 49 individuals participating in sheltered settings, almost all were significantly underachieving socially, emotionally, and vocationally. Hasazi, Gordon, and Roe (1985) also found that students who leave school prior to graduation were inadequately prepared for employment and community access.

Madeleine Will, Assistant Secretary of Education, Office of Special Education and Rehabilitative Services, in a speech delivered at the 1983 conference for The Association for Persons with Severe Handicaps (TASH), stressed that the efforts by school personnel must not be "rendered futile by the failure of the vital transition process." In support of this statement, a similar vocational follow-up study was done that reviewed the status of Madison school leavers with severe disabilities from 1984–1986. These students had received transition services that resulted in 29 of 32 graduates functioning in integrated work settings with support (Brown et al., 1986). The importance of providing systematic, structured transition programming to prepare for an adult life-style has been recognized, therefore, at both local and national levels.

Transition into adult life-styles for persons with severe handicaps requires comprehensive planning and programming. The comprehensiveness of the program will facilitate greater quality of life for the individual. Quality of life issues for adults with severe handicaps has tended to be addressed in terms of success in vocational settings (Bellamy, Sheehan, Horner, & Boles, 1980; Brown et al., 1984; Kerachsky & Thornton, 1987; Wehman, Kregel, Barcus, & Schalock, 1986). The vocational domain is undoubtedly essential in an adult's life, but it must not be viewed as the only critical domain in one's life. Being productive in a daily work setting can assist the individual in developing a quality adult life-style; however, productivity itself will not ensure such a life-style. Bellamy et al. (1984) and Brown et al. (1986) suggest that there should be a 24-hour integration goal that affects an individual's life as a whole. This means that integration with nonhandicapped individuals must exist throughout all aspects of one's life. To facilitate a person's adult life-style development, school programs must attend to all the domains of adult life functioning. Transition programs are encouraged to prepare students to function within the following domains:

1. Domestic
2. Leisure/recreation
3. Community/mobility
4. Community/consumer
5. Vocational

Instruction in basic skills such as communication, motor, academic, and social skills should take place across all of the domains throughout the entire day.

In order to develop comprehensive life-style programming for adults with severe handicaps, siblings, parents, and significant others must be informed about the transition process and become actively involved in facilitating this process. Family members are typically the only stable figures in the life of a person with severe handicaps (Brotherson, Backus, Summers, & Turnbull, 1985); therefore, parents and families are a vital part of the transition. There has typically been a discrepancy in how parents react to adulthood issues for sons or daughters without disabilities as compared to sons or daughters with disabilities (Zetlin & Turner, 1985). According to Zetlin and Turner, parents of adolescents without disabilities responded to the transition to adulthood by recognizing, accommodating, and increasing support for individuation. However, they reported that parents of adolescents with disabilities tended to encourage dependency, obedience, and child-like behaviors. These attitudes should not be surprising. For decades, professionals have encouraged this notion of continual need for protection of persons with disabilities through such developments as segregated schools and sheltered adult programs. Parents need to be educated along with professionals to understand and support services that allow maximal participation in nonsheltered integrated settings.

Siblings, parents, and significant others interact with students predominantly during "nonprogrammed" time. Nonprogrammed time refers to the time the student is not engaged in activities that were set up and/or supervised by school personnel or other service providers (e.g., teachers, social workers, counselors). In order to determine if there has been a positive impact on the quality of a given student's adult life-style, one must carefully evaluate the nonprogrammed activities, environments, and opportunities available to the student. An effective transition program must, therefore, be designed to positively influence the attitudes of others involved in the individual's life to facilitate quality productive opportunities during nonprogrammed time.

This chapter provides guidelines and issues that need to be addressed in developing a successful transition program. Program characteristics are also discussed, as well as curricular issues. Such issues include: specific domains, skills across domains, student and program assessment and evaluation, and strategies related to program implementation. Suggestions for parental and community support agency involvement are included throughout the chapter.

CHARACTERISTICS OF A TRANSITION PROGRAM

Transition programs are designed to prepare students to live and function in their community as independently as possible. Therefore, students should acquire, perform, and maintain skills across a variety of environments. To maximize the effectiveness of such instruction, transition programs must be developed with a framework that includes certain characteristics. For example, the location of the transition program is an important characteristic. High school campuses are not age-appropriate for 18–22-year-olds, but community colleges, adult education campuses, or business settings could be considered as location options.

Another vital characteristic of transition programming is an interagency approach (Wehman et al., 1986). Parents, special education departments, regular education programs, and agencies concerned with vocational education, rehabilitation, and developmental disabilities must work together to plan the transition framework. It is important to identify needed support services and/or resources and then facilitate the procurement of those services and/or resources. The interagency model is one way to ensure a wide range of input into planning and procurement of resources. The interagency team can be expanded when planning more specific program content and community involvement to include representatives from special education, regular education, and postsecondary agencies (e.g., vocational rehabilitation and adult service providers). Additionally, parents, students, students' significant others (e.g., siblings, friends, neighbors), employers, therapists, and recreation/leisure representatives (e.g., YMCA director) could also be included. Each member will bring a perspective that is valuable and can provide insight to program development. Proper planning can prevent implementation difficulties that may threaten program success.

Coordination and collaboration between school and adult service providers has been nonexistent in the past. Edgar, Horton, and Maddox (1984) discussed a number of factors that may impede collaboration if not recognized. These factors include:

1. Inconsistent organizational patterns between agencies
2. Varying geographic areas served by different programs
3. Differing application and eligibility procedures or requirements
4. Varying fiscal years, intake periods, and planning cycles
5. Traditional referral processes based on territorial issues rather than needed services

Providing effective transitioning from school to adult services may then require adult agencies to restructure some of their existing policies and procedures to support the team effort.

Beyond informal supportive relationships between the program and outside agencies, it is important for persons who are implementing transition to develop formal relationships. Specific responsibilities should be developed and should be contracts signed by each responsible party prior to an individual's graduation. Separate contracts may need to be developed for each agency to meet individual needs. Examples of such agencies include: postsecondary agencies (e.g., community colleges, adult education, supported employment agencies), employers, recreation/leisure agencies, and transportation agencies. Contracts with postsecondary agencies should include formal agreements for providing continuing support for adult independence in integrated settings for students after graduation. Such agencies may also agree to assist in financing specific materials that may be necessary for an individual to maintain a certain job. Employers should have contracts that specify the individual student's job responsibilities, work days/hours, and insurance responsibilities. Generally, an employer's responsibilities might include:

Providing a work site and real work tasks for the trainee to perform
Providing the tools, supplies, and equipment necessary for the trainee to perform the assigned work tasks, unless the job is one that requires the employee to supply his or her own tools
Providing instruction on the assigned work tasks
Providing general supervision of the trainee
Completing biweekly training evaluation forms on the trainee's performance
Contacting the school/adult agency immediately and completing required forms in the event of an injury. If the accident occurs after work hours (i.e., evenings, weekends), the employer is responsible for transporting the trainee to a designated medical facility.

The school or adult agency could be responsible for:

Providing vocational training and preparation for the trainee
Prescreening the trainee by assessing his or her work skills, interests, aptitudes, and behavior, and matching these with an appropriate training setting
Providing ongoing counseling and follow-up with the trainee throughout the training period
Providing additional support services as needed (this could involve one-to-one skill or behavior training at the training site)
Providing Workman's Compensation Insurance coverage for those trainees who are not being paid a wage by the employer

The trainee will receive support in demonstrating acceptable work attitudes and in gaining independence or maximal participation in the following areas:

Attendance/punctuality
Appearance
Retaining instruction
Working independently
Initiative
Speed and productivity
Quality of work

Special contracts with recreation/leisure and/or public transportation agencies are necessary when educators are requesting something out of the agency's normal routine (e.g., reduction of fees, provision of special instruction/assistance). Ensuring ongoing communication with employers and agencies will allow for mutually agreed upon modification of initial contracts that will provide smoother programming for all who are involved.

It can be difficult to determine which adult service agencies are most appropriate for a given individual. The following list, adapted from Baumgart, Perino, and Moody (1986), includes questions that parents or educators should ask adult agency representatives to assist in discerning appropriateness:

1. How can your agency help us?
2. What do we need to do to receive your services?
3. When and where should we apply?
4. What other agencies should be involved?
5. Who funds your services?
6. How old must a student be before applying for services?
7. Who decides what services will be offered and what objectives will be targeted?
8. How do you match individuals with jobs?
9. What initial and ongoing support do you provide?
10. Will you provide transportation and/or mobility training?
11. What are your eligibility requirements?
12. At what point do you terminate services?
13. Who is responsible for monitoring Social Security income records?
14. Who is involved in your community network or advisory committees?
15. What is the procedure for maintaining communication with all involved parties?

Development of transition programs must include longitudinal vocational planning that involves employers and educators for students of all ages. To maximize the benefits of the transition into adulthood, general job skills should be introduced into the curriculum for all ages. Employers can provide examples of job-related skills that should be taught throughout the school years. Inventories of nonsheltered jobs can be utilized to determine general job skills (see Chapter 3 of this volume and also the assessment section of this chapter for a more thorough discussion of conducting inventories). General job skills, such as work ethics, breaktime activities, and appropriate dress, are of great importance and should be stressed in the earliest years of education. Longitudinal vocational planning consists of general program and curricular structures for program growth, as well as future oriented individual student goals and objectives. These longitudinal plans will help to prepare the student for his or her next environment, adult life.

CURRICULUM OF TRANSITION PROGRAM

The goal of a secondary transition program is to provide skill instruction and support for a more independent adult life-style. Because secondary transition programs must operate within the parameters of school programs (e.g., number of hours per day, staffing/student ratios), each student's activities must be carefully planned to ensure comprehensive programming. Wehman, Kregel, and Barcus (1985) state that there are three fundamental characteristics of secondary programs that are critical for successful transition. These characteristics are integrated schools, community-based instruction, and functional curriculum. The least effective secondary programs consist of segregated service delivery with classroom-based instruction and a developmental curriculum.

A comprehensive program also includes direct instruction and active participation leading to skill acquisition in each of the following domains: domestic, recreation/leisure, community/mobility, community/consumer, and vocational (Wilcox & Bellamy, 1982). Independence, or at least increased participation, gained in any and all of these areas leads to less responsibility and supervision on the part of parents, siblings, and other members of the community. More importantly, the student can live a more dignified life-style, which typically increases self-esteem.

The *domestic domain* encompasses the areas of personal health care, home care, and interpersonal relationships. Personal health or self-help skills have been traditionally taught in special education programs. These skills should be expanded to include emergency safety skills, medication regulation, nutrition, hygiene, dressing, eating, and toileting. Home care skills are self-explanatory, although those skills must be taught with the assumption that the individual will be living in an integrated environment. Home care must therefore include payment of bills, insurance, room temperature control, and cleaning. (See Chapter 6 of this volume for a more detailed discussion of domestic skills.)

The *recreation/leisure domain* allows for participation in activities that are referred to as play, entertainment, or relaxation during scheduled routines and nonscheduled time. Recreation/leisure activities should reflect the individual's age and interests, as well as family activities, culture, and community facilities. Recreation/leisure activities should span a wide range of activities and should include skills that can involve other people or can be engaged in by oneself. Activities can range from regularly scheduled events, such as swimming, weight lifting, and aerobics classes, to hobbies, such as photography or building collections. (See Chapter 7 of this volume for a more detailed discussion of recreation/leisure skills.)

The area of *community/mobility* should examine all possible means of community access. Each individual should have a variety of means for community mobility. Frequently, persons with severe handicaps are taught one method of mobility and are, therefore, limited in terms of variety of activities and spontaneity. Common reasons for lack of mobility include: not having access to specific transportation due to inclement weather, public transportation strikes, holiday closings, and equipment breakdowns. Examples of various types of transportation include: walking, bicycling (e.g., adult 2- or 3-wheel bikes), wheelchairs, public buses, community vans (e.g., Dial-A-Ride), scooters/carts, private cars/carpools (e.g., parents, siblings, or co-workers), and taxi cabs. More than one type of mobility should be used. (See Chapter 5 of this volume for a more detailed discussion of community/mobility skills.)

The *community/consumer domain* encompasses those purchasing or service-related activities in which an individual participates in his or her community. Consumer skills typically include activities such as grocery shopping, clothes or gift shopping, miscellaneous shopping (e.g., browsing, buying records or plants), or banking. Utilization of the post office, the doctor's or dentist's office, or the Social Security office could also be included. Consumer skill instruction is structured to meet the needs of each individual in his or her local community to the greatest extent possible. (See Chapter 5 of this volume for a more detailed discussion of community/consumer skills.)

The *vocational domain*, without exception, consists of real work experiences in real work settings. Vocational tasks are those that someone else would be paid for doing in that same environment (Brown et al., 1983). The vocational domain also includes job-related skills, such as time management, breaktime and lunchtime behaviors, uniform care, safety procedures, and time clock operation. It must be realized that job-related skills should be taught in conjunction with specific work tasks in the natural environment at the naturally occurring time (Falvey, Brown, Lyon, Baumgart, & Schroeder, 1980). For example, it would not be appropriate to teach coffee break behaviors after work unless that was the time other employees were taking breaks. Use of the time clock would be taught at the work site before and after work as opposed to during scheduled work time or "back in the classroom." (See Chapter 8 of this volume for a more detailed discussion of vocational or employment skills).

There are certain standards that must be reflected in instruction across the curricular domains. Following is a list of those critical standards that are essential for the implementation of a successful transition program:

1. *Chronological age appropriate* Skills, activities, and environments must reflect those typically performed and used by nonhandicapped peers of the same chronological age.
2. *Functional/critical skills* These include skills/activities that are required or expected of nonhandicapped peers. These skills are essential to the student's performance and participation in a variety of community environments.

3. *Natural environmments* Teaching and participation in activities should take place in environments where they would naturally occur.
4. *Zero inferences* Once a student has acquired a skill, inferences would not be made concerning the student's performance of similar skills at a different time or environment. Instruction must occur across a variety of environments, persons, cues, and materials, instead of inferring generalization.
5. *Integration/least restrictive environment* Instruction and participation should include:
   a. Presence of nonhandicapped age peers
   b. Interaction with nonhandicapped peers in natural environments
   c. Ratio of handicapped and nonhandicapped persons has natural proportions
   d. Equal access to community facility (including integrating times and spaces)
   e. Qualified, appropriate personnel to provide the necessary training and support
6. *Student preferences.* Activities and curriculum must emphasize student preferences. Although all students may not be able to verbally communicate preferences, teachers and parents must work together to ascertain such preferences (e.g., examining behavior patterns, affect, eye contact, attention span, and attendance).

Possibly the most difficult aspect of implementing a transition program is *arranging individual schedules* to ensure that each student receives instruction that reflects the comprehensive curriculum. Because transition programs are most often implemented for school-age students, programming will most likely be limited to a typical period of a 6-hour school day. Table 9.1 represents the breakdown of a typical nonhandicapped adult day into time spent in particular domains. This information has then been broken down to provide a structure for a 6-hour school day percentage of curriculum emphasis. Table 9.2 provides this breakdown in specific terms. This provides a basic structure for ensuring instruction in all domains. Individual students may have specific strengths or weaknesses that may necessitate adjusting the percentages to more precisely

Table 9.1. A sample schedule for a typical day

Time	Domain	Amount
6:00–7:30	Domestic	1 1/2 hours
7:30–8:00	Community/mobility	1/2 hour
8:00–5:00	Vocational	9 hours
5:00–5:30	Community/mobility	1/2 hour
5:30–6:30	Community/consumer	1 hour
6:30–8:00	Domestic	1 1/2 hours
8:00–10:00	Recreation/leisure	2 hours

Table 9.2. Percentage of curriculum emphasis

Domain	Percentage	Time for 6-hour day
Domestic	19%	1.14 hours = 1–1½ hours/day
Vocational	56%	3.36 hours = 3–4 hours/day
Recreation/leisure	13%	.78 hour = ½–¾ hour/day
Community/mobility and consumer	13%	.78 hour = ½–¾ hour

meet their needs. As students age, their schedules should reflect a more typical adult day; this requires endurance building (e.g., longer work hours). An extended day might be accomplished with the assistance of school or other agency staff, parents, or employers.

INDIVIDUALIZED TRANSITION PLANS

Individualized transition plans (ITPs) are developed along with individualized education programs (IEPs) when the student turns 18 and enters a transition program. IEPs should reflect all of the domains, be focused on integrated community, work, and living settings, and encompass goals reflecting activities relevant to maximal participation in adult life. The ITP is used to facilitate and encourage the support and involvement of students, parents, employers, postsecondary agencies (e.g., department of rehabilitation, department of developmental disabilities), and other community members (e.g., employers, recreation/leisure supervisors). The purpose of an ITP is to anticipate an individual's needs upon graduation and to determine who will be able to provide the support necessary to help meet those needs. The ITP team participates in long-range planning, determining at what point it would be appropriate to enter into contractual agreements with specified agencies. Involvement and shared responsibility during the transition program will develop a broader and more solid foundation for activities and support after graduation (Nisbet et al., 1982). McDonnell and Hardman (1985) also suggest that the following issues be specifically addressed in the transition plan:

1. Appropriate vocational options
2. Residential options
3. Leisure opportunities that can be completed by the individual with the minimum amount of support necessary from caretakers
4. A program to establish and monitor eligibility
5. Case management services
6. Long term support (e.g., guardianship, establishment of trust funds). (p. 279)

First and foremost, all decisions must reflect the student's preferences, as well as those of the family, school, and supporting agencies.

In transition programs, as well as other programs for students with severe handicaps, IEP and ITP goals should avoid the traditional academic objectives such as isolated math, reading, and writing skills. These skills are of value in the transition program only when they are reflected in domain-related functional activities. Examples of IEP objectives that incorporate basic skills are provided below:

1. Fred will plan, purchase, and prepare three one-course meals independently, as measured by parent and teacher observation. (Incorporating math, reading, mobility, and independent living skills)
2. Sally will locate a telephone in two areas of the local shopping mall, insert an appropriate amount of money, and call Dial-A-Ride to take her home, as measured by teacher and Dial-A-Ride supervisor report. (Incorporating communication, mobility, money management, orientation, and safety skills)
3. Bob will increase his daily work hours to 4 hours per day by adding one new task to his job responsibilities: a) distribute interoffice mail, or b) operate postage meter for outgoing mail, as measured by employer and teacher records. (Incorporating vocational, motor [endurance], and reading skills)
4. Patsy will choose one organized recreational activity in her community and will register, participate, and attend 90% of the time, as measured by recreation instructor and teacher records. (Incorporating motor, communication, money management, mobility, and reading skills)
5. Tyler will carry work materials in his lap while traveling in his electric wheelchair to his work station from the supply room. (Incorporating motor skills and orienting skills)
6. Kelly will independently button the buttons on her work shirt once she has changed into the shirt in the employee restroom before her afternoon shift. (Incorporating fine motor, attention span, math, and grooming skills)

To encourage generalization and to promote more flexibility for community participation, ITP goals should be directed at skills to be taught across domains. Skills taught only in isolation are far less useful than skills that are systematically instructed across environments, activities, and domains (Falvey et al., 1980). For example, learning to use money in a fast food restaurant should not eliminate teaching money use for domestic needs or at a recreation/leisure site. However, it should eliminate teaching money skills at a table in the classroom with play money.

Horner, Sprague, and Wilcox (1982) presented a strategy referred to as general case programming to teach skills that would most likely need to be generalized across a number of environments. The procedure consists of specific teaching strategies for parents and educators to identify and teach in community settings that will result in generalization of those skills to other environments. Instructional strategies such as this should be identified and discussed at the ITP meeting, as well as specific data collection procedures.

The ITP can be separate, above and beyond the IEP process; however, the ITP could be an exact outcome of the IEP, linking appropriate adult agency support(s) to the IEP. Many people feel the ITP is more effective because it is not constrained by the laws and regulations that the IEP must have. Figure 9.1 provides an example of a format used for ITPs.

ASSESSMENT

Within a transition program there are several components of assessment that must be addressed. The components to be assessed consist of initial assessments (e.g., ecological inventories, student repertoire inventories, job match), on-going data collection, and global program evaluations.

Prior to program implementation, several initial functional assessments of students must be conducted. Ecological inventories determine sequences of behaviors that are utilized in performance of specific activities (Brown, Branston, Hamre-Nietupski, Pumpian, Certo, & Gruenewald, 1979). Activities are selected for inventories of skills performed by nonhandicapped age peers in community settings (see Chapter 3 of this volume for a more detailed discussion of ecological inventories). Figure 9.2 provides an example of an ecological inventory that has been completed for one activity (making coffee).

A critical characteristic of developing ecological inventories is that the inventory must be conducted in the actual environment in which the skill will be performed (i.e., the natural environment). Ecological inventories should not consist of "trying to remember" the skill sequences for a McDonald's restaurant while sitting at a desk at school. Instead, the teacher should go to the environment, perform the necessary skills, and record the skill sequence performed. Another critical characteristic of ecological inventories is that they are *nonhandicapped* inventories, that is, they delineate generic, typical routines that have not been adapted or modified for a person with disabilities.

Student repertoire inventories (SRI) provide a measure for comparing a student's current skills against those identified in the ecological inventory, that is, those performed by nonhandicapped age peers (Falvey et al., 1980). A discrepancy analysis is then used as a basis for an instructional plan. (See Chapter 3 of this volume for a more detailed discussion of student repertoire inventories.)

Once ecological inventories and student repertoire inventories have been completed, individual programs can be developed. Figure 9.3 provides an example of a completed student repertoire inventory.

Ongoing data collection provides valuable information regarding student progress, instructional techniques, and trainer effectiveness for these programs. Evaluating data that have been collected on a regular basis provide objective evidence of student progress. In all domains and activities, regular data collection and evaluation provide important instructional information regarding

Individualized Transition Plan

I. **Student information**

Name Address School

Social Security Number Date of birth

Guardianship Name Address

Persons in attendance

II. **Performance profile**

Area	Strengths	Weaknesses	Needs	Interests
Academic				
Domestic				
Home and community management				
Vocational				
Recreation/ leisure				
Communication				
Other functional skills				

(continued)

Figure 9.1. A sample format for an individualized transition plan (ITP).

Figure 9.1. *(continued)*

Area	Projected needs	Goal/activity recommendations	Service provider	Projected timeline	Date action taken	Outcome
Academic						
Domestic						
Home and community management						
Vocational						
Communication						
Other functional skills						
Transportation						
Employment						
Community living options						
Financial, insurance, medical						
Other						

(continued)

We the undersigned have participated in the development of ________________________'s Individualized Transition Plan and agree to carry out the recommendations specified within.

Family / guardian representatives:	Student:
Parent / Date	Student / Date
Careprovider representatives:	
Title / Date	Title / Date
School representatives:	
Title / Date	Title / Date
Title / Date	Title / Date
Title / Date	Title / Date
Adult service providers/funding agencies:	
Title / Date	Title / Date
Title / Date	Title / Date
Title / Date	

Community support representatives:

Employer / Date	Recreation / leisure / Date	Other / Date

Ecological Inventory

Scoring: 0 = Did not perform
1 = Physical
2 = Modeling
3 = Direct verbal
4 = Indirect verbal
5 = Gesture
6 = Independently

Name: *Arlene*
Domain: *Vocational*
Environment: *Nursery school*
Subenvironment: *Kitchen*
Activity: *Making coffee*
Teacher: *Pam Stoner*

Skills	Dates 1/31	2/14	2/19	2/28	3/5	3/7	3/12	3/14
1. *Open the refrigerator*								
2. *Locate coffee*								
3. *Take coffee out and walk to coffee machine*								
4. *Take a filter out of cupboard*								
5. *Place filter in reservoir*								
6. *Measure 5 spoonfuls of coffee from can*								
7. *Put coffee in reservoir*								
8. *Put yellow lid on reservoir*								
9. *Fill decanter with water from the faucet*								
10. *Pour water through top of the coffee machine*								
11. *Put reservoir on top of decanter*								
12. *Replace decanter on top of warmer*								
13. *Turn switch to "on"*								
Total score achieved / Total score possible								
Percentage level of independence								

Comments:

Figure 9.2. An ecological inventory form.

Student Repertoire Inventory

Student: *Arlene* Date: *1/29/86* Teacher: *Pam Stoner*

Environment: *Nursery school* Activity: *Snack preparation, break, clean-up*

Skills	Responses	Discrepancy analyses	Adaptation hypotheses
Enter through gate and close behind self	+		
Greet staff	+		
Go to kitchen through kitchen door	–	*Walks into office—interupts employers*	*Discuss appropriateness of respecting their privacy/time*
Take coat and purse to store room	+		
Read board for snack	–	*Requires verbal prompt*	*Practice skill*
Locate needed utensils and supplies and put in the baskets		*Not familiar with locations*	*Labels on cupboards/drawers*
Locate ingredients for snack	–	*Not familiar with locations*	*Practice skill*
Prepare snack	–	*Requires prompts*	*Practice skills*
Put correct amount of snack in each basket	–	*Cannot judge appropriate amount*	*Quantify amounts for each group*
Clean-up surrounding areas	+	*Requires verbal prompts*	*Practice skill*

(continued)

Figure 9.3. A completed student repertoire inventory.

Figure 9.3. *(continued)*

Student Repertoire Inventory

Student: *Arlene* Date: *1/29/86* Teacher: *Pam Stoner*

Environment: *Nursery school* Activity: *Snack preparation, break, clean-up*

Skills	Responses	Discrepancy analyses	Adaptation hypotheses
Ask employers if they want coffee; prepare coffee if necessary	–	*Requires model and verbal prompts to prepare coffee*	*Practice skill—use checklist*
Locate materials needed for break			
Walk outside and sit on bench	+		
Read magazine and/or watch children Talks to staff outside	+		
Return to kitchen Replace materials in store room	+		
Throw away trash from baskets and put away extra supplies	–	*Requires verbal prompt*	*Practice skill*
Wash dishes and utensils	–	*Doesn't rinse thoroughly Leaves food on some dishes*	*Practice skill—job site and apartment*
Dry and put away dishes/utensils	–	*Doesn't dry completely*	*Practice skill—job site and apartment*

+ = Performed the skill independently and accurately.
– = Did not perform the skill independently or accurately.

techniques, use of adaptations, strengths and weaknesses, and extent of independence and participation in activities. Vocationally, such information is important in determining a student's employability and job compatibility. In all domains, data should be evaluated regularly in order to make any necessary program or instructional strategy changes.

Ongoing assessment will affect both staffing and scheduling issues. Specific information on data collection and assessment has been addressed earlier. However, it is important at this time to reiterate the role of ongoing assessment on the program as a whole. Data collected on a daily basis must be organized and depicted in a way that provides information regarding student, trainer, and program needs and strengths. Data should influence any changes in schedules as well as reflect needs for more or less intensive staffing. Data collection also serves as documentation of accountability. Because community training may be viewed as involving more risk than traditional educational programs, all educational decisions must be based on concrete evidence that is documented and organized in such a way as to support those decisions. Data should demonstrate that direct instruction has occurred and that specified criteria have been met before the student's level of independence increases in community activities. For example, if a student has difficulty independently riding the public bus to work one day, it is valuable for the teacher to be able to provide administrators with data documenting that instruction did occur, and that the student met criteria for independent bus riding on that route. Without appropriate documentation and data collection, liability issues may arise. Following are some examples of data collection instruments used in transition programs. Figure 9.4 is a form used for general community data collection; Figure 9.5 illustrates an ecological inventory form used to collect work training data; Figure 9.6 is an employer worker evaluation; Figure 9.7 is a more general data form used to determine the quality of an individual's daily program.

Assuming all sites are in the community, trainers (or instructional aides) are often working with students without direct teacher supervision. It is therefore important for the teacher to *train and monitor* the instructional strategies and effectiveness of other staff members in the community. In addition, it is valuable to have data documenting and monitoring the trainers' effectiveness in more than one area. Student and program success depends on tasks performed and relationships developed. The trainers' role in each of these areas is critical. Proper monitoring of trainer tasks will maintain program efficiency and effectiveness and will enable trainers to become more highly skilled technicians. Figure 9.8 is an example of a trainer observation form.

Data sheets, cards, or any other type of data collection materials must be adpated to fit the specific needs of each program or individual. Some considerations in the development of data collection materials are:

Transition Community Data

Student name: *Joanna*
Destination: *YMCA*
Mode of Transportation: *Public transit*
Task: *Water exercise*
Observer: *Bruce*

I = Independent — % I: *40% 53%*
Assistance needed due to: — % S: *33% 33%*
B = Behavior — % B: *27% 14%*
S = Skill — Date: *6/5 6/6*

	6/5	6/6						
Dress/grooming appropriately	S	S						
Has ID/$$/materials	I	I						
Leaves home/school on time	S	S						
Walks to work/bus stop safely/appropriately	B	I						
Locates work/bus stop	I	I						
Waits for bus appropriately	B	B						
Boards correct bus	I	I						
Functions on bus ($$, seating, behavior)	B	B						
Locates stop/departs	I	I						
Walks safely to destination	B	I						
Locates destination	I	I						
Initiates task	I	I						
Performs task	I	I						
Completes task/cleans up	S	S						
Leaves on time	S	S						

Figure 9.4. A sample form for general community data collection.

Ecological Inventory

Scoring: 0 = Did not perform
1 = Physical
2 = Modeling
3 = Direct verbal
4 = Indirect verbal
5 = Gesture
6 = Independently

Name: *Arlene*
Domain: *Vocational*
Environment: *Nursery school*
Subenvironment: *Kitchen*
Activity: *Making coffee*
Teacher: *Pam Stoner*

Skills	Dates 1/31	2/14	2/19	2/28	3/5	3/7	3/12	3/14
1. *Open the refrigerator*	3	3	6	6	6	6	6	6
2. *Locate coffee*	6	6	6	6	6	6	6	6
3. *Take coffee out and walk to coffee machine*	6	6	6	6	6	6	4	6
4. *Take a filter out of cupboard*	2	2	3	0	0	3	3	6
5. *Place filter in reservoir*	2	2	2	0	0	1	4	6
6. *Measure 5 spoonfuls of coffee from can*	3	4	3	4	6	6	6	6
7. *Put coffee in reservoir*	3	6	6	6	6	6	6	6
8. *Put yellow lid on reservoir*	2	2	3	4	3	3	3	3
9. *Fill decanter with water from the faucet*	3	3	3	3	4	3	3	3
10. *Pour water through top of the coffee machine*	3	3	3	3	5	5	6	6
11. *Put reservoir on top of decanter*	2	2	3	3	3	4	3	3
12. *Replace decanter on top of warmer*	3	3	3	3	6	6	6	6
13. *Turn switch to "on"*	4	4	4	6	6	6	6	6
Total score achieved / Total score possible	42/78	46/78	51/78	50/78	60/78	61/78	62/78	69/78
Percentage level of independence	54%	59%	65%	64%	77%	78%	79%	88%

Comments:

Figure 9.5. A sample ecological inventory form used for work training data collection.

Worker Evaluation
(to be completed by employer)

Trainee's name: ______________________

Work site: ______________________

Address: ______________________

City: ______________________

Telephone no.: ______________________

Position: ______________________

Site supervisor: ______________________

Evaluations should be made on a realistic basis.

Pay period begins: ______ ends: ______

Assessment categories	100%	90%	80%	70%	60%	50%	40%	30%	20%	10%	Date	Hours		
												In	Out	Total
Punctuality—regularly on time														
Attendance—dependable; notifies in advance, if absent														
Follows instructions—oral and written														
Appearance—appropriately dressed														
Retains instructions—remembers tasks from day to day														
Works independently—does not need continuing supervision; does not waste time														
Initiative—self-starter; works ahead without further direction														
Quality of work—accurate and well done														
Speed and productivity—equivalent to a full-time employee														

Please comment on Trainee's progress: ______________________

Productivity = ______________________

Supervisor's signature: ______________________

Trainee's signature: ______________________

Please have worker evaluation completed and signed by: ______ (Date)

Figure 9.6. A sample employer worker evaluation form.

Individual Daily Program Evaluation

Student Name: *Adam*

Date: *9/3*

Evaluator: *Morgan*

Domain	Activities	No. of environments w/in domain	No. minutes interaction w/NH peers/colleagues	No. NH peers/colleagues present (non-staff)	No. minutes direct instruction in activity	Total time per day
Vocational	*Check membership cards at health club*	*1*	*35*	*25*	*10*	*2 hr*
Consumer	*Watched part of baseball game on TV at health club*	*1*			*15*	*45 min*
Recreation/Leisure	*Watched part of baseball game on TV at health club*	*1*	*45*	*6*	*3*	*45 min*
Mobility	*Dial-A-Ride to/from health club*	*1*	*0*	*1*	*10*	*50 min*
Domestic	*Home: checked cupboards and made grocery list for tomorrow*	*1*	*0*	*0*	*50*	*1 hr*

Most positive part of program day: *Watching the ballgame at the health club with the other members—great interactions!*

Areas of program day needing improvement: *Transportation—need to find more consistent system, hopefully integrated.*

Suggested changes/options: *Check Public Transit routes/times; call and see if buses are accessible.*

Also, need to develop adaptations to help Adam open kitchen cupboards.

Target dates for changes: *9/15: Report on Public Transit options.*
10/1: Complete adaptations and begin training on its use.

Figure 9.7. A sample form for evaluating an individual's daily program.

Observation of Trainer

Date: ______________

Staff: ____________________ Observer: ____________________

Location/Activity: ____

Day/Time: ____

Student objectives:

Activities observed:

Instructional techniques observed:

Suggested strategies:

Figure 9.8. An example of a trainer observation form.

1. Inconspicuousness of materials in the community (e.g., avoid clipboards and kitchen timers)
2. Simplicity of format (i.e., remember that instruction is often occurring at the same time data is being recorded)
3. Content of information collected (i.e., make sure what is being recorded is of value)
4. Compilation capability (i.e., raw data should be easily graphable or depictable in a manner that will be useful)
5. Clarity of instruction (i.e., understandable for others to use, read, and interpret)

Chapter 3 of this volume provides more detailed discussion on strategies for assessing and teaching in the community.

PROGRAM EVALUATION

In order to evaluate the program, in general, there are several factors to consider. If the program goal is to develop an individual's life-style, activities performed outside of programmed time must be considered (i.e., time not scheduled by school/agency personnel). It is no longer sufficient to consider only the activities of a person within school/work hours. To assess a student's total life-style it is essential to receive information from the parents or primary caregiver. Figure 9.9 is an example of a parent inventory of a child's use of time outside of programmed hours. Such information can be gathered several times annually to determine progress and changes. (More examples of parent/guardian inventories can be found in Chapter 3 of this volume.)

Sheehan and Keogh (1984) point out that program impact is not limited to changes that occur only in the students. Other areas to be evaluated include possible effects on parents and significant others, policies, and programs. Burstein and Guiton (1984) developed a conceptual framework for evaluating programs that focuses on program processes. The framework consists of the following six classes of variables:

> 1. "*Entering characteristics* are those preprogram variables that influence individual performance at any given time. These include 1) student characteristics such as type of handicapping condition, ability, etc.; 2) parent variables such as educational level and parenting skills; and 3) teacher and staff variables such as experience, sense of efficacy, and training.
> 2. *Program characteristics* are those variables which influence the definition, implementation, and status of the program. Program characteristics are generally considered to be stable.
> 3. *The IEP* represents those variables that mediate student entering characteristics, program characteristics, and educational processes. Ideally, the IEP functions to select the program and to define the educational processes that are to operate within that program. In practice, the program staff's involvement in

Parent Survey of Student's
Use of Time Outside of School

Please answer the following questions, regarding your son's/daughter's use of spare time, to the best of your knowledge. Please consider what your son/daughter does independently.

I. **Domestic skills**
1. Does his/her own/other's laundry ___ x per week
2. Cooks meals for self/others ___ x per week
3. Bathes/showers independently ___ x per week
4. Cares for other hygiene needs (e.g., shaving, makeup) ___ x per week
5. Selects own clothes from closet ___ x per week
6. Cleans own room/other rooms of house ___ x per week

Examples of domestic activities: ______________________________

____

____

II. **Recreation/leisure activities**
1. Participates in activities with family away from home ___ x per week
2. Participates in activities without family away from home ___ x per week
3. Participates in activities or hobbies at home other than watching television (e.g., sewing, shooting baskets, gardening) ___ x per week
4. Participates in "handicapped only" events ___ x per week
5. Participates in events with nonhandicapped peers ___ x per week

Examples of leisure/recreation activities: ______________________________

____

____

III. **Mobility skills**
1. Walks to places independently ___ x per week
2. Walks to places with family ___ x per week
3. Walks to places with friends (peers) ___ x per week
4. Rides bicycle outside of yard ___ x per week
5. Uses public transportation independently ___ x per week
6. Uses public transportation with family ___ x per week
7. Uses public transportation with friends ___ x per week
8. Is driven by family or friend ___ x per week
9. Uses private transportation (e.g., taxi, Dial-A-Ride, school bus) ___ x per week

IV. **Consumer skills**
1. Does grocery shopping ___ x per week
2. Selects and purchases own clothes ___ x per week
3. Goes to restaurants (independently or with friend/peer) ___ x per week

(continued)

Figure 9.9. An example of a parent inventory used to account for time spent outside of program hours.

Parent Survey of Student's Use of Time Outside of School
(continued)

4. Buys own bus pass ____ x per week
5. Pays bills ____ x per week
6. Utilizes a bank ____ x per week
7. Plans and prepares for leisure activities (e.g., calls theatre for show times, registers for classes) ____ x per week

V. **Vocational skills**

1. Participates in nonpaid jobs outside of school and home ____ x per week
2. Receives pay for work done outside of school time. Specify amount earned. $____ per week

VI. **General Community**

1. Based on your experiences with your son/daughter, how do you think he/she would respond if approached by a police officer (e.g., run away, speak out, refuse to talk) ____
____
____
2. Can your son/daughter tell the difference between a friend and a stranger?
____
____

the development of the IEP shapes its development in terms of existing programs.

4. *Educational processes* are those conditions which directly reflect the instruction received. Instructional variables such as the materials used, pacing, setting, etc. are the primary components of the educational process, but other factors greatly influence instruction (e.g., class composition may determine the grouping that takes place, the instructional activities and materials selected, and the amount of time devoted to an individual student).
5. *Contextual characteristics* include those variables that are not directly involved in the educational process, but can influence program stability and educational continuity. For instance, the nature and quality of schooling received after leaving a treatment program is considered a major factor in the long term effects of the intervention.
6. *The outcome variables* include student outcomes (performance, self-concept, and future school functioning/placement), parent outcomes (skills, attitudes, and advocacy), teacher/staff outcomes (attitudes, professional development), and finally, organizational outcomes (institutionalization of the program, dissemination of the program, interagency collaboration between the program and other service providers)." (p. 33)

Assessment and evaluation practices and procedures may initially appear to be cumbersome and time consuming. However, all procedures should be adapted and refined to meet the individual needs of each program. Once assessment and evaluation procedures are mandated and adapted for a specific program, they become a part of the daily routine, and the benefit far outweighs the initial inconvenience.

An alternative to the indepth process evaluation discussed above is a quality indicator checklist. This checklist is a quick method of determining whether or not basic program components are in place and appropriate techniques are being utilized. The following items are examples of quality indicator components:

ITPs (Features):
- Student involvement
- Parent involvement
- Funding agency involvement
- Adult service provider involvement
- Goals target future environment
- Delineate specific responsibilities and timelines

Students' schedules incorporate all domains
Frequent interaction with nondisabled peers occurs daily
Initial assessment:
- Student interests
- Parent/guardian inventory
- Ecological inventories in all domains
- Student repertoire inventories

Objectives and instruction are based upon initial assessment information
Ongoing assessment and data collection is available
Individual instructional strategies are utilized
Least intrusive instructional strategies are implemented
Behavior management procedures are nonaversive
Decisions are based upon data that are regularly collected and reviewed
Each student has a method of communication
Administrative support is established
Administrative policies and procedures are in place, for example:
- Emergency procedures
- Work experience regulations
- Staffing requirements
- Funding support for consumables

Regular meetings are scheduled and attended by the interagency team
Paid and volunteer staff have received adequate training for assigned tasks
Sites and services are available to and utilized by nondisabled persons of appropriate chronological ages

ADMINISTRATIVE INVOLVEMENT

As is true with attempts to implement innovations in any system, success often depends upon a broad base of immediate and long-term support. In the educational system, a key base of support is the administration. Implementation of a transition program requires the support of district level administrators, as well as local or building administrators. Gaining support from administration generally requires ensuring that they are well informed about the program purposes, content, and strategies. Due to the extremely low incidence nature of students with severe handicaps, such information should be made available in a well organized, concrete manner. Using the Whittier Union High School District as an example, it is important to note that out of a total enrollment of approximately 10,000 high school–age students, there were 35 students with severe handicaps between the ages of 18 and 22 being served by the transition program. These students therefore represent .0035% of the population with which district administrators are concerned. This statistic suggests that it is not reasonable to expect administrators to keep abreast of current trends and best practices for 18–22-year-old students with severe handicaps.

By no means should this imply a lack of interest or commitment to students with severe handicaps on the part of administrators. It simply implies that special education teachers, support staff, parents, and others must assume the responsibility for informing administrators of current best practices. When attempting to gain administrative support, teachers must provide a sound rationale that considers students' best interests and fiscal responsibility and that reflects the basic policies and practices of the district and the community. It is important that administrators receive all relevant information initially and throughout the existence of the program. If the information presented is not complete or ignores potential difficulties or controversies, administrative support is likely to decrease at the first sign of a problem. However, if all of the facts are presented initially, and changes and new information are presented throughout the program's existence, administrators are more likely to feel they are part of the process. Administrators are then personally invested in the goals and successes of the program and the students.

PARENT/FAMILY SUPPORT

Administrative support can often be enhanced by parental support and vice versa. Parental support and involvement is necessary for at least three reasons. First, any new program must involve parents in the program development phase and in maintenance of the program, so that input and understanding is shared from the beginning. Second, parents can promote the growth and success of the program by talking with other parents, administrators, and teachers. Third, parental input is critical to the child's growth and success in the program. To maximize both the potential of the program and it's direct effect on students, parental input and involvement are necessary.

Parental input regarding program planning is valuable for several reasons. Parents bring a perspective of experience and pragmatism that may be overlooked by professionals. Parents often have the ultimate responsibility for their son or daughter throughout their lives, and can express specific hopes and concerns for the present, as well as the future. Frequently, parents serve as the strongest student/child advocate. Parental involvement in the planning phase promotes trust and better understanding of the program. Those parents who are involved can communicate with other parents to develop a stronger base of support for the program.

Support of the program may primarily require the assistance of parents as public relations agents. The value of positive parental input to administrators is immense. Parents are indirect consumers of educational products, and are often the strongest and most effective advocates for the direct consumer, their son or daughter. As is true for any business, the supplier must respond to the needs and demands of the consumer. Parents advocating for more or different services may have more credibility or impact than teachers advocating the same services. The cause is clearly strengthened by both parties working together as a team. Utilizing the strengths of parents as public relations agents is also extremely beneficial because it creates community awareness and support. The more people who become knowledgeable and supportive of the program, the better the chances for immediate and long-term success.

Another level of support needed from parents is that of helping their son or daughter learn and enhance their skills. This level of support is actually more demanding because it is day-to-day support and can be exciting and fulfilling, as well as frightening and anxiety provoking. For the son or daughter, transition to adulthood means greater independence and responsibility; for the family, it means releasing protective strictures (Brotherson et al., 1985). The transition of an individual from childhood to adulthood is stressful for any family, but when the individual has severe handicaps, the transition is even more difficult (Wikler, 1981). The parents' support of their son or daughter within a specific program is only one aspect of the child to adult transition, but it can be a critical aspect.

As an adolescent makes the transition into adulthood, parental involvement should develop into parental support. Typical adolescents demand passage into adulthood that mandates subtle or overt changes in their relationship with their parents. These changes are important for adolescents with severe handicaps as well. It becomes the responsibility of parents and educators to encourage this passage into adulthood by taking on a role that is supportive, rather than directive and authoritative. This may mean that the decisions and preferences of the young adult are considered primarily, with parental preferences being considered second. Parental roles and responsibilies should change relative to their son's or daughter's age; to the family's cultural, ethical, and moral values and needs; and to the relationships of other family members. The following guidelines for parental involvement are suggested as ways to help foster a positive relationship between the individual, his or her parents, and the service provider:

1. Allowing and supporting their son or daughter to participate in the program and be involved in numerous community training sites
2. Providing input into program development and individualized goals for their son or daughter
3. Attending and participating with their son or daughter in meetings
4. Participating in open/honest communication with the staff and providing ongoing input regarding their son's or daughter's program and progress
5. Supporting their son or daughter by following through on requests of school staff regarding gym clothes, materials, functional attendance, necessary paperwork, and so on
6. Encouraging and providing opportunities for use of skills during non-programmed hours
7. Viewing their son or daughter as a young adult and encouraging him or her to make his or her own decisions
8. Informing and including service providers on matters relevant to the student outside of the program (e.g., SSI issues, changes in medications, guardianship, emotional factors that may be affecting the student)

Without continued support from parents, the effects on an individual in a transition program can be significantly minimized. It is beneficial for students to receive consistent messages about themselves, their lives, responsibilities, and potentials from home, school, and the community. Chapter 2 of this volume includes further information about issues involving parents and significant others.

TRAINER ROLES AND RESPONSIBILITIES

Although support for transition programs is important, the development of program trainer expertise is also a key factor. Trainers may consist of teachers or support personnel, and may include therapists, assistants, instructional aides, parents, peer tutors, or any number of outside volunteers. Trainers are directly involved with students, for example, as teachers, supervisors, or observers. Trainers are also directly involved with employers and other community members, thereby requiring the development of positive public relations. Table 9.3 is an example of a trainer's job description used to assist in stressing the trainer's roles, responsibilities, and relationships in the community.

Providing training for the trainers is a time consuming but critical task. Trainers must be familiar with each student's goals and objectives, behavior programs, and skills. Trainers are often required to gain expertise in more than one domain. For example, an aide may be responsible for vocational and do-

Table 9.3. Trainer's roles, responsibilities, and relationship in the community

The trainer will be directly involved with students (e.g., teacher, supervisor, observer) and will also be directly involved with employers and other community members, thereby requiring the development of positive public relations:

As a professional in the community, the trainers represent themselves, the transition program, the school district, and the total profession of special education/rehabilitation. Therefore, it is very important to be aware of your image in the community as a professional.

Appearance is extremely important. Trainers are very visible and must dress in a manner appropriate to the specific community site.

Must maintain close communication with the office; check in every morning to receive any updates to the schedule. If it is necessary to change a schedule of a student/client, the office must be informed.

The trainer's goals are to provide instructional intervention and then fade to the natural supervisor(s). Therefore, it is important to be knowledgeable of the best instructional practices and appropriate behavior management strategies and techniques. This information will be conveyed by the instructors. Ask for assistance any time more information is needed.

The trainer needs to be sensitive and supportive of the student/client and needs to be firm, but not abrasive.

The trainer must be knowledgeable of the emergency procedures and have knowledge of all facets of the program.

mestic skills on Mondays, Wednesday, and Fridays, and vocational and recreation/leisure skills on Tuesdays and Thursdays. Vocational training is often the most difficult task because of the range of training sites that are used. The trainer who is working in the morning with a student at an auto salvage yard must be knowledgeable about auto parts and specific tool use. The same trainer may be assigned to a fast food restaurant and be required to master hot cakes, french fries, and milk shakes. Trainers are also involved with mobility and street safety instruction.

Once a trainer knows his or her students and has analyzed and mastered the task himself or herself, a plan for student instruction is developed. Strategies, task analysis, and data collection systems are developed and implemented. Just as it is important for trainers to collect evaluative data on students, it is important for supervisors or instructors to keep data on trainers. Such information helps maximize instruction time and trainer effectiveness.

Trainer burnout is a very real issue of concern. Trainers in a transition program are generally out in the community for the majority of the time. This means that trainers may have difficulty developing typical relationships with other school staff members. They may be required to take lunch breaks or coffee breaks in the community, and should be encouraged to find comfortable environments for these activities. Often, trainer's hours are scheduled to provide direct service to students without time remaining for planning or conferring with the teacher. Therefore, communication between the trainer and his or her supervisor is more difficult. It may be necessary to use dictating machines or some type of written communication system to keep informed of daily information.

SCHEDULING

Scheduling for students in transition programs may be the most complicated task of all. Each student must receive an appropriate amount of direct instruction in each of the necessary domains. Students who are independent in certain activities may only require spot checking and intermittent instruction on expansion of skills within the activity or expansion of activities. Other students may be scheduled so that they receive direct instruction in small groups. For example, three students may be in the same swimming class or three students may be training at the same vocational site. From that site, the small group may be scheduled to go to the mall for consumer skill instruction with a different trainer.

When developing a working schedule, certain factors must be considered. First, movement between sites depends on available transportation modes, time schedules of public transportation, and availability of a trainer for mobility skills. Second, skills, needs, and interests of students should be accommodated as much as possible. For example, Billy may be with her group at a vocational setting, and her group may then be scheduled for swimming at the recreation center. Because Billy is allergic to chlorine, the schedule must allow for her to participate in a different activity, perhaps an aerobics class. Third, schedules must reflect trainer availability and expertise and allow for student coverage during trainer lunches and breaks. Fourth, schedules must be flexible; they may need revising on a monthly or even weekly basis to reflect changes in student skills, site changes (closure for vacation), trainer changes, or altered bus routes or times. Effective scheduling will require some give and take and a great deal of creativity on the part of the teacher. A sample program schedule is provided in Figure 9.10. Each individual also has his or her own specific schedule (see Figure 9.11). This individual schedule is given to relevant staff members, parents, and students. Student schedules may be adapted using pictures and line drawings instead of written words. Along with each schedule, a student information sheet can be included as well, such as in Figure 9.12.

Implementation needs will vary from program to program. The issues discussed in this section represent typical areas of concern. Regardless of the specific issue, it is almost always beneficial to utilize the support of a number of persons with a variety of skills in developing strategies. Although this initially may be more time consuming, the long-term benefits of other opinions, support, and delegation of responsibilities may far outweigh the initial inconvenience. It can be expected that in one instance, a particular strategy was ex-

	Monday	Tuesday	Wednesday	Thursday	Friday
		A.M.			
Whittwood (P. Stoner/ H. Avalos) Bertha Kelly D. Jeff David M. Craig Arthur Raphael Mark Stacey Arthuro	Boston Store Bertha Jeff David Friendly Hills Bowl Mark Raphael Craig Arthur Pet Haven Arthuro McDonald's Stacey				Community
	Whtr. Community Ctr. (Aerobics) Kelly	Rio Hondo Class Kelly	Whtr. Community Ctr. (Aerobics) Kelly	Rio Hondo Class Kelly	Life Experience Class Kelly
Whtr./So. Whtr. (L. Barrera/ J. Danza) Jose Mario David C. Tiffany Carlos Jackie Dennis Hector Marc Eric	Whittlier College Jose Jackie Eric Dept. of Motor Vehicles Mario Marc Carlos Taco Bell Hector Tiffany Sizzler David				Community Training (TBA) Community Training (TBA)
	Taco Bell Dennis	Community (TBA)	Taco Bell Dennis	Taco Bell Dennis	Life Experience Class Dennis
PR/W. Whtr. D. Gaston/ C. Martinez Lisa Rosalie Allison Tom Sal Louie Rodney Francisco Michelle Jack Patrick	SF S Recreation Ctr. (Aerobics) Michelle Allison Lisa Rosalie SF S Activity Ctr. (Wt. Trng., Basketball Louie Rodney Francisco Pat Jack Tom Community/ Consumer Sal	Community/ Consumer Michelle Allison Lisa Rosalie Domestic (Student's home) Rodney Jack Pat Francisco Community Garden Sal Louie Tom	Domestic (Student's home) Michelle Allison Lisa Rosalie Community Rec. (Student's choice) Louie Rodney Francisco Pat Jack Tom PR Library Sal	Rivera Park (Adult Crafts Class) Louie Rosalie Michelle Lisa Community/ Consumer Tom, Rodney } Vona Sal, Louie } Alpha Beta Pat, Jack, Francisco } Lucky's	Community/ Domestic Allison Rosalie Michelle Lisa Domestic Pat Jack Francisco Louie Life Experience Class Tom Sal Rodney
SF S/Norwalk (S. Larkins)/ B. Schecter/ V. Crumley) Flora Victoria Kelly M. Angie Mary Dionicio Kathy Henry Reynaldo	Domestic (Student's home) Kathy Mary Reynaldo Henry Domestic (Student's home) Victoria Dionicio Angie Kelly Eastman Kodak Flora	SF S Acitivity Ctr. (Wt. Trng., Basketball) Reynaldo Dionicio Henry Rivera Park (Adult Sewing Class) Kathy Victoria Community/ Consumer Mary Kelly Angie	SF S Towne Center (Aerobics) Kathy Victoria Mary Angie Kelly Community/ Consumer Reynaldo Dionicio Henry	SF S Activity Ctr. (Wt. Trng., Basketball) Reynaldo Dionicio Henry Rivera Park (Adult Sewing Class) Kathy Victoria Domestic (Student's home) Mary Angie Kelly	SF S Towne Center (Aerobics) Mary Angie Kelly Life Experience Class Kathy Victoria Community/ Consumer Reynaldo Dionicio Henry

Figure 9.10. A sample transition program schedule for 40 students with severe handicaps.

Monday	Tuesday	Wednesday	Thursday	Friday
		P.M.		
E. Whtr. YMCA (Swimming) Arthur Mark Raphael Jeff Community Stacey Arturo Craig Bertha David Taco Bell Kelly	Domestic (Student's home) Arthur Mark Raphael Jeff E. Whtr. YMCA (Wt. Trng.) Stacey Arthuro Craig Bertha David	Pragmatics Arthuro Stacey David Bertha Jeff Domestic Arthur Mark Raphael Craig	E. Whtr. YMCA (Wt. Trng.) Jeff Arthur Raphael Mark Domestic (Student's home) Arturo Stacey Bertha David Craig	Community Mark Raphael Craig Jeff Arthur E. Whtr. YMCA (Swimming) Arturo Stacey Bertha David
Whittier College (Swimming) Jose Jackie Eric Carlos Domestic (Student's home) Mario Marc David Hector Tiffany ROP Companion Class Dennis	Whtr. Community Ctr. (Gentle Aerobics) Hector David Tiffany Mario Marc Community/ Consumer Jose Jackie Eric Carlos	Whittier College (Swimming) Jose Jackie Eric Carlos Community/ Consumer Mario Marc David Hector Tiffany	Whtr. Community Ctr. (Gentle Aerobics) Hector David Tiffany Mario Marc Domestic (Student's home) Jose Jackie Eric Carlos	Community Training (TBA)
St. Theresa's Convalescent Hosp. Louie Jack Allison Michelle Rosalie Eastman Kodak Tom Jones Chevrolet Rodney Lisa Pat Francisco Rio Hondo Class Sal	Jones Chevrolet Sal	Rio Hondo Class Sal	Jones Chevrolet Sal	Rio Hondo Class Sal
City of SF S: Library Henry Victoria City of SF S: Finance Dept. Kelly Angie Whtr. Boys' and Girls' Club Reynaldo Dionicio Mary Taco Bell Kathy ROP Companion Class Flora				

Juan's Schedule

Monday & Wednesday

Time	*Bus #*	*Activity*
8:10	#104	Leave La Mirada & Hornell
8:36	#104	Arrive Philadelphia & Painter
8:36– 9:00		Walk North on Painter, East on Bailey, South on Friends to Red Cross
9:00–12:00		Office Assistant at American Red Cross (Supervisors: Bill Seery & Doris Ray)
12:12	#104	Leave Philadelphia & Painter
12:20	#104	Arrive Mulberry & Painter
12:30– 1:30		Lunch at Sierra Campus
1:30– 3:10		Senior Care Class at Sierra Campus
3:20	#104	Leave Mulberry & Painter
3:30	#104	Arrive La Mirada & Hornell
		Tuesday & Thursday
9:10		Leave home, walk to Hornell & La Mirada Blvd.
9:20	#104	Leave Hornell & La Mirada
9:35	#104	Arrive Painter & Mar Vista
9:40–11:30		Rio Hondo class at Recreation Center
11:30–11:55		Read in Recreation Center lobby or go to library
11:55–12:05		Walk to Painter & Mar Vista
12:12	#104	Leave Painter & Mar Vista
12:20	#104	Arrive Sierra
12:20– 1:15		Lunch at Sierra or nearby restaurant
1:15– 1:25		Walk to bus at Painter & Mulberry to go to Quad (Tues.) or walk to ROP Class (Thurs.)
1:30– 3:10		ROP Class
3:10– 3:20		Walk to Painter & Mulberry
3:24	#104	Leave Painter & Mulberry
3:35	#104	Arrive Hornell & L Mirada Blvd. Walk home
		Friday
8:10–12:00		Same as Monday
12:00–12:30		Lunch at Park or other selected location uptown
12:30– 1:45		Marinellos hair washed & cut
2:10	#104	Leave Philadelphia & Greenleaf
2:30	#104	Arrive La Mirada & Hornell

(No ROP Class on Friday)

Figure 9.11. An example of a specific transition program schedule.

Name: *Juan*
Date of birth:
Social Security no.:
Height: *5′6″*
Weight: *75 pounds*
Hair color: *black*
Eye color: *brown*
Nationality: *Hispanic*
Communication mode: *communicator or yes/no response*

Home address: ______________________
Telephone no.: ______________________
Home contact person: ______________________
____

Emergency telephone no.: ______________________
Emergency contact person: ______________________
____

Other comments: ______________________
____
____
____

Figure 9.12. An example of a student information sheet.

tremely effective and in the next instance, the same strategy was ineffective or insufficient. All persons involved in developing and implementing a transition program must be willing to be flexible and ready to adapt strategies, as necessary.

SUMMARY

The desire for more independent adult functioning has shaped curriculum school-age students in the last 10 years, providing them with functional, integrated, and community-based educational opportunities. However, a need has been identified in the area of preparing students for the transition from school programs to adult community life. This need can only be met through cooperative planning, implementation, and follow-up of transition services. Longitudinal effectiveness of a transition program can be realized through a comprehensive high school program with early and ongoing involvement and support from school personnel, families, adult service providers, funding agencies, and the general community. The following list is a compilation of summary checkpoints for the development and implementation of transition programs:

1. Communicate, develop cooperative agreements, and encourage planning between students, parents, funding/referral agencies and adult service providers.
2. Facilitate the changing role of parents or care providers.
3. Develop curricula that incorporates basic skills and general job skills across all domains.
4. Develop ITPs that formalize plans and relationships between school-age and adult agencies.
5. Generate ecological inventories and student repertoire inventories for each individual in his or her local community.
6. Develop employment sites and employer evaluation forms.
7. Determine initial and ongoing assessment plans.
8. Establish staffing patterns, roles, and responsibilities.
9. Create schedules that meet program and individual needs.
10. Identify and procure needed support services and resources.
11. Form specific working agreements for each student with the employer.
12. Determine a system for ongoing communication between staff, student, parent/care provider, and employer.

REFERENCES

Baumgart, D., Perino, D., & Moody, G. (1986). *Making transitions work: Long and short term strategies*. Moscow, Idaho: University of Idaho Special Education Department.

Bellamy, G.T., Rhodes, L., Wilcox, B., Albin, J., Mark, D., Boles, S., Horner, R., Collins, M., & Turner, J. (1984). Quality and equality in employment services for adults with severe disabilities. *Journal of The Association for Persons with Severe Handicaps*, *9*(4), 270–277.

Bellamy, G.T., Sheehan, M., Horner, R.H., & Boles, S. (1980). Community programs for severely handicapped adults: An analysis. *Journal of The Association for the Severely Handicapped*, *5*, 307–324.

Brotherson, M., Backus, L., Summers, J., & Turnbull, A. (1985). Transition to adulthood. In J. Summers. *The Right to Grow Up* (pp. 17–45). Baltimore: Paul H. Brookes Publishing Co.

Brown, L., Branston, M.B., Hamre-Nietupski, S., Pumpian, I., Certo, N., & Gruenewald, L. (1979). A strategy for developing chronological age appropriate and functional curricular content for severely handicapped adolescents and young adults. *Journal of Special Education, 13*(1), 81–90.

Brown, L., Rogan, P., Shiraga, B., Albright, K.Z., Kessler, K., Bryson, F., Van Deventer, P., & Loomis, R. (1986). A vocational follow-up evaluation of the 1984–1986 Madison Metropolitan School District graduates with severe intellectual disabilities. *Monograph of The Association for Persons with Severe Handicaps*, *2*, 2. Seattle, WA.

Brown, L., Shiraga, B., Ford, A., Nisbet, J., Van Deventer, P., Sweet, M., York, J., & Loomis, R. (1983). Teaching severely handicapped students to perform meaningful work in nonsheltered vocational environments. In L. Brown, A. Ford, J. Nisbet, M. Sweet, B. Shiraga, J. York, R. Loomis, & P. Van Deventer (Eds.), *Educational programs for SH students*. (Vol. XIII, pp. 1–100) Madison, WI: Madison Metropolitan School Distict.

Brown, L., Shiraga, B., York, J., Kessler, K., Strohm, B., Rogan, P., Sweet, M., Zanella, K., Van Deventer, P., & Loomis, R. (1984). Integrated work opportunities for adults with severe handicaps: The extended training option. *Journal of The Association for Persons with Severe Handicaps*, *9*(4), 262–269.

Burstein, L., & Guiton, G. (1984). Methodological perspectives on documenting program impact. In B. Keogh (Ed.), *Advances in special education* (Vol. 4, pp. 21–42). Greenwich, CT: JAI Press, Inc.

Colvin, G.T., & Horner, R.H. (1983). Exceptional analysis of generalization: An evaluation of a general case program for teaching motor skills to severely handicapped learners. In D. Hogg & P. Miller (Eds.), *Advances in mental handicap research*: Vol. 2: *Aspects of competence in mentally handicapped people* (pp. 309–345). New York: John Wiley & Sons.

Edgar, E., Horton, B., & Maddox, M. (1984). Postschool placements: Planning for public school students with developmental disabilities. *Journal for Vocational Special Needs Education*, *6*(2), 15–18, 26.

Falvey, M., Brown, L., Lyon, S., Baumgart, D., & Schroeder, J. (1980). Strategies for using cues and correction procedures. In W. Sailor, B. Wilcox, & L. Brown (Eds.), *Methods of instruction for severely handicapped students* (pp. 109–133). Baltimore: Paul H. Brookes Publishing Co.

Hasazi, S.B., Gordon, L.R., & Roe, C.A. (1985). Factors associated with the employment status of handicapped youth exiting high school from 1975–1983. *Exceptional Children*, *51*, 455–469.

Horner, R.H., & McDonald, R.S. (1982). A comparison of single instance and general case instruction in teaching of generalized vocational skills. *Journal of The Association for the Severely Handicapped*, *7*(3), 7–20.

Horner, R.H., Sprague, J., & Wilcox, B. (1982). General case programming for community activities. In B. Wilcox & G.T. Bellamy, *Design of high school programs for severely handicapped students* (pp. 61–98). Baltimore: Paul H. Brookes Publishing Co.

Kerachsky, S., & Thornton, C. (1987). Findings from the STETS traditional employment demonstration. *Exceptional Children*, *53*(6), 515–521.

McDonnell, J., & Hardman, M. (1985). Planning the transition of severely handicapped youth from school to adult services: A framework for high school programs. *Education and Training of the Mentally Retarded*, *20*(4), 275–286.

The Merriam-Webster Dictionary. (1974). Springfield, MA: Merriam-Webster Pocket Book edition, p. 725.

Nisbet, J., Shiraga, B., Ford, A., Sweet, M., Kessler, K., & Loomis, R. (1982). Planning and implementing the transitions of severely handicapped students from school to post-school environments. In L. Brown, J. Nisbet, A. Ford, M. Sweet, B. Shiraga, & L. Gruenwald (Eds.), *Educational Programs for SH Students* (Vol. XII, pp. 185–214). University of Wisconsin-Madison and Madison Metropolitan School District.

PL 94-142, The Education for All Handicapped Children Act of 1975.

Sheeham, R., & Keogh, B. (1984). Approaches to evaluation in special education. In B. Keogh (Ed.), *Advances in special education* (Vol. 4, pp. 1–20). Greenwich, CT: JAI Press, Inc.

Stokes, T.F., & Baer, D. M. (1977). An implicit technology of generalization. *Journal of Applied Behavior Analysis, 10,* 349–367.

Van Deventer, P., Yelinek, N., Brown, L., Schroeder, J., Loomis, R., & Gruenewald, L. (1981). A follow-up examination of severely handicapped graduates of the Madison

Metropolitan School District from 1971–1978. In L. Brown, D. Baumgart, I. Pumpian, J. Nisbet, & A. Schroeder (Eds.), *Educational programs for severely handicapped students* (Vol. XI, pp. 1–177). Madison, WI: Madison Metropolitan School District.

Wehman, P., Kregel, J., & Barcus, J.M. (1985). From school to work: A vocational transition model for handicapped students. *Exceptional Children, 52*(1), 25–37.

Wehman, P.H., Kregel, J., Barcus, J.M., & Schalock, R.L. (1986). Vocational transition for students with developmental disabilities. In W.E. Kiernan & J.A. Stark (Eds.), *Pathways to employment for adults with developmental disabilities* (pp. 113–127). Baltimore: Paul H. Brookes Publishing Co.

Wikler, L. (1981). Chronic stresses of families of mentally retarded children. *Family Relations, 30*(2), 281–288.

Wilcox, B., & Bellamy, G.T. (1982). Design of high school programs for severely handicapped students. Baltimore: Paul H. Brookes Publishing Co.

Will, M. (1983, November). *Programming for the transition of youth with disabilities: Bridges from school to working life.* Presented at the National Conference of The Association for Persons with Severe Handicaps, San Francisco.

Zeaman, D., & House, B.J. (1963). The role of attention in retardate discrimination learning. In N.R. Ellis (Ed.), *Handbook of mental deficiency* (pp. 159–223). New York: McGraw-Hill.

Zetlin, A., & Turner, J. (1985). Transition from adolescence to adulthood: Perspectives of mentally retarded individuals and their families. *American Journal of Mental Deficiency, 89*(6), 570–579.

TEN

MOTOR SKILLS

Kathryn D. Bishop, Lori Eshilian, and Mary A. Falvey

THIS CHAPTER PROVIDES educators and parents with a framework from which a sound, comprehensive instructional program can be developed for students with severe physical handicaps. All of the information is based upon the premise that instructing students in community-based functional activities is the most effective means of facilitating increased motor independence.

The chapter includes brief, nontechnical definitions of the most common physical handicaps, as well as terms used to discuss and describe those conditions and related manifestations. Also included are discussions of issues concerning assessment, intervention, therapy models, community training strategies, physical management techniques, self-help, and adaptations and equipment. References cited throughout the chapter can provide additional information in each area.

It is essential that educators become familiar with each student as a complete individual, instead of concentrating solely on the student's mental abilities and disabilities. Knowledge of the physical conditions affecting each student will enable the educator to provide a comprehensive instructional program facilitating each student's maximum independence in society.

DEFINITIONS OF HANDICAPPING CONDITIONS

The eight most common physical handicaps are briefly defined in this section. More technical, medical information regarding each condition is available in the references cited.

Cerebral palsy literally means "paralysis of the brain." It is a nonprogressive disorder resulting in abnormal posture and/or abnormal movement due to brain damage. Eighty-six percent of affected children are diagnosed as having congenital cerebral palsy caused by disturbances during pregnancy or during birth (Bleck & Nagel, 1975). The following is a list of the classifications of cerebral palsy:

Disorders of movement

Spasticity: Tight limb muscles that contract strongly with attempted movement

Athetosis: Uncontrolled, purposeless movement

Rigidity: Severe spasticity, extreme stiffness

Atraxia: Uncoordinated movement due to lack of balance and improper spatial positioning

Tremor: Shakiness in limb(s) upon attempted use

Mixed: More than one type of cerebral palsy; often athetosis and spasticity occur in combination

Limb involvement or disorders

Monoplegia: One limb is involved

Hemiplegia: Arm and leg of the same side are involved

Paraplegia: Legs only are involved

Diplegia: Major involvement in legs, minor involvement in arms

Triplegia: Usually one arm and both legs are involved

Quadriplegia: Both arms and both legs are involved

Double hemiplegia: Arms are more involved than legs, or one side is more involved than the other

Muscular dystrophy is a hereditary condition in which all muscle groups progressively degenerate and are replaced by fat tissue. Males are more frequently affected than females, although the female carries the gene and transmits the condition to her sons. Symptoms, resembling awkwardness or clumsiness, begin to manifest during early childhood years, usually at 3–5 years of age. As muscles deteriorate, respiratory infections increase and ambulation decreases (Bleck & Nagel, 1975).

Spina Bifida (myelomeningocele) is a condition in which a sac of nerve tissue protrudes through the back at the spinal column, which has failed to form properly. The condition usually occurs in the lower back, resulting in decreased or absent sensation in the lower extremities, as well as partial or complete weakness of those muscles. Some students can learn to ambulate with the use of braces, crutches, or wheelchairs. Loss of bladder control is often prevalent. Surgery is usually required in infancy to repair the bulging sac. Spina bifida is frequently associated with hydrocephalus (Bleck & Nagel, 1975).

Hydrocephalus is a condition characterized by an excessive amount of fluid around the brain, often causing enlargement of the head. The condition may result in paralysis of the lower limbs, seizures, and/or retardation. The most successful treatment is to implant a shunt, which is permanently or temporarily inserted for drainage of the fluid (Bleck & Nagel, 1975).

Epilepsy is a change in brain patterns or functions that results in a seizure that begins and ends spontaneously and usually recurs. Most seizures can be controlled with medication. Following are the most common types of seizures, as described by Bigge and O'Donnell (1976):

Grand mal: Violent shaking of the body, loss of consciousness usually lasting 2–5 minutes. May occur more than once a day or as infrequently as once a year.
Petit mal: Staring spell frequently mistaken for daydreaming (may have some eye movement), lasting from a few seconds to a minute. May occur as often as several times during an hour or as infrequently as once a month.
Psychomotor: Inappropriate, purposeless behavior associated with amnesia regarding the behavior (e.g., twitching at the corner of the mouth) (Bleck & Nagel, 1975).

Arthrogryposis literally means "curved joints" (Bleck & Nagel, 1975). It is a condition characterized by stiffness of the limbs and joints. Limb muscles are very weak or are absent, resulting in little or no joint movement. Attempts at treatment through surgery, casting, or bracing are common, with varying degrees of success.

Scoliosis is lateral curvature of the spine (elongated "S" shape), which may involve any segment or length of the spine with varying degrees of severity. This condition is more common in females and may be due to genetic factors, birth abnormalities of the spine, or weakness of muscles in the spine area (Bigge & O'Donnell, 1976). Some cases may be corrected with surgery or body braces.

Down syndrome is a chromosomal disorder that is often associated with hypotonia (weak muscle tone). The individual with Down syndrome may have associated heart defects, which can require reduced physical activity (Batshaw & Perret, 1981).

FREQUENTLY USED TERMS

There are a number of physical manifestations of the conditions described above. Following are some of the more common terms related to these physical manifestations:

Abduction: Movement of limbs away from the midline of the body
Adduction: Movement of limbs toward the midline of the body
Apraxia: Inability to perform specific movements, although there is no muscle or sensory impairment

Atrophy: Deterioration of muscles or nerve cells through nonuse
Clonic: Shaking movements of muscles; repetitive contractions; often resulting from stretching a spastic muscle
Contracture: Permanently tight or frozen muscles and joints that can cause deformities; use of range of motion or surgery can inhibit and/or prevent continued contractures
Hypertonia: Increased muscle tension and tone resulting in stiffness and often the inability to initiate movement. If not treated and/or inhibited, hypertonia can result in increased contractures
Hypotonia: Decreased muscle tension and tone resulting in floppiness and often the inability to initiate movement
Reflexes: Positions or movements that are beyond one's control. Primitive reflexes are those that normally occur during infancy. As the normally developing infant gets older, primitive reflexes either fade or become integrated into more complex positions or movements. Abnormal reflexes are those reflexes not observed at any stage of "typical" development (e.g., tongue thrusting)
Spasm: Sudden tensing of a muscle or muscles

Physical therapists, occupational therapists, and physicians use a number of terms to denote specific techniques and procedures related to positioning or movement. Following are some of the more common terms used to describe characteristics of the physically handicapping conditions previously mentioned (Finnie, 1975):

Asymmetrical: One side of the body is in a different position from the other
Symmetrical: Both sides of the body are in the same position
Extension: Straightening of a muscle(s) at the joint
Flexion: Bending of a muscle(s) at the joint
Prone: Lying on stomach
Supine: Lying on back
Righting: When in uncomfortable or abnormal positions, being able to position head and body in a correct, or right, position
Midline: Toward the center or middle of the body
Tonicity: A measure of the tension in the muscles

ASSESSMENT OF MOTOR SKILLS

In order to determine appropriate goals and objectives, the individualized education program (IEP) team must develop strategies and procedures for acquiring critical and accurate information regarding a student's motor functioning. Assessment procedures that take place in isolated, clinical settings cannot provide a comprehensive picture of a student's functional motor ability. Formal and informal assessments must be conducted in students' natural environments (home, school, and community), settings that more accurately portray students' abilities and difficulties.

Conducting an assessment in the student's natural environments enables educators, parents, and therapists to use the natural materials and cues that are already part of a student's life. For example, a student may discover a way to independently climb the three steps leading to her favorite ice cream shop, but will appear unable to climb the three steps positioned in the middle of a therapy office. To reiterate: accurate assessment involves observing students in familiar activities. Students have often created their own way of adapting in order to accomplish tasks in their daily routines.

Assessing a student across environments provides more complete information than an assessment limited to one environment. Behaviors change as the environment changes, requiring observation of the student's actions in the presence of a variety of people and in a variety of settings. People who are interacting with the student or the setting in which the student is placed may affect the student's motivation, comfort, confidence, and performance.

Specific motor skill abilities and disabilities must be determined, as well as the student's overall daily functioning. Following is a discussion of motor behaviors that must be assessed in natural environments to determine functional motor skill abilities.

Mobility

The extent of the student's independent mobility must be determined. Traditional methods of mobility such as walking and running must be assessed as well as alternative methods, such as rolling, creeping, and crawling. Once independent mobility is evaluated, the need for aided mobility should be determined. Devices such as scooters, braces or crutches, and wheelchairs can significantly increase a student's mobility. Independent or aided mobility provides the student with opportunities to initiate movement, to move to desired locations, to obtain desired materials, and so forth. If a student lacks or has limited mobility, educators, therapists, and parents must together assess his or her current mobility skills and develop opportunities to enhance and increase these skills.

Upright Positioning

Since learning generally occurs when people are in stable, upright sitting or standing positions, the student's ability to obtain and maintain such positions must be assessed. If the student is unable to obtain such a position independently, the amount of assistance necessary for that student to sit or stand must be evaluated. The student's ability to sit or stand in a stabilized manner for a reasonable amount of time must be determined, as well as the amount of assistance necessary to maintain that stable position.

Range of Motion

The extent of the student's range of motion in all joints should be assessed, not only to determine the student's ability to perform specific skills but also to prevent contractures. Range of motion should be evaluated while the student attempts to perform activities such as reaching for the radio, turning his or her head, picking up a shoe, walking to the bus stop, and using his or her hand to activate an electronic wheelchair.

Reflexive Involvement

Any primitive or abnormal reflexes the student is exhibiting must be identified. The goal should be to inhibit the performance of any abnormal or primitive reflexes that may prevent the student from performing functional motor skills.

Structural Deformities

Any structural deformities the student has, such as scoliosis, dislocated hip, or cleft palate, must be determined. Interventions and functional motor programs must consider any structural deformities that are present to ensure appropriate positioning and handling.

Tonal Qualities

The quality of the student's muscle tone should be assessed to determine normal tone, hypertonia, hypotonia, or combinations of tone. Attention should be given to the conditions present when the student's tonal quality changes, so that information can be used when teaching and facilitating functional motor skills.

INTERVENTION

Once the goals, objectives, skills, and activities have been targeted, intervention strategies to enhance movement must be implemented. To facilitate efficient and effective movement, it is often necessary to inhibit abnormal tone, patterns, and/or reflexes. Postural tone must be normalized as much as possible in order for the student to acquire the functional movements necessary to participate in activities involving motor skills (Campbell, 1983). When hypertonicity is involved, postural tone can be stabilized by inhibiting specific reflexes and patterns. To inhibit abnormal patterns and facilitate postural stability, support can be given at the key points of the neck and spine, the shoulder girdle, and the pelvic area (Bobath, 1969). To specifically inhibit rigid muscle tonal quality, flexion should be encouraged and supported. Students' levels of tonicity vary and tend to change or fluctuate in different situations (Campbell, 1983). Factors such as noise levels, familiarity of a task and surroundings, as well as day-to-day mood changes may affect tonal quality. Educators must use a "give and take" method of handling students, which requires sensitivity to those tonal changes (Utley, 1982). Although many techniques for intervention may be similar, each student will have differing needs and should receive intervention with great regard to their individuality.

Overall body stability is crucial to the learning process. Students who experience excessive, uncontrolled movement (e.g., athetoid cerebral palsy) rarely see stimuli in a consistent manner. This excessive, uncontrolled movement must be inhibited so that stimuli appear constant and consistent. Students whose excessive, uncontrolled movements have been stabilized are more likely to learn more rapidly and efficiently. Stability must also be provided to instill a sense of security as well as to provide a base from which movement can be initiated. To accomplish this, the educator must implement good physical management techniques and utilize proper equipment.

Motor skill development must involve appropriate and realistic goals that promote the development of necessary and sufficient movement. To facilitate maximal motor independence, it is important to determine the function of a particular behavior, rather than focusing strictly on the form of the behavior (Campbell, 1983). Necessary and sufficient movement should be facilitated in functional motor activities with active student participation. Table 10.1 provides examples of functional motor acitvities that can be employed to facilitate motor skill acquisition.

It is a normal tendency for peers and adults to do things for students with severe physical handicaps, making them passive recipients of life with little or no control over their environment. This lack of control fosters a sense of learned helplessness. Active participation by each student, to the extent possible, helps the student to maintain a sense of control over his or her environment, usually resulting in increased motivation and a greater awareness of self in relationship to his or her surroundings. Active participation may be expressed through body movements, facial expressions, eye movements, and/or vocalizations (Ford et al., 1982).

Integrated Versus Isolated Therapy Models

Most students with severe handicaps have a need for several types of educational and therapy-based programs. In most cases, the educator has the responsibility for coordinating all of the resources available to a student. As a result, educators must have a broad understanding of the issues involved in providing direct instruction and in securing necessary additional resources. To meet the variety of motor needs of students with severe handicaps, the services of professionals who have diverse areas of expertise (e.g., speech, physical, and occupational therapists) are often necessary.

Students with physical handicaps are usually provided with one of two service delivery models: isolated or integrated therapy (Sternat, Messina, Nietupski, Lyon, & Brown, 1977). In the isolated therapy model, the therapist determines the student's current general developmental motor functioning, uti-

Table 10.1. Functional, age-appropriate motor skills activities

Motor skills	Preschool-age activities
Range of motion	
Upper extremities	Dressing
Lower extremities	Playing language experience activities
Neck and spine	Playing "Simon Says"
Locomotor	
Crawling	Playing "Duck Duck Goose"
Standing	Using drinking fountain
Walking	Walking to dinner table
Climbing stairs	Climbing up slides
Manipulative skills	
Pushing	Punching bags
Pulling	Popping toys on strings or poles
Twisting/turning	Turning on, turning off faucets
Carrying objects	Carrying food to table, toys to bath
Zipping/buttoning	Fastening clothes
Fine motor	
Reaching	Taking toys off shelves
Grasping	Holding toys, foods, parent's hand
Hand to mouth	Eating; brushing teeth
Coordinating both hands/arms	Doing finger plays
Gross motor	
Sitting/trunk control	Eating; playing games
Head control	Activating toys with mercury switch
Righting	Doing movements to songs

Motor skills	Elementary-age activities
Range of motion	
Upper extremities	Manipulating wheelchairs
Lower extremities	Kicking balls; learning karate
Neck and spine	Playing "Simon Says"
Locomotor	
Crawling	Moving to different classroom areas
Standing	Standing for flag salute
Walking	Walking to playground equipment
Climbing stairs	Climbing stairs around school, home, and friend's house
Manipulative skills	
Pushing	Opening doors; pushing in chairs
Pulling	Getting clothes from closet, food from refrigerator
Twisting/turning	Using different doorknobs; opening containers and cabinets
Carrying objects	Taking cafeteria tray to table
Zipping/buttoning	Fastening gym bags, clothes
Fine motor	
Reaching	Pushing doorbells; getting food from shelves
Grasping	Holding pencils; using sports equipment or toys
Hand to mouth	Eating; using napkins; brushing teeth
Coordinating both hands/arms	Playing catch; manipulating wheelchairs
Gross motor	
Sitting/trunk control	Reading; talking with friends
Head control	Activating equipment with a special switch
Righting	Dancing; balancing on bicycles

(continued)

Table 10.1. *(continued)*

Motor skills	Secondary-age activities
Range of motion	
Upper extremities	Sweeping; washing windows; mixing batter
Lower extremities	Riding bicycle (stationary, two or three wheels)
Neck and spine	Doing yoga or other relaxation techniques
Locomotor	
Crawling	Transferring self to and from wheelchair
Standing	Singing the school alma mater
Walking	Moving from car to store; walking to one's seat at the theater
Climbing stairs	Accessing community stores and services
Manipulative skills	
Pushing	Pushing grocery cart; sweeping with a push broom
Pulling	Opening doors; pulling clothes from washer and dryer
Twisting/turning	Turning stereo and television knobs; operating oven or range
Carrying objects	Carrying laundry, bags of groceries, and gym bags
Zipping/buttoning	Fastening food storage bags; opening and closing suitcases
Fine motor	
Reaching	Picking up telephone receiver; turning lights on and off
Grasping	Holding racquet and playing sports; holding telephone receiver
Hand to mouth	Shaving; playing a harmonica
Coordinating both hands/arms	Gardening; weight lifting; manipulating wheelchairs
Gross motor	
Sitting/trunk control	Playing an instrument; watching a movie
Head control	Activating equipment with a special switch; using a head pointer
Righting	Doing aerobic exercises

lizing specialized equipment, materials, and environments. This is done through formal and informal testing. In collaboration with the physician, the therapist develops a program that progresses through normal developmental stages. A schedule for therapy is then established (e.g., 20 minutes twice a week) for motor training. This training is generally conducted in a "therapy room" or other environment separate from the student's classroom or other natural environments. Often, with the isolated therapy model, parents and educators are unaware of the student's progression or of his or her motor needs. Similarly, therapists are frequently unaware of the goals established by the parents and teachers. Then, due to the slow progress exhibited by many students with severe handicaps, therapists may tend to discontinue therapy or provide maintenance therapy only, without informing the parents or educator. Clearly, the isolated therapy model has serious drawbacks in terms of its ability to serve students with severe physical handicaps in the most comprehensive manner possible.

An alternative is the integrated therapy model, in which the therapist observes the student in the classroom, school yard, home, community, and other natural environments. The therapist observes the student engaging in familiar activities. In addition, the therapist administers specific tests in the presence of parents and teachers in the student's natural environments. From this information, the therapist determines the student's primary motor needs and works with parents and educators to develop motor goals and objectives that can be incorporated into a chronological age–appropriate and functional community-based program.

The integrated therapy model may result in a reduction of direct therapist intervention. Direct intervention occurs within the classroom, community, or home settings, and is provided by the educator and/or parent under the supervision of the therapist. The therapist trains the parents, educators, and other support personnel to implement the program at home, in the community, and at school on a regular basis. At regular intervals, the educators, parents, support personnel, and therapists meet to review progress and design changes to maximize the effectiveness of programs.

A pilot study by Giangreco (1986) compared the effectiveness of direct/isolated therapy with therapeutic techniques that were incorporated into a functional activity in the regular teaching plan. The study resulted in significantly improved performance on the activity through integrated therapy, but there was minimal change with isolated direct therapy. In order for students to acquire maximum support service benefits, the concept of integrated therapy must be utilized. This model facilitates a team approach to the development of motor goals, objectives, and strategies for organizing and implementing an integrated team approach with all support personnel.

To maximize the effectiveness of the team approach, the team members must share relevant information regarding each student. Following are some of the most important areas of information to share:

1. Medical information (past and present)
2. Home living environment, including information related to cultural and linguistic characteristics of the family
3. Behavioral interventions
4. Effective reinforcers
5. Mode(s) of communication
6. Optimal and naturally occurring times for the student to work on specific goals and objectives
7. Amount of time in the classroom for mobility/movement
8. Any relevant changes that might affect the student's behavior

In summary, the integrated therapy model provides program implementation throughout a student's daily routine by those regularly involved with the student. The model relies on communication and a team orientation to deliver the most effective programming. However, Auerswald (1968) cautions that to be most effective, each member of the interdisciplinary team must be able to broaden the perspective of their discipline enough to consider the holistic being of the individual. Averswald suggests an ecological approach which challenges each contributor to use the vantage point of his or her discipline and at the same time interface and bridge the gaps between the structural frameworks of each discipline. The educator can play a key role in facilitating this ecological perspective and in encouraging collaboration to provide the holistic model of intervention for each student.

Community Training Strategies

The importance of providing community training for students with severe handicaps is emphasized throughout this book and in numerous other publications (Sailor & Guess, 1983; Sailor, Wilcox, & Brown, 1980; Snell, 1983; Wilcox & Bellamy, 1982; Wilcox & York, 1980). To provide students with severe physical handicaps the critical skills necessary to be a part of the community, educators must facilitate community training by creating optimal instructional strategies. The logistics and planning of such training can be challenging, due to the inaccessibility of some environments, students' transportation needs, health and safety issues, and so forth.

Before developing a community training program, ecological inventories of the community must be completed. The inventories should be conducted in environments in which students can acquire beneficial recreation/leisure, vocational, and domestic skills. The community inventory should be focused on current as well as subsequent needs, so that training can be meaningful now and in the future (Falvey, Brown, Lyon, Baumgart, & Schroeder, 1980). Specific needs such as oxygen tanks and wheelchairs must be considered when surveying possible training sites. In order to identify appropriate training sites, the accessibility of each specific site and the routes to and from home, school, and work must be determined. Factors that need to be analyzed when determining accessibilty have been identified in *Access Seattle* (1979) and are listed as follows:

1. Parking
2. Locations of bus stops
3. Ramps and curb cuts
4. Entrances, doorways (widths and thresholds)
5. Stairs (steepness, handrails)
6. Elevators (door openings, cab size, height of controls)
7. Aisle width and floor space
8. Restrooms (marked and accessible)
9. Lighting
10. Intersections (controlled or uncontrolled)
11. Sidewalks (existence and condition)

Sites not considered optimally accessible should not be eliminated immediately. School district personnel can be influential in affecting changes within their communities that allow for greater accessibility for students with handicaps. Documentation of the need for wheelchair access on public transportation, for curb cuts, and for widening public sidewalks and aisle ways in stores and public areas should be made. Presentation of documentation to city councils, newspapers, city planners, and commissions on transportation and safety can help to bring about the necessary changes. Minor changes by shopkeepers or creative adaptations by the educator may make a site accessible. When educators and community members work together, much can be accomplished. For example, a high school wood shop class built a ramp that was attached to the side of entryway stairs in a highly frequented movie theatre, allowing students with severe physical handicaps to enter the theatre in proximity to their nonhandicapped peers and enabling interaction between the students. Parent teacher associations (PTAs) and business associations have written letters to local government officials requesting the repair of dangerous sidewalks. Students enrolled in community college courses have designed product displays and arrangements in stores allowing for more floor and aisle space. With cooperation and imagination, many needless barriers in local school and community environments can be reduced or eliminated.

Once sites have been targeted on the basis of accessibility and other factors, transportation methods must be studied. Many public transportation systems are installing lifts to accomodate persons in wheelchairs. Numerous cities also have "Dial-a-Ride" systems that provide vans to serve as inexpensive taxis for persons with handicaps. In addition, community training sites are often within walking distance of schools. The width of sidewalks, the presence of curb cuts, and the condition of streets must also be evaluated for their accessibility. Students who have difficulty walking long distances can be taught to sit in a wheelchair and to wheel it to and from the training sites, and then walk independently while at the site. Once inside some training sites, such as grocery stores, walkers and crutches could be replaced by grocery carts for easier mobility. Many supermarkets have specially designed grocery carts that are intended to make shopping easier and more accessible for persons in wheelchairs.

As frequently stressed in this book, community training should reflect natural environmental proportions as much as possible. If, for example, five persons with physical handicaps are being trained by five supervisors in the same grocery store at the same time, an artificial environment has been created; it has become a "handicapped shopping day." The training environments and all the conditions within those environments should reflect environments utilized by all community members.

Another factor that needs to be considered in community training is the development and provision of appropriate student/staff ratios. Many students with physical handicaps may initially or continually require 1:1 assistance in the community. Since most classrooms are staffed with ratios such as 2 staff for 8–12 students, educators must develop methods and resources to meet the staff ratio needs. Creating heterogeneous groupings of students so that all the students with severe physical handicaps are not in the same class is one of the most effective strategies. Nonhandicapped friends can also be included in community training by providing mobility assistance—for example, by pushing a wheelchair or sight guiding a person with a visual impairment. In addition, friends can serve as appropriate social models and can provide opportunities for social interaction. Support personnel such as speech therapists, occupational therapists, and physical therapists are also valuable resources to assist in community training while teaching in their specialty area (e.g., speech therapists can facilitate communication in community environments). Parents can be a resource for added assistance, as can school PTAs, local service organizations, senior citizens groups, or fraternities and sororities from local colleges and universities. Thorough training should be given to all volunteers and participants before they assist in the community training program.

When providing training in the business community or in the regular school, the image of each student and the program as a whole should be positive, healthy, and as normal as possible. Involvement in activities should be unobtrusive, allowing students to learn independent skills without drawing undue negative attention to them. For example, Betsy, a 10-year-old student with cerebral palsy who is learning to feed herself, often spills food onto her blouse when eating "spoon foods." To enhance her self-image and provide unobtrusive instruction, careful selection of the food she eats (sandwiches versus applesauce) and the use of extra napkins rather than wearing a bib will create a more positive experience for both Betsy and her nonhandicapped peers. The actual teaching environments should also be taken into account. Betsy can comfortably dine with her peers in any restaurant and in the regular school cafeteria by selecting finger food menu items, while continuing to work on her spoon feeding skills in the classroom. As another illustration, a student who is gavage fed may eat in the classroom prior to the regular lunchtime and still be able to participate socially in the cafeteria with other students.

For students who will require assistance at mealtime in the community, it is important to remember that assistance should be offered with dignity and respect for the individual. Regardless of age, considerations should be made as to the student's choice of food, what he or she wants to eat next, and when he or she is full. It is also important to sit naturally beside the student, rather than facing him or her, as one would do with an infant, to use one's dominant hand in feeding so as to demonstrate good control, to pace eating according to the student's needs for chewing and swallowing, and to bring food to the student at an appropriate level (not swooping down as if it were an airplane). Other personal dignity, social acceptance, and hygienic considerations to be aware of are: not blowing or tasting for the temperature of a student's food, using a napkin rather than a bib, towel, or spoon to wipe around a student's mouth, wiping gently around the mouth and not the whole face, getting a wet napkin rather than spitting on a napkin to clean dried food, and not mashing the foods or mixing foods together so that they lose their sensorial appeal. Again the dignity of each student should be the priority consideration for determining whether assisted eating, self-eating, and/or social integration are the appropriate mealtime objectives.

When assessing the image of each student, careful evaluation of the appearance of any special equipment—for example, cleanliness of wheelchairs—is necessary. Many students can be taught to clean their own wheelchairs or parts of their wheelchairs. Wheelchairs and tray tables should be clear of outdated and age-inappropriate bumper stickers and decals that would portray a "square" or age-inappropriate image. In addition, clothing could be worn on the outside of braces. In effect, students with physical handicaps not only have the right to be educated in the least restrictive environment but they have the right to be taught in the least obtrusive manner.

Physical Management Techniques

Students with physical handicaps may temporarily or permanently require assistance with positioning and ambulating. Physical management techniques such as positioning, transferring, and carrying of students must be provided in an effective manner. Physical management techniques have been widely reviewed in the literature (Finnie, 1975; Fraser & Hensinger, 1983; Utley, 1982; Utley, Holvoet, & Barnes, 1977).

When physically managing a student, educators and others must consider the following several factors:

1. Students' positions should be changed regularly to allow more comfort and prevent sores or stiffness.
2. Students should be positioned so that they are able to view other people in the room and are in proximity to classroom activities.
3. Students should be told when they are going to be handled, where they will be moved, and what their activity will be.
4. Students' preferences for positions should be valued.
5. Positions must be changed to facilitate various skill training tasks (e.g., the student may be placed on a wedge to participate in an activity requiring head control and then be positioned upright with a head brace to participate in activities requiring reaching skills).
6. Students should be positioned in a manner that will not indirectly encourage negative patterns (e.g., a student with a strong extension pattern placed with his or her back to a television set may cause the extension to become stronger because of the distraction going on out of his or her view).

Effective physical management techniques involve attending to the student's overall well-being in addition to the safety of the educator. Whenever a student is transferred or moved from one situation to another, a systematic, well-planned approach must be used. Educators must know how the movement will be done and where the student will be moved. Following are some important points to consider when preparing to move a student:

1. Communicate movement intentions to the student.
2. Encourage the student to help in any way possible.
3. Obtain help from others when necessary. Undertaking a task that is too difficult may result in injury to the person lifting as well as to the student.
4. Bend knees when lifting a student. Lifting should be done with the entire body, as opposed to using only the back.
5. Establish a broad base of support by keeping feet apart (approximately shoulder width) when bending and lifting.
6. Avoid reaching, by positioning oneself near the student.
7. Take small steps in order to turn or rotate while moving a student. Do not rely on twisting or turning at the trunk while lifting or carrying.

Proper physical management techniques on the part of the educator provide the safest and most effective method of handling students. Positioning and handling techniques can facilitate movement that leads to functional skill acquisition. A goal parallel to proper management is activity-based functional skill acquisition. Positioning a 16-year old student at a desk and giving him or her a set of stacking rings would be nonproductive as well as chronological age inappropriate. Optimal physical management techniques must be used to facilitate participation in age-appropriate and functional activities.

Emergency Procedures

It is highly recommended that educators and parents be trained in basic first aid and cardiopulmonary resuscitation (CPR). Classes are frequently offered by the American Red Cross at convenient sites such as hospitals, YMCAs/YWCAs, college campuses, and elsewhere. The classes are usually inexpensive, demand little time, and offer extremely valuable information.

A major medical concern of educators of students with severe handicaps is that of responding to seizures. Students with known seizure disorders should have accompanying records indicating the type, length, and severity of seizures. Anticipatory signs of seizures and length of recovery time should also be noted, as well as any special emergency procedures. Many seizure disorders are treated with medication. It is important that educators be aware of the type of medication being used and of any present or possible side effects (including toxic effects) of that medication. Basic procedures to aid a student who is having a grand mal seizure are:

1. If the student is likely to fall, assist him or her to lie down.
2. Clear area of furniture and/or other harmful objects.
3. If the student is lying down, roll the student on his or her side to prevent choking and loosen any restrictive clothing.
4. Do not try to restrain the student or attempt to stop the seizure.
5. Do not force anything into his or her mouth.
6. Record the incident as accurately as possible.
7. Notify the parents, the physician, and the school nurse.

Much of the training for students with severe handicaps occurs in the community, away from the availability of the school nurse. When community training takes place, a policy for emergency procedures must be established.

Self-Help Skills

Beyond visible gross and fine motor difficulties, students with physical handicaps may need extensive aid and instruction in areas such as hygiene, eating, and toileting. Again, numerous strategies can assist the student to develop these specific skills. A team approach should be utilized to determine which stategies are most effective for a given student. Factors to consider across all skill areas are: the student's age, motivation, type and degree of disability, amount of present independence, and obtrusiveness of the intervention.

Poor oral muscle coordination can severely impede normal eating patterns. Students with physical handicaps often have nutritional deficits related to eating difficulties. Specific eating techniques must be used to inhibit abnormal patterns and to ensure an appropriate intake of nutrients. Strategies for eating include, among others: proper positioning for chewing and swallowing (Utley, 1982), using the Mueller (1975) techniques for mouth opening, jaw control, lip closure, and swallowing, and tongue exercises that will increase tone (Bigge & O'Donnell, 1976). There are also issues to consider beyond specific intervention techniques. Foods should be chosen in accordance with student preference, family food and cultural norms, nutritional value, texture, and specific eating goals (e.g., peanut butter can be used to encourage tongue lateralization).

Eating patterns often deteriorate while students are learning to eat independently (Utley, 1982). Consideration of a student's age, motivation, and application of ideas, such as Campbell's (1983) theory of independence (i.e., providing the least amount of assistance that will result in a sufficient level of independent skill performance), as well as the concept of least intrusive interventions, are important to consider when determining when to initiate teaching a student to eat independently. For example, proper lip closure may be sacrificed for independent eating, particularly for older students. Facilitating independent eating to the maximal extent possible allows for greater independence, less invasion of personal space, and probably, an increased self-concept.

Lack of independent toileting skills is often the reason students with severe handicaps are excluded from appropriate school, living, recreation/leisure, and work environments. Toilet training instructional programs developed for persons with severe handicaps have, within the last 15 years, proven highly successful (Azrin & Foxx, 1971, 1974; Copeland, Ford, & Solon, 1976; Fredericks et al., 1975). However, for some students with severe physical handicaps, the issue is not always one of implementing programs to teach control. It is physically impossible for some students to have bladder and/or bowel control. When this is the case, it is critical that educators work with the physician, parent, and student in determining the most appropriate means of bladder/bowel care.

Goals for bladder and bowel care must include cleanliness and comfort, prevention of urinary tract or bowel infections, prevention of skin irritation, social acceptance, and maximal independence (McCubbin, 1983). The student's age, degree of control, movement capabilities, and intellectual functioning are all important considerations when deciding the most appropriate method of care. Self-catheterization, ostomies, and other techniques can be used to aid in healthy, socially appropriate means of bladder and bowel control (Bigge & O'Donnell, 1976; McCubbin, 1983).

Incontinence should not exclude a student from participation in community activities. Students who do not have bowel/bladder control should be given support in using restrooms before, during, and after community activities. If a student requires changing while in the community, he or she can be changed in a private stall in a public restroom. If a student needs access to a table for changing, then one option for a nonfacility based program (e.g. transition program) is to transport the student home to be changed, since community instruction occurs in the individual's local community. Another option is to arrange with one or two community businesses to make the employee restroom available, if that provides a clean, private area. At no time should a student be changed on the floor of a public restroom that is neither private nor clean.

Hygiene, grooming, and dressing skills are all necessary for maintaining a healthy body and positive self-image. Cleanliness is an important health factor as well as a critical aspect in developing and maintaining social relationships. Students should be taught skills that will lead to the greatest independence, whether that means use of adaptive equipmemt or opting for the simplest care (e.g., a male student may choose to grow a beard rather than struggle with shaving). Students should be taught to select their own clothing, with instruction being provided where necessary regarding ease of dressing, current peer styles, seasons/weather, comfort, fit (with special equipment such as braces or casts), and appropriateness for specific occasions. Again, the main goals are maximal independence, with a healthy, positive self-image.

Another important consideration when dealing with toileting, hygiene, grooming, and dressing skills is the issue of privacy. All students should learn to participate in the care of their personal needs as independently as possible and be cared for when necessary with respect to their privacy. The issue of privacy should include age-appropriate and normalized use of toilet facilities and dressing areas in the natural environment. For example, males over the age of 5 generally do not use women's restrooms, students do not dress in their classrooms, and the dressing area of a school gym is usually less private than the department store dressing rooms). The right of privacy must also include ownership of personal clothing and grooming articles, and the right of confidentiality about a student's personal needs between staff members.

ADAPTATIONS

The "principle of partial participation" (Baumgart et al., 1982) refers to the assumption that a person has a right to participate in any and all activities to any extent possible. Often, persons with severe handicaps are denied activity-oriented opportunities because of their inability to fully perform all the skills required. Instead of excluding students from activities, individualized adaptations can be developed and provided for those students to allow participation in a variety of natural environments.

Frequently, the concept of adaptations is correlated with the design and utilization of materials and devices. Baumgart et al. (1982) have expanded the concept of adaptations to include:

1. Adapting skill sequences—rearranging the typical order of steps within a task
2. Adapting rules—changing certain rules to allow more participation
3. Utilizing personal assistance—providing aides, peer tutors, using buddy systems, crew labor, and so forth, to accomplish tasks
4. Fostering social/attitudinal changes—changing assumptions and beliefs of the student, family, professionals, and/or community members
5. Creating or using materials and devices to meet specific needs of specific students—microswitches, mechanical devices, calculators, computers, communciation devices, special handles, lifts, and so on

Included in Table 10.2 are examples of adaptations to facilitate independence in a variety of skills for various ages.

When determining whether or not to use an adaptation and what adaptation should be used, several factors must be considered. York, Nietupski, and Hamre-Nietupski (1985), outlined the "decision-making process" of determining the use of microswitches. Microswitches are control devices that allow access to electrical or battery operated equipment by persons who cannot activate the equipment in the manner most frequently used. Types of microswitches include: mercury tilt switch, pillow switch, pedal switch, chin switch, push on/off switch, or puff switch. Microswitches are used with an alco relay or battery

Table 10.2. Examples of adaptations to facilitate independence

Student	Task	Adaptation
	Adapting Skill Sequences	
Needs pureed food.	Eating with peers in cafeteria.	Pick up lunch tray early; prepare in classroom; take to cafeteria.
5-year-old student has ataxic cerebral palsy; has no mobility; unable to crawl.	Being independently mobile in all events.	Student may pass over crawling stage and learn to be mobile by walking.
Fatigues extremely easily.	Cleaning apartment.	Do one task a day instead of doing all cleaning one day a week.
Has short attention span.	Playing table games.	Provide reinforcement throughout the game instead of just at the end.
Has difficulty with balance.	Using toilet independently.	Sit on toilet, then remove pants.
Is unable to maintain balance while bending and reaching.	Bathing independently.	Sit in bathtub, then adjust water faucets.
	Adapting Rules	
Has difficulty eating quickly.	Eating with peers in cafeteria.	Allow a longer lunch period for this student by starting earlier.
Is unable to locate bus stop landmarks.	Riding the bus independently.	Student asks bus driver to tell him or her when they are at the right stop.
Has difficulty bending and maintaining balance.	Sweeping floors	Sweeps dirt out the door instead of using a dustpan.
Is unable to write name.	Signing checks.	Signs name with assistance and has a rubber stamp made.
Cannot discriminate between written numbers.	Playing table games.	Uses one denomination of money.
Uses a wheelchair.	Using restroom in a public place.	Student uses employee restroom if public one is not accessible.
	Utilizing Personal Assistance	
Uses crutches.	Using school cafeteria.	Ask peer to carry tray of food.
Has limited cooking skills.	Eating a complete meal.	Have a team meal where each person prepares one course.
Has poor fine motor skills.	Using household appliances.	Ask family member to plug in appliance.

(continued)

Table 10.2. *(continued)*

Student	Task	Adaptation
Has low reading ability.	Playing table games.	Peer reads all questions while student and peer take turns answering.
Has poor fine motor skills.	Marketing.	Ask a neighbor to assist with cutting out coupons.
Uses a wheelchair.	Riding in an elevator.	Ask someone to push button for correct floor if button out of reach.
	Materials and Devices	
Is unable to add or subtract amounts.	Marketing with a limited amount of money.	Use calculator to add amounts.
Has low reading ability.	Setting temperatures on range or setting time on alarm clock.	Use color-coded dials or gauges.
Uses wheelchair.	Cleaning house.	Use long-handled brushes/sponges.
Has difficulty matching colors.	Dressing independently.	Tag clothes that match with coded labels.
Poor fine motor skills.	Playing table games.	Use enlarged pieces and adapting switches.
Difficulty with balance.	Bathing.	Use nonslip mats, handrails, hand-held shower heads.

adapter that functions as a remote control unit so that the equipment can be controlled by the microswitch. The purpose for developing a microswitch is to allow a person with physical handicaps access to equipment, which increases that person's independence in functional activities. The same considerations for determining the use of microswitches can and should be used in determining the use of any adaptation.

The first consideration is establishing the validity of the educational activity. The goal should not be the successful development of an adaptation or its use. The goal should be the gaining of a functional movement or control over one's environment that leads to greater independence. If it is an activity a student will participate in daily (e.g., dressing), several adaptations may be necessary to allow for independence. However, if the activity occurs infrequently (e.g., changing a light bulb) it may be a waste of valuable instructional time to develop and train the student to use a large number of adaptations to complete the task.

The second consideration is whether this activity can be taught directly without the use of an adaptation. There is no need to develop an elaborate adaptation if the skill can be taught without it. Students with severe physical handicaps need to be encouraged to use as much of their motor skills as possible rather than relying on microswitch adaptations and devices that may allow other muscles to become weak or contracted. Creating adaptations may be challenging for professionals, and they may be fun for students to use. However, it is important not to overuse or foster dependence on nonfunctional or unnecessary devices. The goal for the student remains independence in the most unobtrusive and appropriate manner.

The third consideration is determining what adaptation is appropriate. As mentioned earlier, there are many possible types of adaptations. The ideal adaptation allows for greater participation and control over one's environment and compensates for one's motor deficiencies. A student's current skills, strengths, weaknesses, and motivation will also determine the appropriate adaptation to use. Whether an adaptation will be permanent or temporary will also have a major effect on decisions regarding the kind of adaptation used. If, for example, it will take longer to train the student to use an adaptation than it does to wait for a leg cast to be removed, the adaptation should not be developed. If, however, the adaptation is temporary and can be used to teach other skills, it would be more appropriate to develop and teach the student to use it. Permanent adaptations must be expanded or adjusted as students become older or more skilled (i.e., instead of continuing to push a student in a wheelchair, the student can learn to independently operate a motorized wheelchair). The care and upkeep of long-term adaptations must be considered, and students should be taught to perform the upkeep to the maximum extent possible. Accessibility, convenience, and reliability of the adaptation is also important. For instance, a microswitch that works sporadically is of no value. Similarly, there is little worth in an adaptation whose use is restricted to a limited area or to a limited number of people (e.g., the use of sign language in the community).

The fourth consideration is the development of the educational program around the use of the adaptation(s) selected. Included in designing an appropriate program is assessment to determine the appropriate instructional position and dominant motor movement(s) of the student. It is also necessary to determine the most appropriate environment and materials for instruction, determine the instructional procedures (e.g., teaching sequences, natural cues, a system for fading), and develop a data-based measurement system.

The final consideration is ensuring the safety of all students using adaptations. This is especially important when using electrical adaptions and equipment. There are several "how to" manuals (e.g., Burkhart, 1980, 1982, 1987) that provide information on the construction of microswitches. Although they are quite simple, it is important to follow safety tips such as those recommended by York et al. (1985):

1. Always seek expert advice from an electrician, an electrical engineer, or a qualified radio/electronic technician when questions arise or when equipment is malfunctioning.

2. When using microswitches to activate plug-in devices, either use an optical isolator or a power relay (also called a voltage regulator) in your circuit to decrease the 110V from your household electrical outlet to a safe level for the microswitch. The amount of voltage which typically goes to the microswitches is 6V. Caution should be taken when using devices with heating elements, such as a hair dryer or popcorn popper; a power relay that can handle a higher number of watts must be used.
3. Always check for frayed and exposed wires and replace/repair as necessary.
4. Be careful that wires and cords are positioned such that they do not become wet and students cannot become tangled in them. If there is possibility of becoming wet, precautions should be taken so that wires and cords remain waterproof.
5. Use tin solder, not lead solder, when assembling microswitches.
6. Secure small microswitches so they cannot be inhaled or swallowed.
7. Batteries contain acid, so be sure damaged or used batteries are disposed of properly.
8. Mercury is a poison. Encase mercury microswitches in plastic tubing or glue. Use caution when handling mercury switches and keep them safely stored when not in use.
9. Check to be sure that microswitches and other equipment are free of rough and sharp edges to avoid abrasions and puncture wounds.
10. Check with a physician prior to using any electrical devices with students who have heart problems or use electrical medical equipment.

Equipment and adaptations should be selected to achieve the goals of facilitating or inhibiting movement, supporting posture, and aiding independence in motor tasks across all curricular domains. Educators, parents, and therapists should work closely with physicians and orthotists to ensure that the student's equipment is appropriate.

The fit and function of any equipment or adaptation must be continually reevaluated (Venn, Morganstern, & Dykes, 1979). The major purpose of reevaluation is to determine if the equipment or adaptation can or should be discontinued. Fading the use of special equipment as soon as possible will lead to a more normalized appearance in the individual and more convenient functioning in daily tasks.

With the help of special equipment and creative adaptations, students with severe physical handicaps are often able to accomplish the same tasks as their peers. Following is a list of some of the most commonly used equipment. For more detailed information, refer to Burkhart (1980, 1982), Finnie (1975), and Fraser and Hensinger (1983).

Positioning

1. Bolsters/sand bags: pillow-like objects used to support desired positions
2. Triangle/corner chairs: provide three-sided support in upright position; can also be used with table
3. Bean bags: comfortable positioning; adjust to individual
4. Wedges: wedge-shaped foam pads used in prone position; allow work on head control, use of hands/arms
5. Car seats: provide safety and appropriate positioning
6. Wheelchairs/inserts: upright positioning and mobility inserts, individually designed and fitted
7. Prone boards: standing positioning, allowing use of hands/arms

Mobility

1. Scooters: used by young children from many positions
2. Walkers: style varies with need
3. Crutches: style varies with need
4. Bicycles (two or three wheels): can have adapted seats, handle bars, or pedals, as necessary
5. Wheelchairs (power and regular):
   a. Standard: with specific equipment such as footrests, neckrests, headrests, side supports, and inserts
   b. Travel chairs: serve as both therapeutic chairs and car seats (rear wheels are collapsible)

Isolated Support

1. Braces: plastic, fiberglass, or cloth; are removable support for scoliosis or joint strengthening; metal braces are being used less frequently
2. Splints: used on hands, wrists, arms, knees, and ankles; used for support or to help inhibit contractures

Self-Help Aids: Eating

1. Nonslip mats: rubbery material preventing bowls and plates from sliding on tables
2. High-sided bowls: allow for easier scooping
3. Plastic or rubber handles on utensils: for easier grip
4. Hard plastic utensils: used with students who have a bite reflex (metal may damage teeth, light plastic will break)
5. Cups with cutouts: allow room for nose while drinking if unable to tilt head back

Self-Help Aids: Toileting

1. Wet pants signalers: sound off as student begins to urinate in pants, allowing teacher to implement toileting procedures
2. Toileting signalers: sound off when student urinates in toilet, allowing teacher to immediately reinforce
3. Supportive seats: fit onto regular toilet seat, adding height, side, or back support
4. Medical procedures: ostomies, ileal conduits, catheterizations, and other procedures

Self-Help Aids: Bathing

1. Nonslip mats: placed beside tub and in bottom of tub
2. Bath seats/benches: placed inside tub to provide access and support
3. Webbed slings: strap attaches to faucet and reaches around back of student for support
4. Slatted frame or other false bottom, making tub shallower
5. Hand-held soap holders, sponges with straps
6. Hand-held shower heads

Self-Help Aids: Dressing

1. Velcro: used as substitute for fasteners
2. Clothes that are looser fitting may be easier to put on and remove
3. Foot stools: provide stability, make it easier to reach shoes, and so forth

Activity-Oriented Equipment

1. Mercury switches: device worn on part of student's body where movement is desired; attaches to radio or device that switches on when body part moves
2. Other switches controlled by hands, feet, cheeks, voice, breath
3. Battery-operated devices: toys, wheelchairs, communication systems adapted with special switches
4. Computer aids: communication, leisure/recreation, calculators for shopping, and so forth
5. Toy modifications: larger handles, switches, controls, adapted to be operated by different modalities (e.g., by voice)
6. Radio-controlled device: door openers, phone answering machines, toys
7. Mobility devices: battery-operated riding toys, power wheelchairs, scooters.

SUMMARY

The development of a comprehensive motor skills program for persons with physical handicaps must include the following components: an understanding of conditions and related terms; assessment of functional skills in natural environments; determination of functional chronological age–appropriate goals; consideration of related issues, such as community training and therapy models; and implementation of teaching strategies, which may include adaptations. Motor skills programming must be integrated into all aspects of the student's daily routine by educators, therapists, and parents. Once programming has been integrated, a student's motor functioning will enhance his or her potential for independent functioning across all curricular domains.

REFERENCES

Access Seattle: A guidebook for disabled persons. (1979). Seattle: Junior League of Seattle and Easter Seal Society of Washington.

Auerswald, E.H. (1968). Interdisciplinary versus ecological approach. *Family Process, 6,* 202–215.

Azrin, N.H., & Foxx, R. (1971). A rapid method of toilet training the institutionalized retarded. *Journal of Applied Behavior Analysis, 4,* 89–99.

Azrin, N.H., & Foxx, R.M. (1974). *Toilet training in less than a day.* New York: Simon & Schuster.

Batshaw, M.L., & Perret, Y.M. (1981). *Children with handicaps: A medical primer.* Baltimore: Paul H. Brookes Publishing Co.

Baumgart, D., Brown, L., Pumpian, I., Nisbet, J., Ford, A., Sweet, M., Messina, R., & Schroeder, J. (1982). Principle of partial participation and individualized adaptations in educational programs for severely handicapped students. *Journal of The Association for the Severely Handicapped, 7*(2), 17–27.

Bigge, J.L., & O'Donnell, P.A. (1976). *Teaching individuals with physical and multiple disabilities.* Columbus, OH: Charles E. Merrill.

Bleck, E.E., & Nagel, D.A. (Eds.). (1975). *Physically handicapped children: A medical atlas for teachers.* New York: Grune & Stratton.

Bobath, B. (1969). The treatment of neuromuscular disorders by improving patterns of coordination. *Physiotherapy,* 55, 18–22.

Burkhart, L.J. (1980). *Homemade battery powered toys and educational devices for severely handicapped children.* Millville, PA: Author.

Burkhart, L.J. (1982). *More homemade battery devices for severely handicapped children, with suggested activities.* Millville, PA: Author.

Burkhart, L.J. (1987). *Using computers and speech synthesis to facilitate communicative interaction with young and/or severely handicapped children.* College Park, MD: Author.

Campbell P. (1983). Basic considerations in programming for students with movement difficulties. In M. Snell (Ed.), *Systematic instruction of the moderately and severely handicapped* (2nd ed., pp. 168–201). Columbus: Charles E. Merrill.

Copeland, M., Ford, L., & Solon, N. (1976). *Occupational therapy for mentally retarded children.* Baltimore: University Park Press.

Falvey, M., Brown, L., Lyon, S., Baumgart, D., & Schroeder, J. (1980). Strategies for using cues and correction procedures. In W. Sailor, B. Wilcox, & L. Brown (Eds.), *Methods of instruction for severely handicapped students* (pp. 109–133). Baltimore: Paul H. Brookes Publishing Co.

Finnie, N.R. (1975). *Handling the young cerebral palsied child at home.* New York: E.P. Dutton.

Ford, A., Davis, J., Messina, R., Ranieri, L., Nisbet, J., & Sweet, M. (1982). Arranging instruction to ensure the active participation of severely multihandicapped students. In L. Brown, J. Nisbet, A. Ford, M. Sweet, B. Shiraga, & L. Gruenewald (Eds.), *Educational programs for severely handicapped students* (Vol. 12, pp. 31–80). Madison, WI: Madison Metropolitan School District.

Fraser, B.A., & Hensinger, R.N. (1983). *Managing physical handicaps: A practical guide for parents, care providers, and educators.* Baltimore: Paul H. Brookes Publishing Co.

Fredericks, H.D., Baldwin, V.L., Grove, D.N., Riggs, C., Furey, V., Moore, W., Jordan, E., Gage, M.A., Levak, L., Alrick, G., & Wadlow, P. (1975). *A data-based classroom for the moderately and severely handicapped.* Monmouth, OR: Instructional Development Corp.

Giangreco, M.F. (1986). Effects of integrated therapy: A pilot study. *Journal of The Association for Persons with Severe Handicaps, 11*(3), 205–208.

McCubbin, T. (1983). Routine and emergency medical procedures. In M. Snell (Ed.), *Systematic instruction of the moderately and severely handicapped* (2nd ed.). Columbus, OH: Charles E. Merrill.

Mueller, H. (1975). Feeding. In N. Finnie, *Handling the young cerebral palsied child at home*. New York: E.P. Dutton.

Sailor, W., & Guess, D. (1983). *Severely handicapped students: An instructional design.* Boston: Houghton Mifflin.

Sailor, W., Wilcox, B., & Brown, L. (Eds.). (1980). *Methods of instruction for severely handicapped students*. Baltimore: Paul H. Brookes Publishing Co.

Snell, M.E. (1983). Self care skills. In M. Snell (Ed.), *Systematic instruction of the moderately and severely handicapped* (2nd ed., pp. 358–409). Columbus: Charles E. Merrill.

Sternat, J., Messina, R., Nietupski, J., Lyon, S., & Brown, L. (1977). In E. Sontag (Ed.), *Educational programming for the severely and profoundly handicapped* (pp. 263–278). Reston, VA: Council for Exceptional Children, Division on Mental Retardation.

Utley, B. (1982). Motor skills and adaptation. In L. Sternberg & G. Adams (Eds.), *Educating severely and profoundly handicapped students* (pp. 163–204). Rockville, MD: Aspen Systems.

Utley, B., Holvoet, J., & Barnes, K. (1977). Handling, positioning, and feeding the physically handicapped. In E. Sontag (Ed.), *Educational programming for the severely and profoundly handicapped* (pp. 279–299). Reston, VA: Council for Exceptional Children, Division on Mental Retardation.

Venn, J., Morganstern, L., & Dykes, M. (1979). Checklists for evaluating the fit and function of orthoses, prostheses, and wheelchairs in the classroom. *Teaching Exceptional Children, 11*(2), 51–56.

Wilcox, B., & Bellamy, G.T. (1982). *Design of high school programs for severely handicapped students*. Baltimore: Paul H. Brookes Publishing Co.

Wilcox, B., & York, R. (Eds.). (1980). *Quality education for the severely handicapped.* Falls Church, VA: Counterpoint Handcraft Book.

York, J., Nietupski, J., & Hamre-Nietupski, S. (1985). A decision-making process for using microswitches. *Journal of The Association for Persons with Severe Handicaps, 10*(4), 214–223.

ELEVEN

COMMUNICATION SKILLS

Jennifer Coots and Mary A. Falvey

THE FOLLOWING IS a description of methods for determining the most appropriate and functional interventions to employ in developing the communicative competence of persons with severe handicaps. In previous chapters, the rationale for developing chronological age–appropriate and functional activities within a wide variety of vocational/employment, domestic, recreation/leisure, and community environments was delineated. One of the most essential basic skills necessary for participation in activities across all domains is the ability to communicate.

Students with severe handicaps exhibit significant difficulties and delays in the area of communication skills. Students with autism, for example, experience major problems in the use of language, both in being understood and in being able to understand the communications of others (Kanner, 1943; Prizant, 1983; Schuler, 1979; Wing, 1981). Students with severe retardation exhibit substantial delays in communication and are often unable to verbally express even simple thoughts. Other students with retardation are characterized by prompt dependency, passivity, or learned helplessness (Calculator, 1988; Seligman, 1975). Students with physical handicaps may have substantial difficulties in producing the sounds necessary to communicate verbally. In addition, some students exhibit communication difficulties associated with several or all three of the disabilities just mentioned.

ELEMENTS OF COMMUNICATION

Communication involves certain elements. First, the use of a *system* is essential—for example, spoken language, manual signs, pictures, and objects.

Second, the communicator must be able to employ *mode(s)* for delivering a message with these symbols (e.g., speech, pointing, gesturing, eye blinking). Third, *social interaction* skills are necessary for the message to be understood by the message receiver, and for comprehension of the rules that dictate the reciprocal nature of interacting. Finally, the vocabulary or *communicative content* necessary to communicate is an essential component. It is critical that readers understand that communication can involve speech and language, although it is not dependent upon those components. Rather, communication is defined as "occurring when people interact in some way (verbally or nonverbally) so that a message passes from one person to another and a response is given in return" (Musselwhite & St. Louis, 1982, p. 48). The strategies emphasized in this chapter are those that teach students with severe handicaps to communicate and interact with others within a variety of environments.

COMMUNICATION INTERVENTION: PAST RESEARCH

Traditionally, speech and communication have been viewed as synonymous (Calculator, 1988). This has led to isolated intervention efforts that focused on drill in comprehension and articulation skills within didactic, noncontingent interactions (Bedrosian, 1988). In addition, intervention has traditionally focused on teaching students to label, and has relegated students to limited respondent roles. Teachers have also reported that this focus on the development and refinement of "speech" led to the exclusion of many students from speech/language services. Students with severe handicaps were often described as not being ready for speech services due to their delay.

Another practice interfering with the effectiveness of communication intervention has been over-reliance and dependence upon developmental models. The difficulties that result from relying upon developmental models are discussed in Chapter 3 of this volume. In the area of communication, reliance upon these models has been especially problematic, as the models were based upon limited or restricted information, thus producing a skewed view of language development. This limited information base was due to a bias in early language acquisition research; rather than examine individual differences, early studies sought to determine the universals in development (Goldfield & Snow, 1985).

PRESENT TRENDS IN COMMUNICATION INTERVENTION

Research that has expanded the focus of communication intervention has occurred in the area of pragmatics, or the function of communication. Halliday (1975), for example, found that beginning communicators communicated about many things with different purposes before language occurred. Keogh and Reichle (1985) stated that even newborn babies exert some control over what happens to them by communicating, whether intentionally or not. Current intervention programs are beginning to target these prelinguistic and presymbolic forms of communication as the beginning points of communication training rather than waiting for speech or other "prerequisites" of communication to occur (Owens & Rogerson, 1988; Siegel-Causey & Downing, 1987). Communication intervention no longer targets speech alone, but rather focuses on the comprehensive development of these functions along with the forms and content that will have the greatest impact upon the person's life (Falvey, Bishop, Grenot-Scheyer, & Coots, 1988; McLean & Snyder-McLean, 1978).

Studies examining natural language acquisition have identified several characteristics of early interactions which seem ideally suited to assisting children in acquiring language. "Child directed speech" and parent/child interactions are characterized by patient, contingent, nondirective, responsive child-centered interactions which maximize the child's attention to the task at hand. In addition, these interactions are active, involve prompts, assign meaning, occur within routines and joint activities, and involve varied stimuli (Ainsworth, 1973; Hart, 1985; MacDonald, 1985; Snow, 1972; Snow & Ferguson, 1978; Vygotsky, 1978).

It can be stated that for a child who did not develop speech as an infant and whose communication skills are therefore delayed, these naturally occurring strategies and contexts were not sufficient or effective in assisting that child in acquiring language. The child may then require vastly different intervention strategies such as the isolated, drill-based intervention programs mentioned earlier. Other researchers have stated that instead, the natural contexts and contingencies characteristic of "child directed speech" and natural language acquisition need to guide intervention. The natural cues and stimulus dimensions available in these contexts need to be made more salient. Alternatively, they can be adapted in an age-appropriate manner rather than changed or isolated, in order to avoid teaching skills out of context (Hart, 1985; MacDonald, 1985; McLean & Snyder-McLean, 1978; Warren & Rogers-Warren, 1985).

This expanded view of communication has also changed perceptions regarding who is responsible for developing and implementing communication intervention programs. Because the focus is no longer on developing speech skills in isolation, assessment and intervention are no longer viewed as the sole responsibility of a speech or language therapist (Warren & Rogers-Warren, 1985). Instead, cooperative assessment, planning, and intervention efforts involving families, communication specialists, teachers, and students and/or clients, have been determined to be critical in developing programs that maximize the communicative competence of persons with severe handicaps across domains and environments (Falvey, McLean, & Rosenberg, 1988).

REQUISITES TO COMMUNICATION

Behaviors such as attending, imitating, and following simple directions have traditionally been viewed as prerequisites to communication (Kent, 1974).

While these behaviors and skills are important, many are not truly prerequisites to communicating. Insistence upon mastering a behavior like imitation as a prerequisite may delay teaching of functional communication behaviors. The emphasis on prerequisite skill hierarchies has been identified by Brown et al. (1979) as the "not ready for" hypothesis. The only prerequisite behavior that seems reasonable to consider before developing a student's communication training program is that he or she is able to breathe, either independently or through artificial means. No other prerequisite behaviors are reasonable or appropriate to the development of a communication training program for a student. However, several behaviors or skills must be taught concurrently with specific communication skills. These have been referred to as "requisites" for communication (Gruenewald, Schroeder, & Yoder, 1982), and are defined and described in the following paragraphs.

Reasons for Communicating

Unfortunately, many students with severe handicaps are often inadvertently discouraged from producing appropriate communicative behaviors. Frequently, well meaning educators and families anticipate the needs and wants of students to such an extent that the student finds little or no reason to communicate. In addition, traditional programs that emphasize speech production in isolation of communication frequently produce the perception by the students that there is no purpose for those speech behaviors. Because students often have little control over their own lives, they may also develop "learned helplessness," resulting in a lack of motivation to control their environment by communicating. Finally, students exhibiting such behaviors as temper tantrums or abuse of self, of others, or of property, are frequently placed on strict extinction programs to eliminate such behaviors. Recent research has demonstrated that such inappropriate behaviors might serve as the student's only attempts at communicating, and should therefore be shaped into more appropriate responses rather than extinguished (Donnellan, Mirenda, Mesaros, & Fassbender, 1984; Prizant & Duchan, 1981; Rein, 1984; Schuler & Goetz, 1983). Educators and parents must determine what motivates a student in order to provide that student with reasons to communicate (Gruenewald et al., 1982).

Communication: Content

Once the student has developed reasons to communicate, he or she must have something to communicate, that is, communicative content. To determine the communicative content that must be taught, ecological inventories, parent and significant other interviews, and systematic observation of the student should be considered. The communicative content taught to a student must focus on the content necessary to interact with nonhandicapped peers, family members, community members, neighbors, co-workers, and employers (Wulz, Myers, Klein, Hall, & Waldo, 1982). Emphasis must be placed on communicative content that will assist the student to become as independent as possible with the widest range of people in a variety of environments (Gruenewald et al., 1982). Content should also reflect vocabulary that will have the greatest impact upon the individual student's life. The content should also allow the student to exhibit control over what occurs in his or her life, and should reflect the ideas the student most wants to communicate. Moreover, too much stress has been placed upon teaching students to respond to someone else's initiation. Emphasis must also be placed on teaching students to initiate interactions.

Communication: Methods

Since many students with severe handicaps are at risk for not developing intelligible speech, providing an augmentative or alternative means to communicate is essential. When possible, speech should always be the first choice, as it is the most convenient and adaptable mode available. However, many students will not be able to acquire enough intelligible speech to allow for a functional communication system (Gruenewald et al., 1982). When analyzing communicative behavior exhibited by the general population, it becomes apparent that several means of communicating are often used (e.g., gesturing, facial and body movement, writing, verbal expression). It is logical, therefore, to teach students with severe handicaps to initiate and respond in a variety of ways, since such variety is apparent in the general population. In addition, providing the student with a means to signal someone else's attention is essential. For some students with severe handicaps, particularly those with severe communication difficulties and delays, alternative and often nonverbal modes of expression are their primary means of communicating.

Communication: Environments

Once the student is motivated to use a communication system, environments or places to communicate must be made available. Environments often dictate the communicative behaviors expected and can serve as discriminative stimuli for students displaying appropriate communicative behaviors (Gruenewald et al., 1982). If generalized communicative competence is the goal of intervention, then integrated community environments provide the most appropriate environments in which to assess, instruct, and evaluate a student's skills and behaviors (Horner & Budd, 1985).

Communication: Audience

Since communication implies interaction, a second person must be involved. That person can be the one who initiates or the one who responds. In either case, the second person can serve as the discriminative stimulus, as can the environment (Gruenewald et al., 1982). Systematic instruction must be provided in such a way that students have opportunities to learn to interact with others, particularly with nonspecialized staff persons. In addition, training must emphasize teaching the student to initiate interactions with familiar and unfamiliar people at appropriate times.

An unfortunate result of traditional service delivery models has been the placement of students with severe handicaps into segregated educational environments. These students then had limited access to appropriate communication models and persons with whom to interact effectively. Therefore, social interaction and communication behaviors may have been extinguished or inhibited (McHale, Simeonsson, Marcus, & Olley, 1980; Strain, 1983). As stated by Schuler (1981), a segregated situation in which students with severe handicaps are communicating and interacting solely with one another will not be conducive to behavior change, nor to the maintenance or generalization of communication skills. Access to nonhandicapped peers who are competent communicators is therefore essential to the development of effective communication skills.

ASSESSMENT PROCEDURES AND TECHNIQUES

In the past, assessments have been limited to group or individual standardized measures conducted in artificial environments and at the beginning of a program. Assessments should be modified to emphasize the use of various measures and techniques in order to determine critical needs for individual students and their present levels of performance in those areas. Assessment of the present level of performance and current communication ability is undertaken so that present abilities can be built upon. Specifically, assessment strategies have been broadened to include critical information with regard to when, where, what, and how assessments should be conducted.

When to Assess

Detailed and thorough assessments must be conducted in order to determine relevant and functional programs that will facilitate the student's acquisition and performance of communicative behaviors. These behaviors should enhance interactions and interaction opportunities and should provide appropriate ways to control one's environment. Assessment is the first component in developing and determining programs, but assessments must continue to be conducted in order to verify that the student is acquiring skills and that the skills are continuing to be functional for that student.

Where to Assess

A critical part of the assessment process is determining the environments that will be used for assessment and instruction. In order to determine how the student is currently communicating, what the student is communicating, and what the student needs to communicate, assessment of those behaviors must be conducted in the student's natural environments (e.g., home, school playground, work, bus, classroom, school cafeteria, neighborhood, community recreation center). It is essential to assess a student across a variety of environments to determine the conditions that exist when the student is exhibiting communicative behaviors. Assessment is also essential for evaluating the student's ability to generalize communicative behaviors across environments, persons, cues, and other stimulus dimensions.

What to Assess

Needless to say, determining what to assess in order to develop a comprehensive communication program for a student must be done prior to the actual assessment. Several areas that should be addressed in order to develop such a communication program are addressed in the following list:

1. **Receptive understanding** The student's understanding of the critical communicative concepts and terms that occur in his or her environments must be assessed. This should involve presenting communicative concepts and terms in familiar and functional ways for the student.
2. **Expressive communicative behaviors** The student's attempts at communicating, verbally and nonverbally, must be assessed. Differences in frequency and type should be noted; when the student is responding and when the student is initiating the interaction should be determined. Emphasis should be placed upon identifying as many different communicative behaviors as the student is able to produce (e.g., signing, talking, pointing, smiling, eye blinking, grunting). In addition, attempts to communicate through inappropriate behavior must be carefully examined (Donnellan et al., 1984). For many students with severe handicaps, assessment of communicative behaviors needs to target the initial presymbolic level of increasing/decreasing activity level on seeing/touching an interesting object, using a differentiated cry, and/or vocalizing to indicate states such as fear, contentment, and anger (Siegel-Causey & Downing, 1987).
3. **Cognitive understanding** The student's understanding of cognitive concepts must be assessed. Specifically, assessment must be conducted to determine the student's abilities with regard to paralinguistic skills such as memory, perceptual discrimination, and attending. Similarly, symbolic and representational skills, understanding of cause and effect and anticipation of events, and imitative skills should be assessed. This information will be essential in the selection of the appropriate symbol set, method, and content for communication.
4. **Communicative functions** The student's understanding of the functions of communication must be evaluated. Determining for what purposes the student uses communication is an important part of the assessment. Following is a list of the functions of communication as described by Chapman (1981) that should be assessed: gives information; gets information; describes an ongoing activity; gets the listener to do something, believe

something, or feel something; expresses one's own intentions, beliefs, or feelings; indicates readiness for further communication; solves problems; entertains. Request, refusal, and recurrence (e.g., "more") are additional initial functions of communication (Keogh & Reichle, 1985; Reichle, Piche-Cragoe, Sigafoss, & Doss, 1988; Reichle, Rogers, & Barret, 1984).

5. **Interaction skills** The frequencies and types of interactions the student exhibits across settings with others must be assessed. Specifically, the following questions must be addressed:
   Does the student attempt to interact?
   How often does the student interact?
   What communication modes does the student use to interact?
   With whom does the student interact (e.g., siblings, familiar and unfamiliar peers, adults)?
   In what contexts (e.g., what materials and persons are present, what environments) does the student interact?
   What content does the student use in interacting?
6. **Physical, motor and sensory skills** The student's overall physical, motor, and sensory abilities must be assessed, particularly when considering augmentative communication systems and when teaching interacting skills. Following is a listing of physical, motor, and sensory skills that should be assessed:
   Fine motor skills and coordination (e.g., reaching, pointing, grasping)
   Degree of control over extremities (i.e., head, arms, and legs)
   Mobility skills (e.g., crawls, walks, uses wheelchair)
   Overall positioning (both optimal and usual position)
   Range of motion in all joints
   Amount and type of exploring, interacting and/or manipulating motorically
   Visual acuity and discrimination
   Hearing acuity and discrimination

How to Assess

Several methods must be considered when assessing students' communicative behaviors and abilities. These methods should be used in combination rather than in isolation. The major question that needs to be answered by the assessment process is: "What does the student usually do with regard to communicating?" so that those skills can serve as the basis for an intervention program. Following is a discussion of these methods.

Developmental Measures First, the use of *developmental measures* must be considered. Developmental sequences of communication contain critical information for assessment. Determining the normal developmental sequence of communication can assist educators in assessing and understanding the student's level and abilities.

Some cautionary remarks must be delineated concerning the appropriate use of developmental measures. First, developmental measures often ignore the variance that occurs between individuals in the acquisition of skills (Hecht, 1986). Second, much attention has been placed on the correlation between cognitive development and language development. The term "cognitive hypothesis" has been used to refer to the supposition that a particular conceptual achievement or mental age is necessary to a linguistic achievement (Bloom, 1970; Brown, 1973; Chapman & Miller, 1980; Cromer, 1974, 1976). Recent developments in the study and acquisition of communication behaviors have demonstrated that language acquisition cannot be adequately understood apart from achievements in the areas of cognitive, social, and motor skills (Vincent & Branston, 1979). However, the difficulties involved in measuring cognitive level makes the discussion concerning the relationship between language, cognition, and other areas of development problematic. The use of developmental assessments in determining communicative performance and needs may therefore be problematic. In order to increase accuracy and validity in determining the most functional communication program for a given student, developmental assessment should be used in conjunction with other assessment procedures, particularly the results from informal measures.

Systematic Observational Procedures The second type of assessment that should be used is *systematic observational procedures*. Gruenewald et al. (1982) stated that the major purpose of using observational techniques is to determine the relationship of a predetermined set of expectations to a student's skill proficiency, rather than comparing that student to other students or groups of students. This procedure is designed to tell educators how the student learns best, and what the student should be learning.

Observations should be conducted in the student's natural environments (e.g., home, classroom, playground, work, community). Materials, cues, and familiar and unfamiliar people should be present. The data that are collected should reflect environments, familiar and unfamiliar persons and materials, natural cues used, and any other stimulus dimensions. Observation should first be conducted in the student's natural environments without manipulation of those environments. Assuming additional assessment information is necessary, manipulation of the stimulus dimensions within those environments should take place in order to determine the extent of the student's communicative behaviors and abilities. Figure 11.1 provides an example of a communication and social skills survey that can be used in order to obtain the necessary information about the conditions present when students communicate.

Language sampling is an observation technique involving the observation of the student in his or her own natural environments and the recording of a sample of that student's spontaneous use of language. Each utterance is recorded along with the context in which it is made. The sample is then analyzed

Utterances	Initiated	Responses	Persons present	Materials present	Time of day
"Want more"	✓		Mom	Cookies and milk	3:30 P.M.
"Boo" (for book)		✓	Older sibling asked student, "What do you want?"	Book, doll, and radio	7:30 P.M.
"Night"		✓	Dad said, "Goodnight."	Bed, toys, bed sheets, and light	8:45 P.M.

Figure 11.1. Example of a communication and social skills survey.

for the communicative function and intent. Syntactic and semantic categories, vocabulary, and the mean length of utterance (MLU) (which refers to the average length of a student's utterances) are also examined.

Ecological and Student Repertoire Inventory The third type of assessment method that should be used is the *ecological and student repertoire inventory*. These inventories are used to identify functional communicative content for students. They are also used to determine the student's understanding and skill proficiency with regard to communication in his or her current and subsequent natural environments. An in-depth discussion of ecological and student repertoire inventories is presented in Chapter 3 of this volume. An ecological inventory is conducted within the student's current and subsequent natural environments to determine the communicative content and expectations within those environments. Specifically, the ecological inventory of communicative behaviors and content delineates the following information:

1. The curricular domains (i.e., domestic, vocational/employment, recreation/leisure, and community domain)
2. The current and subsequent environments
3. The subenvironments
4. The activities that occur in those environments
5. The communication skills required in those environments and exhibited by same age nonhandicapped peers
6. The natural cues and correction procedures available
7. The communicative content used and expected (i.e., vocabulary) by nonhandicapped same age peers

Once this information has been determined, the *student repertoire inventory* must be conducted. The student repertoire inventory is conducted by taking the student to those environments that have been inventoried and comparing his or her communicative performance to those delineated in the ecological inventory of the nonhandicapped same-age peers. This information is analyzed with regard to the student's abilities to perform the specific communicative behaviors expected within the natural environments, and to utilize the communicative content present in those environments. The discrepancies that exist in behaviors and content between the performance of the student with severe handicaps and nonhandicapped individuals are then targeted for instruction.

Interviews and Questionnaires The fourth assessment method, using *interviews and questionnaires*, must be employed with parents and significant others. Although observation and other forms of direct assessment can yield critical information, parents and significant others can be an essential source of assessment information concerning the student's critical needs and present level of performance (Klein et al., 1981). A sample survey is presented in Figure 11.2.

Parents can be initially surveyed or called upon to assist in the determination of who (other than themselves), would be appropriate to complete the

1. Describe the way your son/daughter communicates.
2. Which do you see as being your son's/daughter's preference?
3. Does your son/daughter exhibit the following behaviors when communicating: smiling, frowning, eye blinking, looking at objects/persons, gesturing/pointing, signing, touching, pulling person, banging objects, laughing, crying/whining, screaming, making sounds, words, other?
4. Describe conditions, including times, events, people, places, and materials present when your son/daughter communicates.
5. Does your son/daughter respond to commands? If yes, give examples.
6. Does your son/daughter answer questions? If yes, give examples.
7. Does your son/daughter functionally use objects? If yes, give examples.
8. List the objects, persons, places, activities, and emotions that you wish your son/daughter to be able to communicate.
9. What objects, food, toys, materials, music, expressions, persons, and so forth, are positively reinforcing to your son/daughter?
10. What body parts does your son/daughter use voluntarily when participating in activities and/or manipulating objects?
11. List adaptive equipment and/or physical assistance needed by your son/daughter. Describe his or her preferred position(s).
12. Does your son/daughter have visual or auditory difficulties? If yes, describe.
13. What language(s) are spoken at home?

Figure 11.2. Sample parent survey questionnaire to determine student's communication repertoire and skills.

questionnaire. This questionnaire should be completed by parents and by anyone else who is significant to the student—for example, those who interact with, have responsibility for, or have a special relationship with the student. Siblings, grandparents, other relatives, neighbors, friends, respite care workers, co-workers, bosses, and tutors could be significant others for a student.

Referral *Referral of parents to other experts* might be necessary. Since students with severe handicaps exhibit numerous and diverse difficulties and delays in learning, a collaborative, transdisciplinary approach is necessary. Although teachers should be the primary case managers for their students, they should solicit the input and expertise of the appropriate disciplines when necessary. For example, when a hearing problem is suspected, the student should be referred to an audiologist or teacher of the hearing impaired for a functional hearing assessment. When a vision problem is suspected or known, the student should be referred to an opthalmologist, optometrist, or teacher of the visually impaired for a functional vision assessment. When significant motor problems are present, the student should be referred to an occupational or physical therapist. When significant speech, language, and communication problems are present, the student should be referred to a speech or communication therapist. And when significant psychological or social service problems are present, the student should be referred to a psychologist or social worker. Making appropriate and needed referrals is essential so that valuable time is not wasted in the absence of critical information that can be provided by such specialists.

How Often to Assess

Before a program is instituted, data should be collected using the various methods of assessment just described. However, once a program has started, continual data collection must occur in order to determine program effectiveness on a consistent and regular basis.

COMMUNICATION MODES

The most commonly used mode of communication among the general population is speech, although all persons augment their use of speech with nonverbal communication modes (e.g., gestures, body language, expressions, writing) (Vanderheiden & Yoder, 1986). Speech is often impossible for a large number of students with severe handicaps, because they lack the motor, linguistic, and/or cognitive skills necessary to produce sounds in a manner that can be understood by others. This section therefore begins with a brief overview of speech as a communication mode, followed by a more detailed description of augmentative and/or alternative methods of communication.

Speech

For those students who are developing speech or who already have speech, several issues should be considered. First, speech must not be assessed and analyzed apart from the context in which it is produced. Some students, particularly those with autism, exhibit speech with reasonable to good articulation skills, but produce the speech only in an echoic form, that is, modeling someone else's speech. This form of speech is referred to as *echolalia*. Schuler (1979) has contributed extensively to our understanding of echolalia, classifying it into several categories along a continuum from noncommunicative to communicative. Schuler identified "delayed noncommunicative echolalia" as the least functional echolalia. Echolalia can also be classified as "delayed," "immediate," and "mitigated," and as having communicative functions. The results of Schuler's work and that of others (Prizant, 1983; Prizant & Duchan,

1981; Rein, 1984) strongly suggest that intervention strategies for students who exhibit echolalia should be used to carefully analyze the communicative functions of the student's speech. Additionally, shaping and other procedures should be used to facilitate their production of appropriate communicative speech.

The second issue that needs to be considered in speech assessment is that of the student's primary language. Students who are non–English-speaking or who use English as a second language should be assessed in their own language. Intervention programs should reflect the student's most familiar language, as well as the language(s) used in their home, neighborhood, school, and work environments.

Augmentative and Alternative Communication Modes

Once a student has been identified as having severe communication handicaps, the student can be considered to be at risk for not developing intelligible speech. Educators and parents must consider developing and teaching augmentative and/or alternative communication modes to students.

In order to determine and develop appropriate augmentative or alternative communication modes for students who do not have intelligible speech, educators and parents must be familiar with the variety of modes available. Following is a discussion of some of the most commonly used modes.

Gestures Gesturing is a common form of nonverbal communication among the general population; therefore, it is a commonly understood augmentative mode of communication that may be useful for persons with severe handicaps. Generally understood gestures refer to motor movements that are topographically similar to the object or action they represent (e.g., motioning someone to go in a different direction by pointing in that direction). In addition, gestures might consist of body language that is generally understood within a cultural group or across several cultural groups (e.g., smiling when happy or content). Hamre-Nietupski et al. (1977) delineated over 150 generally understood gestures that are used by persons with and without handicaps to communicate. Gestures should be taught within the context in which they will be used—that is, the student should be taught how, with whom, and when to use what gestures. Several limitations must be considered when teaching the use of gestures. First of all, not all concepts, feelings, and other information that a student might want to communicate can be communicated with a gesture; therefore, using gestures as the only communicative mode would limit the student's available communicative content. Second, although many gestures are widely understood, many can also be ambiguous and may not clearly communicate a message. Third, certain gestures may be understood only by a specific group and not by the general population.

Manual Signing Manual signing refers to the use of fingers, hands, and arms to communicate. There are various forms of manual signing; the most frequently used systems are American Sign Language (ASL) (Wilbur, 1976) and Signing Exact English (SEE) (Mayberry, 1976). Several issues need to be considered when using manual signing. First, manual signing is not understood or used by the general population. Therefore, caution should be used when teaching students to use manual signing as the sole form of communication, as it limits the people with whom the student can communicate. Second, students with significant motor difficulties might not be able to produce all of the signs. Third, since manual signing involves the use of fingers, hands, and arms, students will need to limit the use of their fingers, hands, and arms in other communicative manners when communicating. Fourth, although signing has been successfully used as an augmentative mode for some persons with severe handicaps, care must be taken in deciding that signing is the best, most efficient mode of communication for each individual student. It has not been an effective mode for all students.

System Displays In order to determine, design, and develop appropriate functional system displays for students with severe communication handicaps, several categories of information must be considered. First, the *symbol system* that will be used must be determined—that is, whether it will involve objects, photos, black and white line drawings, abstract symbols, or traditional orthography. Second, the *selecting/activating response*, for example, pointing, gazing, head movement, or switch activation, must be determined. Third, the form of the *system display* (e.g., single cards, wallet displays, books, manual boards, or electronic aids) must be determined. Each of these issues is discussed in the following paragraphs.

Symbol System The most concrete form of communication is to use actual objects. This form eliminates ambiguity and requires little or no abstract cognitive ability on the part of the student. Therefore, this form of communication can be used initially to assess the student's receptive understanding and object preferences, and as a beginning form of communication. However, objects can be cumbersome, and if they are not in sight (i.e., if they are in the other room, outside, or across town), they cannot be discussed or used to communicate. In addition, if objects are used as the only form of communication, the student has no way of communicating abstract concepts such as feelings. As a result, objects should be used only when other more abstract forms of communication are unsuccessful or impossible. In addition, as the student becomes proficient at using objects to communicate, those objects should be paired with more abstract forms (e.g., miniature objects, pictures, and words). The objects should then be gradually faded so that the student is able to use a more expandable, abstract, and flexible system.

Photographs, line drawings, and other pictures of objects, actions, and places can be used for students who require a nonverbal form of communication. One of the advantages of using photographs of actual objects, actions, and places is that they can be used to reduce ambiguity and to individualize for each student (e.g., using an actual photograph of the student's jacket). A number of issues should be considered when using pictures. First, when using actual photographs versus line drawings, when determining the appropriate size of the pictures, and when determining the location and placement of pictures on a display, educators must determine the student's preferences and visual discrimination skills. Second, as unnecessary and irrelevant stimuli within photographs may be confusing to some students and/or message receivers, the actual pictures must be carefully selected for individual students. For example, when using a photograph of a woman holding an apple to represent "apple," the student or the message receiver might attend to the woman, to the type of clothing she is wearing, or to other irrelevant stimulus dimensions. In this instance, a picture featuring only an apple would be preferable. Third, pictures should be paired with words so that the message receiver is able to interpret the communicative referent for each picture.

Abstract symbols such as Blissymbols (Vanderheiden & Grilley, 1976) and non-SLIP (Non-Speech Language Initiation Program) symbols (Carrier, 1976) have been taught to students who required a nonverbal form of communication. The term "abstract symbols" refers to symbols that represent objects, actions, feelings, or concepts. Several issues need to be considered when using abstract symbols. First, because these symbol systems do not resemble their actual referents, they often appear to be confusing and too visually complex to the student or the message receiver. Second, if the student is able to understand and use an abstract symbol system, educators should consider using a more commonly used form of abstract symbols, such as traditional orthography.

The term traditional orthography refers to the use of written words for communication. Because this form of communication is used among the general population, it should be encouraged and taught if the student has the capacity to use this form. Several factors must be considered when using traditional orthography as a nonverbal form of communication. First, traditional orthography cannot be used as a communication system with message receivers who are nonreaders within the language being used. This might eliminate communicating with young siblings or peers who have not acquired reading skills, or with family members, neighbors, and friends who are nonreaders of the language being used. Second, traditional orthography involves using specific materials (e.g., pencils, pens, paper, typewriters, computers, memorywriters); some environments may not contain those materials or may not be conducive to the use of those materials. For example, when working as a janitor mopping the floor, the activity of floor mopping would need to stop if the student wanted to communicate with a co-worker using traditional orthography.

Selecting/Activating Response Selecting responses refer to the action the student makes when using an augmentative and/or alternative communication system. Students' skills must be assessed in order to determine the most appropriate response that the student can voluntarily control. Following is a list of the most common selecting responses used in order to communicate:

Pointing
Head movements
Eyegazing

In addition to selecting responses, educators and parents must consider responses that activate switches that can interface with a scanning device or direct selection device. Vanderheiden and Grilley (1976) have delineated some of the more common switch-activating devices, as follows:

1. Mechanical switches for the extremities, such as buttons or keys on keyboards, paddles and levers, pillow switches, wobblesticks, joysticks, sliding or trolley switches, poke switches, tip or tilt switches
2. Mechanical switches for specific body parts, such as: head, chin, eyebrow, knee, palate, splint (finger), tongue, thumb, or wrist
3. Pneumatic (air or breath) switches, such as suck and puff switch or air paddles
4. Touch switches requiring contact by no physical pressure, such as touchplates or cybergloves and cyberplates
5. Moisture-sensitive switches
6. Proximity switches sensitive to the body or to a special trigger element (e.g., metal, magnet, circuit) when brought within a certain range of the switch
7. Optical switches, such as a lightspot (a light source attached to a head pointer or some other body part), or interrupted-beam switches
8. Sonic switches that are activated by sound
9. Bioelectric switches that are activated by the electric impulses generated in nerves and muscles of the body.

System Display Form Several of the forms of communication already described require the use of devices or materials to display available symbols. Following is a discussion of some of the most commonly used devices and materials.

Pictures, symbols, and/or words can be used in single card or wallet display augmentative communication systems. Single cards and wallet displays can contain pictures, symbols, or words that students can carry in their pockets, handbags, knapsacks, or the like. Single cards and wallet displays can be used by the student in order to nonverbally communicate about a specific object, action, place, feeling, or concept. The single card can be smaller than a credit card or as large as needed for an individual student. The specific size of the single card should be determined on the basis of the student's visual discrimination skills. The finer the student's skills, the smaller the single card should be.

The student's motor abilities should also be considered when selecting the size of the card and the type of display (e.g., book, wallet). Wallet display pictures, symbols, and words are generally credit card size and allow for communication about several ideas. Additional credit-card holders can be added as the student's abilities and vocabulary needs increase.

Communication books can be used to allow for a large number of ideas. Communication books can contain one or more pages, each page allowing for one or several referents. Pictures, symbols, and/or words can be used to represent objects, actions, places, feelings, or concepts and can be displayed in a communication book. Such books can be carried by the student in his or her arms, bookbag, handbag, or knapsack. They can also be placed on revolving hooks attached to the front of a walker. The student's ability to turn pages and hold the book so that someone else can see it must be assessed before a communication book is determined as the appropriate augmentative system. Students using communication books need to be taught to locate the desired referent as quickly as possible and to indicate through pointing or gesturing, in order for the message receiver to get the message. (See Mirenda, 1985, for a complete description of issues to consider in selecting and designing pictorial display systems.)

Manual communication boards can be designed to fit on wheelchair trays or can be the actual wheelchair tray. Pictures, symbols, and/or words can be displayed on a communication board so that the student can, through pointing or gesturing, communicate with others. The student's range of motion, ability to cross midline, and visual discriminative abilities must be assessed before determining if and how a manual communication board can meet a student's communicative needs. Boards must also be designed in order to facilitate interactions with other students.

The most sophisticated nonverbal communication systems available are electronic communication aids. These aids can be designed to fit on a communication tray (e.g., Zygo communicator), to be carried in a pocket (e.g., Canon communicator), or to be carried in one's arms, bookbag, knapsack, or handbag. These electronic communication aids can allow a student to communicate simple and complex messages expediently. Some of the most commonly used devices are described in Table 11.1.

In addition, computer technology continues to be refined and the use of voice synthesizers and switches has made computers easier to use as augmentative communication devices for persons with severe handicaps. Readers are referred to Chapter 12 of this volume for a discussion of the use of computers by persons with severe handicaps.

DECISION-MAKING CRITERIA

Decision-making criteria have been developed in order to determine candidacy for augmentative system use and to select systems of augmentative communi-

Table 11.1. Sample electronic communication aids

Name	Purpose	Supplier
Phonic Mirror	Speech synthesizer	HC Electronics, Inc. 250 Camino Alto Mill Valley, CA 94941
Handivoice	Speech synthesizer	HC Electronics, Inc. 250 Camino Alto Mill Valley, CA 94941
Canon Communicator	Phonetic alphabet system	Canon, Inc. Saburo Nagata, Director Audio Visual Aids Department P.O. Box 50 Tokyo Airport, Japan
Zygo Communicator	Scanner on electronic aid	Zygo Industries, Inc. P.O. Box 1008 Portland, OR 97207
Verascan	Rotary scanner	Prentke Romich Co. 1022 Heyl Road Wooster, OH 44691
Touchtalker and Light Talker	Programmable electronic aids with speech	Prentke Romich Co. 1022 Heyl Road Wooster, OH 44691

cation for persons with severe handicaps (Chapman & Miller, 1980; Nietupski & Hamre-Nietupski, 1979; Sailor et al., 1980; Shane, 1980). Unfortunately, some of these decision-making criteria eliminate persons with severe handicaps from candidacy for the use of an augmentative system (Reichle & Karlan, 1985). The participation model of assessment (Beukelman & Mirenda, 1987) differs from those previously developed in that the model's goal is to meet the communication needs of any person. The participation model involves assessing communicative needs by means of an activity inventory, including a nonhandicapped peer inventory and student repertoire inventory, and then assessing the communicative barriers to participation in the targeted environments. The barriers are divided into opportunity and access barriers. Opportunity barriers include such factors as the lack of competent communicative partners due to participation in a segregated educational placement, or the lack of communicative partners knowledgeable concerning adaptations necessary to make in order to communicate with an augmentative communication device user. Each of these barriers interferes with participation in identified activities and with successful use of augmentative devices. The identification of access barriers includes the assessment of student mobility, manipulation, communication, and cognitive/linguistic and sensory/perceptual abilities in order to determine how those are barriers to participation in activities. Potential intervention options are examined so as to meet the abilities and needs of the student and to increase the student's participation in the identified activities. Decision-making criteria and models concerning appropriate augmentative communication systems for persons with severe handicaps should meet all of the student's needs in the most effective manner possible.

Another decision-making factor involves the selection of components of an augmentative system. In the past, the focus has been on the selection of a single best augmentative device for an individual; currently, the multimodal approach to communication typical of the general population is applied to augmentative device users. In other words, decisions concerning augmentative communication have begun to focus on the development of multimodal systems of communication. These can include: a communication board, gestures, grunts, and/or vocalizations. This issue becomes critical when considering, for instance, an augmentative system user whose system of communication includes a communication board. This person must have a method for getting the attention of others (e.g., by grunting or by using a buzzer.) In this manner, communicators are urged to use whichever mode "gets the message across" in the most efficient manner in each environment and activity, rather than focusing on using a single mode that may not be efficient in all environments. Though probably no system can meet all requirements of an effective augmentative system, Vanderheiden and Lloyd (1986) delineated the following requirements to be used in evaluating the systems of individual persons:

Provides a full range of communicative functions
Is compatible with other aspects of individual's life
Does not restrict communication partners
Is usable in all environments and physical positions
Does not restrict topic or scope of communication
Is effective
Allows and fosters growth and change
Is acceptable and motivating to user and others
Is affordable

INTERVENTION

As mentioned earlier in this chapter, recent research has suggested that the optimal environment for acquisition of communication is interactive, active, student centered, and contingent upon what is of interest to the student. In addition, the optimal environment is characterized as being responsive, nondidactic, nondirective, varied in stimuli, and fine-tuned to provide sufficient prompts to the learner while allowing for maximal independence, and involving assignment of meaning to early communicative attempts (Ainsworth, 1974; Hart, 1985; MacDonald, 1985; Snow, 1972; Snow & Ferguson, 1978; Vygotsky, 1978). Language intervention strategies should reflect these characteristics, while at the same time providing systematic instruction in the identified areas of need within the environments where the communication is most needed. This determination is based upon natural cues, corrections and prompts.

While general instructional strategies such as shaping and chaining are discussed in Chapter 4 of this volume, the present chapter delineates systematic instructional strategies that can be used in developing the communication competencies of persons with severe handicaps.

Nonsymbolic Communication

Siegel-Causey and Downing (1987) suggest that beginning communicators must first acquire physical and social *control* over their environments in order to learn the purpose of communication. Some of the specific strategies these authors describe for use in developing such skills include responding consistently to the possible communicative intent of any intentional behavior of the student or adult, such as change in muscle tone, while positioning and providing the individual with an activity or item that is not preferred to allow them the opportunity to develop refusal skills. Mirenda (1987) suggests using *gestural dictionaries* to allow all interactive partners involved with the beginning communicator to respond to idiosyncratic gestures in a consistent manner. A board can be posted on the wall that lists the gestures, the communicative intent, and the appropriate response for each gesture made by the particular student. Over time, all significant others, such as parents, siblings, and teachers, can shape the gestures by responding to more specific and refined gestures by the individual.

Mirenda (1988) also suggests using *scripted routines* with beginning communicators. This strategy can be implemented by first teaching a student a regular routine for an activity such as eating or drinking. Once the script for the routine is established, pauses can be inserted into the routine at specific points to allow the individual to communicate by change in body tone, vocalization, or gesture that they expect or want the activity to continue. Whatever behavior the student engages in should be assigned a communicative meaning by the interactive partner. This allows the student the opportunity to develop the ability to anticipate activities and/or events and to communicate acceptance or refusal of those events.

Choice and decision-making skills are also important for beginning communicators to develop in order to learn that they can control events occurring around them (Guess, Benson, & Siegel-Causey, 1985; Shevin & Klein, 1984). Choice-making opportunities can be offered throughout the natural course of a day. Examples include: choice of clothes, snacks, lunch foods, toys, jobs, activities, playmates, or living situations. Choices can initially be made between two actual objects, then three objects, and so on. Choice making can later be used to help the student develop symbolic communicative abilities by having him or her choose between two symbols of desired items. Klein et al. (1981) referred to this as "requesting through choice response" (p. 20). Initially, student preferences will need to be identified so that appropriate choices can be delineated. Figure 11.3 provides a sample survey to be used in identifying student preferences. Because "learned helplessness" and passivity are problem behavior patterns for many persons with severe handicaps (Calculator, 1988), it is critical that the student develop the ability to control his or her environment. Students beginning to learn to communicate must then be allowed the opportunity to terminate an activity, to refuse to engage in an activity, or to choose between activities. Later, students may need to learn that they may not always receive what they want; however, initially, it is critical that accept and reject signals be responded to appropriately and consistently.

Moving to Symbolic Communication

Incidental Teaching Strategies **Incidental teaching strategies** (Hart & Risley, 1975; Peck, 1985) make use of naturally occurring environments, activities, and initiations of activities by beginning communicators. While incidental teaching strategies can also be used in developing nonsymbolic communication skills, teachers can use these strategies to develop use of symbols. This is achieved by looking for opportunities to teach, model, or prompt the use of previously identified symbols within ongoing activites. Teachers can also arrange environments and activities in order to facilitate the use of incidental teaching strategies. For example, teachers can give the student the wrong toy or food when a request is made, can perform a routine activity incorrectly or in a nonroutine fashion, can place toys or food within sight but just out of reach, or can provide a symbol when a student communicates nonsymbolically that he or she would like a different item at a fast food restaurant. Each of these examples sets up an opportunity for a student to use a symbol or other communicative behavior.

Time Delay Procedures **Time delay procedures** have proven effective with students who have become dependent upon prompts to communicate (Halle, Baer, & Spradlin, 1981; Halle, Marshall, & Spradlin, 1979). When using this strategy, the teacher will pause rather than prompt when the student has an opportunity to request or respond. For example, while playing with toys preferred by a student, the teacher may pause rather than ask: "What do you want?" when the child is ready to request the toy. The teacher can prompt the request by showing the toy, but he or she should not verbally or physically prompt the request, as the goal is to develop spontaneous requesting skills. On the job, the job coach or co-workers can pause to allow the student to request assistance or a desired item rather than prompt the student by asking: "Do you need assistance?"

Verbal Prompt-Free Strategies **Verbal prompt-free strategies** have also proven effective with students who are beginning symbol users and who are either prompt-dependent or are at risk for developing prompt-dependency (Mirenda & Dattilo, 1987; Mirenda & Santogrossi, 1985). This strategy is implemented by presenting a symbol of a desired item to the student and waiting

Person completing questionnaire: ____________ Date: ____________
Student's name: ________________________

1. What are the student's favorite toys or games?

2. What are the student's favorite foods?

3. What does the student dislike doing?

4. What kinds of foods does the student dislike?

5. What actions by you result in the student laughing, smiling, or showing other signs of enjoyment?

Figure 11.3. Sample survey of student preferences, to be completed by persons significant to the student across settings.

until he or she intentionally or unintentionally touches the symbol. Once the student touches the symbol, he or she may be given the item. A physical prompt may be required initially, but over time, the student should be reinforced only for intentional touches and the number of choices should be increased.

Interrupted Behavior Chain Strategy The **interrupted behavior chain strategy** has also been effective in teaching initial symbol users (Goetz, Gee, & Sailor, 1985; Hunt, Goetz, Alwell, & Sailor, 1986). The first step in this strategy is to identify and teach a routine activity to a student. Once the student has learned the routine or the chain of steps, the teacher attempts to identify appropriate steps for interruption by rating the student's level of distress and desire to complete the activity at possible points of interruption. Once a point of interruption is identified that does not cause undue distress but which reflects a point at which the student desires to complete the activity, the chain of steps is implemented. The teacher interrupts at the predetermined point, and a symbol for the next step is presented. For example, once a student has learned to wash dishes, the activity is interrupted at the point at which he or she is to obtain the dish soap, and a picture of the dish soap is presented. The teacher then models or prompts the student to select the symbol and obtains the requested item, and the chain continues. If the student does not touch the symbol with assistance, the chain is either stopped, or in some instances, the student is assisted in completing the activity. The researchers involved in developing the interrupted chain strategy have found that acquisition of symbol use is attained within four to five trials when used with chains that occur several times per day.

Dimensions to Consider

When developing and implementing a communication program, a number of additional dimensions should be considered. Following are listed 11 of the more essential dimensions presented in this chapter:

1. The communication program, including the determination of an augmentative and/or alternative communicative system, should be based upon *individualized needs* across all the student's natural environments.
2. The communicative content, symbol set, mode, and instructional program should reflect a student's *primary language and cultural values*.
3. The communicative behaviors should be taught directly in all the student's *natural environments*.
4. The communicative content to be taught should be *relevant and functional* to the student.
5. Communication intervention should focus on developing the skills of both *initiating and responding*.
6. The communicative program, including the determination of a communication mode, should *facilitate interactions* with others, particularly with nonhandicapped peers, nonspecialized staff, and community members.
7. The most *efficient* mode(s) and systems possible for a given student should be taught.
8. The communication program, including the determination of a communication mode, should reflect the student's and his or her family's *preferences*.
9. Communication modes should be developed that are *flexible* enough for "add-ons"; if appropriate, they should allow for communicating simple as well as complex messages.
10. Directions to the *message receiver* should be included for all augmentative and alternative communicative modes.
11. Pictures, symbols, and words should be *self-explanatory* to the message receiver.

12. Communication programs should be developed that facilitate *generalized communicative competence*. This is achieved by loosely training, and by training multiple exemplars and behaviors, with multiple trainers in multiple settings with natural contingencies (Horner & Budd, 1985; Stremel-Campbell & Campbell, 1985).

Issues involved in training to facilitate generalization of skills are discussed in more detail in Chapters 4 and 5 of this volume.

EVALUATION

Data need to be collected over time in order to determine the effectiveness of a communication training program and the appropriateness of augmentative and/or alternative communication systems for a student. Following are several types of data that should be collected:

1. The *modes* used to communicate a message
2. The *frequency* of the communicative behaviors
3. The frequency of communicative behaviors that were *initiations* and *responses*
4. The *communicative intent*
5. The *conditions* present when the communicative response was made (e.g., location, number of people, structured/unstructured)
6. The *exact* and the *intended message*
7. The *reinforcers/consequences* that were provided after the response

Figure 11.4 provides a sample of a data sheet that can be used to collect data.

SUMMARY

This chapter reviews issues and strategies related to the determination, development, implementation, and evaluation of educational programs designed to facilitate the acquisition and maintenance of communicative behaviors in natural environments. Specific procedures for assessing students' present communicative repertories and preferences, as well as the effectiveness of communicative programs, are delineated. Since students with severe handicaps are at risk for not developing intelligible speech, this chapter emphasizes developing augmentative and alternative communicative modes. Finally, procedures for teaching communicative behaviors are described.

REFERENCES

Ainsworth, M.,O.,S. (1973). The development of infant-mother attachment. In B.M. Caldwell & H.N. Ricutti (Eds.), *Review of child development research* (Vol. 3, pp. 1–94). Chicago: University of Chicago.

Communicative mode	Frequency		Communicative intent	Conditions present	Exact message	Reinforcement consequence
	Initiated	Responses				
Verbal and gestural	✓		Wanted the towel	In kitchen with sister	"Wa ta" and pointed to towel	Got the towel
Gestured using communication booklet		✓	To indicate desire to go outside	In classroom; recess bell has rung	Pointed to picture of "outside"	Positive reinforcement; got to go outside
Blinked eye		✓	To indicate desire to eat carrots	In school cafeteria with nonhandicapped students and teacher.	Blinked eyes once after teacher asked, "Do you want your carrots?"	Positive reinforcement; got the carrots

Figure 11.4. Sample data sheet for determining communicative competence.

Bedrosian, J.L. (1988). Adults who are mildly to moderately mentally retarded: Communicative performance, assessment and intervention. In S.N. Calculator & J.L. Bedrosian (Eds.), *Communication assessment and intervention for adults with mental retardation* (pp. 265–307). Boston: College-Hill Press.

Beukelman, D., & Miranda, P. (1987). *Communication options for persons who cannot speak: Assessment and evaluation.* Proceedings of the National Planners Conference of Assistive Device Service Delivery. Columbus, OH: Great Lakes Area Regional Resource Center.

Bloom, L. (1970). *Language development: Form and function of emerging grammars.* Cambridge, MA: MIT Press.

Brown, L., Branston, M.B., Hamre-Nietupski, S., Pumpian, I., Certo, N., & Gruenewald, L. (1979). A strategy for developing chronological age appropriate and functional curricular content for severely handicapped adolescents and young adults. *Journal of Special Education 13*(1), 81–90.

Brown, R. (1973). *A first language.* Cambridge, MA: Harvard University Press.

Calculator, S.N. (1988). Exploring the language of adults with mental retardation. In S.N. Calculator & J.L. Bedrosian (Eds.), *Communication assessment and intervention for adults with mental retardation* (pp. 95–106). Boston: College-Hill Press.

Carrier, J. (1976). Application of a nonspeech language system with the severely language handicapped. In L.L. Lloyd (Ed.), *Communication assessment and intervention strategies* (pp. 523–547). Baltimore: University Park Press.

Chapman, R. (1981). Exploring children's communicative intents. In J.F. Miller (Ed.), *Assessing language production in children: Experimental procedures.* Baltimore: University Park Press.

Chapman, R., & Miller, J. (1980). Analyzing language and communication in the child. In R.L. Schiefelbusch (Ed.), *Nonspeech language intervention* (pp. 159–196). Baltimore: University Park Press.

Cromer, R.F. (1974). Receptive language in the mentally retarded: Processes and diagnostic. In R.L. Schiefelbusch & L.L. Lloyd (Eds.), *Language perspectives—Acquisition, retardation, and intervention.* Baltimore: University Park Press.

Cromer, R. (1976). The cognitive hypothesis of language acquisition and its implication for child language deficiency. In D. Morehead & A. Morehead (Eds.), *Normal and deficient child language.* Baltimore: University Park Press.

Donnellan, A.M., Mirenda, P.L., Mesaros, R.A., & Fassbender, L.L. (1984). Analyzing the communicative functions of aberrant behavior. *Journal of The Association for Persons with Severe Handicaps, 9,* 201–202.

Falvey, M.A., Bishop, K.B., Grenot-Scheyer, M., & Coots, J.J. (1988). Issues and trends in mental retardation. In S.N. Calculator & J.L. Bedrosian (Eds.), *Communication assessment and intervention for adults with mental retardation* (pp. 45–65). Boston: College-Hill Press.

Falvey, M.A., McLean, D., & Rosenberg, R. (1988). Transition from school to adult life: Communication strategies. *Topics in Language Disorders.*

Goetz, L., Gee, K., & Sailor, W. (1985). Using a behavior chain interruption strategy to teach communication skills to students with severe disabilities. *Journal of The Association for Persons with Severe Handicaps, 10,* 21–30.

Goldfield, B., & Snow, C. (1985). Individual differences in language acquisition. In J.B. Gleason (Ed.), *The development of language* (pp. 307–330). Columbus, OH: Charles E. Merrill.

Gruenewald, L., Schroeder, J., & Yoder, D. (1982). Considerations for curriculum development and implementation. In B. Campbell & V. Baldwin (Eds.), *Severely handicapped/hearing impaired students* (pp. 163–180). Baltimore: Paul H. Brookes Publishing Co.

Guess, D., Benson, H.A., & Siegel-Causey, E. (1985). Concepts and issues related to choice-making and autonomy among persons with severe disabilities. *Journal of The Association for Persons with Severe Handicaps*, *10*, 79–86.

Halle, J., Baer, D., & Spradlin, J. (1981). Teachers' generalized use of delay as a stimulus control procedure to increase language use by handicapped children. *Journal of Applied Behavior Analysis*, *14*, 389–409.

Halle, J., Marshall, A., & Spradlin, J. (1979). Time delay: A technique to increase language use and facilitate generalization in retarded children. *Journal of Applied Behavior Analysis*, *12*, 431–439.

Halliday, M. (1975). *Learning how to mean: Explorations in the development of language*. New York: Elsevier/North Holland.

Hamre-Nietupski, S., Stoll, A., Holtz, K., Fullerton, P., Flottum-Ryan, M., & Brown, L. (1977). Curricular strategies for teaching nonverbal communication skills to verbal and nonverbal severely handicapped students. In L. Brown, J. Nietupski, S. Lyon, S. Hamre-Nietupski, T. Crowner, & L. Gruenewald (Eds.), *Curricular strategies for teaching functional object use, nonverbal communication, problem solving and mealtime skills to severely handicapped students* (Vol. 8, pp. 95–250). Madison, WI: Madison Metropolitan School District.

Hart, B. (1985). Naturalistic language training techniques. In S.F. Warren & A.K. Rogers-Warren (Eds.), *Teaching functional language* (pp. 63–88). Baltimore: University Park Press.

Hart, B., & Risley, T. (1975). Incidental teaching of language in the preschool. *Journal of Applied Behavior Analysis*, *8*, 411–420.

Hecht, B.F. (1986). Language disorders in preschool children. *Advances in Special Education*, *5*, 95–119.

Horner, R.M., & Budd, C.M. (1985). Acquisition of manual sign use: Collateral reduction of maladaptive behavior and factors limiting generalization. *Education and Training in Mental Retardation*, *20*, 39–47.

Hunt, P., Goetz, L., Alwell, M., & Sailor, W. (1986). Using an interrupted behavior chain strategy to teach generalized communication responses. *Journal of The Association for Persons with Severe Handicaps*, *11*, 196–204.

Kanner, L. (1943). Autistic disturbances of affective contact. *Nervous Child*, *2*, 217–250.

Kent, L. (1974). *Language acquisition program for the severely retarded*. Champaign, IL: Research Press.

Keogh, W.J., & Reichle, J. (1985). Communication intervention for the "difficult-to-teach" severely handicapped. In S.F. Warren & A.K. Rogers-Warren (Eds.), *Teaching functional language* (pp. 157–194). Baltimore: University Park Press.

Klein, M.D., Myers, S.P., Hogue, B., Waldo, L.J., Marshall, A.M., & Hall, M.K. (1981). *Parent's guide: Classroom involvement, communication training resources*. Lawrence, KS: Early Childhood Institute, Comprehensive Communication Curriculum.

MacDonald, J.D. (1985). Language through conversation: A model of intervention with language-delayed persons. In S.F. Warren & A.K. Rogers-Warren (Eds.), *Teaching functional language* (pp. 89–122). Baltimore: University Park Press.

Mayberry, R. (1976). If a chimp can learn sign language, surely my nonverbal client can too. *Asha*, *18*, 228–233.

McHale, S.M., Simeonsson, R.J., Marcus, L.M., & Olley, J.G. (1980). The social and symbolic qualities of autistic children's communication. *Journal of Autism and Developmental Disorders*, *10*, 229–310.

McLean, J.E., & Snyder-McLean, L.K. (1978). *A transactional approach to early language training*. Columbus, OH: Charles E. Merrill.

Mirenda, P. (1985). Designing pictorial communication systems for physically able-bodied students with severe handicaps. *Augmentative and Alternative Communication, 1*, 58–64.

Mirenda, P. (1987, November). *Facilitating augmentative communication: A public school model*. Paper presented at the Annual Conference of The Association for Persons with Severe Handicaps, Chicago.

Mirenda, P. (1988, August). *Instructional techniques for communication*. Paper presented at the Augmentative and Alternative Communication for Students with Severe Disabilities Special Education Innovative Institute, Fremont, CA.

Mirenda, P., & Dattilo, J. (1987). Instructional techniques in alternative communication for students with severe intellectual disabilities. *Augmentative and Alternative Communication, 3*, 143–152.

Mirenda, P., & Santogrossi, J. (1985). A prompt-free strategy to teach pictorial communication system use. *Augmentative and Alternative Communication, 1*, 143–150.

Musselwhite, C.R., & St. Louis, K.W. (1982). *Communication programming for severely handicapped: Vocal and non-vocal strategies*. Houston: College-Hill Press.

Nietupski, J., & Hamre-Nietupski, S. (1979). Teaching auxiliary communication skills to severely handicapped learners. *AAESPH Review, 4*, 107–124.

Owens, R.E., & Rogerson, B.S. (1988). Adults at the presymbolic level. In S.N. Calculator & J.L. Bedrosian (Eds.), *Communication assessment and intervention for adults with mental retardation* (pp. 189–238). Boston: College-Hill Press.

Peck, C.A. (1985). Increasing opportunities for social control by children with autism and severe handicaps: Effects of student behavior and perceived classroom climate. *Journal of The Association for Persons with Severe Handicaps, 10*, 183–193.

Prizant, B.M. (1983). Echolalia in autism: Assessment and intervention. *Seminars in speech and language, 4*, 63–77.

Prizant, B.M., & Duchan, J.F. (1981). The functions of immediate echolalia in autistic children. *Journal of Speech and Hearing Disorders, 46*, 241–249.

Reichle, J., & Karlan, G. (1985). The selection of an augmentative system in communication intervention: A critique of decision rules. *Journal of The Association for Persons with Severe Handicaps, 10*, 146–156.

Reichle, J., Piche-Cragoe, L., Sigafoss, J., & Doss, S. (1988). Optimizing functional communication for persons with severe handicaps. In S.N. Calculator & J.L. Bedrosian (Eds.), *Communication assessment and intervention for adults with mental retardation* (pp. 239–264). Boston: College-Hill Press.

Reichle, J., Rogers, N., & Barret, C. (1984). Establishing pragmatic discriminations among the communicative functions of requesting, rejecting and commenting in an adolescent. *Journal of The Association for Persons with Severe Handicaps, 9*, 31–36.

Rein, R.L. (1984). *Observational study of the use of verbal perservations by persons with autism*. Unpublished doctoral dissertation, University of California, Los Angeles, and California State University, Los Angeles.

Sailor, W., Guess, D., Goetz, L., Schuler, A., Utley, B., & Baldwin, M. (1980). Language and severely handicapped persons: Deciding what to teach whom. In W. Sailor, B. Wilcox, & L. Brown (Eds.), *Methods of instruction for severely handicapped students* (pp. 71–108). Baltimore: Paul H. Brookes Publishing Co.

Schuler, A.L. (1979). Echolalia: Issues and clinical applications. *Journal of Speech and Hearing Disorders, 4*, 411–434.

Schuler, A.L. (1981). Teaching functional language. In B. Wilcox & A. Thompson (Eds.), *Educating autistic children and youth* (pp. 154–178). Washington, DC: U.S. Department of Education.

Schuler, A.L., & Goetz, L. (1983). Toward communicative competence: Matters of method, content, and mode of instruction. *Seminars in Speech and Language, 4*, 79–91.

Seligman, M. (1975). *Helplessness: On depression, development, and death.* San Francisco: W.H. Freeman.

Shane, H. (1980). Approaches to assessing the communication of nonoral persons. In R.L. Schiefelbusch (Ed.), *Nonspeech language and communication* (pp. 197–224). Baltimore: University Park Press.

Shevin, M., & Klein, N.K. (1984). The importance of choice-making skills for students with severe disabilities. *Journal of The Association for Persons with Severe Handicaps, 9*, 159–166.

Siegel-Causey, E., & Downing, J. (1987). Nonsymbolic communication development: Theoretical concepts and educational strategies. In L. Goetz, D. Guess, & K. Stremel-Campbell (Eds.), *Innovative program design for individuals with dual sensory impairments* (pp. 15–48). Baltimore: Paul H. Brookes Publishing Co.

Snow, C. (1972). Mother's speech to children learning language. *Child Development, 43*, 549–565.

Snow, C., & Ferguson, C. (1978). *Talking to children.* London: Cambridge University Press.

Strain, P.S. (1983). Generalization of autistic children's social behavior change: Effects of developmentally integrated and segregated settings. *Analysis and Intervention in Developmental Disabilities, 3*, 23–34.

Stremel-Campbell, K., & Campbell, C.R. (1985). Training techniques that may facilitate generalization. In S.F. Warren & A.K. Rogers-Warren (Eds.), *Teaching functional language* (pp. 251–285). Baltimore: University Park Press.

Vanderheiden, G., & Grilley, K. (Eds.). (1976). *Non-vocal communication techniques and aids for the severely physically handicapped.* Baltimore: University Park Press.

Vanderheiden, G.C., & Lloyd, L.L. (1986). Communication systems and their components. In S.W. Blackstone & D.M. Bruskin (Eds.), *Augmentative communication: An introduction* (pp. 49–162). Rockville, MD: American Speech-Language-Hearing Association.

Vanderheiden, G.C., & Yoder, D.E. (1986). Overview. In S.W. Blackstone & D.W. Bruskin (Eds.), *Augmentative Communication: An introduction.* Rockville, MD: American Speech-Language-Hearing Association.

Vincent, L., & Branston, M.B. (1979). *Teacher competency in the area of communication.* Unpublished manuscript, University of Wisconsin at Madison, Department of Studies in Behavioral Disabilities.

Vygotsky, L.S. (1978). *Mind in society.* Cambridge, MA: Harvard University Press.

Warren, S.F., & Rogers-Warren, A.K. (1985). Teaching functional language: An introduction. In S.F. Warren & A.K. Rogers-Warren (Eds.), *Teaching functional language* (pp. 3–23). Baltimore: University Park Press.

Wilbur, R.B. (1976). The linguistics of manual languages and manual systems. In L.L. Lloyd (Ed.), *Communication assessment and intervention strategies* (pp. 423–500). Baltimore: University Park Press.

Wing, L. (1981). Language, social, and cognitive impairments in autism and severe mental retardation. *Journal of Autism and Developmental Disorders, 11*, 31–44.

Wulz, S.V., Myers, S.P., Klein, M.D., Hall, M.K., & Waldo, L.J. (1982). Unobtrusive training: A home-centered model for communication training. *Journal of The Association for the Severely Handicapped, 7*, 36–47.

Twelve

FUNCTIONAL ACADEMIC SKILLS

Marquita Grenot-Scheyer, Lori Eshilian, and Mary A. Falvey

THE CRITERION OF ULTIMATE functioning requires that educators assist students with severe handicaps to develop and acquire the skills necessary to allow them to function as independently as possible in as many environments as possible (Brown, Nietupski, & Hamre-Nietupski, 1976). Since the ultimate educational goal for students is achieving the ability to function in demanding adult environments, students must be taught directly in those environments. For instance, there is little point in a student's being able to make change on a desk top across from her teacher if that same student cannot pay for her soft drink in a fast food restaurant. Similarly, it is important that a student learn to use a calculator to add grocery prices in the grocery store, rather than only during mathematics sessions in the classroom. Furthermore, it makes little difference that a student can read "Don't Walk" from a photocard illustrating this sign, if the same student cannot demonstrate comprehension of this concept by waiting at a street corner for the signal to change to "Walk."

This chapter includes a framework for selecting academic curricular content, and a delineation of reading, writing, and mathematic developmental sequences that have functional application across the four curricular domains: vocational, domestic, recreation/leisure, and community. In addition, the use of computer technology to facilitate the acquisition and practice of functional academic skills is presented.

Traditionally, curricula for students with severe handicaps have included academics and/or preacademics as part of the educational sequence. This sequence is typically based upon a traditional model—in other words, it is based upon those skills and skill sequences to which nonhandicapped students are exposed as they acquire and develop academic skills.

Duffy and Sherman (1973) presented a developmental sequence skill list for both word recognition and comprehension skills. Many academic skills, such as reading, mathematics, and writing progress in a logical and sequential developmental order. The teaching sequence for students with severe handicaps may be identical to that used with nonhandicapped students. However, the task analysis of the skill sequence may require finer analyses, and the development and use of adaptations. In addition, given the difficulties that these students have in generalizing skills, academic teaching activities and materials must be functional and chronological age appropriate.

Commercially available sequences, packages, and kits are typically divided into various cognitive areas such as matching, categorizing, identifying vowels and consonants, numeral recognition, quantity, and identification of time and measurement. Teachers of students with severe handicaps often teach directly from these sequences. As a result, they identify and use chronological age–inappropriate tasks, because students with severe handicaps generally function substantially below their chronological age peers. It is therefore the responsibility of educators to critically evaluate traditional curriculum materials, in order to select and utilize only those skill components that are meaningful, functional, and chronological age appropriate for a given student.

Frequently, instructional strategies presented in such sequences, packages, and kits dictate teaching according to the curriculum sequence, with little or no deviation allowed or advised. The underlying assumption is that in order for learning to occur, students must move along the entire presented sequence. For most students with severe handicaps, movement along such a continuum does not occur in a timely manner. That is, many students acquire skills along the continuum at very different rates by using various materials and activities. Some students may not have time for instruction in all the prerequisite skills typically performed by nonhandicapped students; rather, these students will need direct instruction in the skills required for performing the activities within natural environments. For example, it is more important to teach an adolescent a functional reading vocabulary that will allow him to function within his community than it is to "get the student ready" by having him trace letters made of sand, match two-dimensional shapes to three-dimensional shapes, or match identical shapes according to size.

As increasing numbers of teachers reject the "not ready for" hypothesis in favor of adapting curriculum sequences, packages, and kits to develop curricula that are relevant and meaningful, specific considerations and strategies are necessary (Brown et al., 1979). This chapter includes a delineation of such considerations and presents strategies that can be used to develop relevant and meaningful curricula.

CONSIDERATIONS FOR DETERMINING ACADEMIC CONTENT FOR INSTRUCTION

Developing functional academic curricular content requires the consideration of several important characteristics. These characteristics are delineated and discussed below:

1. **Age of Student** There are at least three reasons why it is critical that teachers consider the chronological age of the student when developing any functional academic content. First, academic content is likely to be more meaningful and functional for the student if it is age appropriate. It may be necessary to acquire and/or develop high-interest, low-level activities and materials in order to motivate the student and to match his or her chronological age. Second, the student with severe handicaps may be more willing to accept assistance from a nonhandicapped peer if the content is age appropriate. Third, the nonhandicapped peer is likely to be more familiar with and motiviated to provide tutorial assistance if chronological age–appropriate material is used.
2. **Present Levels of Ability** It is important for educators to build upon the strengths of the student and to inventory any academic content with which the student has had success in the past. Educators should determine that student's current functional academic ability and the environments in which those abilities have been demonstrated. For example, a teacher determines that a 10-year-old student with severe handicaps has the following functional academic skills: possesses a safety-sight vocabulary of 30 words, matches pictures to the preceding words both at home and at school, identifies numerals 1–25, is able to make purchases up to $5.00, and is able to write simple words in manuscript form. Given this information, the teacher is able to develop appropriate functional academic content for the student that builds upon his safety-sight vocabulary. The academic content also improves his ability to match pictures to words, and increases his ability to make purchases independently.
3. **Language and/or Communication Ability** The way in which the student communicates his or her needs, wants, and desires to others is an important consideration when determining functional academic content. Language and/or communication abilities are especially important when determining appropriate methods for measuring comprehension skills for a given student. Specifically: how will the student communicate to others that he or she understands written words and mathematical concepts? A student with severe handicaps may demonstrate such comprehension by using words and/or symbols in an appropriate context (i.e., the student verbally explains or demonstrates comprehension of his or her job duties at a local nursery by using key vocabulary words he or she has learned, such as hoe, rake, sweep, and plant).

4. **Preferred Learning Modality** During assessment, educators need to determine the preferred learning modalities or approaches for each student. Students who easily recognize the similarities and differences between many objects in their environment, or who enjoy, for example, looking through magazines and record jackets, are likely to learn using their visual modalities. Other students who often listen to records, hum popular songs, or follow verbal directions easily are likely to learn using their auditory modalities. Still other students who indicate a need for physical materials or who manipulate materials or objects in order to comprehend a concept learn by using their kinesthetic modalities. Finally, many students learn most effectively by using a variety of approaches, incorporating each of the modalities. The challenge to educators is to assess and determine the student's preferred learning modality and then to structure activities and tasks accordingly. Frequently, students will demonstrate a preference for more than one modality, so educators must determine and match the most effective learning modality to the most appropriate activity and task for a particular student.
5. **Functionality** The degree of functionality of academic content and materials across environments is a major consideration when determining curricular content. Concepts, words, phrases, materials, and activities that are meaningful for a given student are more likely to be retained and used than those that are meaningless or nonfunctional to the student. For example, it is functional and more meaningful for a student to generate and write out a grocery shopping list with his parents at home, to practice these words at school, and subsequently, to purchase these items in the store, than it is for the student to learn 10 nonrelated words from a primary word list and complete a math computation worksheet.
6. **Principle of Partial Participation** The principle of partial participation is an especially critical instructional consideration when determining functional academic content and curricular strategies. The principle suggests that rather than requiring 100% accuracy and independence for all skills in a sequence, adaptations might be developed instead that allow the student to engage in as many activities as possible (Baumgart et al., 1982). In many commercially available curriculum packages, sequences, and kits, specific skills and objectives must be accomplished independently and accurately before the student is permitted to move to the next skill. Historically, this has meant that many students have been denied the opportunity to even attempt to participate in activities involving reading skills.
7. **Use of Adaptations** A final consideration when determining functional academic content is to use adaptations to increase student participation across a wide variety of activities and environments. Using adaptations to teach various concepts to students represents a valuable resource to educators and students. Traditionally, students with severe handicaps were de-

nied the opportunity to even attempt academic skills due to the popular "notion" of their lower cognitive capabilities. The use of adaptations can allow the student to at least partially participate in various academic skills and activities. Adaptations can be made in the presentation of information, in the sequencing of information, in the completion of tasks, and in materials.

There are many academic skills that students with severe handicaps can best accomplish and more fully participate in if adaptations are developed and utilized. Examples of adaptations that can be developed for each of the major functional academic content areas follow in this chapter.

FRAMEWORK FOR SELECTING ACADEMIC CURRICULAR CONTENT

Browder and Snell, 1987, have suggested four approaches for selecting academic curricular content for students with severe handicaps: the generalized academic approach, the specific academic approach, the academic adaptation approach, and the partial participation approach. Each of these approaches is primarily concerned with teaching academics that are subcomponents of functional activities, and with assisting students in meeting the academic demands of their daily lives. Ecological inventories (Brown et al., 1979) should be completed for each approach to determine what academic skills are required to function as independently as possible in the activities and environments relevant for each student. Examples of ecological inventories for determining reading, math, and writing content, and methods for developing ecological inventories are delineated later in this chapter.

The generalized, specific, adaptation, and partial participation academic approaches focus on critical skills necessary for students to function in integrated school, community, and vocational environments. Each of the approaches described below should be considered when determining the academic curricular content for each student. The age of the student, present levels of ability, communication and/or language ability, preferred learning modality, and functionality of the academic content should all be examined when determining which approach is best for the individual student. It is important to remember that all students have different skill levels in each academic content area. For example, a student may be better in reading than in math or writing, or may be more skilled in handling money than in telling time. The opportunity to learn the highest level of academic curricular content should be afforded to all students.

Generalized Academic Approach

In the generalized academic approach, skills that can be used across environments are examined. Examples of such skills include: matching, word analysis, spelling, writing, money, time telling, computation, and measurement. Although these skills can be found within traditional curriculum sequences, in the generalized academic approach, they are evaluated and taught within functional activities that have current and future significance to the individual student. For example, the matching of colors may be taught as part of the generalized reading curricula. Instruction could take place during such activities as matching and folding clothes, locating items to be purchased in a grocery store, or stocking paints on a shelf in an art supply store. When using the generalized academic approach, traditional curriculum sequence steps that have no current functional application may be disregarded. For example, roman numerals may not be taught to all elementary-age students with severe handicaps as part of their math curriculum. However, roman numerals may be taught to an older student with severe handicaps if it is a skill necessary for his or her job success (e.g., a job sorting and organizing boxes in a warehouse that uses roman numerals to label its merchandise).

The teaching of generalized academic skills requires a longitudinal commitment from students with severe handicaps, their teachers, and families. As previously suggested, the rate of the student's previous academic progress, the age of the student, and the number of years he or she will be remaining in school are important considerations when selecting the generalized academic approach.

The generalized academic approach can lead to increased integrated academic opportunities in regular education classrooms, since the instruction generally resembles that received by nonhandicapped peers. In addition, there are numerous commercially available materials for teaching generalized academic curricular content (e.g., Edmark Sight Word Vocabulary, Lakeshore Time Flash Cards, D'nealian Handwriting Books). Caution must be taken so that students with severe handicaps are using age-appropriate commercial materials and that mastery of generalized skills is not assumed based solely on their use. Mastery of generalized academic skills must be tested within functional activities, using natural materials and in a variety of environments, where those skills are naturally required.

Specific Academic Approach

When a student's learning history indicates that it is not feasible to use a generalized academic approach, or if the student is older and does not have the time it would take to learn a generalized academic skill, or if a student's other skill needs are greater than on the academic skill need of a particular activity, then other approaches to academic instruction should be considered. In the specific academic approach, the focus is on the activity rather than on the academic skill response. For example, if an individual needs to ride public transportation to work and does not have the generalized reading, money, or time telling skills required for this activity, specific academic instruction might be appropriate.

That is, the individual would be assisted in learning the specific time to be at the bus stop, the specific bus stop to wait, the specific bus number to look for, and the specific amount of change needed. Thus, the specific academic approach is highly individualized to the needs of each student and each activity.

In contrast to the generalized academic approach that teaches skills that could be used across environments, the specific academic approach emphasizes those skills an individual needs to be more independent in a particular functional activity. Teachers should develop detailed ecological inventories that specify the exact words or pictures to be read, or the exact amounts of money required for purchases in that activity. Additionally, any possible writing that may be required (e.g., signature, date, phone number) should be outlined, and a specific time schedule to be followed should be provided. There are few commercially available materials appropriate for instruction utilizing the specific academic approach. Instructional aids can be developed or obtained to assist students to practice and learn academic skills. For example, the student can be provided with pictures of the menu at McDonald's, empty containers that match the desired items to be purchased in a grocery store, actual coins taped to a card to show the amount needed to purchase soda from a vending machine, or a written card with the bus arrival time to match to a digital watch. Efforts should be made so that instructional materials are age-appropriate and assist students in demonstrating their competencies. The goal in developing instructional aids is to fade their use as the student develops independent academic skills.

Academic Adaptation Approach

Some students with severe handicaps will require continual use of instructional aids, technical equipment, or adaptations to materials, skills sequences, or physical environments. Other students with handicaps may require simplification of the skill itself to allow for successful academic performance and increased independence in functional activities. The academic adaptation approach is useful for students who are unlikely to become independent without some sort of adaptation, or for students who have very little time to learn the academic skills necessary to function independently. For example, an individual with severe handicaps may need an adaptation for writing the time on his or her time card at a new job (e.g., a time stamp, a model to copy from, or a job coach writing in the time). This academic approach is also useful for skills that are important to the individual but that are not used often enough to justify long-term instruction. For example, if the skill of writing one's signature is useful only when signing the back of a paycheck that is obtained bimonthly, it may be more appropriate to purchase a name stamp for that purpose rather than spending years training the individuals to write his or her name.

Once again, ecological inventories should be used to determine which skills or materials could be adapted, how the physical environment could be changed, or what technical equipment or instructional aids need to be developed for increased academic functioning. All adaptations and prostheses should be age appropriate and developed with the plan of how they could be faded in the future, if and or when the student demonstrates the ability to function without their use.

Partial Participation Approach

The fourth approach for selecting academic curricular content is the partial participation approach. In this approach, those academic skills that are within functional activities are not specifically taught. Utilizing this approach, academic tasks are performed for the student, while the student participates in the functional activity at the highest level possible. For example, during a cooking activity, the instructor or another student may measure the ingredients and verbally describe and demonstrate that skill, while the student partially participates by pouring the ingredients into a mixing bowl. This approach is used for students whose other skill needs are currently greater than their academic skill needs (e.g., motor skill development has been identified as having priority over academic skill development).

The partial participation approach requires the educator to conduct ecological inventories, as in all other academic approaches, so that the student who is partially participating can function as independently as possible. That is, for students who cannot discriminate or match correct change, appropriate coins can be given to them prior to the purchasing activity; for students who cannot read a menu in a restaurant, pictures of the choices can be used by the student to indicate to the waiter by pointing to his or her order. The assistance provided and the materials used by the student who is partially participating should be age appropriate (e.g., the student should remove the precounted coins from an age-appropriate wallet). This approach can assist in the development of a positive interdependency between a student with severe handicaps and the person who is providing the academic support. It also allows for participation in functional activities, which is preferable to nonparticipation, or to participation in activities that have no signficance to the student's current or future life.

When developing an individual student's academic curricular content, it is important to remember that each of the preceding approaches is not exclusive of one another, and that one approach is not always appropriate for a particular student when teaching across all functional activities or in different academic areas. For example, a student may be quite capable of learning *generalized* time telling skills when using an *adapted* digital watch. This same student may be able to read *words specific* to ordering food in the school cafeteria, yet may need to be given the exact amount of money required in order to *partially participate* in purchasing the food. As illustrated, each of the four approaches has been utilized in order to maximize the student's level of independence.

Functional academic skills are an integral part of independent living activities across all domains. Table 12.1 is a list of sample instructional objectives illustrating the four approaches to teaching functional academics across the four domains. The instruction of academic skills within functional activities, whether generalized or specific academic skills, or those taught through the use of adaptations or partial participation, should reflect the appropriate instructional strategies addressed in Chapter 4 of this volume.

READING

A variety of strategies can be utilized to generate functional and appropriate reading content. In this section, several of these strategies are discussed. Also, examples of activities, materials, and tasks are presented to illustrate reading skills as they are required across the four curricular domain areas.

In developing and determining appropriate reading curricula, educators must examine a number of important issues, such as: student ability and desire, parent/guardian preferences, district/curriculum requirements, and reading requirements across the student's environments. Reading requirements across the student's current and subsequent environments are the most critical aspect of curriculum to the student; such requirements will serve as the foundation for generating reading content for that student. As previously suggested, it may be important for special educators to have knowledge of a typical reading sequence and of the skills that are taught at each grade level. Students with severe handicaps should be able to participate in reading programs in the regular classroom with the necessary support. Therefore, educators must incorporate these skills and sequences into the student's reading program.

The importance of being able to read within the various domains is examined and discussed in this book as a prerequisite to functional literacy. Functional literacy is the ability to comprehend written words sufficiently enough to read. Such literacy may include the following reading skills:

1. Reading to gain information (e.g., interpreting signs, locating a favorite program in the television guide, or reading about the weather in the local newspaper)
2. Reading to complete tasks (e.g., following recipe directions, locating items on a shopping list, finding a telephone number in the directory, or following directions for a card game)
3. Reading for leisure (e.g., choosing a favorite movie from the listings, selecting a magazine from the magazine racks, or choosing a favorite record at the record store)
4. Reading to locate and maintain a job (e.g., using the want ads from the newspaper to locate possible places of employment, using a time clock appropriately, locating the appropriate bus line, or choosing a snack from the vending machine at breaktime) (Johnson, 1982)

Table 12.1. Sample instructional objectives

The student will	Domestic	Community	Recreation/Leisure	Vocational
Generalized:	Learn to read, identify and measure using 1 cp, 1/2 cp, 1 Tb, 1 tsp, 1/2 tsp, 1/4 tsp, completing 2 cookie recipes of choice, 100% over 4 trials.	Learn to ride public transportation at a variety of times to all locations in the community that are utilized on a regular basis (e.g., school, work, the mall, grocery store, YMCA, grandparents' or friends' houses), 100% over 5 trials.	Identify the movie section of the newspaper and select a movie to go see, reading the time(s) it is showing, and preparing to go to the movie theatre (e.g., correct amount of money), 100% over 5 trials.	Work in a record/video store categorizing records, C.D.s, and tapes according to the type of music: (classical, western, rock, pop, jazz and musicals), and alphabetizing them according to the recording artist's name, earning minimum wage over 6 months with positive evaluations from the supervisors.
Specific:	Learn to make a box cookie mix of choice measuring 1/2 cp of hot water and 1/2 cp oil, 100% independent over 4 trials.	Learn to ride the #410 bus at 7:50 A.M. from the corner of 1st & Main to school and return home at 2:50 P.M., 100% accuracy over 10 trials.	Will be able to call the theatre nearest to his/her house to hear what movies are showing and the times, 4/5 times per 5 trials.	Work in a record/video store matching records, C.D.s, and tapes to those items already on the shelves, restocking and organizing the shelves, earning subminimum wage for completing a portion of the job tasks, over 6 months with positive evaluations.

Adaptation:	(Same as Specific) using a measuring cup with a red line indicating $1/2$ cup mark and following a picture task sequence card, 100% over 4 trials.	Learn to ride public transportation from home to school and return, to the mall, and YMCA using cards with the correct times to catch the bus to each location to be matched to the time on a digital watch, 100% accuracy over 5 trials.	(Same as Generalized Approach) utilizing the $1 over method of purchase to buy the theatre ticket and to purchase a soda and popcorn/candy, 4/5 times over 5 trials.	Work in a record/video store with a job coach to assist in locating the correct aisles and bins and utilizing picture cues and alphabet list to assist in the alphabetizing of the records, earning subminimum wage, according to the percentage of speed compared to other employees over 6 months.
Partial participation:	Assist in choosing a cookie mix, pouring premeasured ingredients and stirring (at least 25 strokes) with verbal prompts for each task over 4 trials.	Utilize public transportation for community training with assistance, within 15 seconds and pulling the cord to indicate departure with 1 indirect prompt, 4/5 times over 5 trials.	Attend a movie in a local theatre demonstrating appropriate behavior when waiting in line to purchase a ticket and maintaining appropriate verbalizations during the movie, 90% of the time over 5 trials.	Work in a record/video store dusting the shelves, records, and tapes, vacuuming the store, and emptying trash, earning a minimum wage over 6 months with positive evaluations from the supervisors.

Table 12.2 is an example of a typical reading sequence that might be found in a traditional curriculum series, package, or kit. Presented in conjunction with this sequence is a list of functional and chronological age–appropriate activities that could be used to assess and teach the associated reading skills.

Educators must be familiar with all teaching strategies and methods when determining the ones that are the most appropriate for an individual student. There is no "one way" to best teach reading; however, some strategies and methods have been found to be more effective than others when teaching reading to students with severe handicaps. In addition, these strategies and methods may be used in conjunction with each other, and should not be considered in isolation. Several teaching strategies and methods are presented in the following pages.

Ecological Inventory Strategy

The ecological inventory strategy is a process by which essential reading information pertaining to an individual student and to the environments in which he or she functions is identified and delineated. Regardless of the approach or particular reading method to be utilized, the ecological inventory strategy can be used with any of the strategies to develop reading content. Specifically, this strategy delineates the essential reading vocabulary required in a particular activity or environment.

There are several reasons for using the ecological inventory strategy to develop reading content. Following are several of the most crucial reasons:

1. Developing reading content provides a unique way in which to generate meaningful curricular content for individual students (Brown et al., 1979)
2. Examining vocabulary encountered in a given student's environment reveals the receptive comprehension required in that student's environment (Johnson, 1982)
3. Examining vocabulary encountered in a given student's environment reveals the functional object use required (Johnson, 1982)
4. Examining vocabulary encountered in a given student's environment reveals the structure of the words required (Johnson, 1982)
5. Examining vocabulary encountered in a given student's environment reveals the phonics and context skills required (Johnson, 1982)
6. Examining vocabulary encountered in a given student's environment reveals the relevant written and verbal vocabulary necessary for that environment (Johnson, 1982)

Educators can develop appropriate individualized reading programs by generating key vocabulary drawn from specific environments that the student frequents or will frequent in the future. The steps for conducting an ecological inventory to generate reading content include the following:

1. Delineate the curricular domains.
2. Delineate the environments.
3. Delineate the subenvironments.
4. Delineate the activities that occur in the environments.

Two examples of this strategy are presented here. The first example describes a student who participates in woodshop at his junior high school; the second example describes a student who participates in a recreation program at a YMCA.

Domain: Vocational
Environment: Junior high school
Subenvironment: Woodshop
Activity: Working on wood projects
Ecological inventory sequence/development of key vocabulary

1. List objects (nouns) used in activity.
   a. Equipment names: jigsaw, vise, workbench
   b. Tool names: sandpaper, ruler, file
   c. Safety signs: "FLAMMABLE," "DO NOT TOUCH," "EXIT"
2. List actions (verbs) performed in activity.
   a. Working: sand, cut, file, rasp
   b. Cleaning: sweep, dust, put away, wash
3. List modifiers and descriptors (adjectives and adverbs) used in activity.
   a. Adjectives: hard, rough, smooth
   b. Adverbs: slowly, quickly
4. List prepositions used in activity.
   a. Working: rasp around, gouge in
   b. Cleaning: sweep behind, clean under
5. List titles used in activity.
   a. Names of woodshop teacher, aides, peers

Domain: Recreation/leisure
Environment: YMCA summer program
Subenvironment: Concession stand
Activity: Buying lunch
Ecological inventory sequence/development of key vocabulary

1. Inventory information vocabulary needed.
   a. Nouns: pizza, burrito, hamburger, french fries, juice, milk, cookie, trash, cashier
   b. Verbs: throw, wait here
   c. Adjectives/adverbs: behind, in front, this side

As the preceding examples illustrate, critical vocabulary from the student's environment can be obtained for use within a reading program. To par-

Table 12.2. Sequence of typical reading skills and corresponding functional and chronological age–appropriate activities to inventory and teach these skills

Skill area	Preschool	Elementary	High school	Adult
Visual discrimination:				
1. Matches concrete shapes one to one	Matches pairs of cookie cutters while baking cookies with Mom	Selects Frisbee to match friend's Frisbee, to take to the park.	Selects and matches group of garden tools to match necessary ones for that day	Selects and matches necessary cleaning items to match job adaptation to clean motel rooms
2. Selects matching object from given set of concrete objects	Chooses red glass during nutrition that matches friend's glass	Selects yellow tetherball to match friend's selection	Selects appropriate cleaning materials from storage room to clean cafeteria tables	Stacks paper cups of various sizes according to appropriate size at job at McDonald's
3. Matches real object to picture of object	Recognizes Grandma at airport from photo and gives her a hug	Using a children's cookbook, with pictures, selects necessary items to make pudding	In grocery store, selects appropriate grocery item from array of food pictures	Selects dusting materials to match job photo adaptation to clean pews in church
4. Matches color one to one.	Arranges pegs in pegboard according to rows of different colors	Distributes color pennies to team members according to their color	Matches socks by color, folds together, and puts in drawer	Matches lid to appropriate paint cans after painting is finished
5. Sorts by color	Sorts blocks into different color piles before building	Arranges and sorts construction paper by color in teacher workroom	Arranges and sorts flowerpots by color in junior high room	Sorts laundry by color before washing clothes
6. Identifies color	Points to red when asked what color he or she would like to make a valentine	Selects and attaches appropriate color ribbons to rows of chairs in auditorium to match class colors	Verbally identifies correct colors using color wheel in art class	Points to appropriate international danger colors (red, yellow) when asked to identify for a roommate
7. Sorts by shapes	Sorts Christmas cookies by shape after baking	Stacks pillows in linen department according to size and shape	Removes utensils from dishwasher and places into appropriate section of utensil tray	Sorts and hangs gaskets by shape in auto repair shop

8. Matches by size	Selects appropriate size doll clothing for two different dolls	Places spoonful of vegetables onto cafeteria tray to match designated amount	Selects kitchen-size trash bag for garbage can in kitchen from different sizes	Selects appropriate size box to accommodate gift item in store
9. Sorts by size	Picks up toys and puts blocks into "big" and "little" containers	Collects balls after recess and puts away according to size in ballbox	Puts dishes away in cupboard according to size	Sorts and folds laundry from nursing home according to bed size
10. Identifies by size	Arranges little chairs for dolls and big chair for self at "tea party"	Requests a "big" slice of cake when asked at party	Measures and weighs self in health office	Identifies and selects appropriate size clothing in department store
11. Identifies objects by color, shape, and size	Using communication book, asks for "double-scoop" of chocolate ice-cream not just one scoop	Cuts and pastes picture of red bicycle into Christmas "wish list"	Selects a "Michael Jackson look-alike jacket" from several on rack	Verbally describes jacket to person at lost and found counter in shopping mall (e.g., "red, shiny, and size 7")
Decoding skills:				
1. Identifies letters of alphabet	Sequences and matches letter of alphabet while singing alphabet song with a friend	Arranges letters of school name in appropriate order to prepare for typesetting of school newspaper	Matches names on letters to teachers' mail boxes	Is able to select personal card with name imprinted on it from other cards in wallet
2. Identifies consonant sounds in both initial and final position	Plays rhyming game in preschool room, matching a picture to the sound the teacher makes (e.g., ball for "b")	In fourth-grade classroom, plays game to identify consonant sounds, during language arts	Not chronological age appropriate	Not chronological age appropriate
3. Identifies short and long vowel sounds	Practices saying vowel sounds in unison with other children in preschool room	Completes worksheet in library learning lab that emphasizes short and long vowel sounds	Not chronological age appropriate	Not chronological age appropriate
4. Recognizes and blends consonant-vowel-consonant (CVC) words	Arranges magnetic letters on board to form new words	Plays word game in fourth-grade classroom during language arts	Fills in words of crossword puzzle	Plays "Scrabble" with several roommates

(continued)

Table 12.2. *(continued)*

Skill area	Preschool	Elementary	High school	Adult
Vocabulary development:				
1. Recognizes name	Looks at teacher while teacher is writing letters of her [the child's] name on board	Raises hand when name is called in classroom	Checks off name on class roster as it is passed around in woodshop class	Selects appropriate time card to punch at grocery store
2. Recognizes color and number words	Listens for teacher to call "all those with red on" to line up for recess	Completes "paint by number" color sheet at a friend's house (e.g., paints number 1 red, number 2 green, and so forth)	In art class, develops a design that uses the word "blue" repeatedly with blue ink	Writes check in store, spelling out the cash amount in number words (e.g. "five dollars")
3. Recognizes and follows directional words and prepositions	Not chronological age appropriate	Selects door with the sign that has "IN" on it, to enter the store	Follows directions on photocopier machine in school office that indicates, "Right Side Down," before positioning paper	Presses the "UP" button to go to third floor while on first floor
4. Recognizes and utilizes words/abbreviations for days, months, and dates	Not chronological age appropriate	Writes date on board in morning to help teacher	Writes day and date to begin entry in diary	Calls up friend on his or her birthday to send birthday greetings
5. Recognizes and utilizes safety-functional vocabulary	While walking with dad to the store, stops at "STOP" sign, points to it, and says, "Stop"	At YMCA, reads sign, "MEN," and enters the appropriate restroom	Reads sign, "DO NOT TOUCH," in woodshop class and removes wood from machinery	Reads signs on container, "POISON," and puts this box on top shelf away from young children

ticipate to the greatest extent possible within the two preceding environments, the student needs to have as many opportunities as possible to practice the vocabulary, engage in activities requiring the vocabulary, demonstrate comprehension of the vocabulary, and use the new vocabulary in different situations and environments.

In the two preceding examples, the educator must consider the relevancy of the selected vocabulary and its importance to the student both now and in the future. Falvey and Anderson (1983) identified dimensions to consider when selecting priorities for curricular content. Educators can use such similar dimensions when determining and selecting reading vocabulary from various environments. Based upon these dimensions, several questions that educators must ask themselves when determining reading vocabulary follow:

1. What reading vocabulary will be taught?
   a. Is the vocabulary functional?
   b. Is the vocabulary chronological age appropriate?
   c. Will the vocabulary meet the current and subsequent needs of the student?
   d. Can the vocabulary cross environments?
   e. Is the vocabulary similar to vacabulary that nonhandicapped peers utilize?
   f. Does the vocabulary promote independence?
   g. Will the vocabulary meet the largest variety of student's needs?
   h. Does the vocabulary consider cultural/familial needs and characteristics?
   i. Can the vocabulary be utilized frequently?
2. How will the vocabulary be taught?
   a. Can the vocabulary be used with a variety of reading strategies?
   b. Is the vocabulary motivating to the student?
   c. Can the vocabulary be taught in accordance with the student's preferred learning modality?
   d. Can the vocabulary be taught with, by, or in the presence of nonhandicapped peers?
3. Where will the vocabulary be taught?
   a. Will the vocabulary be taught in the natural context in which it occurs?
   b. Can the vocabulary be taught/utilized by a variety of people in the student's environment?
   c. Can the student use the vocabulary to communicate across a wide variety of environments?

Given the considerations just described, it may be important for a particular student to learn, for example, the general verbs used when working in woodshop (such as sand, file, stamp), but not the verbs he or she would rarely encounter or be expected to know (such as chisel, edge, plane). For another student, it may be important to teach nouns he or she will use during lunch, and to concentrate instructional efforts on the words that are most frequently used and that have the most relevance to the student (e.g., words the student would need to use to order, buy, or receive lunch). For yet another student, instructional time may best be spent emphasizing all the related prepositions, adjectives, adverbs, and other vocabulary encountered in the workshop environment. In this manner, the students' functional vocabulary can be increased, and his or her ability to interact successfully during occasional lecture periods can be further enhanced.

A final consideration for selecting vocabulary that is relevant and meaningful to the student involves correlating the cognitive/intellectual abilities of the student with the vocabulary and concepts selected. That is, in addition to considering the preceding questions when determining reading vocabulary, the educator should select concepts, vocabulary, and reading material that will match the student's cognitive/intellectural abilities. Depending upon the student's ability, vocabulary is selected that ranges from concepts easiest to grasp to concepts most difficult to grasp, and from vocabulary representing concrete objects to vocabulary representing abstract concepts. It is essential that the educator be aware of the student's cognitive/intellectual ability in relation to his or her chronological age. The educator must develop and select reading concepts, vocabulary, and materials that match the student's needs in a chronological age–appropriate, functional, and meaningful manner.

The use of an ecological inventory strategy for generating reading content involves acquiring the reading content from as many of the students' present and anticipated environments as possible. To assist in the determination and delineation of such information, parents/ guardians, teachers, nonhandicapped peers, and community members can be interviewed and observed. All available resources should be utilized.

Basal Reading Method

Teachers of students with severe handicaps may find it helpful to use the local school district's basal readers as guides for information regarding sequence and content of reading skills. There are at least two reasons why educators should consider using basal readers. First, it is important that educators understand the sequence of reading skills purported to be necessary for movement along a continuum, particularly for those students who are acquiring skills in accordance with the sequence of the continuum. Second, for those students who are participating in academic classes in regular education programs, special educators should be knowledgeable about basal readers so as to enhance and facilitate the integration of students with handicaps into regular classroom reading programs.

Piernok (1979) suggested that educators might use the basal reader manual as a basis for developing a reading program. A basal reader manual often includes components such as concept development, word recognition, comprehension goals, directed reading, and follow-up.

Educators who work exclusively with basal readers must consider a number of critical variables. First, the stories in basal readers are often unrealistic. Second, the stories are frequently chronological age inappropriate. Third, the stories are often based upon assumptions and actions typically present in only one culture, making comprehension difficult for students who represent other cultures. Fourth, the sequences suggested in basal readers usually assume the student will progress from one level to the next as he or she acquires skills. However, for many students who have severe handicaps, it is unrealistic, inappropriate, and restrictive to expect movement along this continuum. For example, in the authors' experience, a 15-year-old student was able to learn to sight read "No Swimming Allowed" and to demonstrate comprehension of these words by performing the correct action of not swimming in the designated section of the river. However, the same student was unable to read a paragraph describing safe water activities during the summer in the basal reader. For this student, building and developing a functional vocabulary would be more appropriate than adhering to the developmental reading sequence described in a basal reader manual. Valuable instructional time would be wasted on "getting the student ready" to learn.

Phonetic Method

A phonetic method for teaching reading skills involves sounding out letters, letter combinations, or words (i.e., identifying consonant sounds in the initial and final position of a word), identifying vowel sounds, and recognizing and blending consonant-vowel-consonant (CVC) words. When deciding whether to use this method with a student, it is important to consider the student's learning style. Students who are strong auditory learners are likely to respond more rapidly to the phonetic method than those who are not. Students who line up when the bell rings, who prefer to listen to a cassette player during breaktime, and who comprehend and follow multistep directions, are able to respond to auditory stimuli and are likely to learn through their auditory modalities.

A major advantage of the phonetic method is that it can be easily used across a wide variety of activities, materials, and environments. Employing the materials available in the student's natural environment, educators can design and implement a reading program using a phonetic method. For example, a 6-year-old student with severe handicaps may use phonics to participate in reading activities at home, in the special education classroom, and in the adjoining regular kindergarten. Special materials or kits are not required for this student to be successful. The materials and activities needed to teach words utilizing phonics are readily available in the student's different environments. In addition, instructional strategies can easily be implemented by various people, including teachers, parents, and nonhandicapped peers.

Several issues must be taken into account when implementing the phonetic method. As previously suggested, chronological age–appropriate tasks and materials should be developed and used to teach reading. Instead of utilizing commercially developed materials that are generally nonfunctional and often chronological age inappropriate (e.g., primary grade worksheets for adolescents), educators could develop pictures of materials, activities, environments, concepts, and so forth that the student encounters, and employ these in instruction. Second, a phonetic method to teaching reading may take too long for some students to grasp and, thus, may not serve the immediate or subsequent needs of this student in the most timely manner. For example, for the last 3 years, Mark, a 12-year-old student with autism, has had an annual educational goal of being able to "identify the initial consonant sound for 10 new pictures." Unfortunately, Mark has only acquired five beginning consonant sounds during that 3-year period. He has not had the opportunity to develop reading skills using any other reading methods. The challenge to educators is to identify the reading methods that will develop reading skills in the most efficient and timely manner possible, and that will have the greatest impact on the student's ability to function in as many environments as possible.

Sight-Word Method

A third method that can be used to teach reading is a sight-word method involving the presentation of a stimulus (e.g., the word "ENTER" written on a card) and then a response (e.g., student says or signs "enter" or points to a picture of a girl entering a store). Snell (1983) describes this process as a "whole-word" approach; that is, it emphasizes the whole word as a meaningful unit. Further, the main focus of instruction involves associating a spoken word with the printed word match.

A sight-word method can easily be used in many environments. For example, a student can practice reading lunch menu items from the lunch board and then purchase what she desires. After lunch, that same student can continue working on this lesson by writing or matching pictures of what she had for lunch. The student can then take the activity home to share with her parents as a follow-up or as an extension to the original lesson. Finally, the student can accompany her parents to a neighborhood delicatessen to continue practicing the skills. Another student can practice at school matching names of his favorite television programs to the television guide, then select the programs he would like to watch that evening at home.

The sight-word method can be particularly useful and adaptable when teaching reading skills in different community environments (e.g., stores, restaurants, and buses). This can easily be used in a grocery store, where the student is required, for example, to read the label on a bottle of apple juice and demonstrate comprehension of it by selecting the juice on the shelf that corresponds to the word on her grocery list. As another illustration, the sight-word method can be taught in a restaurant, where the student is required to match his menu list with the actual items on the menu and then order from the waiter. This method is useful only if educators select meaningful vocabulary and functional reading content and activities within which to present the sight words.

Language Experience Method

The language experience method can be used with students of varying ages and abilities. The method utilizes experiences, activities, environments, people, and materials most familiar to the student. Snell (1978) indicated that the use of the language experience method integrates expressive and receptive language skills and provides experiences that contribute to vocabulary development. In addition, the vocabulary that is used originates from the language, communication, and experiences of the student and thus, is meaningful and functional for that student.

The experiences selected should be based upon relevant vocabulary and experiences available in the students' own home, school, neighborhood, work, recreation, or general community environments. A review of an experience should be provided through the use of discussion, slides, photos, pictures, objects, or other materials related to the experience. Presentation of vocabulary could include use of slides, flashcards, worksheets, transparencies, chalkboards, tape recorders, and so on. Using the key vocabulary, the students generate a story or essay based upon their experiences. It is critical to elicit responses from all the students so that the story/essay has direct meaning for them and is based upon their perceptions of the experience, and not those of the teacher or of one student only. A review of key vocabulary words is conducted following the development of the story/essay. Checking the students' comprehension of key vocabulary concepts is another essential component of the language experience method. Language experience stories/essays should not occur in isolation; rather, they should form a network of related and relevant reading experiences for students. As stated by Hall (1976), the cornerstone of the language experience method is the interrelatedness of language and experience.

There are several advantages to this method. First, since this method allows for individualizing for each student or group of students, the content, material, and vocabulary can be chronological age appropriate. Second, since reading content is based upon the unique activities and experiences of the student, the content is generally more meaningful and motivating to the student. Third, the language experience method stresses functional reading content and facilitates the development of a functional reading vocabulary. Fourth, the method provides opportunities for peer interaction through cooperative reading experiences and projects.

When a decision has been made to utilize a language experience method to develop reading content, educators should consider a number of variables. First, the students should be heterogeneously grouped; when students of various ability levels are grouped together, they have the opportunity to learn from and assist each other. Second, instruction must truly be individualized, even if instruction occurs within a group. Students of varying ability levels will have different learning objectives that will need to be met during instructional time. Third, the key vocabulary identified during the development of the language story/essay should be used and reinforced in as many situations as possible, so as to encourage generalized use of the vocabulary. Fourth, for some students, acquisition of reading skills may occur in a developmental manner and at a rate comparable to their nonhandicapped peers. For these students, supplemental reading activities should be provided. Decoding skills and/or concept development skills from a basal reader system may supplement a language experience method and provide a "total" reading program for such students.

As has been demonstrated, special educators have at their disposal several reading methods for teaching reading content. These methods should not be considered mutually exclusive and should be used in combination with each other to provide a comprehensive and functional reading approach for students with severe handicaps. In addition, the ecological inventory strategy can be used with any of the methods to determine reading content. A vital component in any reading approach is that of assessing, teaching, and evaluating comprehension skills; these skills are addressed in the following section.

Comprehension Skills

Comprehension has been defined as "a skill that rests primarily on the student's ability to conceptualize, to classify or to determine relationships between concepts, and to answer factual questions about or make inferences from what is read" (Snell, 1983, p. 455). Specific strategies for teaching comprehension are often an elusive component in commercially available reading programs. A functional reading comprehension sequence may include the following skills:

1. Functional use of objects
2. Appropriate motor response to stimuli
3. Pairing of word to picture/photo
4. Identifying the main concept (verbal or written)
5. Classifying of information
6. Sequencing of information
7. Interpreting information
8. Drawing conclusions regarding information

For educators, the challenge is to assess, teach, and evaluate these comprehension skills in a measurable way. Although some students have good sight-word abilities (i.e., they can visually recognize certain words and use these words to communicate), many students lack the skills necessary to demonstrate their understanding or comprehension of these words. It is critical that students develop a meaningful vocabulary, that is, a set of words that have conceptually meaningful mental associations. For example, one may think it impressive that a student can read all of the grocery item labels presented in television commercials. The real test of functionality however, resides in this student's ability to select from the shelves the grocery items that are written on his/her grocery list. This ability requires that selection of vocabulary and demonstration of comprehension of this vocabulary be performed in the natural setting requiring the skill.

For some students with severe handicaps it may not be important to focus instructional time on acquisition of all of the possible comprehension skills. Rather, instructional efforts should be devoted to assessing, teaching, and evaluating those comprehension skills that best match the student's current needs and abilities. For example, an elementary-age student who is multiply handicapped demonstrates comprehension by functionally using an object that a reading word represents by pointing to the game "Simon" when presented with three leisure activities (including "Simon") written on her communication board. Table 12.3 presents a sequence of comprehension skills in conjunction with the functional demonstration/application of these skills across environments.

MATHEMATICS

In this section strategies for generating mathematics content for students with severe handicaps are described. The emphasis will be upon identifying those mathematics skills that are critical for students to possess and use in order to acquire, maintain, and generalize skills necessary to participate as independent members of their community. Specific strategies, activities, materials, and examples are provided that illustrate how mathematics skills are required and can be taught across a variety of environments.

It is essential that educators be knowledgeable about the developmental/sequential mathematics sequence, so that they can use it as a reference guide for those students who are acquiring mathematics skills in a manner comparable to their nonhandicapped peers. Furthermore, students with severe handicaps can participate in the regular mathematics program if they recieve instruction in typical mathematics skills utilizing the sequence, skills, and materials available in the regular classroom. There are many mathematical skills that students can best accomplish, and can more fully participate in, if adaptations are developed and utilized. It is important that the educator consider the chronological age and abilities of the student when selecting and developing such adaptations. Table 12.4 presents a variety of adaptations and the mathematical skills for which they are appropriate.

A crucial element in the curriculum decision-making process is the anal-

Table 12.3. Examples of general comprehension and functional skills

Identifying Main Concept/Idea

An elementary student selects four oranges and three apples, as pictorially described on his shopping list to purchase.

A junior high student verbally explains the important points of a slide presentation explaining sexual reproduction.

An adult female verbally repeats to the physician the medication dosage she must take, in order to clarify his statements.

Identifying Details

An elementary student "finely" chops the apples for a fruit salad, according to the recipe's instructions.

A junior high student follows the woodshop teacher's instructions to gouge his bowl "deeply" and then to sand the bowl until it is "smooth."

An adult male follows his job sequence of edging the lawn by trimming *all* edges and corners evenly.

Classifying Information

An elementary student who works as the ball monitor puts all balls away after recess in the appropriate place (e.g., all softballs together, all handballs together, all volleyballs together).

A teenage student prepares to do her family's laundry by sorting the clothes that go together (e.g., all dark clothes, light clothes, hand-washable clothes).

An adult male participates in the development of a grocery list for his group home by classifying necessary items according to the store classifications (e.g., dairy, fruits, vegetables, dry goods, bakery items, canned goods).

Sequencing Information

A young preschool student arranges the sequence of food items needed to make a salad for his family.

A teenage student verbally explains the sequence of the card game "UNO" to a nonhandicapped peer.

An adult male chambermaid sequences his job photo adaptation according to personal preference (e.g., make bed, clean toilet, clean sink, sweep, empty trash cans) before beginning his job.

Interpreting Information

A teenage male reads the sign "EMPLOYEES ONLY." Since he does not work at this fast-food restaurant, he decides to try another door.

A teenage male reads the sign: "EMPLOYEES ONLY." Since he does not work at this fast-food restaurant, he decides to try another door.

Am adult determines that he will need to catch bus number 6 on Normandie Avenue at 10:05 A.M. to get to his job site on time.

ysis of skills in a given area in order to determine the importance and relevancy of those skills. This analysis must include: what mathematics skills will be taught, how the skills will be taught, and, if necessary, how the skills and/or sequences will be adapted so that they are functional and meaningful for a given student. For example, in a junior high classroom, the following mathematics skills were identified as part of the instructional activities:

Table 12.4. Adaptations and appropriate mathematics skills

Adaptation/description	Math skill application	Example	Advantages	Disadvantages
Jig: Tray or other device that assists an individual to separate and count items	Counting Sorting Matching Sequencing One-to-one Correspondence	A young woman with severe handicaps collates cards at the American Red Cross using a tray with six sections to assist her in counting the correct number of cards to put in each envelope.	Allows individual to partially participate in activity.	Some jigs may not be portable and/or may not be appropriate for various materials.
Tally card: Card with lines or blocks on it that the individual marks or fills in upon completing a task, to assist him or her to keep track of work	Counting Sequencing One-to-one Correspondence Rationale Counting	An elementary age student with severe handicaps uses a tally card to assist him in counting bulletins to be given to each classroom.	Student does not have to know how to rationally count independently to participate in an activity.	Student may become prompt dependent. Need to fade system as appropriate.
Hand-held calculator: Electronic device with digital readout that enables an individual to perform mathematical computations	Computation Estimation	A young man with severe handicaps uses a calculator to determine if he has enough money for the groceries he has chosen. He enters the amount of money he is carrying (e.g., $20.00) and then subtracts each item.	Allows individual to participate in activities requiring computation skills with or without (additional) assistance from a nonhandicapped individual. Calculators are portable, nonintrusive and dignified, since nonhandicapped individuals use them also.	The individual must be taught specific strategies to check and recheck himself or herself, to ensure appropriate computation.
Coin cards: Small wallet or purse-size cards with amount of money represented on card (e.g., face of coins stamped on cards or drawn on cards)	One-to-one Correspondence More versus less Estimation Measurement Computation	A young girl uses her coin cards in her wallet to purchase a soft drink at McDonald's independently. She matches the actual coins needed (55¢) to the money card and puts the extra coins back into her wallet before giving the money to the cashier.	Allows student to purchase predetermined item independently. An inventory of the price of items must be completed prior to purchasing.	The actual amounts on coin cards will vary across environments and settings.

1. Standing second in line at assembly, as required
2. Identifying date on personal calendar
3. Identifying time to go to work
4. Collating 50 packages of school forms for the office
5. Counting out or matching coins on coin cards for lunch
6. Using calculator to determine price of supplies at store
7. Using time card to decide when breaktime is over at job site

Students with severe handicaps have demonstrated that they can acquire and utilize various mathematics skills, if these math skills are functional and meaningful for them. Williams, Brown, and Certo (1975) attempted to teach students with moderate and severe handicaps a variety of mathematics skills. Given the nature of the sequence used, the students acquired skills slowly and did not easily generalize or use these skills. As a result, the original mathematics sequence was adapted and skills were successfully taught using functional materials and activities.

Commercially available mathematics sequences may provide mathematics content. These sequences are typically divided into various components and skills and are arranged hierarchically. They provide important information regarding concept development. However, caution must be exercised when utilizing such sequences to develop mathematics content. Often, if the sequences are used in isolation to teach mathematics skills, the result is that the students are required to learn and master nonfunctional and chronological age–inappropriate tasks to which they have been artifically "matched."

A second method for generating mathematics content is to utilize an ecological inventory strategy. An ecological inventory strategy is an appropriate strategy that can be used to generate relevant and functional mathematics content. The steps for conducting an ecological inventory for mathematics content, according to Ford et al. (1977), are:

1. Delineate the curricular domains.
2. Delineate the environments.
3. Delineate the subenvironments.
4. Delineate the activities.
5. Inventory money concepts needed to perform the activities.
6. Inventory time concepts needed to perform the activities.
7. Inventory measurement concepts needed to perform the activities.
8. Inventory problem-solving skills needed to perform the activities.

Figure 12.1 provides an example of an ecological inventory. The inventory was conducted to determine the mathematics skills required for an elementary-age student with severe handicaps to participate in dinner preparation in his group home.

It is suggested that educators utilize the preceding two strategies and implement necessary modifications of them in order to generate appropriate and

Domain: Domestic
Environment: Group home
Subenvironment: Kitchen
Activity: Dinner preparation

Activity 1:	Planning dinner menu
Skill 1:	Determine meal (hamburgers, potato salad, beverage).
Skill 2:	Determine amount of food necessary.
Activity 2:	Meal preparation—potato salad
Skill 1:	Read recipe.
Skill 2:	Assemble ingredients; assemble utensils.
Skill 3:	Obtain 6 potatoes; put in water to boil.
Skill 4:	Set timer for 35 minutes.
Skill 5:	Cut onion in half; chop.
Skill 6:	Wash 3 stalks celery; cut in pieces about 3 inches long; chop.
Skill 7:	Peel cooled potatoes; cut in halfs, fourths, and eighths; put in bowl with celery and onion.
Skill 8:	Measure 4 tablespoons mayonnaise; measure ½ teaspoon pepper.
Skill 9:	Mix all ingredients together.

Figure 12.1. Example of an ecological inventory to delineate mathematics skills necessary for food preparation.

meaningful mathematics content. Based upon information derived from the ecological inventory strategy and from commercially available mathematics sequences, appropriate mathematics objectives and activities that will meet current and subsequent needs of the student can be developed. Table 12.5. provides a sequence of typical mathematics skills in conjunction with activities and materials across ages that can be used to inventory and teach these skills in various environments.

Students with severe handicaps represent a heterogeneous group of individuals with various abilities and needs. As is true across all curricular areas, educators must determine appropriate instructional methods and strategies for teaching mathematics content and skills to each student based upon that student's learning strategies. Chapter 4 of this volume provides a comprehensive discussion of various instructional approaches.

WRITING

Year after year, many students with severe handicaps have educational objectives that include at least one fine motor/handwriting skill. For example:

Alex will copy three basic shapes independently, 100% of the time.

Vanessa will write all of the letters in her first name legibly, and in accordance with the size of the paper, 100% of the time.

Nathan will address an envelope legibly, using cursive handwriting, 100% of the time.

Table 12.5. Sequence of typical mathematics skills and corresponding functional and chronological age–appropriate activities to inventory and teach these skills

Skill area	Preschool	Elementary	High school	Adult
Object manipulation	Pouring sand into containers	Putting groceries away	Playing game of checkers	Pushing cart through supermarket
Spatial and perceptual skills	Working on jigsaw puzzle	Looking at a magazine	Inserting coin in vending machine	Matching socks to wear
Classification/ categorization	Sorting toys to put away (e.g., all dolls, books, in separate piles)	Emptying dishwasher of utensils and sorting them into tray	Sorting clothes to be washed at the laundromat	Putting groceries back on appropriate shelves as part of work training
One-to-one correspondence	Passing out one cookie to each friend at snacktime	Setting table: putting one plate, one glass on each placemat	Matching appropriate number of coins to coin card adaptation to buy a soft drink	Dealing cards to players during game of "UNO"
More and less	Figuring out how many blocks to put on "SKY-SCRAPER" before it falls	Helping Dad water plants (e.g., not too much water)	Adjusting time schedule to ensure enough time to catch bus to YMCA	Determining amount of extra food needed for two more friends at dinner
Rote counting	Singing a number song (e.g., "One little, two little, three little Indians . . .")	Counting to 20 before finding friends in "Hide and Seek" game	Counting to 5 before playing drums in school band	Counting to 10 before saying anything when angry

Rational counting	Counting out six apples for friends during snacktime	Selecting and counting teams for baseball game	Counting correct number of chairs to set up for meeting at the library	Counting out correct number of donuts (12) to put in box for customer
Ordinal numbers	Waiting in line until it is your turn to jump rope	Playing game during recess (e.g., everyone who is third in line run to the wall)	Finding the end of the line at the movies	Determining the sequence of ingredients to use in a recipe (e.g., first peel the apples, second, cut apples, third, add mayonnaise)
Identifying numbers	Standing in line while teacher identifies second person to be ball monitor	Locating a new friend's house by reading his address	Writing today's date in personal diary	Recognizing price tag on shirt in department store
Computation	Playing dominoes with big brother	Keeping score at baseball game	Figuring cost of lunch at McDonald's Restaurant	Budgeting paycheck
Measurement; fractions; money; time	Helping Dad cut the pie into equal pieces for everyone	Helping Mom buy 2 pounds of apples in the grocery store	Determining how long the football game will last after school in order to tell Dad	Selecting the appropriate size of gift box for a customer's items
Estimation	Helping big sister figure out how many party favors to make for your birthday party	Estimating how far you can broad jump (e.g., 2 feet, 3 feet)	Deciding how much punch to make for the Halloween dance	Estimating how long it will take to get to your new job by bus

For those students whose chronological age matches the characteristics of the task, the preceding objectives may be appropriate. For example, it is chronological age appropriate for 4-year-old students to copy shapes, for 6-year-old students to write their names, and for 10-year-old students to address envelopes for a party invitation. For other students, who are faced year after year with nonfunctional chronological age-inappropriate tasks, adaptations in objectives, materials, and instruction must be developed. This section of the chapter focuses on the wide variety of functional and chronological age–appropriate writing activities and adaptations that are available for use with students with severe handicaps.

Before the educator selects specific writing activities and adaptations, several important issues must be considered. Traditionally, the issue of cursive writing (handwriting in which successive letters connect and the angles are rounded) versus manuscript writing (printing) and adaptations (computers and typewriters) has been given much attention. Several factors must be evaluated when deciding which strategies to teach and when to use them. First, the student who has indicated a particular preference or who has demonstrated greater proficiency with one system should be encouraged to use that system. The motor components for one system may be easier for a particular student to master than for another student. For example, a 13-year-old student may write more legibly when using cursive writing than when using manuscript writing. For this student, the characteristic stopping and starting inherent in manuscript writing interferes with the student's ability to write.

Second, the purpose of the activity for the student must be considered when determining the writing system. For example, for students who are not likely to use writing as a communication system, a manuscript writing system is preferred, since most words available in community environments appear in a printed form, thus allowing for generalization of the printed words and information.

A third issue that must be considered when determining a writing system is the use of typewriters and computers. For many students, typewriters and computers offer an alternative to more traditional methods of instruction and communication. For the student with multiple and physical handicaps who, because of motor involvement, is not able to communicate successfully using writing skills, computer software is available that allows the student to create, request, and communicate using one key. For another student who prefers not to communicate by means of paper and pencil, the use of a computer may be a motivating strategy to encourage and develop written communication skills.

Another major issue to consider when determining writing systems for students is the development and use of adaptations. As noted previously, adaptations may be made in instruction, materials, and objectives. In this section, adaptations are presented in terms of materials only. Table 12.6 lists writing

Table 12.6. Adaptations and appropriate writing skills

Adaptation/description	Writing skill application	Advantages
Adapted Credit Card: Cut a rectangle from the bottom third of a credit card to form a "frame" to help guide the individual in signing his or her name.	General writing skills; copying; tracing; and refining handwriting.	Credit card is portable and is used by nonhandicapped persons across many environments.
Business Card: Business cards printed with an individual's name and including important information (e.g., address, phone number, Social Security number, emergency information).	Appropriate to use as a substitute for writing skills for individuals for whom writing is not necessary or possible (e.g., those with physical limitations, illegible writing skills, no writing skills).	Business card allows individual with limited or no writing skills to communicate information to others; card is portable; and is used by nonhandicapped people across many environments.
Writing Stamp: Stamp printed with an individual's signature, name, address, or other important information.	Appropriate to use as a substitute for writing skills for individuals for whom writing is not necessary or possible (e.g., those with physical limitations, illegible writing skills, no writing skills).	Writing stamp allows individual with limited or no writing skills to communicate information to others; stamp is portable.

adaptations that can be used to teach students with severe handicaps of varying abilities.

Numerous writing activities may be developed and utilized by teachers to assist students with severe handicaps to acquire and/or refine writing skills. Table 12.7 lists examples of such activities across ages and curricular domains.

COMPUTER TECHNOLOGY

There are numerous ways that computer technology can be utilized in programs for students with severe handicaps. As previously suggested, technological advancements have enabled students with severe learning and motor difficulties to communicate needs, to express ideas, to interact with peers, and ultimately, to have an impact on their environments (Meyers, 1984). In this section, a review of the use of computers to assist students to learn and utilize skills, in particular functional academic skills, is presented.

Computer Managed Instruction

There are many ways that computers can be used in school programs. Computor managed instruction (CMI) can include tutorials, drill and practice, problem solving and evaluation, simulation and demonstration, remediation,

Table 12.7. Examples of functional writing activities across ages and curricular domains

Skill area	Preschool	Elementary	High school	Adult
General writing skills	Uses crayon to scribble; uses thin paintbrush; draws shapes with chalk	Uses pencil when attempting signatures; requires adaptation to stay on lines of paper; colors in art designs with felt markers	Requires adaptation to complete signature on passport; begins typewriter and computer use Puts on make up	Begins typewriter/ computer use
Tracing skills	Traces random letters in sandbox using forms; traces name on birthday card to Dad	Traces name onto letter using adaptation if necessary; traces numbers onto paper to form abstract design; traces address into personal directory	Traces name on hall pass sign-in/out sheet; traces abstract design onto paper in art class; traces shirt pattern onto fabric; uses template to make signs for art club	Continues typewriter/ computer use and application
Copying skills	Copies alphabet letters and numbers onto paper; copies big sister's spelling words at home	Copies "Daily Events" from chalkboard into personal calendar; copies party invitation onto invitations	Copies title of book onto library card to check it out; copies abstract pop designs onto school folder	Copies hours from time card to record in personal records; copies date into diary; copies favorite recipe to send to friend; copies a favorite song from record jacket; continues typewriter and computer use and application
Independent writing skills	Writes name on chalkboard during morning circle; writes name with finger paint during art period	Writes name on ball checkout sheet for after-school playground; records temperature data on class chart; keeps baseball scores at games; writes letter to relatives	Signs up for after-school dance; writes and sends "love-grams" on Valentine's Day; writes fan letter to Michael Jackson; signs yearbook at end of school year	Writes daily "happenings" in personal journal; develops grocery list; keeps score during card game; writes and sends holiday cards to relatives and friends; continues typewriter/computer use and application

word processing, and computer graphics and music. CMI can also be of assistance in testing, classroom management, and computer-assisted instruction (CAI). CMI can be of assistance in the development, administration, and analysis of test material. Computers may be utilized by educational personnel to assist in classroom management. For example, they can be used in record keeping, IEP planning and development, and in generating schedules for community-based instruction, homework assignments, data sheets, and curricular revisions.

CAI involves the use of computers to present instruction to students. The interaction between the computer and the student is designed to assist students to learn new concepts or to improve upon their knowledge of concepts previously learned (Chan, 1984). There are many advantages of CAI, including the following:

Provides immediate feedback and reinforcement
Allows for trial-and-error learning
Requires active responding
Utilizes and builds upon the learner's previous experiences
Provides students with some sense of control, and allows students to be decision makers
Facilitates self-pacing and individualization
Provides opportunities for student to student interaction and cooperative learning experiences
Allows students to be independent, that is, to learn and succeed without direct teacher intervention
Allows students to practice functional academic skills utilizing age-appropriate and high status equipment
Stimulates communication and self-expression
Motivates students to learn more quickly

CAI may assist educational personnel to develop and practice a variety of functional academic skills. In reading and math, CAI has been utilized to read survival signs, sequence items on grocery lists, and practice functional reading words. In writing, CAI can be use to compose letters to friends, type recipes, and develop signs and posters. In vocational and employment skill development, CAI can be used to practice keyboarding and data entry.

Computer Peripherals/Add-Ons

There are a variety of peripherals/add-ons to computers that facilitate more active and independent participation by students with severe handicaps. *Speech synthesizers,* for example, enable students to communicate more easily with others. Speech synthesizers make it possible for students to hear and "speak" information (either verbally or through augmentative communication devices) typed in at the keyboard, to hear digitized lessons, texts, and procedure prompts, and to send and receive electronic mail (banking and shopping) by voice over the phone (Bowe, 1984). A similar technology, *speech recognition,* allows the computer to "hear." This particular technology is especially useful for those individuals with severe physical or motor impairments who may experience difficulty manipulating the keyboard. Utilizing speech recognition technology, computers are capable of recognizing and responding to a few hundred words, usually words spoken by a single person (Bowe, 1984). Those having difficulty manipulating the standard computer keyboard can use specialized keyboards and switches that make the microcomputer available to the student with severe handicaps (Meyers, 1984). *Emulators,* or alternative devices for entering the information into the computer, make the computer "think" that its own keyboard is being used; in effect, the peripheral product is activated by the student, who in turn, activates the keyboard (Bowe, 1984). Examples of such emulators include: joysticks, paddles, power pads, manual switches, light pens, mouth sticks, tongue switches, and pneumatic puff and sip switches. *Keyboard modifications,* such as keyguards, provide holes over the keys so that other keys are not accidentally struck. Finally, a *printer* attached to the computer makes printed paper copy available to the student who may have difficulty with traditional writing implements. A printed copy provides immediate reinforcement to the student, and allows him or her to communicate information, for example, in response to questions in a social science class.

Considerations for Selecting Software

Educational personnel have a wealth of software programs available. Various software programs allow nonreaders to "read" text on the monitor screen using synthesized voice output, and to make the keyboard "talk," thus providing an opportunity for the user to create written language by talking. It is critical that teachers and families consider the following characteristics as guidelines in the selection of software and peripherals. These considerations are adapted from Dutton (1987):

1. Is it chronological age appropriate for the student?
2. Is it motivating and fun for the student?
3. Is it appropriate as a recreation-leisure or interaction activity with nonhandicapped peers?
4. Does it empower the student to do something he or she needs to do, or enjoys doing, more independently (or better or faster) than before?
5. Does it promote decision making?
6. Does it allow the student to take control of the goal of the activity, the strategy to reach the goal, or both?
7. Will it help the student to engage in real work, now or in the future?
8. Are there appropriate cues for the student?
9. Is it adaptable? Can the teacher, parent, or student adapt it to meet individual needs?

10. Is it easy for student *and* teacher to use?
11. Is it challenging enough to be interesting but not so challenging that it is frustrating?

Computer Assisted Cooperative Interaction and Learning

Computers may provide opportunities for students with severe handicaps and their nonhandicapped peers to interact with one another while they learn skills. However, Johnson and Johnson (1986) have suggested that such interactions are often a neglected component of CAI. There are at least three basic ways that students may interact with one another while using the computer. First, students can compete with each other to determine who is "best" at a particular skill or game. Second, students can work individually toward goals, sitting side by side. Finally, students can work cooperatively toward a goal with an interest in their own learning as well as their partner's learning (Johnson & Johnson, 1986). Cooperative learning strategies are effective in assisting educational personnel to meet the wide variety of curricular needs present in students with severe handicaps. They are also effective in fostering positive social relationships between students with severe handicaps and their nonhandicapped peers (Falvey, Coots, Bishop, & Grenot-Scheyer, 1989; Johnson & Johnson, 1986).

While traditional educational curricula have focused on individualistic or competitive learning experiences, cooperative learning is characterized by positive interdependence, individual accountability, and heterogeneous groupings (Falvey et al., in press; Johnson & Johnson, 1986). (For a more detailed discussion of cooperative learning see Chapter 13 of this volume.) Often, students with severe handicaps who are skilled in the use of computers can provide inservice training to nonhandicapped peers regarding the use of the computer's software.

SUMMARY

This chapter presents a framework for selecting functional academic content as well as a delineation of reading, writing, and mathematics skills that are required across various environments and curricular domains. Specific information regarding sequences, instructional strategies, adaptations, materials, and information regarding the use of computer technology is provided to assist the educator in developing appropriate educational programs for students with severe handicaps.

REFERENCES

Baumgart, D., Brown, L., Pumpian, I., Nisbet, J., Ford, A., Sweet, M., Messina, R., & Schroeder, J. (1982). The principle of partial participation and individualized adaptations in educational programs for severely handicapped students. *Journal of The Association for the Severely Handicapped, 7*(2), 17–27.

Bowe, F. (1984, October). Micros and special education. *Popular Computing*, (pp. 121–128.

Browder, D.M., & Snell, M.E. (1987). Functional academics. In M.E. Snell (Ed.), *Systematic instruction of persons with severe handicaps* (3rd ed., pp. 436–468). Columbus, OH: Charles E. Merrill.

Brown, L., Branston, M.B., Hamre-Nietupski, S., Pumpian, I., Certo, N., & Gruenewald, L. (1979). A strategy for developing chronological age appropriate and functional curricular content for severely handicapped adolescents and young adults. *Journal of Special Education, 13*(1), 81–90.

Brown, L., Neitupski, J., & Hamre-Nietupski, S. (1976). The criterion of ultimate functioning and public school services for severely handicapped students. In M.A. Thomas (Ed.), *Hey, don't forget about me! Education's investment in the severely, profoundly and multiply handicapped* (pp. 2–15). Reston, Virginia: Council for Exceptional Children.

Chan, Y. (1984). *Uses of microcomputers in schools.* Unpublished manuscript, Los Angeles Unified School District, Los Angeles.

Duffy, G.G., & Sherman, G.B. (1973). *How to teach reading systematically.* New York: Harper & Row.

Dutton, D. (1987). *Food for thought while selecting software and peripherals for students with severe handicaps.* Unpublished manuscript, Computer Access Center, Santa Monica.

Falvey, M.A., & Anderson, J. (1983). Prioritizing curricular content. In A. Donnellan, J. Anderson, L. Brown, M. Falvey, G. LaVigna, L. Marcus, R. Mesaros, P. Mirenda, G. Olley, & L. Schuler (Eds.), *National Society for Children and Adults with Autism: National Personnel Training,* (Module 3). Unpublished manuscript.

Falvey, M.A., Coots, J., Bishop, K., & Grenot-Scheyer, M. (1989). In W. Stainback, S. Stainback, & M. Forest (Eds.), *Educating all children in the mainstream of regular education.* Baltimore: Paul H. Brookes Publishing Co.

Ford, A., Huppler, B., Marks, J., Scheuerman, N., Swetlick, B., Van Deventer, P., & Wheeler, J. (1977). *Curriculum outlines of reading, phonics, penmanship, math, money and time for the moderately retarded.* Unpublished manuscript, Madison Metropolitan School District, Madison, WI.

Hall, M.A. (1976). *Teaching reading as a language experience* (2nd ed.). Columbus, OH: Charles E. Merrill.

Johnson, D.W., & Johnson, R.T. (1986, January). Computer-assisted cooperative learning. *Educational Technology,* pp. 12–18.

Johnson, F. (1982). Strategies to delineate related skill components of specific activities within subenvironments of specific environments. Unpublished manuscript, University of Wisconsin at Madison.

Meyers, L.F. (1984). Unique contributions of micro-computers to language intervention with handicapped children. *Seminars in Speech and Language, 5*(1), 23–34.

Piernok, F. T. (1979). Using basal guide books—the ideal integrated lesson plan. *Reading Teacher, 3*(2), 167–172.

Snell, M.E. (1978). Functional reading. In M.E. Snell (Ed.), *Systematic instruction of the moderately and severely handicapped* (1st ed., pp. 324–390). Columbus, OH: Charles E. Merrill.

Snell, M.E. (1983). Functional reading. In M.E. Snell (Ed.), *Systematic instruction of the moderately and severely handicapped* (2nd ed., pp. 445–487). Columbus, OH: Charles E. Merrill.

Williams, W., Brown, L., & Certo, N. (1975). Basic components of instructional programs. *Theory Into Practice, 14*(2), 123–136.

THIRTEEN

INTEGRATION ISSUES AND STRATEGIES

Marquita Grenot-Scheyer, Jennifer Coots, and Mary A. Falvey

LEGAL IMPETUS FOR integrating students with severe handicaps with their nonhandicapped peers is mandated by Public Law 94-142, the Education for All Handicapped Children Act of 1975, and its amendments (PL 99-457, the Education of the Handicapped Amendments of 1986). These landmark legislative actions require that students with handicaps must be educated with their nonhandicapped peers, to the maximum extent appropriate, in the least restrictive environment.

Ultimately, however, the concept of least restrictive environment must extend beyond school walls. Nonhandicapped adults live, work, and recreate in heterogeneous environments, relying upon members of their community for various types of assistance. This "interdependence" may take many forms. For example, relying on a neighbor for a ride to the doctor's office when one is ill, requesting assistance from a librarian to fill out a library card, depending upon the neighborhood grocer to deliver groceries when the weather is inclement, or hiring a neighborhood girl to trim one's grass are all illustrations of nonhandicapped individuals' reliance on neighbors and community members. If students with severe handicaps are to become interdependent and productive members of their community, it is crucial that they and their nonhandicapped peers learn to function together throughout their educational years (Brown, Nietupski, & Hamre-Nietupski, 1976; Voeltz, 1983). Individuals with and without severe handicaps must be provided with opportunities to develop the skills and attitudes that are critical for successful interactions both now and in the future.

In the first section of this chapter, definitions and categories of integration are delineated; a description of the various types of interactions that can and should occur between students with and without severe handicaps is also provided. In the second section, frequently cited barriers to integration, and strategies to overcome such barriers, are described. In the final section of this chapter, the changing role of the special education teacher is examined, and curricular strategies for facilitating integrated educational opportunities for all students are discussed.

DEFINITIONS OF INTEGRATION

The definitions of such terms as: "least restrictive environment," "integration," and "mainstreaming" have developed, evolved, and changed as individuals with severe handicaps have been provided the right and opportunity to utilize their communities. However, there are still places in this country where educational placement is not based upon where one lives but, rather, based upon disability without regard for educational needs. This has generally resulted in segregated educational settings that are located long distances from home. More and more students with severe handicaps and their families are compelling school administrators to provide appropriate educational services in neighborhood schools and communities (Stainback, Stainback, & Forest, 1989). However, there are regional discrepancies that exist in service delivery for students with severe handicaps. For example, in a survey conducted in 1987, California educated approximately 57% of students with severe handicaps at segregated "special" centers that did not include nonhandicapped students (California Research Institute, 1987). In Virginia, 33% of students with severe handicaps were educated on segregated sites, 33% were educated on separate/secluded sites adjacent to regular education facilities, and 33% were educated within site locations common to regular education classes (Roth & Nardi, 1987). In Vermont, only 5% of the students with severe handicaps were educated on segregated sites, while 95% of students with severe handicaps were educated in integrated public schools. Currently, plans are being made in Vermont to increase the number of students in integrated settings to 100% (Williams et al., 1986). These contrasting data support the contention that geographic location, rather than educational need, often determines the restrictiveness of educational placements for students with severe handicaps.

Previously, integration was defined as placement into regular education sites with opportunities for interaction, while mainstreaming generally referred to placement in general education programs (Grenot-Scheyer & Falvey, 1986). But a new vision of integration and mainstreaming that allows all students with severe handicaps to be educated within their communities and neighborhood schools has emerged. As Biklen and Knoll (1987) have suggested, educational programs and services must be pluralistic and must avoid the exclusion that has characterized programs and services for so many years. Traditionally, students have been excluded from services because they did not meet certain criteria, or because services were provided in such a manner as to disregard the "whole" person. This practice of exclusion and compartmentalization of persons resulted in services that did not effectively meet the total needs of persons with severe handicaps (Biklen & Knoll, 1987).

School integration is defined here as placement in age-appropriate neighborhood or community schools and classrooms. The simplicity of this definition conceals the complexity inherent in providing appropriate educational services and support for students with severe handicaps. However, there are numerous instances across the United States wherein families, educators, administrators, and others have demonstrated their willingness and ability to design educational programs and services that provide optimal learning environments. Such programs and services truly meet the spirit and intent of the least restrictive environment mandate of PL 94-142 (Stainback et al., 1989; Taylor, 1982; Taylor, Biklen, & Knoll, 1987).

CATEGORIES OF INTEGRATION

The definition of integration can be further clarified by reviewing levels of integration that are typically found within programs providing integrated services to students with severe handicaps. The levels of integration identified by the Iowa State Department of Instruction are an integral component of that state's position statement regarding interaction opportunities (Benton, 1985). The proposal suggests that interaction opportunities between students with and without severe handicaps must reflect at least the following levels in order to provide a full range of interaction opportunities for all students:

1. **Physical Integration** Students with severe handicaps should attend school with their nonhandicapped peers on age-appropriate neighborhood or community school sites. For maximal interaction opportunities, instruction should occur in regular education classrooms, nonclassroom settings, and in home and community settings. Some examples are: pre-school-age children with severe handicaps attend programs at their local daycare center; elementary-age children with severe handicaps attend their neighborhood elementary school; adults with severe handicaps work and live in communities of their choice.
2. **Functional Integration** Integration opportunities should include the concurrent use of school facilities and resources by students with and without severe handicaps. Some examples are: changing in the locker room for physical education class; checking out a book from the library; passing in

the hallway; purchasing a school pin at the student store; eating lunch in the cafeteria together.

3. **Social Integration** This type of integration allows for interactions between students with and without severe handicaps. In addition to the opportunities provided by functional integration, social integration allows for the development of age-appropriate social and communication skills and friendships with a wide variety of people. Some examples are: attending a school dance with friends; playing in the school band together; completing an art mural for the front office with students from one's homeroom; making holiday cookies together.
4. **Societal Integration** This type of integration allows for the development of support systems to assist persons to become active, contributing members of their communities. It requires systematic planning and effort so that students with severe handicaps can ultimately work, live, and recreate alongside nonhandicapped citizens. Examples of such efforts include: development of a transition program to provide vocational opportunities in the community; utilization of the local community college campus by adults with severe handicaps; living opportunities within normalized community settings for citizens with severe handicaps.

TYPES OF INTERACTIONS

In addition to providing for a full range of integration opportunities, educators must systematically facilitate interactions between students with and without severe handicaps in order to maximize the benefits of integration. If the goal of education for students is lifelong integration, then it is necessary for students to have opportunities to interact with one another. Following are definitions of the various types of interactions based upon the work of Hamre-Nietupski, Branston, Ford, Gruenewald, and Brown (1978):

1. **Proximal interactions** are interactions during which sensory contact is made between a student with severe handicaps and a nonhandicapped student. Examples include: collating papers in the school office side by side, sitting next to each other in class, and using the same bathroom facilities.
2. **Helping interactions** are interactions in which a student voluntarily provides direct assistance or instruction to another student. Examples include: pushing a friend in a wheelchair to his or her next period, being a "buddy" during morning circle in preschool, instructing a friend in the use of a new woodworking tool, and showing a friend how to use the latest pocket calculator game. It is critical to the self-concept and self-esteem of both the students with and without severe handicaps that each have an opportunity to help and be helped.
3. **Service interactions** are interactions in which direct services are provided

to another person as part of one's job responsibilities. Examples of such interactions include: requesting and receiving assistance from the store manager, receiving assistance from a school crossing safety guard, and following the instructions of a teacher on school yard duty.

4. **Reciprocal interactions** are interactions in which students with and without severe handicaps benefit from the experience or activity. Typically, these types of interactions are not service-oriented or of a helping nature. Rather, they provide opportunities for students to learn from each other about one another. Each student makes a contribution to the interaction or activity. Examples include: completing a cooking activity together, playing a computer game together, listening to favorite records together, and attending a soccer game with classmates.

INTEGRATION BARRIERS AND STRATEGIES

Individuals who are working toward the full integration of persons with severe handicaps into schools and communities often encounter barriers to their efforts in the areas of attitudes, fiscal, and logistical constraints, and accessibility. Families, educators, administrators, researchers, and community members involved in providing integrated educational opportunities have identified specific strategies to use in overcoming or avoiding such barriers. In this section, barriers to integrating are discussed, and successful strategies that may be employed in overcoming such barriers are delineated.

Attitudinal Issues

Resistance to integration may be due to the perception that students with severe handicaps will be teased, isolated, and/or exploited by peers, will be exposed to social and emotional harm, and may suffer from lack of opportunities to socialize with "their own kind" (Brown et al., 1979). Other fears that hinder integration include the concerns that the educational programs of the nonhandicapped students may suffer, and that regular education programs may not effectively meet the needs of the students with severe handicaps (Brown et al., 1979).

The response to these attitudinal barriers to integration may be approached from two perspectives. First, the human cost of segregating individuals with severe handicaps is too great if the ultimate goal of education is to facilitate the development of contributing citizens. Secondly, there is a growing body of empirical data that suggests integration is beneficial; it fosters positive attitude changes, provides communication and social interaction opportunities, and introduces age-appropriate models of behaviors and skills (Anderson, 1983; Certo & Kohl, 1984; Coots, 1985; Falvey, 1980; Gaylord-Ross & Pitts-Conway, 1984; Guralnick & Paul-Brown, 1980; Meyer & Kishi, 1985; Ragland, Kerr, & Strain, 1978; Stainback & Stainback, 1981, 1985; Strain, 1983; Strain, Kerr, & Ragland, 1979). There are no empirical data to support the notion that students with severe handicaps and their nonhandicapped peers will be harmed educationally, emotionally, or physically when allowed to attend school together. On the contrary, with adequate planning and support, integration benefits students with and without severe handicaps.

Specific strategies to overcome attitudinal barriers include the following recommendations:

1. If students with severe handicaps are to be expected to function effectively in heterogeneous community environments in the future, as many **preceding experiences** as possible should be conducted in heterogeneous community environments (Brown et al., 1976). Examples include: attending school together, participating in the same scout troops, attending camp together, participating in the same after-school programs, and "hanging out" in the same settings in the community.
2. **Advance preparation** is crucial for successful integration efforts. Sufficient time should be allotted to develop well planned and comprehensive integration. In the past, the "dump and hope" method was used repeatedly; the obvious shortcomings of this method have been consistently demonstrated.
3. **Task forces** organized to plan integration efforts, activities, and timeliness should include members of all groups affected by integration. Students, family members, special and regular education teachers, administrators, facilities and transportation representatives, and related services staff should be included. In this manner, all persons can be involved, have input, assist in problem solving, and gain information, so that the decisions that are made meet all concerns from the beginning of the process.
4. It is recommended that **credible and committed staff and administrators** be selected to implement the integration plan. Critical to successful integration efforts is a sense of "ownership" and a belief that the students with severe handicaps are an essential part of the larger student body population and not simply the responsibility of the special education staff. Special education teachers involved in the integration plan should exhibit the following characteristics: a desire to make the transition to a new site, good interpersonal skills, good instructional capabilities, and the ability to share their enthusiasm toward integration with others.
5. **Inservice training sessions** should be conducted before integration occurs. Such sessions should take place on an ongoing basis for parents, significant others, teachers, administrators, and students. Inservice training can provide factual information and opportunities for individuals to develop awareness of, and appreciation for, individual differences. Negative attitudes are often a result of inaccurate or missing information (Stainback & Stainback, 1982). Therefore, informal and formal inservices or opportunities to share accurate information should be provided. Visits to regular

school sites that take place before the move from a segregated site occurs can also alleviate concerns and provide information.

Fiscal and Logistical Issues

Logistical and fiscal barriers regarding the "how to" of providing integrated educational services arise out of concerns regarding higher operating and transportation costs and costs attributed to the decentralization of related services (e.g., speech therapy, physical therapy, adaptive physical education, orientation and mobility, and nursing services). Additional fiscal and logistical barriers include availability of space on regular education campuses and the use of existing segregated sites.

In 1985, Piuma conducted a study of four classrooms in a northern California school program to determine the cost differential in the provision of integrated and segregated educational programs. Piuma found that it cost 8.4% less to educate students on an integrated site than to educate students on a segregated site. The costs involved in transporting students with severe handicaps to centralized locations, often at great distances from their homes, are great. Such costs could be reduced by placing students with severe handicaps in their neighborhood schools. Many of these students could also make use of the transportation services offered to nonhandicapped students who are attending the same school; this would avoid the cost of duplicating transportation services within a district. An additional difficulty involved in transporting students to centralized, segregated locations concerns medical needs. Students who have severe handicaps may have medical difficulties that make long bus rides difficult.

In response to the inefficiency involved in decentralizing related services, recent research has questioned the effectiveness of centralized service delivery. Traditionally, therapy or other ancillary services for students with severe handicaps have been artificial, isolated, and episodic (Bishop & Falvey, 1986; Rainforth & York, 1987; Sternat, Messina, Nietupski, Lyon, & Brown, 1977). Research has demonstrated that students with severe handicaps do not easily transfer or generalize the skills learned in isolated therapy situations to the environments and activities that demand such skills (Donnellan & Mirenda, 1983; Falvey, Brown, Lyon, Baumgart, & Schroeder, 1980; Warren, Rogers-Warren, Baer, & Guess, 1980). Therefore, related services should be conducted in the natural contexts within which the skills will be needed. This requires the use of a decentralized model of service delivery (Campbell, 1987; Gee, Harrell, & Rosenberg, 1987; Goetz & Gee, 1987).

Specific recommendations to address fiscal and logistical concerns include the following:

1. Carefully and thoroughly **analyze cost differences** so the data can be used to illustrate to those involved the actual costs of integrated settings.
2. Allot **sufficient time** to develop plans and strategies to effect the transition

of students to integrated environments. The task force approach can assist participants regarding the appropriate use of district financial resources. District transportation and facilities representatives, knowledgeable about current district practices and resources, can assist in optimal utilization of resources while ensuring a maximum amount of integration.

3. An **integrated therapy model** for the provision of related services should be utilized (Heron & Harris, 1987; Rainforth & York, 1987; Sternat et al., 1977). Many school districts have encouraged their related services personnel to provide services to students utilizing an integrated therapy or consultation model rather than using a direct service model exclusively (Heron & Harris, 1987). Utilizing the integrated therapy model, related services staff guide, model, and instruct teachers, family members, aides, bus drivers, and others, to directly provide the intervention while engaging in a functional activity. This allows the student to practice necessary skills more frequently in natural contexts. Proper planning and coordination of personnel can ensure that utilization of this model does not result in a lessening of services. (See Chapter 3 of this volume for a more detailed discussion concerning the integration of basic skills into functional activities. For a discussion of the utilization of an integrated therapy model, see Chapter 10 of this volume.)
4. Carefully examine where additional services are required and **reassign existing related services staff**. For example, nursing services for medically fragile students can be provided by reassigning nurses from segregated sites to the integrated sites that are attended by the students who are medically fragile. In schools, city emergency services personnel (e.g., paramedics) can be used as needed, just as they would on the segregated site. Other services can be provided by assigning related services staff to several schools so that they distribute their services equally among the students at those sites.
5. A **plan for the effective use of school space** should be developed with input from district personnel and facilities personnel. Strategies for locating space on regular campuses could include using underenrolled school sites, school sites with supportive/committed administrative and/or teaching staff, and neighborhood schools. In addition, developing fiscally responsible and educationally sound plans for segregated school building usage is critical. Strategies and plans that have been developed and used by several different school districts include converting segregated schools into regular neighborhood schools or "magnet" schools used by students with and without handicaps, and using the site as a preschool setting for serving students with and without handicaps. Additional strategies include: using the school site for adult education classes for members of the community, using the site for school district office space, or selling the building and using the profits to upgrade other schools within the district.

Individual school district plans must be developed to consider the current and projected demographics of the community.

Accessibility Issues

Although a legal imperative exists that requires accessibility to public places (Section 504 of the Rehabilitation Act of 1973), an argument used to maintain segregated sites is that of inaccessibility of regular education campuses. Limited accessibility to special education curricular resources and special education personnel support are also cited as reasons to maintain segregated sites.

There are several responses to these barriers. First, the law (Section 504 of the Rehabilitiation Act of 1973) clearly prohibits excluding students with any handicaps from attending a regular education campus or classroom on the basis of their handicap. Second, not all students with severe handicaps require barrier-free environments. Third, the reorganization of resources can often benefit all concerned.

Specific strategies that assist in addressing accessibility issues include the following:

1. **Sufficient time** must be allotted to plan integration efforts so that sites can be modified to be as accessible as necessary in an effective and efficient manner. In order to make the best use of existing facilities, it is critical to have input from district personnel knowledgeable about facilities.
2. **Determine which students require barrier-free environments** when identifying regular education sites. All students should be provided with opportunities to practice and learn to traverse naturally occurring barriers across a variety of environments, no matter what their motor abilities are, or what adaptive equipment they use for mobility. For example, a student who has multiple handicaps including muscular dystrophy may need to develop stair climbing abilities when he moves to an integrated site that features many stairs. He will have many opportunities to develop those skills in a natural context once he has moved to the site. However, installation of ramps or elevators will be critical for his long-term success at the school site.
3. Special education **resources can be made available** on regular education sites. One medium sized district reassigned a special education resource teacher who had been assigned to the segregated site, to three integrated sites (two junior highs and one senior high) where students with severe handicaps attended. This resource teacher assisted in making resources available to the special education teachers. By rethinking the division of resources, districts can develop plans that effectively make the best use of resources to the benefit of all students without duplication of efforts. For example, the segregated site may have a wealth of computer resources while the integrated site does not. These resources can be made available

to students with and without handicaps by dividing them among the integrated sites.

4. Special education and regular education staff can **provide assistance** to each other as needed to facilitate the integration process. Special educators may be able to assist regular education teachers in individualizing curriculum or in designing behavioral intervention programs for students who are having difficulty in regular education classes. The special educator may need to provide information through inservice training regarding the goals and objectives of the special education program, just as the regular educator may provide information to the special educator on the protocol and rules of the regular education school. The regular education teacher can also assist the special education teacher in working with large groups, in learning about the school community, in working with the parent teacher association, and in becoming familiar with the scope and sequence of the district curriculum.

TEACHER STRATEGIES FOR FACILITATING INTERACTION

As the special education teacher is often responsible for the day-to-day interaction between students with and without severe handicaps, several strategies specific to teachers are delineated here. Specifically, teacher roles and responsibilities in addition to curricular strategies and considerations are discussed.

Roles and Responsibilities

Special education teachers at integrated sites can serve in a variety of roles, each of which may affect the amount and type of interaction opportunities that are provided to their students. The setting most familiar to special education teachers is that of a *self-contained special education classroom*. In this situation, the teacher has primary responsibility for planning and implementing curriculum and instruction to meet student needs. Such needs include interaction opportunities. The difficulty with providing interaction opportunities for students with severe handicaps in a self-contained special education classroom is that the interaction opportunities are invariably intermittent, as nonhandicapped peers spend the majority of their day in regular education classes. Teachers must keep in mind that successful integration efforts depend upon frequent, regularly scheduled, and systematic interaction opportunities.

Team teaching arrangements developed between regular education and special education teachers can be used effectively to meet student educational needs while maximizing opportunities for interactions. In this model, students previously served exclusively by the special education teacher are placed in age-appropriate regular education classrooms in natural proportions. Specifically, the percentage of students with disabilities in any one classroom would reflect the percentage of people with disabilities in the general community. The regular and special educator would then share curriculum and instruction responsibilities. The strengths of each teacher are then available to all students, and the teachers themselves are able to share and learn from each other (Falvey, Coots, Bishop, & Grenot-Scheyer, 1989). Through teaming, teachers can arrange student groupings that maximize the benefits of heterogeneity, so that students with differing abilities work to assist and learn from each other. In addition, students can be encouraged to learn from each other through interaction by employing group and cooperative learning strategies (Johnson & Johnson, 1981; Johnson, Johnson, Warring, & Maruyama, 1986; Yager, Johnson, Johnson, & Snider, 1985). For a more detailed discussion of cooperative learning strategies, see Chapter 14 of this volume.

Other special educators have become *consultant teachers* who bring their particular expertise to the learning situation for all students (Falvey et al., 1989). In this model, the students typically served by the special education teacher are placed into age-appropriate regular education classes and are provided with consultant services as required for those educational needs not met by the standard curriculum. Consultant services can be delivered in a direct or indirect manner to both regular education and special education students and teachers (Heron & Harris, 1987). For example, a computer consultant (formerly, this might have been a special education teacher with expertise in computers) developed and facilitated an interactive lesson on the computer among several junior high school students. This activity provided an age-appropriate opportunity to work on initiation skills within a peer group for all of the students, including a student with autism. In another example, the community-based instruction consultant (formerly, this might have been a special education teacher with expertise in community-based instruction), provided direct instruction to students in natural community environments. By carefully planning instructional opportunities while employing a consultant model, the individual education needs of all students can be met while maximizing interaction opportunities.

The degree to which students are integrated depends in part upon the role of the special education teacher. As educational systems continue to move toward full integration, teachers must adapt and expand their expectations and roles in order to maximize interaction between students with and without severe handicaps. School responsibilities that teachers have found helpful to fulfill in order to facilitate integration have included:

1. Sharing in the school duties and responsibilities such as recess duty
2. Becoming involved in school activities such as the Parent Teacher Association
3. Meeting with the regular education teachers and having an open door policy to encourage sharing information with teachers
4. Observing school protocol

Curricular Strategies

In order to maximize the benefits of integration, interaction opportunities must occur frequently, at regularly scheduled times, and in a systematic manner. In this section, strategies teachers may employ in developing interaction opportunities are presented.

In any integration effort, it is important to identify and *inventory chronological age–appropriate activities*. The regular education staff can be excellent resources for identifying chronological age–appropriate activities that students engage in during the school day. Furthermore, school rules regarding such matters as dress codes, types of music, types of games played during recess, behaviors exhibited during free time, and appropriate classroom set-up and decoration must be identified. Nonhandicapped peers can also provide input into these areas of concern. Figure 13.1 provides an example of an ecological inventory of the activities in which students engage during recess at an elementary school.

A time analysis approach to conducting ecological inventories of chrono-

Domain: Recreation/leisure
Environment: Regular education elementary school
Subenvironment: Playground

Activity 1: Playing 4-Square

1. Locate 4-Square area.
2. Stand in line appropriately; move up in line.
3. When turn comes up, move into appropriate square.
4. Bounce ball to partner, receive ball from partner.
5. Continue playing until you miss a ball or bounce ball outside square.
6. Stand in line appropriately; move up in line.

Activity 2: Jumping Rope

1. Locate jump rope area.
2. Stand in line appropriately; move up in line.
3. When turn comes up, jump rope.
4. Continue jumping rope until you miss or until end of song.
5. Take turn, turning rope; continue until it is someone else's turn.
6. Stand in line appropriately; move up in line.

Activity 3: "Hanging Out"

1. Locate group of friends.
2. Stand or sit with friends.
3. Talk with friends appropriately.
4. Look "cool" (hands down, appropriate gestures).
5. Continue until bell rings.

Figure 13.1. Example of an ecological inventory of recess activities for elementary-age students.

logical age–appropriate activities can be used to determine appropriate interaction opportunities. This information serves as a basis for developing integration activities. The steps involved in a time analysis approach to conducting ecological inventories include: delineating all the naturally occurring time periods during the day (e.g., before school, passing each other in the hall, recess, nutrition, lunch); delineating all of the chronological age–appropriate activities that occur during these time periods; delineating the skills necessary to participate in these activities. A more detailed discussion of the strategies for conducting ecological inventories is provided in Chapter 3 of this volume.

If the long-range goal is full integration, then teachers must *identify and plan for the interaction opportunities* that occur frequently throughout the course of a day. In the past, integration often occurred only during planned programs, such as "Special Friends at Lunch" or during weekly games in the special education classroom. Unfortunately, reliance on special programs to facilitate interactions may only increase beliefs that students with severe handicaps are different; the result may be that persons may not be interacting with these students during the course of a day. The goal of planned integration efforts is for students with severe handicaps to be members of regular education schools and classrooms. Additionally, students with severe handicaps should have opportunities to engage in all activities with classmates relying upon naturally occurring support systems, such as friends, and should have the benefit of support from specialized consultants and teachers, as needed.

While working toward this goal, teachers may need to *plan specific integration opportunities* that will assist students to become acquainted. Such opportunities will also help students to learn about and value their similarities and differences, and subsequently help them to develop friendships. When scheduling integration opportunities, special educators should be knowledgeable about the regular school. Regular education teachers may be more willing to participate in integration activities if the activities occur at convenient times. These scheduling issues may differ greatly between individual teachers. For example, one third-grade teacher may want assistance with her Physical Education program in the afternoon, while a second-grade teacher may want a portion of his class to participate in an activity supervised by the special education teacher during morning reading time. Similarly, the woodshop teacher may be more willing to have students with severe handicaps participate in the fifth-period Basic Woodworking class, rather than in the third-period Advanced Design Class. Table 13.1 delineates successful integration activities implemented by teachers both in special and regular education classrooms across ages.

Integration opportunities can and should be used to teach, maintain, and generalize skills that nonhandicapped students are learning. For example, a nonhandicapped student who is having difficulty with mathematic skills participates in grocery shopping with students with severe handicaps. This pro-

Table 13.1. Successful integration activities implemented in special and regular education classrooms.

Elementary	High school	Adult
Cooking →	→	→
Opening →		
	Homeroom →	
Nutrition/snack/lunch →	→	→
School and community libraries →	→	→
Computers →	→	→
Peer tutoring →	→	→
Student council/student recognition →	→	
Safety patrol →	→	
Field trips →	→	
Physical education/aerobics →	→	→
Arts and crafts →	→	→
Playground games →	School sports →	
Recesses/breaks →	→	→
Special festivals/parties →	→	→
Work sites (i.e., cafeteria, grounds, office maintenance) →	→	→
Assemblies, special programs →	→	
Music/dances →	→	→
Boys Scouts, Eagle Scouts, Girl Scouts, etc. →		
Making student movies, tapes, and so forth →	→	→
	Classes at community colleges →	→
	Wood shop, metal shop, auto mechanics, vocational classes, home economics, driver training, and so forth →	→
	Yearbook, pep rallies →	
	Gym assistants →	→
Church groups →	→	→
Youth clubs →	→	
Participating in Little League →	→	
	Coaching and/or assisting in Little League →	→
After School programming at YMCA, YWCA, and so forth →	→	→
		Day and night programming at YWCA, YMCA, and so forth
	Work at Head Start →	→
	Competitive training and employment →	→

(continued)

Table 13.1. *(continued)*

Elementary	High school	Adult
Home recreational activities: TV, radio, reading, drawing, and so forth →	→	→
Community recreation activities: bowling, movies, shopping, browsing, video arcades, gym, parks, pools, beach, and so forth →	→	→
Community activities: laundromats, grocery stores, restaurants, banks, and so forth →	→	→
	Assist with mailings for political campaigns, and so forth →	→
	Volunteer work (i.e., Red Cross, child care, hospitals, and so forth) →	→

vides him with the opportunity to practice his mathematics skills in a functional manner. The same student also provides a model for age-appropriate social interaction behaviors for the students with severe handicaps.

Selecting Appropriate Integration Opportunities

When *selecting appropriate integration opportunities*, several issues should be considered. Following is a discussion of these issues.

Select Activities that Enhance the Student's Abilities and Self-Image Integration opportunities should be selected and designed so as to enhance the abilities of students with severe handicaps, rather than highlighting their disabilities. For example, a group of students with severe handicaps had the opportunity to acquire cooking skills in their school program while their nonhandicapped peers had not. The students with severe handicaps taught and demonstrated their skills to nonhandicapped students. In addition to highlighting abilities, the activities that are selected should maintain the students' dignity. Situations in which nonhandicapped students participate in activities such as feeding and toileting, for example, should generally be avoided, as this would likely violate the right of the student with disabilities to dignified interactions. Identifying activities that demonstrate abilities and skills valued by society are critical for integration efforts.

Emphasize Similarities Teachers often inadvertently emphasize the differences, rather than the similarities, between students with severe handicaps and their nonhandicapped peers. Acceptance and friendship can be facilitated by emphasizing similarities (Asher, Odom, & Gottman, 1977). Examples include:

Answering students' questions about disabilities factually, without including unnecessary details

Providing information using positive terminology, and emphasizing abilities and similarities

Using instances of teasing as opportunities to teach values, provide factual information, and teach students how to respond to teasing

Intervening with the entire group when working with students with and without handicaps (e.g., "What do you all need to do next?" or, "Great working together"), rather than focusing on intervening with the student with severe handicaps

Facilitate Interaction and Communication In some instances, human differences training (Stainback, Stainback, & Jaben, 1981) has been used to promote understanding and increased interactions between students with severe handicaps and their nonhandicapped peers. This training can be provided through simulation of handicaps or through integration into the regular education curriculum (e.g., reading about an individual with a handicap during a social science class). Discussions about individual differences should be objective and should focus on the positive aspects of human differences, rather than exclusively focusing on differences that result from disabilities.

Since many students with severe handicaps use alternative and augmentative modes of communication, or other adaptive devices, students with and without disabilities must receive sufficient instruction and training in the use of these devices. Nonhandicapped students can learn to communicate and respond with a student with severe handicaps using Zygo boards, sign language, communication booklets, typewriters, and so on. Fortunately, nonhandicapped students often express interest in learning new language systems. In addition, learning to use adaptive equipment (e.g., wheelchairs, walkers) or assisting a student to use his/her adaptive equipment often removes the apprehensiveness that many nonhandicapped students feel about interacting with students who are using such equipment.

Provide Students with Severe Handicaps Systematic and Direct Instruction Regarding Appropriate Interaction Such instruction can best occur in naturally occurring interactions. *Role playing, rehearsing, and coaching* can be effective instructional techniques for some students with severe handicaps. Students can rehearse and practice the communication skills necessary for various social interactions prior to interacting. Examples include:

Communicating with a new friend by direct eye gaze and smiling

Requesting the scissors and crayons from another student through gestures

Determining appropriate topics for conversation at lunchtime

Requesting assistance from the horticulture teacher

Requesting that peers join in on a baseball game

Asking a friend to dance at the Halloween Dance

After practicing communication skills, students can then receive feedback, which may assist them in engaging in those interactions when they naturally occur.

Utilize the Natural Activities that Occur during the School Day Educators should utilize the *natural activities that occur* during the school day to teach and have students practice appropriate communication and social skills. For example, while waiting for the bell to ring in the morning, a student can practice "looking cool" or "hanging out" (e.g., the student stands with hands in his or her pockets or holds a backpack while interacting with a friend). Waiting in line to buy lunch, the student can practice standing at an appropriate distance from other students, moving in the line appropriately, and putting food items on thc tray at a reasonable rate. Similarly, delivering messages to teachers and to the school office staff can provide opportunities for students to practice communication and mobility skills.

Frequent opportunities for *choice and decision making* can encourage the development of communication skills and can lead to positive interaction activities. Seating arrangements, playground activities, hallway mobility patterns, classroom academic activities, and so forth, can all be structured to facilitate interactions and cooperation between all students.

Intervene and Shape Interactions as they Occur It is often most effective to *intervene and shape interactions* as they occur. However, teachers must keep in mind that teacher intrusion into interactions can also limit the number of interactions that occur (Meyer et al., 1987). Teachers may find their efforts most successful if they carefully plan and then evaluate interaction opportunities to ensure that their actions are not inadvertently interfering with interactions.

General considerations for teachers facilitating interactions within integration opportunities include the following:

1. Facilitate "reciprocal" rather than "helping" interactions.
2. Allow all students varied opportunities to help.
3. Stress cooperation rather than "helping."
4. Provide opportunities to "show off" competencies and strengths.
5. Encourage maximum participation of all students.
6. Set up interaction opportunities that are valued activities for all students.
7. Fade teacher intervention/intrusion as quickly as possible.
8. Avoid having nonhandicapped peers implement nonfunctional or undignified teaching programs (e.g., toileting)
9. Encourage choice and decision making.
10. Structure seating arrangements, playground activities, hallway mobility and positioning to facilitate interactions.
11. When students are working or playing together in a group, reinforce and intervene with the entire group.
12. Use opportunities like teasing to teach values and appropriate responses to teasing, and to provide factual information.

13. Develop a school interaction project for all students.
14. Answer students' questions about disabilities factually without unnecessary detail or additional information. Use positive terminology, focus on abilities, and emphasize similarities.
15. Encourage after-school relationships and activities.
16. Conduct evaluations and determine quality of interactions (e.g., amount of time, quality/type of interactions, perceptions, and attitudes of students, teachers).
17. Facilitate interactions, relationships, and friendships rather than "programs."

EVALUATING INTEGRATION

As with every component of the curriculum, evaluation of integration is a critical and necessary procedure for determining program effectiveness and program modification needs. (Haring & Billingsley, 1984). Integration efforts should not be evaluated in isolation of other program components. Rather, comprehensive evaluation procedures should result in the collection of data reflecting the following components (L. Meyer, personal communication, January 21, 1986). Integrated educational programs should result in:

1. The acquisition of skills by students with severe handicaps in at least the following areas: communication; recreation/leisure; domestic; vocational; community; self-determination and decision making; independence and interdependence
2. A range of social relationships for students including friendships
3. Positive attitudes toward individual differences in students with and without severe handicaps.
4. Positive self-concepts for students with and without severe handicaps.
5. Expanded curricular and social interaction opportunities.

In addition to determining program effectiveness, evaluation procedures also provide a powerful data base to validate and support integration efforts. Specifically, systematic evaluation procedures might include the following methods:

1. **Attitude surveys** can be used to examine the attitudes of nonhandicapped students, parents, regular education staff, and special education staff toward students with severe handicaps. These surveys may prove useful in documenting attitude changes over time, and they may indicate areas in which students, parents, and staff require information.
2. **Data collection procedures**, such as anecdotal recording, behavior or frequency counts, and/or language sampling, can provide teachers and program managers with important information regarding the frequency and

quality of interactions that occur between students with severe handicaps and their nonhandicapped peers (Falvey, Grenot-Scheyer & Luddy, 1986). The "SIOS: Social Interaction Observation System" (Voeltz, Kishi, & Brennan, 1981) is an example of an instrument designed to use when systematically observing various behaviors and factors important for successful integration. Teacher-developed instruments have been used successfully to evaluate such behaviors and integration efforts. Information obtained from instruments such as these can assist teachers in identifying successful integration efforts and can help identify when increased facilitation of interactions between students with and without severe handicaps is needed.

3. **Videotaping** integration activities can facilitate the data collection process by providing a permanent product of the interactions. The analysis of these videotapes can provide a detailed and critical view of the integration process over time (Coots, 1985; Falvey, 1980; Strain, 1983).
4. **Interviews** with staff, parents, students, community members, and other participants in integration activities can be used to determine understanding and acceptance of the integration activities (Rosenberg, 1980).
5. **Checklists and other criterion-referenced measures** can be used by teachers, administrators, parents, board of education members, and others to help determine the degree to which students with severe handicaps placed into regular education settings are integrated into various components of the regular education program. The Severely Handicapped Integration Checklist (SHIC) developed by Stainback and Stainback (1983) is a comprehensive and useful checklist of quality indicators of integration.

SUMMARY

As suggested by Falvey et al. (1989), the challenge for educators is to develop and facilitate curricular and instructional options that allow all students to learn in the most beneficial manner. The creative examples that currently exist in neighborhood schools must be supported and expanded to ensure that all students receive the most appropriate and beneficial education possible in settings that support the development of a wide range of social interactions and relationships. Biklen and Knoll (1987) and Voeltz (1984) suggest that phrases such as "integration" and "integration programs" must and will become obsolete when full integration is achieved. Until all students are provided appropriate education in neighborhood and community schools alongside their nonhandicapped peers, integration strategies and considerations are both logical and necessary.

Specific strategies for facilitating integration are included in this chapter. In addition, barriers and solutions to those barriers are delineated. Integration in school is essential to facilitate lifelong integration into all aspects of neighborhoods and communities.

REFERENCES

Anderson, J.L. (1983). *An observational study of the interaction of autistic children and their families in the natural home environment*. Unpublished doctoral dissertation, University of Wisconsin at Madison.

Asher, S.R., Odom, S.L., & Gottman, J.M. (1977). Children's friendships in school settings. In L.G. Katz (Ed.), *Current topics in early childhood education* (Vol. 1, pp. 33–61). Norwood, NJ: Ablex.

Benton, R.D. (1985). *Department of public instruction position statement regarding integration of children with moderate and severe handicaps*. Des Moines, IA: Department of Public Instruction.

Biklen, D., & Knoll, J. (1987). The disabled minority. In S.J. Taylor, D. Biklen, & J. Knoll (Eds.), *Community integration for people with severe disabilities* (pp. 3–24). New York: Teacher's College Press.

Bishop, K., & Falvey, M. (1986). Motor skills. In M. Falvey, *Community-based curriculum: Instructional strategies for students with severe handicaps* (pp. 139–161). Baltimore: Paul H. Brookes Publishing Co.

Brown, L., Branston, M.B., Hamre-Nietupski, S., Johnson, F., Wilcox, B., & Gruenewald, L. (1979). A rationale for comprehensive longitudinal interactions between severely handicapped students and other citizens. *AAESPH Review*, *4*(1), 3–14.

Brown, L., Nietupski, J., & Hamre-Nietupski, S. (1976). The criterion of ultimate functioning and public school services for severely handicapped children. In M.A. Thomas (Ed.), *Hey don't forget about me: Education's investment in the severely, profoundly and multiply handicapped* (pp. 2–15). Reston, VA: Council for Exceptional Children.

California Research Institute. (1987). *Survey of severely disabled students in California*. Unpublished manuscript, California Research Institute on the Integration of Students with Severe Disabilities, San Francisco State University.

Campbell, P.H. (1987). Integrated programming for students with multiple handicaps. In L. Goetz, D. Guess, & K. Stremel-Campbell (Eds.), *Innovative program design for individuals with dual sensory impairments* (pp. 159–188). Baltimore: Paul H. Brookes Publishing Co.

Certo, N., & Kohl, F.L. (1984). A strategy for developing interpersonal interaction instructional content for severely handicapped students. In N. Certo, N. Haring, & R. York (Eds.), *Public school integration of severely handicapped students: Rational issues and progressive alternatives* (pp. 221–244). Baltimore: Paul H. Brookes Publishing Co.

Coots, J. (1985). *The effects of integration on the functional nature of the communicative/interactive attempts of students with severe handicaps*. Unpublished master's thesis, California State University, Los Angeles.

Donnellan, A., & Mirenda, P. (1983). A model for analyzing instructional components to facilitate generalization for severely handicapped students. *Journal of Special Education*, *17*, 317–331.

Falvey, M. (1980). *Changes in academic and social competence of kindergarten-aged handicapped children as a result of an integrated classroom*. Unpublished doctoral dissertation, University of Wisconsin at Madison.

Falvey, M., Brown, L., Lyon, S., Baumgart, D., & Schroeder, J. (1980). Strategies for using cues and correction procedures. In W. Sailor, B. Wilcox, & L. Brown (Eds.), *Methods of instruction for severely handicapped students* (pp. 109–133). Baltimore: Paul H. Brookes Publishing Co.

Falvey, M., Coots, J., Bishop, K., & Grenot-Scheyer, M. (1989). Educational and curricular adaptations. In S. Stainback, W. Stainback, & M. Forest (Eds.), *Educating all students in the mainstream of regular education* (pp. 143–158). Baltimore: Paul H. Brookes Publishing Co.

Falvey, M., Grenot-Scheyer, M., & Luddy, E. (1986). Developing and implementing integrated community referenced curriculum. In A. Donnellan, A. Cohen, & R. Paul (Eds.), *Handbook of autism and disorders of atypical development* (pp. 238–250). New York: John Wiley & Sons.

Gaylord-Ross, R.J., & Pitts-Conway, V. (1984). Social behavior development in integrated secondary autistic programs. In N. Certo, N. Haring, & R. York (Eds.), *Public school integration of severely handicapped students: Rational issues and progressive alternatives* (pp. 197–219). Baltimore: Paul H. Brookes Publishing Co.

Gee, K., Harrell, R., & Rosenberg, R. (1987). Teaching orientation and mobility skills within and across natural opportunities for travel: A model design for learners with multiple severe disabilities. In L. Goetz, D. Guess, & K. Stremel-Campbell (Eds.), *Innovative program design for individuals with dual sensory impairments* (pp. 127–157). Baltimore: Paul H. Brookes Publishing Co.

Goetz, L., & Gee, K. (1987). Functional vision programming: A model for teaching visual behaviors in natural contexts. In L. Goetz, D. Guess, & K. Stremel-Campbell (Eds.), *Innovative program design for individuals with dual sensory impairments* (pp. 77–97). Baltimore: Paul H. Brookes Publishing Co.

Grenot-Scheyer, M., & Falvey, M.A. (1986). Integration issues and strategies. In M.A. Falvey, *Community-based curriculum: Instructional strategies for students with severe handicaps* (pp. 217–233). Baltimore: Paul H. Brookes Publishing Co.

Guralnick, M., & Paul-Brown, D. (1980). Functional and discourse analysis of nonhandicapped preschool children's speech to handicapped children. *American Journal of Mental Deficiency*, *84*(5), 444–454.

Hamre-Nietupski, S., Branston, M.B., Ford, A., Gruenewald, L., & Brown, L. (1978). Curricular strategies for developing longitudinal interactions between severely handicapped and nonhandicapped individuals in school and nonschool environments. In L. Brown, S. Hamre-Nietupski, M.B. Branston, M.A. Falvey, S. Lyon, & L. Gruenewald (Eds.), *Curricular strategies for developing longitudinal interactions between severely handicapped students and others and curricular strategies for teaching severely handicapped students to acquire and perform skills in response to naturally-occurring cues and correction procedures* (Vol. 8, pp. 27–177). Madison, WI: Madison Metropolitan School District.

Haring, N., & Billingsley, F.F. (1984). Systems-change strategies to ensure the future of integration. In N. Certo, N. Haring, & R. York (Eds.), *Public school integration of severely handicapped students: Rational issues and progressive alternatives* (pp. 83–105). Baltimore: Paul H. Brookes Publishing Co.

Heron, T.E., & Harris, K.C. (1987). *Educational consultant: Helping professionals, parents, and mainstreamed students*. Boston: Allyn & Bacon.

Johnson, D.W., Johnson, R.T., Warring, D., & Maruyama, G. (1986). Different cooperative learning procedures and cross handicap relationships. *Exceptional Children*, *53*, 247–252.

Johnson, R.T., & Johnson, D.W. (1981). Building friendships between handicapped and nonhandicapped students: Effects of cooperative and individualistic instruction. *American Educational Research Journal*, *18*, 415–423.

Meyer, L.H., Fox, A., Schermer, A., Ketelsen, D., Montan, N., Maley, K., & Cole, D. (1987). The effects of teacher intrusion on social play interactions between children with autism and their nonhandicapped peers. *Journal of Autism and Developmental Disorders, 17*(3), 315–332.

Meyer, L.H., & Kishi, G.S. (1985). School integration strategies. In K.C. Lakin & R.H. Bruininks (Eds.), *Strategies for achieving community integration of developmentally disabled citizens* (pp. 231–252). Baltimore: Paul H. Brookes Publishing Co.

Piuma, C. (1985). *A case study: Cost analysis study of selected San Mateo County Office of Education integrated and segregated classrooms serving severely disabled students.* Unpublished manuscript, California Research Institute on the Integration of Students with Severe Disabilities, San Francisco State University.

Ragland, E.U., Kerr, M.N., & Strain, P.S. (1978). Behavior of withdrawn autistic children. *Behavior Modification, 2*, 565–578.

Rainforth, B., & York, J. (1987). Integrating related services in community instruction. *Journal of The Association for Persons with Severe Handicaps, 12*(3), 190–198.

Rosenberg, R.L. (1980). *A multidimensional case study exploring the dynamics of the integration of mildly handicapped students.* Unpublished doctoral dissertation, University of Madison at Wisconsin.

Roth, M.A., & Nardi, G.A. (1987). A comparison of program locations and opportunities for public school students with severe handicaps. *Education and Training in Mental Retardation, 22*(4), 236–243.

Stainback, S., & Stainback, W. (1985). *Integration of students with severe handicaps into regular schools.* Reston, VA: Council for Exceptional Children.

Stainback, S., Stainback, W., & Forest, M. (1989). *Educating all students in the mainstream of regular education.* Baltimore: Paul H. Brookes Publishing Co.

Stainback, W., & Stainback, S. (1981). A review of research on interactions between severely handicapped and nonhandicapped students. *Teaching Exceptional Children, 13*, 172–175.

Stainback, W., & Stainback, S. (1982). Nonhandicapped students' perceptions of severely handicapped and nonhandicapped students. *Education and Training in Mental Retardation, 17*, 177–182.

Stainback, W., & Stainback, S. (1983). A severely handicapped integration checklist. *Teaching Exceptional Children, 15*(3), 168–171.

Stainback, W., Stainback, S., & Jaben, T. (1981). Providing opportunities for interaction between severely handicapped and nonhandicapped students. *Teaching Exceptional Children. 13*, 172–175.

Sternat, J., Messina, R., Nietupski, J., Lyon, S., & Brown, L. (1977). Educational programming for the severely and profoundly handicapped. In E. Sontag (Ed.), *Occupational and physical therapy services for severely handicapped students: Toward a naturalized public school service delivery model* (pp. 263–278). Reston, VA: Council for Exceptional Children, Division on Mental Retardation.

Strain, P.S. (1983). Generalization of autistic children's social behavior change: Effects of developmentally integrated and segregated settings. *Analysis and Intervention in Developmental Disabilities, 3*, 23–34.

Strain, P.S., Kerr, M.M., & Ragland, E.U. (1979). Effects of peer-mediated social initiations and prompting/reinforcement procedures on the social behavior of autistic children. *Journal of Autism and Developmental Disorders, 9*, 41–54.

Taylor, S. (1982). From segregation to integration: Strategies for integrating severely handicapped students in normal school and community settings. *Journal of The Association for the Severely Handicapped, 7*(3), 42–49.

Taylor, S., Biklen, D., & Knoll, J. (Eds.). (1987). *Community integration for people with severe disabilities*. New York: Teachers College Press.

Voeltz, L.M. (1983). *Why integrate?* Unpublished manuscript, University of Minnesota Consortium Institute for the Education of Severely Handicapped Learners, Minnesota.

Voeltz, L.M. (1984). Program and curriculum innovations to prepare children for integration. In N. Certo, N. Haring, & R. York (Eds.), *Public school integration of severely handicapped students: Rational issues and progressive alternatives* (pp. 155–183). Baltimore: Paul H. Brookes Publishing Co.

Voeltz, L.M., Kishi, G.M., & Brennan, J. (1981). *SIOS: Social interaction observation system*. Unpublished document, Honolulu: Hawaii Integration Project, Department of Special Education, University of Hawaii.

Warren, S.F., Rogers-Warren, A.M., Baer, D.M., & Guess, D. (1980). Assessment and facilitation of language generalization. In W. Sailor, B. Wilcox, & L. Brown (Eds.), *Methods of instruction for severely handicapped students* (pp. 227–258). Baltimore: Paul H. Brookes Publishing Co.

Williams, W., Fox, W., Christie, L., Thousand, J., Conn-Powers, M., Carmichael, L., Vogelsberg, R.T., & Hull, M. (1986). Community integration in Vermont. *Journal of The Association for Persons with Severe Handicaps, 11*(4), 294–299.

Yager, S., Johnson, R.T., Johnson, D.W., & Snider, B. (1985). The effect of cooperative and individualistic learning experiences on positive and negative cross-handicap relationships. *Contemporary Educational Psychology, 10*, 127–138.

FOURTEEN

DEVELOPING AND FOSTERING FRIENDSHIPS

Marquita Grenot-Scheyer, Jennifer Coots, and Mary A. Falvey

THE PURPOSE OF THIS chapter is to provide an overview of the process whereby friendships are developed and supported among individuals with and without severe handicaps. Historically, services for individuals labeled as severely handicapped have been characterized by segregation and isolation. In effect, specialized programs remove individuals with severe handicaps from community life and involvement. This situation has been slowly changing. As more and more students with severe handicaps move into their neighborhood schools, and as increasing numbers of adults with severe handicaps live and work in their communities, the importance of social relationships, and in particular, friendships, becomes increasingly clear to professionals and families who organize and deliver such services (Stainback, Stainback, & Forest, 1989).

SUPPORTING THE DEVELOPMENT OF FRIENDSHIPS: A RATIONALE

Families of individuals with severe handicaps, in particular, have requested, challenged, and compelled professionals to realize the importance of friendships to their sons and daughters; parents have urged professionals to facilitate the development and maintenance of friendships between their children and nonhandicapped peers. According to various professionals and numerous families across the United States, full integration leads to relationships that can support individuals with severe handicaps in their neighborhoods, schools, and communities (Strully & Bartholomew-Lorimer, 1988; Taylor, Biklen, & Knoll, 1987). However, the integration that is found in specialized interaction programs may not be sufficient if it does not encourage the development and support of friendships between individuals with and without severe handicaps. "Special friends" and peer tutoring programs must be viewed as temporary instructional arrangements that may allow individuals to develop the attitudes and skills necessary to interact with one another (Voeltz, 1983). As the parents of a young women who is labeled severely handicapped commented, 'special' is not good enough, if a special program prevents the development of friendships between individuals with severe handicaps and their nonhandicapped peers" (Strully & Strully, 1985).

Stainback and Stainback (1987) have noted that, for many years, educators and researchers have been interested in the social interactions that occur between individuals labeled severely handicapped and their nonhandicapped peers. Research on the attitudes of nonhandicapped students toward their peers with severe handicaps has shown that positive attitudes can and do result when students are provided opportunities to interact (Condon, York, Heal, & Fortschneider, 1986; Esposito & Reed, 1986; McHale & Simeonsson, 1980; Rynders, Johnson, Johnson, & Schmidt, 1980; Voeltz, 1980; Ziegler & Hambleton, 1976). In addition, research on the interactions between individuals with and without severe handicaps has demonstrated that frequent, productive, and effective interactions do occur when individuals are provided with opportunities to interact with one another (Anderson, 1983; Baumgart, 1981; Breen, Haring, Pitts-Conway, & Gaylord-Ross, 1985; Coots, 1985; Falvey, 1980; Guralnick & Paul-Brown, 1980; Haring, Breen, Pitts-Conway, Lee, & Gaylord-Ross, 1987; Storey & Gaylord-Ross, 1987; Strain, 1983). Finally, research on the effects of having nonhandicapped students provide peer tutoring and demonstration for students with severe handicaps has revealed that these students have developed skills as a result of the tutoring (Chin-Perez et al., 1986; Haring et al., 1987; Johnson, Johnson, Deweerdt, Lyons, & Zaidman, 1983; Kohl, Moses, & Stettner-Eaton, 1984; McHale, Olley, Marcus, & Simmeonsson, 1981), as well as from observing nonhandicapped peers engage in activities (Egel, Richmond, & Koegel, 1981).

Only recently have researchers examined the development of friendships between individuals labeled severely handicapped and their nonhandicapped peers. Although there are numerous examples of friendships in school, work, and community settings, there are few studies that have systematically examined friendships between individuals with and without severe handicaps (Cole, 1988; Field, 1984; Howes, 1983; Strain, 1984a; Voeltz & Brennan, 1982). Although the preceding studies have shed some light on the nature of friendships between children with severe handicaps and their nonhandicapped peers, the findings from these studies present equivocal data. Specifically, it is unclear whether friendships between children with and without severe handicaps resemble the friendships of nonhandicapped children, which are characterized by mutual enjoyment and reciprocal interaction (Howes, 1983; Roopnarine & Field, 1984), or whether such friendships are characterized by more physical efforts and nonreciprocal exchanges (Cole, 1988; Strain, 1984a).

Much of what professionals know about friendships comes from the rich and informative literature describing the friendships of typical children and adolescents, and from observations of such friendships in communities across the United States. Based upon these sources, one may suggest that the major prerequisite for the development and maintenance of friendship is *opportunity* (Hartup, 1975; Howes, 1983). Opportunity, composed of *proximity* and *frequency,* allows peers to practice and elaborate upon skills (Lewis & Rosenblaum, 1975), to get to know one another (Asher, Odem, & Gottman, 1977), and subsequently, to develop friendships. The service delivery model that removes individuals from their neighborhoods and communities for the sake of specialized services, and therefore restricts the types of relationships available to those individuals, is untenable when one considers the enormous importance of friendships for all individuals (Falvey, Coots, Bishop, & Grenot-Scheyer, 1989). In one large western state, the majority of students with severe handicaps spend most of their days in segregated schools or in self-contained programs (California Research Institute, 1987). Professionals need to remember that friendship opportunities increase as interaction opportunities increase. Clearly, the greatest barrier to friendships between individuals with and without severe handicaps is lack of opportunity, and not individual characteristics, skills, abilities, and/or disabilities.

FRIENDSHIP DEFINED

Friendship is an elusive yet familiar concept to all (Perske, 1987). In addition, friendship means different things to different people at different times and at different ages (Stainback & Stainback, 1987). Depending upon one's age, a friend may be someone with whom to play, or someone with whom to share lunch (Hayes, 1978; Howes, 1983), someone with whom to share secrets, or someone to be trusted and with whom one may be intimate (Berndt, 1982). Typically, friendships among children and adolescents are of the same gender, although this changes over time (Damon, 1977; Eder & Hallinan, 1978; Schofield, 1981).

Friendship has been defined in a number of ways. Before defining friendship, it is important to differentiate between popularity and friendship since, oftentimes, these terms are used interchangeably when, in fact, their meanings are very different (Grenot-Scheyer, in preparation). Popularity, usually measured by sociometrics, indicates if one is liked or accepted by a number of peers (Hartup, 1970). There are popular children who do not have friends (Hymel & Asher, 1977) and children who have friends, but are not necessarily popular or accomplished in social skills (Masters & Furman, 1981). The definition of friendship that appears to be the most pragmatic to educators and researchers is that friendship is a bond between two individuals that is characterized by mutual preference for one another, a positive affective style, and an ability to engage in social interactions, and to have interactions that last over a period of time (Hartup, 1975; Howes, 1983).

Friendships are characterized by a range of social interactions. Friends engage not only in reciprocal interactions (e.g., give and take), but also in helping and proximal interactions. For example, Ryan, a 10-year-old boy labeled as severely multiply handicapped, and his nonhandicapped friend, Sam, enjoy playing games on the adapted computer. In addition, they sit together at lunch, and Sam sometimes helps Ryan with his straw and milk. Ryan and Sam are often observed just "hanging out" together, with no apparent interaction evident. Finally, Ryan and Sam often walk home together after school, since they live in the same neighborhood. As this example illustrates, friends engage in reciprocal activities, help each other, and sometimes, just spend time together. All of these types of interactions are essential, and no single type is more important than another. When interactions between two individuals involve only helping or proximal interactions exclusively, attempts should be made to foster reciprocal interactions. All types of interactions exist in most friendships, and professionals should foster the expression of a range of interactions between friends.

BENEFITS OF FRIENDSHIP

There are numerous developmental, psychological, and sociological reasons for fostering friendships between individuals with and without severe handicaps. First, friendships provide the opportunity to develop, practice, and maintain a variety of communicative, cognitive, and social-emotional skills (Field 1984; Guralnick, 1980; Hartup, 1983; Howes, 1983; Rubin, 1982). Second, friendships can provide individuals with nurturance and support (Berndt & Perry, 1986; Howes & Mueller, 1980; Rubin, 1982; Weiss, 1974). Third, lack of friendships in the early years is correlated with maladjustment in later years (Buhrmester & Furman, 1986; Cowen, Pederson, Babigian, Izzo, & Trost, 1973; Robins, 1966; Roff, Sells, & Golden, 1972; Sullivan, 1953). Finally, friendships may be at the base of a network of relationships that allow individuals with severe handicaps to grow up, go to school, live, work, and recreate within their own neighborhoods and communities (Strully & Bartholomew-Lorimer, 1988; Strully & Strully, 1985; Taylor et al., 1987; Weiss, 1974).

Given the complex needs of individuals with severe handicaps, one may question the importance of examining peer relationships, and friendships in particular, for these individuals. As stated by Strain (1984b), "While the case has been made by others . . . of the developmental significance of friendships for normally developing children, it may be argued that friendships are even more important for handicapped children's language, cognitive, sexual, and academic development" (p. 193). Furthermore, Taylor et al. (1987) have suggested that if there has been one thing lacking in the lives of individuals with severe handicaps, it is the opportunity for close, mutual, and ongoing relationships with other individuals. As voiced by one parent of a teenager with severe handicaps, "Friendships are important for Dusty because I don't want her to be lonely" (D. Dutton, personal communication, January 15, 1988). Individuals with severe handicaps often find themselves in the company of those who are paid to be with them (Lutfiyya, 1988; Strully & Bartholomew-Lorimer, 1988). It is critical that everyone have people in their lives who are there because they want to be in a relationship, not because they are obligated to do so.

Finally, friendships between individuals with severe handicaps and their nonhandicapped peers may be the best illustration of a true sense of community. Although individuals with severe handicaps may have increased dependency and vulnerability, nonhandicapped individuals can come to recognize such vulnerability as a characteristic shared in one way or another by everyone at various times in our lives, rather than as something that divides people (Strully & Bartholomew-Lorimer, 1988). Given the opportunity to become acquainted, to interact with one another, and subsequently, to develop friendships, individuals labeled as severely handicapped and their nonhandicapped peers can grow past acceptance of each other, and begin to cherish one another for their unique contributions (L. Vincent, personnel communication, January 15, 1988).

FOSTERING FRIENDSHIPS

In spite of all the technology available to human services professionals, friendship cannot be taught. Professionals cannot "program" friendships, although variables can be manipulated in such a manner as to allow for the opportunity for individuals to be friends (Perske, 1987). Thus, professionals can build connections to foster and support friendships between individuals with and without severe handicaps.

For all individuals, the skills necessary to interact with one another and to get along in a community are acquired through social relationships, including friendships. Friendships provide unique opportunities for individuals to acquire and practice skills that would be extremely difficult, if not impossible, for professionals to teach. Several important curricular considerations that professionals should keep in mind when developing and supporting friendships between individuals with severe handicaps and their nonhandicapped peers are delineated in the next section.

Curricular Considerations

Professionals can assist individuals with severe handicaps to develop and maintain friendships with their nonhandicapped peers by utilizing natural, age-appropriate, and culturally relevant activities, materials, and settings (Falvey, Brown, Lyon, Baumgart, & Schroeder, 1980). For example, naturally occurring times and activities in which children can develop friendships are present at the neighborhood school or playground. Such opportunities may also be found at the community after school recreation program or on the weekends in the local park. When adults with severe handicaps live and work in their communities, local social/recreation opportunities are available. Social and recreation opportunities are available by participating in activities sponsored by religious and community youth and adult groups, service organizations, community college events, and sorority and fraternity functions. Chapter 7 of this volume includes a discussion of strategies to facilitate access to integrated community recreation programs and services.

Professionals should deemphasize the "special-ness" of programs and highlight and emphasize the similarities of individuals with and without severe handicaps. It has been suggested that friendships are based upon the similarities and compatibilities of individuals (Asher et al., 1977). Professionals should, therefore, assist individuals with severe handicaps to demonstrate and/or express areas of interest and similarity that they share with potential friends. Factual information regarding handicaps can be provided to nonhandicapped individuals as appropriate, but natural opportunities for individuals to learn about each other should be encouraged. At some point in the relationship, information regarding an individual's disability may be important to provide to the individual's friend, such as, "This is what we need to do in case Yolanda has a seizure."

Finally, individuals with severe handicaps and their nonhandicapped peers need varied and regular opportunities to develop friendships and to be with one another. As suggested by Lutfiyya (1988), nonhandicapped individuals have numerous opportunities to become acquainted with others and to develop friendships. Professionals can develop and structure such opportunities in a variety of ways. For example, teachers of children and adolescents with severe handicaps can facilitate the development of friendships during school hours and after-school events. Community recreation leaders can assist students with severe handicaps to develop friendships during after-school and weekend recreation activities. Job coaches can assist adults with severe handicaps to develop friendships at their job sites by such activities as joining baseball leagues and attending after-work functions. It is important that professionals identify and analyze the age-appropriate social activities in which nonhandicapped individuals participate in order to best utilize naturally occurring opportunities.

Social Skills and Friendship

As previously suggested, even though one cannot teach friendship, there are a number of social skills that professionals can foster that are associated with having friends. Skills associated with friendship can be practiced and enhanced like any other skill (Stainback & Stainback, 1987). Outlined below are several of the skills and actions often expressed by friends.

Displays Positive Interaction Style Positive interactions are those that are enjoyed by others and make others feel good to be around you. Positive interactions can include a smile, a laugh, a soft touch, or a special gaze in a friend's direction. Professionals can assist individuals with severe handicaps to interact with their friends and acquaintances in a positive manner.

Gets the Message Across An intended message can be communicated to a friend utilizing verbal, nonverbal, gestural, or pictorial means. A smile or eye gaze as greeting and as a way to say, "I like you," are examples of communicating a message. Professionals can assist individuals to communicate in the clearest and most efficient manner in order to facilitate the individual's interactions with friends.

Is Reinforcing to Others Friends demonstrate a positive affective style that reflects their enjoyment of being with one another. Professionals can assist individuals with severe handicaps to express their feelings to friends in positive and reinforcing ways. In addition, professionals can assist nonhandicapped individuals to notice the subtle cues and reinforcers that their friends might use or provide.

Initiates Thoughtful Actions Thoughtful actions are important within friendships. Such actions remind someone that a friend is thinking about them and is concerned about his or her welfare. Examples of such actions include sending a greeting card, calling a friend to send a birthday wish, or just to say, "Hi." Professionals can assist individuals with severe handicaps to engage in such thoughtful actions.

Is a Good Listener Critical to a friendship is attentiveness and responsiveness to the other person's needs. Professionals can assist individuals with severe handicaps to be attentive by demonstrating good listening behaviors and by identifying the appropriate times to listen and to share information or feelings.

Shares Belongings and Feelings Friends often share a variety of belongings and feelings. Depending upon their ages, friends can share, among other things, toys, food, feelings, and secrets. Professionals can assist individuals by arranging opportunities to share activities and belongings. Such opportunities include: playing in the same sandbox, eating lunch on the same lunch bench, and working at the same job location. Furthermore, professionals can facilitate communication between friends by developing augmentative communication devices to assist the individual with severe handicaps to share thoughts and feelings with nonhandicapped friends.

Has Similar Likes and Dislikes Friends are often described as having similar likes and dislikes. Professionals can highlight areas of compatibility between friends, and/or structure opportunities to develop similar interests. For example, professionals can inventory the recreation leisure choices of individuals with severe handicaps and then develop opportunities for the student to engage in such activities. For instance, one young man with severe handicaps who was very proficient with computers joined a community computer club to share his interest and expertise with others.

Takes the Perspectives of Others Being able to see the joys and challenges of life through the eyes of a friend is a unique characteristic of friendship. Professionals can assist individuals to see life from their friends' perspectives. One woman, whose friend with severe handicaps used a wheelchair to move around, sometimes needed to push her around street obstacles and up hills. From this perspective, she had the opportunity to experience some of the challenges that her friend met every day.

Is Trustworthy and Loyal A friend is someone to count on, and who will be there when needed. Professionals can assist individuals to develop trusting and loyal attitudes and behaviors towards their friends. Examples of such behaviors are: differentiating when something is important enough to keep a secret, demonstrating ones' loyalty by sitting by a friend when he or she appears sad, and helping a friend when he or she is in need.

Instructional Strategies

There are a number of instructional strategies that professionals may utilize to facilitate and enhance friendships between individuals with severe handicaps and their nonhandicapped peers. As previously noted, friendships are highly complex and unique relationships and do not lend themselves to systematic task analyses. In light of this caution, professionals may utilize instructional strategies to assist individuals with and without handicaps to engage in the social skills usually expressed by friends.

Shaping As described in Chapter 4 of this volume, shaping involves the systematic reinforcement of a desirable behavior. Individuals with severe handicaps can be systematically reinforced for engaging in those social skills used by friends. This reinforcement can come from professionals or from the individual's friend. For example, Elizabeth, a teenager labeled as multiply handicapped was taught to hold her head up and to turn her head intentionally toward her friends upon their arrival. Initially, her teacher had used a headband mercury switch attached to a tape recorder to shape and reinforce the behavior. As Elizabeth's endurance increased the use of the mercury switch was faded. In another example, Nathan, a 6-year-old boy with autism, received systematic reinforcement from his teacher for playing kickball appropriately with his friends. Over time, the teacher systematically faded the use of social praise, as well as her presence, as Nathan's friends helped and encouraged him to play kickball appropriately.

Modeling Modeling is a more direct way to teach some of the complex skills that are part of being a friend. Modeling consists of demonstrating a behavior for the student to imitate (Snell, 1987). Nonhandicapped friends may serve as excellent models of age-appropriate behaviors. Professionals can structure activities so that individuals with severe handicaps can benefit from watching their friends. For example, Nancy, a young woman with severe handicaps, had difficulty joining groups of co-workers during break time. To assist Nancy to develop appropriate entry skills, she and her job coach observed Nancy's co-workers. The job coach pointed out to Nancy the most effective behaviors for "successful entry." Nancy was advised to locate a group where one of her friends was present, to approach this friend, to greet other members of the group, and so forth. In another example, Anthony, a young boy with severe handicaps, often exhibited aggressive behaviors to indicate his desire to play on the gym bars. In addition to developing an augmentative communication booklet to assist Anthony to express his desires in an age-appropriate manner, his teacher also structured opportunities for him to observe the age-appropriate behavior of his peers on the gym bars. Specifically, Anthony's teacher pointed out the appropriate ways of playing on the bars. As he became more successful at playing appropriately with his peers, Anthony's teacher faded her cues as well as her proximity to him.

Coaching Coaching may assist some individuals with severe handicaps to practice the social skills important to friendships. Coaching typically involves direct instruction, opportunities to practice the skill(s) with peers, and a "postreview" session to review the skill (Gottlieb & Leyser, 1981; Oden & Asher, 1977). Coaching is a beneficial strategy in that specific social skills/behaviors can be targeted for improvement (Gottlieb & Leyser, 1981). For example, a rehabilitation counselor utilized coaching strategies to teach Brian, a young man with severe handicaps, the finer nuances of asking someone to dance at a company party. First, Brian and his counselor practiced what Brian would say and do, Brian then tried the suggestions; afterward, they reviewed how the interaction went.

Not all of the preceding strategies will work with all individuals with severe handicaps. Professionals should assess the situation carefully to determine the appropriate type and amount of instructional support that is necessary. Although professionals may choose to be direct in their efforts, they can also hinder the development of friendships between individuals with and without handicaps (Lutfiyya, 1988). Therefore, as previously suggested, professionals should fade their assistance as soon as naturally occurring supports are available. The challenge to professionals is to create the optimal environment that encourages individuals with and without handicaps to want to be friends with one another.

IMPLICATIONS FOR SERVICE DELIVERY

In addition to continuing to provide services that adhere to the criterion of ultimate functioning (Brown, Nietupski, & Hamre-Nietupski, 1976), professionals must ensure that such services allow for friendships between individuals with and without severe handicaps. The acquisition of functional skills alone will not ensure that individuals with severe handicaps will be active and integral members of their communities (Strully & Strully, 1985). Although school and adult programs have traditionally valued independence for individuals with severe handicaps, such a goal is neither realistic nor normalized (Voeltz, 1983). Specifically, for a number of individuals with severe handicaps, independent performance 100% of the time is not a viable expectation, given the severity and multiplicity of their handicapping conditions (Strully & Strully, 1985). Furthermore, nonhandicapped individuals depend upon one another for a variety of activities throughout life. Professionals should reconsider this notion of interdependence, and should develop services that allow and foster interdependence among individuals with severe handicaps and their nonhandicapped peers. As suggested by Bersani (1988), specialized services should foster relationships; furthermore, a balance between natural supports (family, friends, co-workers, etc.) and "systems" support should be sought.

Although most of this chapter focuses on what individuals with severe handicaps can do to have and be a friend, professionals should not limit their efforts to fostering friendships exclusively between persons with severe handicaps. As Gold (1980) has noted, the quality of life of individuals with severe handicaps often rests on the commitment and resources of nonhandicapped individuals. Professionals can help the individual with severe handicaps to identify those nonhandicapped individuals who, if given the opportunity, would like to become acquainted and develop friendships with individuals with severe handicaps.

As previously indicated, there is little empirical documentation of friendships between individuals with severe handicaps and their nonhandicapped peers. Additional research is necessary to assist professionals to delineate those characteristics and variables that will provide optimal support for individuals with and without handicaps to develop and maintain friendships.

Clearly, the setting in which services are provided is critical in the development and maintenance of friendships. When individuals with severe handicaps leave their neighborhoods and communities to receive specialized services, a clear message is sent to their nonhandicapped peers, "They don't belong." If the goal of professional efforts is indeed full integration and a true sense of community for all, then children and adolescents with severe handicaps must attend their neighborhood schools and adults with severe handicaps must live and work in communities of their choice.

SUMMARY

In this chapter, an overview is presented of the process whereby friendships among individuals with and without severe handicaps are developed and supported. Rationales for friendships, as well as definitions of friendship, are provided. Specific curricular suggestions and strategies that professionals should consider when facilitating friendships are also provided. Finally, implications for the delivery of services so as to best maximize friendship opportunities between individuals with and without severe handicaps are described.

REFERENCES

Anderson, J.L. (1983). *An observational study of the interaction of autistic children and their families in the natural home environment.* Unpublished doctoral dissertation, University of Wisconsin, Madison.

Asher, S.R., Oden, S.L., & Gottman, J. M. (1977). Children's friendships in school settings. In L.G. Katz (Ed.), *Current topics in early chilhood education* (Vol. 1, pp. 33–61). Norwood, N.J.: Ablex.

Baumgart, D. (1981). *Activities and interactions of severely handicapped and nonhandicapped students during recess at two integrated elementary schools.* Unpublished doctoral dissertation, University of Wisconsin, Madison.

Berndt, T.J. (1982). The features and effects of friendship in early adolescence. *Child Development, 53,* 1447–1460.

Berndt, T.J. & Perry, T.B. (1986). Children's perceptions of friendships as supportive relationships. *Developmental Psychology, 22*(5), 64–648.

DBersani, H. (1988, April). *Promising practices in quality assurance of integrated community living options.* Keynote presentation at a meeting of the Division of Developmental Disabilities: "Choices: Community Integration and Family Support Conference," Phoenix, AZ.

Breen, C., Haring, T., Pitts-Conway, V., & Gaylord-Ross, R. (1985). The training and generalization of social interaction during breaktime at two job sites in the natural environment. *Journal of the Association for Persons with Severe Handicaps, 10*(1), 41–50.

Brown, L., Nietupski, J., & Hamre-Nietupski, S. (1976). The criterion of ultimate functioning and public school services for severely handicapped children. In M.A. Thomas (Ed.), *Hey, don't forget about me: Education's investment in the severely, profoundly and multiply handicapped* (pp. 2–15). Reston, VA: Council for Exceptional Children.

Buhrmester, D., & Furman, W. (1986). The changing functions of friends in childhood: A neo-Sullivan perspective. In V.J. Derlaga & B.A. Winstead (Eds.), *Friendship and social interaction* (pp. 41–61). New York: Springer-Verlag.

California Research Institute. (1987). *Survey of severely disabled students in California.* Unpublished manuscript, San Francisco State University, California Research Institute on the Integration of Students with Severe Disabilities.

Chin-Perez, G., Hartman, D., Park, H.S., Sacks, S., Wershing, A., & Gaylord-Ross, R. (1986). *Maximizing social contact for secondary students with severe handicaps. Journal of the Association for Persons with Severe Handicaps, 11*(2), 118–124.

Cole, D.A. (1988). Difficulties in relationships between nonhandicapped and severely mentally retarded children: The effect of physical impairments. *Research in Developmental Disabilities, 9,* 55–72.

Condon, M.E., York, R., Heal, L.W., & Fortschneider, J. (1986). Acceptance of severely handicapped students by nonhandicapped peers. *Journal of The Association for Persons with Severe Handicaps, 11*(3), 216–219.

Coots, J.J. (1985). *The effects of integration on the functional nature of the communicative/interactive attempts of students with severe handicaps.* Unpublished master's thesis, California State University, Los Angeles.

Cowen, E.L., Pederson, A., Babigian, M., Izzo, L.D., & Trost, M.R. (1973). Long-term follow-up of early detected vulnerable children. *Journal of Consulting and Clinical Psychology, 41,* 438–446.

Damon, W. (1977). *The social world of the child.* San Francisco: Jossey-Bass.

Eder, D., & Hallinan, M.T. (1978, April). Sex differences in children's friendships. *American Sociological Review, 43,* 237–250.

Egel, A.L., Richmond, G.S., & Koegel, R.L. (1981). Normal peer models and autistic children's learning. *Journal of Applied Behavior Analysis, 14,* (1), 3–12.

Esposito, B.G., & Reed, T.M. (1986). The effect of contact with handicapped persons on young children's attitudes. *Exceptional Chiildren, 53*(3), 224–229.

Falvey, M.A. (1980). *Changes in academic and social competence of kindergarten aged children as a result of an integrated classroom.* Unpublished doctoral dissertation, University of Wisconsin, Madison.

Falvey, M.A., Brown, L., Lyon, S., Baumgart, D., & Schroeder, J. (1980). Strategies for using cues and correction procedures. In W. Sailor, B. Wilcox, & L. Brown (Eds.), *Methods of instruction for severely handicapped students* (pp. 109–133). Baltimore: Paul H. Brookes Publishing Co.

Falvey, M.A., Coots, J.J., Bishop, K., & Grenot-Scheyer, M. (1989). Educational and curricular adaptations. In. W. Stainback, S. Stainback, & M. Forest (Eds.), *Educating all students in the mainstream of regular education* (pp. 143–158). Baltimore: Paul H. Brookes Publishing Co.

Field, T. (1984). Play behavior of handicapped children who have friends. In T. Field, J.L. Roopnarine, & M. Segal (Eds.), *Friendships in normal and handicapped children* (pp. 153–162). Norwood, NJ: Ablex.

Gold, M.W. (1980). *Try another way training manual.* Champaign, IL: Research Press.

Gottlieb, J., & Leyser, Y. (1981). Friendship between mentally retarded and nonretarded children. In S.R. Asher & J.M. Gottman (Eds.), *The development of children's friendships* (pp. 150–181). Cambridge: Cambridge University Press.

Grenot-Scheyer, M. (in preparation). *Friendships between children with severe handicaps and their nonhandicapped peers.* Unpublished manuscript, California State University Los Angeles.

Guralnick, M.J. (1980). Social interactions among preschool children. *Exceptional Children, 46*(4), 248–253.

Guralnick, M.J., & Paul-Brown, D.P. (1980). Functional and discourse analysis of nonhandicapped preschool children's speech to handicapped children. *American Journal of Mental Deficiency, 84*(5), 444–454.

Haring, T.G., Breen, C., Pitts-Conway, V., Lee, M., & Gaylord-Ross, R. (1987). Adolescent peer tutoring and special friend experiences. *Journal of The Association for Persons with Severe Handicaps, 12*(4), 280–286.

Hartup, W.W. (1970). Peer interaction and social organization. In P.H. Mussen (Ed.), *Carmichael's manual of child psychology* (3rd ed., pp. 361–456). New York: John Wiley & Sons.
Hartup, W.W. (1975). The origins of friendship. In M. Lewis & L.A. Rosenblum (Eds.), *Friendships and peer relations* (pp. 11–26). New York: John Wiley & Sons.
Hartup, W.W. (1983). Peer relations. In E.M. Hethermgton (Ed.), *Socialization, personality, and social development* (pp. 104–196). New York: John Wiley & Sons.
Hayes, D.A. (1978). Cognitive bases for liking and disliking among preschool children. *Child Development, 49,* 906–909.
Howes, C. (1983). Patterns of friendship. *Child Development, 54,* 1041–1053.
Howes, C., & Mueller, D. (1980). Early peer friendships: Their significance for development. In W. Spiel (Ed.), *The psychology of the twentieth century.* Zurich: Kindler.
Hymel, S., & Asher, S.R. (1977). *Assessment and training of isolated children's social skills.* (ERIC Document Reproduction Service No. ED 136 930)
Johnson, R., Johnson, D.W., DeWeerdt, N., Lyons, V., & Zaidman, B. (1983). Integrating severely adaptively handicapped seventh grade students into constructive relationships with nonhandicapped peers in science class. *American Journal of Mental Deficiency, 87,* 611–619.
Kohl, F.L., Moses, L.G., & Stettner-Eaton, B.A. (1984). A systematic training program for teaching nonhandicapped students to be instructional trainers of severely handicapped schoolmates. In N. Certo, N. Haring, & R. York (Eds.), *Public school integration of severely handicapped students: Rational issues and progressive alternatives* (pp. 185–195). Baltimore: Paul H. Brookes Publishing Co.
Lewis, M., & Rosenblaum, L.A. (1975). *Friendships and peer relations.* New York: John Wiley & Sons.
Lutfiyya, Z.M. (1988, September). Other than clients: reflections on relationships between people with disabilities and typical people. *Newsletter: The Association for Persons with Severe Handicaps, 14*(9), 3–5.
Masters, J.C., & Furman, W. (1981). Popularity, individual friendship selection and specific peer interaction among children. *Developmental Psychology, 17*(3), 344–350.
McHale, S.M., Olley, J.G., Marcus, L.M., & Simeonsson, R.J. (1981). Nonhandicapped peers as tutors for autistic children. *Exceptional Children, 48*(3), 263–265.
McHale, S.M., & Simeonsson, R.J. (1980). Effects of interaction on nonhandicapped children's attitudes toward autistic children. *American Journal of Mental Deficiency, 85*(1), 18–24.
Oden, S., & Asher, S.R. (1977). Coaching children in social skills for friendship making. *Child Development, 48,* 495–506.
Perske, R. (1987, October). *Why friendship?* Presentation at the meeting of The Association for Persons with Severe Handicaps conference, Chicago.
Robins, L.N. (1966). *Deviant children grown up.* Baltimore: Williams & Wilkins.
Roff, M., Sells, S.B., & Golden, M.M. (1972). *Social adjustment and personality development in children.* Minnesota: University of Minnesota Press.
Roopnarine, J.L., & Field, T. (1984). Play interaction of friends and acquaintances in nursery school. In T. Field, J.L. Roopnarine, & M. Segal (Eds.), *Friendships in normal and handicapped children* (pp. 89–98). Norwood, NJ: Ablex.
Rubin, Z. (1982). *Children's friendships.* Cambridge: Harvard University Press.
Rynders, J.E., Johnson, R.T., Johnson, D.W., & Schmidt, B. (1980). Producing positive interactions among Down Syndrome and nonhandicapped students through cooperative goal structuring. *American Journal of Mental Deficiency, 85,* 268–273.
Schofield, J.W. (1981). Complementary and conflicting identities: Images and interac-

tion in an interracial school. In S. Asher & J. Gottman (Eds.), *The development of children's friendships* (pp. 53–90). Cambridge: Cambridge University Press.

Snell, M.E. (1987). *Systematic instruction of persons with severe handicaps.* Columbus, OH: Charles E. Merrill.

Stainback, S., Stainback, W., & Forest, M. (Eds.). (1989). *Educating all students in the mainstream of regular education.* Baltimore: Paul H. Brookes Publishing Co.

Stainback, W., & Stainback, S. (1987, March). Facilitating friendships. *Education and Training in Mental Retardation* pp. 18–25.

Storey, K., & Gaylord-Ross, R. (1987). Increasing positive social interactions by handicapped individuals during a recreational activity using a multicomponent treatment package. *Research in Developmental Disabilities, 8,* 627–649.

Strain, P.S. (1983). Generalization of autistic children's social behavior change: Effects of developmentally integrated and segregated settings. *Analysis and Intervention in Developmental Disabilities, 3,* 23–34.

Strain, P.S. (1984a). Social behavior patterns of nonhandicapped and developmentally disabled friend pairs in mainstream preschools. *Analysis and Intervention in Developmental Disabilities, 4,* 15–28.

Strain, P.S. (1984b). Social interactions of handicapped preschoolers. In T. Field, J.L. Roopnarine, & M. Segal, (Eds.), *Friendships in normal and handicapped children* (pp. 187–207). Norwood, NJ: Ablex.

Strully, J.L., & Bartholomew-Lorimer, K. (1988). Social integration and friendship. In S.M. Pueschel (Ed.), *The young person with Down syndrome: Transition from adolescence to adulthood* (pp. 65–76). Baltimore: Paul H. Brookes Publishing Co.

Strully, J., & Strully, C. (1985). Friendship and our children. *Journal of The Association for Persons with Severe Handicaps, 10*(4), 224–227.

Sullivan, H.S. (1953). *The interpersonal theory of psychiatry.* New York: Norton.

Taylor, S.J., Biklen, D., & Knoll, J. (Eds.). (1987). *Community integration for people with severe disabilities.* New York: Teacher's College Press.

Voeltz, L.M. (1980). Children's attitudes toward handicapped peers. *American Journal of Mental Deficiency, 84*(5), 455–464.

Voeltz, L.M. (1983). *Why Integrate?* Unpublished manuscript, University of Minnesota Consortium Institute for the Education of Severely Handicapped Learners, Minneapolis, MN.

Voeltz, L.M., & Brennan, J. (1982, August). *Analysis of interactions between nonhandicapped and severely handicapped peers using multiple measures.* Paper presented at the 6th International Congress of the International Association for the Scientific Study of Mental Deficiency, Toronto, Canada.

Weiss, R.S. (1974). The provisions of social relationships. In Z. Rubin (Ed.), *Doing unto others* (pp. 17–26). Englewood Cliffs, NJ: Prentice-Hall.

Ziegler, S., & Hambleton, D. (1976, May). Integration of young TMR children into a regular elementary school. *Exceptional Children,* 459–461.

INDEX